Practical Python Programming for IoT

Build advanced IoT projects using a Raspberry Pi 4, MQTT, RESTful APIs, WebSockets, and Python 3

Gary Smart

BIRMINGHAM - MUMBAI

Practical Python Programming for IoT

Commissioning Editor: Karan Sadawana
Acquisition Editor: Shrilekha Inani
Content Development Editor: Romy Dias
Senior Editor: Rahul Dsouza
Technical Editor: Aurobindo Kar
Copy Editor: Safis Editing
Project Coordinator: Neil Dmello
Proofreader: Safis Editing
Indexer: Manju Arasan
Production Designer: Joshua Misquitta

First published: October 2020

Production reference: 1151020

Published by Packt Publishing Ltd.
Livery Place
35 Livery Street
Birmingham
B3 2PB, UK.

ISBN 978-1-83898-246-1

www.packt.com

Contributors

About the author

Gary Smart is a senior software engineer and an IoT and integration expert. The commencement of Gary's IT career coincided with the birth of the World Wide Web and has grown in line with the internet and emerging technologies ever since, including the rise of mobile phones and tablets, embedded technologies, SaaS and business migration to the cloud, and in recent years, the IoT revolution. Gary's practical experience includes both technical and management positions and experience in both small and large organizations, including Hewlett-Packard, Deakin University, and Pacific Hydro-Tango, boutique consulting firms, and innovative internet and IoT start-ups.

> *A big and loving thanks to my wife, Kylie. Without your encouragement and support, this book and the opportunity to share my passion and knowledge with others would not have happened. And a big thanks also to my friends and colleagues who along the journey have likewise provided encouragement and expressed sincere interest in the material I was producing. You've all helped me understand that I have something valuable to share! Thank you!*

About the reviewer

Federico Gonzalez is an Argentinian-based cooperative developer and teacher. He studies information systems engineering at UTN with a focus on development. He is part of Devecoop, a cooperative where he works on projects using a broad range of technologies, currently focusing on developing software and teaching React.js. He contributes to open source projects such as Lelylan (an IoT cloud platform with microservices architecture), EventoL (conference and installfest management software), and some minor contributions to projects with a Docker environment, Python, or JavaScript code. He also gives various workshops at universities, conferences, and companies in Argentina featuring React.js, Python, Docker, open source free software, and cooperatives.

> *Devecoop is my company. It lets me work on many interesting projects and sponsors me to go to conferences and give workshops and talks, and also helps me grow my teaching skills. I've learned a lot from the people that contribute to free software communities (USLA, GNUTN, CAFELUG, and more) and I'm a contributor too.*

Packt is searching for authors like you

If you're interested in becoming an author for Packt, please visit `authors.packtpub.com` and apply today. We have worked with thousands of developers and tech professionals, just like you, to help them share their insight with the global tech community. You can make a general application, apply for a specific hot topic that we are recruiting an author for, or submit your own idea.

Table of Contents

Preface

Welcome to *Practical Python Programming for IoT*. The focus of this book is centered around Raspberry Pis, electronics, computer networking, the Python programming language, and how we combine all these elements to build complex and multifaceted IoT projects.

We will be looking at these elements from many angles, comparing and contrasting different options, and discussing the *how* and *why* behind the electronic circuits we build. By the time you reach the end of this book, you will have a broad toolkit comprised of electronic interfacing code examples, networking code examples, and electronic circuit examples that you can borrow from, adapt, and reengineer for your own needs and projects.

I look forward to joining you on this IoT journey.

Who this book is for

This book is for application developers, IoT professionals, and hobbyists interested in building IoT applications leveraging the Python programming language. It is written with mid-to senior-level software engineers in mind who are experienced in desktop, web, and mobile development, but who have little to no exposure to electronics, physical computing, and IoT.

What this book covers

Chapter 1, *Setting Up Your Development Environment*, explores the Python ecosystem in the context of the Raspberry Pi OS and teaches you how to correctly set up a Python development project for success. You will also learn alternative ways of starting Python programs and how to configure your Raspberry Pi for GPIO interfacing.

Chapter 2, *Getting Started with Python and IoT*, teaches you the basics of electronics and GPIO interfacing with Python. You will build and experiment with simple electronic circuits that are controlled using Python, and combine this learning to build a simple yet complete internet-controllable IoT application from the ground up using the dweet.io platform.

Chapter 3, *Networking with RESTful APIs and Web Sockets Using Flask*, explores how to build network servers in Python using two approaches – RESTful APIs and Web Sockets. You will learn how to use these servers in conjunction with Python and an HTML/JavaScript user interface to control electronic circuits over a network from a web browser.

Chapter 4, *Networking with MQTT, Python, and the Mosquitto MQTT Broker*, teaches networking approaches using Message Queue Telemetry Transport, a popular choice for distributed IoT applications. You will learn how to use MQTT in conjunction with Python and an HTML/JavaScript user interface to control electronic circuits over a network and from a web browser.

Chapter 5, *Connecting Your Raspberry Pi to the Physical World*, explores different Python-based software options and techniques used to interface and control electronics using a Raspberry Pi's GPIO pins. You will also build and learn to use an ADS1115 analog-to-digital converter module to expand your Raspberry Pi's native interfacing options, and be introduced to **Pulse Width Modulation** (**PWM**), an important electronic and interfacing concept that you'll be using in later chapters.

Chapter 6, *Electronics 101 for the Software Engineer*, teaches you core electronic concepts and fundamentals. You will learn the essential *how* and *why* behind common electronic and interfacing circuits and how they are used practically to correctly and safely interface sensors and actuators to your Raspberry Pi. You will also learn the differences between digital and analog electronics and how each applies to and influences interfacing circuit requirements. Many of the fundamentals you learn about in this chapter are seen applied practically in subsequent chapters as we work with different electronic components and modules.

Chapter 7, *Turning Things On and Off*, teaches you how to use optocouplers, MOSFET transistors, and relays to turn other circuits on and off using your Raspberry Pi and Python. You will also learn about circuit loads, how they are measured, and how this influences the choice and use of optocouplers, MOSFET transistors, and relays in circuits.

Chapter 8, *Lights, Indicators, and Displaying Information*, teaches you how to use an APA102 LED lighting strip, RGB LEDs, OLED displays, and buzzers in conjunction with Python to create visual and auditable orientated circuits and applications.

Chapter 9, *Measuring Temperature, Humidity, and Light Levels*, teaches you how to measure common environmental attributes with your Raspberry Pi and Python. You will build a circuit using a DHT11/22 temperature and humidity sensor and learn about and use **Light-Dependent-Resistors** (**LDRs**) to detect the presence or absence of light. In this chapter, you will also deepen your practical understanding and experience of analog electronics, and apply the basic principle to build a moisture detection circuit and application.

Chapter 10, *Movement with Servos, Motors, and Steppers*, teaches you how to create movement using popular mechanical devices together with your Raspberry Pi and Python. You will learn how to control a servo using PWM to create angular movement, use an H-bridge IC circuit together with a motor to control its speed and direction of rotation. Plus, you will learn how to adapt the H-bridge IC circuit for use with a stepper motor for those projects where you need precise control over movement.

Chapter 11, *Measuring Distance and Detecting Movement*, teaches you the principles behind distance measurements using an HC-SR04 ultrasonic distance sensor and how to use an HC-SR501 PIR sensor to detect movement on a macro scale. You will also learn how to use both a ratiometric and switch-type Hall-effect sensor to detect movement and measure relative distance on micro scales.

Chapter 12, *Advanced IoT Programming Concepts – Threads, AsyncIO, and Event Loops*, is an advanced programming chapter that looks at alternative approaches to structuring complex Python programs. You will learn about Python threading, asynchronous I/O, classic event loops, and publisher-subscriber patterns, all within the context of electronic interfacing. By the end of the chapter, you will have experimented with and understood four functionally equivalent applications that are written in four very different ways.

Chapter 13, *IoT Visualization and Automation Platforms*, is a journey into the world of IoT-related online services and integration. You will be creating two environmental-monitoring applications based on the DHT11/22 temperature and humidity circuit from Chapter 9, *Measuring Temperature, Humidity, and Light Levels*. First, you will leverage your MQTT understanding from Chapter 4, *Networking with MQTT, Python, and the Mosquitto MQTT Broker*, to create an online dashboard at ThingSpeak.com to display and graph both temperature and humidity data. Then, you will also apply RESTful API concepts from Chapter 4, *Networking with MQTT, Python, and the Mosquitto MQTT Broker*, and build an If-This-Then-That (IFTTT.com) workflow Applet that sends you an email whenever the temperature rises above or falls below a certain point.

Chapter 14, *Tying It All Together – An IoT Christmas Tree*, pulls together many of the themes and concepts you have learned about in earlier chapters with a multifaceted example centered around an internet-connected Christmas tree. From an electronics perspective, you will revisit the APA102 LED strip from Chapter 8, *Lights, Indicators, and Displaying Information* (this will be the Christmas tree lights), and servos from Chapter 10, *Movement with Servos, Motors, and Steppers* (this is used to provide a mechanism to shake or rock the tree). From a networking perspective, you will revisit dweet.io from Chapter 2, *Getting Started with Python and IoT*; RESTful-APIs from Chapter 3, *Networking with RESTful APIs and Web Sockets Using Flask*; and MQTT from Chapter 4, *Networking with MQTT, Python, and the Mosquitto MQTT Broker,* and learn how to combine techniques to achieve complex integrations that need to bridge different technologies. Finally, you will revisit IFTTT from Chapter 13, *IoT Visualization and Automation Platforms*, and create two Applets that let you control your tree's lights and make the tree shake or rock over the internet. These three Applets include email control, and voice-activated control using Google Assistant.

To get the most out of this book

The following headings provide an overview of the hardware, software, electronics, and peripherals you will require to successfully work through and complete the exercises found in this book.

- **Hardware and software**: All of the exercises and code in this book were built and tested on the following hardware and software versions:

  - Raspberry Pi 4 Model B
  - Raspberry Pi OS Buster (with desktop and recommended software)
  - Python version 3.5

  It will be my assumption that you will be using an equivalent setup; however, it is reasonable to expect that the code examples should work without modification on a Raspberry Pi 3 Model B or a different version of Raspbian OS or Raspberry Pi OS as long as your Python version is 3.5 or higher.

  If you are not too sure about your Python version, don't worry. One of our first tasks in Chapter 1, *Setting Up Your Development Environment*, will be understanding Python on your Raspberry Pi and working out which versions are available.

- **Electronic Parts and Equipment**: We will be using many electronic parts throughout this book. At the start of each chapter, I list the specific parts and quantities you will require for the chapter's examples. In addition to the parts listed, an electronic breadboard and a mixture of jumper/dupont cables will also be required.

For your convenience, a table cataloging all the electronic parts used throughout the book, the chapters where they are used, plus the minimum quantities you will require follows. If you are new to buying electronic parts, you'll also find tips to help get you started after the table:

Part Name	Minimum Quantity	Description / Notes	Used in Chapter(s)
Red LED	2 *	5mm red LED. Different-colored LEDs can have different electrical characters. Most of our examples in the book will assume a red LED.	2, 3, 4, 5, 6, 7, 9, 12, 13
15Ω Resistor	2 *	Color bands (4-band resistor) will be brown, green, black, silver/gold	8
200Ω Resistor	2 *	Color bands (4-band resistor) will be red, black brown, silver/gold	2, 3, 4, 5, 6, 8, 9, 12, 13
1kΩ Resistor	2 *	Color bands (4-band resistor) will be brown, brown, red, silver/gold	6, 7, 9, 8, 11
2kΩ Resistor	2 *	Color bands (4-band resistor) will be red, black, red, silver/gold	6, 11
10kΩ Resistor	1 *	Color bands (4-band resistor) will be brown, black, orange, silver/gold	9, 13
51kΩ Resistor	1 *	Color bands (4-band resistor) will be green, brown, orange, silver/gold	6
100kΩ Resistor	1 *	Color bands (4-band resistor) will be brown, black, yellow, silver/gold	7, 8, 9
Momentary Push-Button Switch	1	To source a push-button switch that is breadboard friendly, try searching for a *large tactile switch*.	1, 6, 12
10kΩ *Linear* Potentiometers	2	Larger potentiometers that you can adjust with your fingers will be easier to work with in the book's examples than small potentiometers that will require a screwdriver to adjust. Make sure you have *linear* potentiometers (not logarithmic).	5, 6, 12
2N7000 MOSFET	1 *	This is a logic-level compatible MOSFET transistor.	7, 8
FQP30N06L Power MOSFET	1 *	Optional. When purchasing, make sure the part number ends with L, indicating that it is a logic-level compatible MOSFET (otherwise, it will not reliably work your Raspberry Pi).	7
PC817 Opto-Coupler	1 *	Also known as an opto-isolator.	7

SDR-5VDC-SL-C Relay	1	These relays are very popular and easy to come by; however, they are not breadboard friendly. You will need to solder terminals or wires to them so you can plug them into your breadboard.	7
1N4001 Diode	1 *	We will be using a diode in the role of a fly-back suppression diode to protect other electrical components from voltage spikes.	7, 8
Size R130 5-volt DC Hobby Motor	2	Size R130 is just a suggestion. What we need are 5-volt compatible DC motors with a stall current (ideally) less than 800 mA. While these motors are easy to come by on auction sites, their current and operating currents can be poorly documented so it can be a gamble as to what you get. Chapter 7, *Turning Things On and Off,* will take you through an exercise to measure the operating currents of your motors.	7, 10
RGBLED, Common Cathode type	1 *	This is an LED that is capable of making different colors.	8
Passive Buzzer	1	A *passive* buzzer that will work with 5 volts.	8
SSD1306 OLED Display	1	This is a small monochrome pixel-based display.	8
APA102 RGBLED Strip	1	This is a strip of addressable APA102 RGBLEDs. You will just need the LED strip, not a power supply or a remote control for our exercises. Be careful to make sure it is the APA102 LEDs that you are purchasing as there are different (and incompatible) types of addressable LEDs available.	8, 14
DHT11 or DHT22 Temperature/Humidity Sensor	1	The DHT11 and DHT22 are interchangeable. The DHT22 is slightly more expensive but offers more accuracy and can measure sub-zero temperatures.	9, 13
LDR	1 *	Light-Dependent-Resistor	9
MG90S Hobby Servo	1	This is a suggestion. Any 5-volt hobby servo with 3 wires (+, GND, Signal) should be suitable.	10, 14
L293D H-Bridge IC	1 *	Make sure the part number you purchase ends in D, meaning the IC includes embedded fly-back suppression diodes.	10
28BYJ-48 Stepper Motor	1	Make sure you purchase the 5-volt stepper motor variety, with a 1:64 gearing ratio.	10
HC-SR501 PIR Sensor	1	A PIR sensor detects movement. It works on heat, so it can detect the presence of people and animals.	11
HC-SR04 Ultrasonic Distance Sensor	1	An Ultrasonic Distance Sensor estimates distances using sound waves.	11
A3144 Hall-Effect Sensor	1 *	This is a non-latching switch-type Hall-effect sensor that turns on in the presence of a magnetic field.	11

AH3503 Hall-Effect Sensor	1 *	This is a ratiometric-type Hall-effect sensor that can detect how close (relatively) it is to a magnetic field.	11
Magnet	1	A small magnet is required for use with the Hall-effect sensors.	11
ADS1115 Analog-to-Digital (ADC) Converter Breakout Module	1	This module will allow us to interface analog components with our Raspberry Pi.	5, 9, 12
Logic Level Shifter/Converter Breakout Module	1	This module will allow us to interface 5-volt electrical components with our Raspberry Pi. Search for a Logic Level Shifter/Converter Breakout Module and look for a bi-directional (preferred) module when 4 or 8 channels.	6, 8, 14
Breadboard	1	All our electronic examples will be built on a breadboard. I recommend purchasing two full-size breadboards and joining them together – more breadboard working areas will make building circuits easier.	2 - 14
Dupont / Jumper Cables	3 sets *	These cables are used to wire components together on your breadboard. I recommend purchasing sets of male-to-male, male-to-female, and female-to-female types.	2 - 14
Raspberry Pi GPIO Breadboard Breakout	1	This is optional, however, it will make it easier to interface your Raspberry Pi GPIO pins with your breadboard.	2 - 14
Digital Multimeter	1	As a guide, a digital multimeter in the price range of $30-50 USD should be more than suitable. Avoid the very-low and cheapest multi-meters.	6, 7
External Power Supply	2	Some of the circuits in this book will require more power than we can expect our Raspberry Pi to provide. As a minimum source, a 3.3/5-volt breadboard-compatible power supply capable of outputting 1 amp will be suitable. You might also like to research lab power supplies as a more capable and general alternative.	7, 8, 9, 10, 14
Soldering Iron and Solder	1	There will be cases where you need to solder wires and terminals onto components – for example, it is highly likely that you will need to solder terminal legs on to the ADS1115 and logic level converter/shifter modules that you purchase. You will also need to solder terminals or wires onto your SDR-5VDC-SL-C relay so you can plug it into your breadboard.	

* Spares recommended. These are components that can be damaged if incorrectly connected or powered or can physically break with use (for example, legs breaking off).

These parts have been selected due to their low price points, and their general availability on websites such as eBay.com, Bangood.com, AliExpress.com, and electronics retailers.

Before making your purchases, please consider the following:

- The **Minimum Quantity** column is what you will need for the exercises in this book, however, it's highly recommended that you purchase spares, especially of LEDs, resistors, and MOSFETs as these components are easily damaged.
- You will find that many components will need to be purchased in bulk lots.
- Search around for *Electronic Component Starter Kits* and compare what they include against the parts listed in the table. You may be able to purchase many of the parts together in a single (and discounted) transaction.
- The many available plug-and-play *Sensor Module Starter Kits* that are available will, for the most part, not be compatible with the circuit and code exercises presented throughout this book. The depth of our electronic and code examples means we will need to work with core electrical components. After completing this book, however, you will be in a great position to understand how these plug-and-play sensor modules are built and work!

If you are using the digital version of this book, we advise you to type the code yourself or access the code via the GitHub repository (link available in the next section). Doing so will help you avoid any potential errors related to the copying and pasting of code.

Download the example code files

You can download the example code files for this book from your account at `www.packt.com`. If you purchased this book elsewhere, you can visit `www.packtpub.com/support` and register to have the files emailed directly to you.

You can download the code files by following these steps:

1. Log in or register at `www.packt.com`.
2. Select the **Support** tab.
3. Click on **Code Downloads**.
4. Enter the name of the book in the **Search** box and follow the onscreen instructions.

Once the file is downloaded, please make sure that you unzip or extract the folder using the latest version of:

- WinRAR/7-Zip for Windows
- Zipeg/iZip/UnRarX for Mac
- 7-Zip/PeaZip for Linux

The code bundle for the book is also hosted on GitHub at `https://github.com/PacktPublishing/Practical-Python-Programming-for-IoT`. In case there's an update to the code, it will be updated on the existing GitHub repository.

We also have other code bundles from our rich catalog of books and videos available at `https://github.com/PacktPublishing/`. Check them out!

Code in Action

Code in Action videos for this book can be viewed at `https://bit.ly/316OvNu`

Download the color images

We also provide a PDF file that has color images of the screenshots/diagrams used in this book. You can download it here: `https://static.packt-cdn.com/downloads/9781838982461_ColorImages.pdf`.

Conventions used

There are a number of text conventions used throughout this book.

`CodeInText`: Indicates code words in text, database table names, folder names, filenames, file extensions, pathnames, dummy URLs, user input, and Twitter handles. Here is an example: "Let's check for the availability of GPIO packages using `gpio_pkg_check.py` and `pip`."

A block of code is set as follows:

```
# Global Variables
...
BROKER_HOST = "localhost"    # (2)
BROKER_PORT = 1883
CLIENT_ID = "LEDClient"      # (3)
TOPIC = "led"                # (4)
client = None # MQTT client instance. See init_mqtt()    # (5)
...
```

When we wish to draw your attention to a particular part of a code block, the relevant lines or items are set in bold:

```
# Global Variables
...
BROKER_HOST = "localhost"     # (2)
BROKER_PORT = 1883
CLIENT_ID = "LEDClient"       # (3)
TOPIC = "led"                 # (4)
client = None # MQTT client instance. See init_mqtt()    # (5)
...
```

Any command-line input or output is written as follows:

```
$ python --version
Python 2.7.16
```

Bold: Indicates a new term, an important word, or words that you see onscreen. For example, words in menus or dialog boxes appear in the text like this. Here is an example: "From your Raspbian desktop, navigate to the **Raspberry** menu | **Preferences** | **Raspberry Pi Configuration.**"

 Warnings or important notes appear like this.

 Tips and tricks appear like this.

Get in touch

Feedback from our readers is always welcome.

General feedback: If you have questions about any aspect of this book, mention the book title in the subject of your message and email us at customercare@packtpub.com.

Errata: Although we have taken every care to ensure the accuracy of our content, mistakes do happen. If you have found a mistake in this book, we would be grateful if you would report this to us. Please visit www.packtpub.com/support/errata, selecting your book, clicking on the Errata Submission Form link, and entering the details.

Piracy: If you come across any illegal copies of our works in any form on the Internet, we would be grateful if you would provide us with the location address or website name. Please contact us at `copyright@packt.com` with a link to the material.

If you are interested in becoming an author: If there is a topic that you have expertise in and you are interested in either writing or contributing to a book, please visit `authors.packtpub.com`.

Reviews

Please leave a review. Once you have read and used this book, why not leave a review on the site that you purchased it from? Potential readers can then see and use your unbiased opinion to make purchase decisions, we at Packt can understand what you think about our products, and our authors can see your feedback on their book. Thank you!

For more information about Packt, please visit `packt.com`.

Section 1: Programming with Python and the Raspberry Pi

In this first section of our journey, our primary focus will be on the *Internet* part of IoT.

We'll start by learning how to properly set up your Python development environment, before exploring and playing with a variety of networking techniques using Python to build network- and internet-connected services and applications. We will also create simple web user interfaces that work with the techniques and examples we will learn about.

However, I am sure if you are reading this book you are eager to jump right in, learn about and play with electronics, and start building and tinkering. I know I would be! So, Chapter 2, *Getting Started with Python and IoT* is dedicated to building a simple internet-connected IoT project from the ground up – electronics and all – so that we have a reference example for later chapters (and something to tinker with!).

Let's get started!

This section comprises the following chapters:

- Chapter 1, *Setting Up Your Development Environment*
- Chapter 2, *Getting Started with Python and IoT*
- Chapter 3, *Networking with RESTful APIs and Web Sockets using Flask*
- Chapter 4, *Networking with MQTT, Python, and the Mosquitto MQTT Broker*

Setting Up your Development Environment 1

An important yet often overlooked aspect of Python programming is how to correctly set up and maintain a Python project and its runtime environment. It is often overlooked because it presents as an optional step for the Python ecosystem. And while this might be fine for learning Python language fundamentals, it can quickly become a problem for more complex projects where we need to maintain separate code bases and dependencies to ensure our projects do not interfere with one another, or worse as we will discuss, break operating system tools and utilities.

So, before we jump into **IoT** code and examples in later chapters, it is so very important for us to cover the steps required to set up a Python project and its run time environment.

In this chapter, we will cover the following topics:

- Understanding your Python installation
- Setting up a Python virtual environment
- Installing Python GPIO packages with `pip`
- Alternative methods of executing a Python script
- Raspberry Pi GPIO interface configuration

Technical requirements

To perform the hands-0n exercises in this chapter, you will need the following:

- Raspberry Pi 4 Model B
- Raspbian OS Buster (with desktop and recommended software)
- Minimum Python version 3.5

These requirements are what the code examples in this book are based on. It's reasonable to expect that the code examples should work without modification on a Raspberry Pi 3 Model B or a different version of Raspbian OS as long as your Python version is 3.5 or higher.

The full source code for this book can be found on GitHub at the following URL: `https://github.com/PacktPublishing/Practical-Python-Programming-for-IoT`. We will clone this repository shortly when we come to the *Setting up a Python virtual environment* section.

Understanding your Python installation

In this section, we will find out which versions of Python you have installed on your Raspberry Pi. As we will discover, there are two versions of Python that come pre-installed on Raspbian OS. Unix-based operating systems (such as Raspbian OS) typically have Python version 2 and 3 pre-installed because there are operating-system-level utilities built with Python.

To find out which versions of Python you have on your Raspberry Pi, follow these steps:

1. Open a new Terminal and execute the `python --version` command:

    ```
    $ python --version
    Python 2.7.16
    ```

    In my example, we see that Python version 2.7.16 has been installed.

2. Next, run the `python3 --version` command:

    ```
    $ python3 --version
    Python 3.7.3
    ```

In my example, we see that the second version of Python (that is, `python3`, with the 3) that is installed is version 3.7.3.

Don't worry if the minor versions (the numbers .7.16 after the 2 and .7.3 after 3) are not the same; it is the major versions 2 and 3 that are of interest. Python 2 is a legacy version of Python, while Python 3 is the current and supported version of Python at the time of writing. When we are starting a new Python development, we will practically always use Python 3 unless there are legacy issues we need to contend with.

 Python 2 officially became end-of-life in January 2020. It is no longer maintained and will not receive any further enhancements, bug fixes, or security patches.

If you are an experienced Python programmer, you may be able to discern whether a script is written for Python 2 or 3, but it's not always obvious by simply looking at a piece of code. Many new-to-Python developers experience frustrations by mixing up Python programs and code fragments that are meant for different Python versions. Always remember that code written for Python 2 is not guaranteed to be upward-comparable with Python 3 without modification.

A quick tip I can share to visually help to determine which Python version a code fragment is written for (if the programmer has not made it clear in the code comments) is to look for a `print` statement.

If you look at the following example, you will see that there are two `print` statements. The first `print` statement without the parentheses is a give-away that it will only work with Python 2:

```
print "Hello"  # No parentheses - This only works in Python 2, a dead give-
away that this script is for Python 2.

print("Hello") # With parentheses - this will work in Python 2 and Python 3
```

Of course, you can always run the code against both Python 2 and 3 and see what happens.

We have now seen that there are two Python versions available by default on Raspbian OS, and made mention that there are system-level utilities that are written in Python that reply on these versions. As Python developers, we must take care not to disrupt the global Python installations as this can potentially break system-level utilities.

We will now turn our attention to a very important Python concept, the Python virtual environment, which is the way we isolate or *sandbox* our own Python projects from the global installation.

Setting up a Python virtual environment

In this section, we will discuss how Python interacts with your operating system installation and cover the steps necessary to set up and configure a Python development environment. In addition, as part of our setup process, we will clone the GitHub repository that contains all of the code (organized by chapter) for this book.

By default, Python and its package management tool, `pip`, operate globally at the system level and can create some confusion for Python beginners because this global default is in contrast to many other language ecosystems that operate locally on a project folder level by default. Unwearyingly working and making changes to the global Python environment can break Python-based system-level tools, and remedying the situation can become a major headache.

As a Python developer, we use Python virtual environments to sandbox our Python projects so they will not adversely interfere with system-level Python utilities or other Python projects.

In this book, we will be using a virtual environment tool known as `venv`, which comes bundled as a built-in module with Python 3.3 and above. There are other virtual environment tools around, all with their relative strengths and weaknesses, but they all share the common goal of keeping Python dependencies isolated to a project.

 `virtualenv` and `pipenv` are two alternative virtual environment tool options that offer more features than `venv`. These alternatives are well suited for complex Python projects and deployments. You'll find links to these in the *Further reading* section at the end of this chapter.

Let's begin and clone the GitHub repository and create a new Python virtual environment for this chapter's source code. Open a new Terminal window and work through the following steps:

1. Change into or create a folder where you want to store this book's source code and execute the following commands. With the last command, we rename the cloned folder to be `pyiot`. This has been done to help shorten Terminal command examples throughout the book:

```
$ cd ~
$ git clone
https://github.com/PacktPublishing/Practical-Python-Programming-for
-IoT
$ mv Practical-Python-Programming-for-IoT pyiot
```

2. Next, change into the `chapter01` folder, which contains the code relating to this chapter:

    $ cd ~/pyiot/chapter01

3. Execute the following command, which creates a new Python virtual environment using the `venv` tool. It's important that you type `python3` (with the 3) and remember that `venv` is only available with Python 3.3 and above:

    $ python3 -m venv venv

    The options that we are passing to `python3` include `-m venv`, which tells the Python interpreter that we want to run the module named `venv`. The `venv` parameter is the name of the *folder* where your virtual environment will be created.

> While it might look confusing at first glance in the preceding command, it's a common convention to name a virtual environment's folder `venv`. Later in this chapter, in the *Anatomy of a virtual environment* section, we will explore what lies beneath the `venv` folder we just created.

4. To use a Python virtual environment, we must *activate* it, which is accomplished with the `activate` command:

    ```
    # From with in the folder ~/pyiot/chapter01
    $ source venv/bin/activate
    (venv) $
    ```

    When your Terminal has a Python virtual environment activated, all Python-related activity is sandboxed to your virtual environment.

> Notice in the preceding code that, after activation, the name of the virtual environment, `venv`, is shown as part of the Terminal prompt text, that is, `(venv) $`. In this book, whenever you see Terminal examples where the prompt is `(venv) $`, it's a reminder that commands need to be executed from within an activated Python virtual environment.

5. Next, execute `which python` (*without* the 3) in your Terminal, and notice that the location of the Python executable is beneath your `venv` folder and if you check the version of Python, it's Python version 3:

```
(venv) $ which python
/home/pi/pyiot/chapter01/venv/bin/python

(venv) $ python --version
Python 3.7.3
```

6. To leave an activated virtual environment, use the `deactivate` command as illustrated here:

```
(venv) $ deactivate
$
```

Notice also that `(venv) $` is no longer part of the Terminal prompt text once the virtual environment has been deactivated.

Remember to type `deactivate` to leave a virtual environment, not `exit`. If you type `exit` in a virtual environment, it will exit the Terminal.

7. Finally, now that you are outside of our Python virtual environment if you execute `which python` (*without* the 3) and `python --version` again, notice we're back to the default system-level Python interpreter, which is version 2:

```
$ which python
/usr/bin/python

$ python --version
Python 2.7.13
```

As we just illustrated in the preceding examples, when we ran `python --version` in an *activated* virtual environment, we see that it's Python version 3 whereas in the last example, at the start of this chapter, the system level, `python --version`, was version 2, and we needed to type `python3 --version` for version 3. In practice, `python` (with no number) relates to the default version of Python. Globally, this is version 2. In your virtual environment, we only have one version of Python, which is version 3, so it becomes the default.

A virtual environment created with `venv` inherits (via a symbolic link) the global Python interpreter version that it was invoked with (in our case, version 3 because the command was `python3 -m venv venv`). If you ever need to target a specific Python version that is different from the global version, investigate the `virtualenv` and `pipenv` virtual environment alternatives.

We have now seen how to create, activate, and deactivate a Python virtual environment and why it is important to use a virtual environment to sandbox Python projects. This sandboxing means we can isolate our own Python projects and their library dependencies from one another, and it prevents us from potentially disrupting the system-level installation of Python and breaking any system-level tools and utilities that rely on them.

Next, we will see how to install and manage Python packages in a virtual environment using `pip`.

Installing Python GPIO packages with pip

In this section, we learn how to install and manage Python *packages* in a Python virtual environment you created and explored in the previous section. A Python *package* (or *library* if you prefer that term) allows us to extend the core Python language with new features and functionality.

We will need to install many different packages throughout this book, however, for starters and to explore and learn the basic concepts related to package installation and management, we will be installing two common GPIO-related packages in this section that we will use throughout this book. These two packages are the following:

- The `GPIOZero` library, an entry-level and easy to use GPIO library for controlling simple electronics
- The `PiGPIO` library, an advanced GPIO library with many features for more complex electronic interfacing

In the Python ecosystem, package management is done with the `pip` command (`pip` stands for *Python installs packages*). The official public package repository that `pip` queries is known as the *Python Package Index*, or simply *PyPi*, and it is available for browsing on the web at `https://pypi.org`.

Similarly to `python` and `python3`, there is `pip` and `pip3`. `pip` (without the number) will be the *default* `pip` command that is matched to the *default* `python` command in a given virtual environment.

There will be code examples in this book where we will be interacting with your Raspberry Pi's GPIO pins, so we need to install a Python package (or two) so that your Python code can work with your Raspberry Pi's GPIO pins. For now, we are just going to check for and install two GPIO-related packages. In `Chapter 2`, *Getting Started with Python and IoT*, and `Chapter 5`, *Connecting Your Raspberry Pi to the Physical World,* we will cover these GPIO packages and other alternatives in greater detail.

In your `chapter01` source code folder, you will find a file named `gpio_pkg_check.py`, which is replicated in the following. We will use this file as the basis to learn about `pip` and package management in the context of a Python virtual environment. This script simply reports the availability of a Python package depending on whether using `import` succeeds or raises an exception:

```
"""
Source File: chapter01/gpio_pkg_check.py
"""
try:
    import gpiozero
    print('GPIOZero Available')
except:
    print('GPIOZero Unavailable. Install with "pip install
gpiozero"')

try:
    import pigpio
    print('pigpio Available')
except:
    print('pigpio Unavailable. Install with "pip install pigpio"')
```

Let's check for the availability of GPIO packages using `gpio_pkg_check.py` and with `pip`. I'll kill the suspense by telling you that they're not going to be available in your freshly-created virtual environment (yet), however, we are going to install them!

Note: They *are* already installed at the system level if you want to check yourself by running this script outside of your virtual environment.

The following steps will walk us through the process of upgrading `pip`, exploring the tool's options, and installing packages:

1. As the first step, we will upgrade the `pip` tool. In a Terminal window, run the following command, remembering that all commands that follow must be performed in an *activated* virtual environment—meaning you should see the text `(venv)` in the Terminal prompt:

   ```
   (venv) $ pip install --upgrade pip
   ...output truncated...
   ```

   The preceding `upgrade` command may take a minute or two complete and will potentially output a lot of text to the Terminal.

   Are you facing `pip` problems? If you're getting a sea of red errors and exceptions when trying to install a package with `pip`, try upgrading the `pip` version as a first step using `pip install --upgrade pip`. It is a recommended first step after creating a fresh Python virtual environment to upgrade `pip`.

2. With `pip` now upgraded, we can see what Python packages are already installed in our virtual environment using the `pip list` command:

   ```
   (venv) $ pip list
   pip (9.0.1)
   pkg-resources (0.0.0)
   setuptools (33.1.1)
   ```

   What we see in the preceding are the default Python packages in our fresh virtual environment. Do not worry if the exact package list or version numbers do not match exactly with the example.

3. Run our Python script with the `python gpio_pkg_check.py` command and observe that our GPIO packages are *not* installed:

   ```
   (venv) $ python gpio_pkg_check.py
   GPIOZero Unavailable. Install with "pip install gpiozero"
   pigpio Unavailable. Install with "pip install pigpio"
   ```

4. To install our two required GPIO packages, we use the `pip install` command as shown in the following example:

```
(venv) $ pip install gpiozero pigpio
Collecting gpiozero...
... output truncated ...
```

5. Now, run the `pip list` command again; we will see these new packages are now installed in our virtual environment:

```
(venv) $ pip list
colorzero (1.1)
gpiozero (1.5.0)      # GPIOZero
pigpio (1.42)         # PiGPIO
pip (9.0.1)
pkg-resources (0.0.0)
setuptools (33.1.1)
```

You may have noticed that there is a package called `colorzero` (this is a color manipulation library) that we did not install. `gpiozero` (version 1.5.0) has a dependency on `colorzero`, so `pip` has installed it for us automatically.

6. Re-run `python gpio_pkg_check.py` and we now see that our Python modules are available for import:

```
(venv) $ python gpio_pkg_check.py
GPIOZero Available
pigpio Available
```

Great! We now have a virtual environment with two GPIO packages installed. As you work on Python projects, you will inevitably install more and more packages and want to keep track of them.

7. Take a snapshot of the packages you have previously installed with the `pip freeze` command:

```
(venv) $ pip freeze > requirements.txt
```

The preceding example *freezes* all installed packages into a file named `requirements.txt`, which is a common filename to use for this purpose.

8. Look inside the `requirements.txt` file and you will see all of the Python packages listed together with their version numbers:

```
(venv) $ cat requirements.txt
colorzero==1.1
gpiozero==1.5.0
pigpio==1.42
pkg-resources==0.0.0
```

In the future, if you move your Python project to another machine or a new virtual environment, you can use your `requirement.txt` file to install all of your captured packages in one go using the `pip install -r requirements.txt` command.

Our `requirements.txt` example shows we have installed GPIOZero version 1.5.0, the current version at the time of writing. This version has a dependency on ColorZero version 1.1. It is possible that different (past or future) versions of GPIOZero may have different dependencies than those shown in our example, so your own `requirements.txt` file when performing the example exercise may be different.

We've now completed the basic installation life cycle of Python packages using `pip`. Note that whenever you install new packages with `pip install`, you also need to re-run `pip freeze > requirements.txt` to capture the new packages and their dependencies.

To finish our exploration of `pip` and package management, here are a few other common `pip` commands:

```
# Remove a package
(venv) $ pip uninstall <package name>

# Search PyPi for a package (or point your web browser at
https://pypi.org)
(venv) $ pip search <query text>

# See all pip commands and options (also see Further Reading at the
end of the chapter).
(venv) $ pip --help
```

Congratulations! We've reached a milestone and covered the essential virtual environment principles that you can use for any Python project, even ones that are not Raspberry Pi related!

During your Python journey, you will also come across other package installers and tools named `easy_install` and `setuptools`. Both have their uses; however, it's `pip` that you will rely on most of the time.

Now that we have seen how to create a virtual environment and install packages, let's take a look at a typical Python project folder structure such as `~/pyiot/chapter01` and discover what lies beneath the `venv` folder.

Anatomy of a virtual environment

This section relates to `venv`, which we have been using in this chapter, and will apply to `virtualenv` *but not* `pipenv`, which we listed as alternative virtual environment tools. The example is also specific to a Raspbian OS and is typical of a standard Unix-based OS. It's important to, at a minimum, understand the basic structure of a virtual environment deployment since we will be mixing our own Python programming code in with the files and folders that make up the virtual environment.

 The light weight `venv` tool that comes with Python 3.3 and above is a subset of `virtualenv`.

Here is the folder structure of our virtual environment. Yep, its a screenshot from a Mac. That's so I could get everything on screen at once:

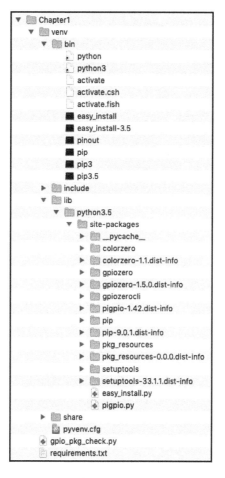

Figure 1.1 – Contents of a typical venv virtual environment folder

The following points explain the core subfolders that are found within our `~/pyiot/chapter01` folder after we ran `python3 -m venv venv` and installed packages using `pip`:

- The `venv` folder contains all of the Python virtual environment files. There is no real practical need to be touching anything under this folder manually—let the tools do that for you. Remember that the folder is named `venv` only because that's what we called it when it was created.

- The venv/bin folder contains the Python interpreter (in the venv case, there are symbolic links to the system interpreter) and other core Python tools, including pip.
- Underneath the venv/lib folder are all the sandboxed Python packages for the virtual environment, including the GPIOZero and PiGPIO packages we installed using pip install.
- Our Python source file, gpio_pkg_check.py, is in the top-level folder, ~/pyiot/chapter01; however, you can create sub-folders here to help to organize your code and non-code files.
- Finally, requirements.txt lives by convention in the top project folder.

The virtual environment folder venv does not actually need to be kept in the project folder; however, it's often convenient to have it there for activation with the activate command.

 Your venv folder and anything below it *should not* be added to your source version control system, but you should add requirements.txt. As long as you have a current requirements.txt file, you can always recreate your virtual environment and reinstate packages to a known state.

It's important to understand that, as a Python developer, you will be mixing in your own programming code with files and folders that form part of the virtual environment system and that you should be pragmatic when selecting which files and folders are added to your version control system, should you be using one.

This last point is important since the virtual environment system can amount to many megabytes in size (and often many times larger than your program code) that does not need versioning (since we can always recreate the virtual environment as long as we have a requirements.txt file), plus it's host platform-specific (that is, there will be differences between Windows, Mac, and Linux), plus there will be differences between different virtual environment tools (for example, venv versus pipenv). As such, virtual environments are not generally portable in projects that involve many developers working on different computers.

Now that we have briefly explored the file and folders structure and the importance of understanding this structure, we will continue and look at alternative ways of running a script that is sandboxed to a virtual environment.

Alternative methods of executing a Python script

Let's briefly turn our attention to the alternative ways that we can execute a Python script. As we will learn, choosing the appropriate method is all based around how and from where you intend to start your script and whether your code requires elevated permissions.

The most common way of running a Python script is from within its virtual environment and with the permissions of the currently logged in user. However, there will be scenarios where we need to run a script as the root user or from outside an activated virtual environment.

Here are the ways we will explore:

- Using `sudo` with virtual environments
- Executing Python scripts outside of their virtual environments
- Running a Python script at boot

Let's start by learning how to run a Python script with root user permissions.

Using sudo within virtual environments

I'm sure that while working on your Raspberry Pi you have had to execute commands in a Terminal with the `sudo` prefix because they required root privileges. If you ever need to run a Python script that is in a virtual environment as root, you must use the full path to your virtual environment's Python interpreter.

Simply prefixing `sudo` before `python`, as shown in the following example, does not work under most circumstances, even if we are in the virtual environment. The `sudo` action will use the default Python that's available to the root user, as shown in the second half of the example:

```
# Won't work as you might expect!
(venv) $ sudo python my_script.py

# Here is what the root user uses as 'python' (which is actually
Python version 2).
(venv) $ sudo which python
/usr/bin/python
```

The correct way to run a script as root is to pass the absolute path to your virtual environment's Python interpreter. We can find the absolute path using the `which python` command from inside an activated virtual environment:

```
(venv) $ which python
/home/pi/pyiot/chapter01/venv/bin/python
```

Now, we `sudo` our virtual environment's Python interpreter and the script will run *as* the root user and *within* the content of our virtual environment:

```
(venv) $ sudo /home/pi/pyiot/chapter01/venv/bin/python my_script.py
```

Next, we'll see how to run a Python script that's sandboxed in a virtual environment from outside of its virtual environment.

Executing Python scripts outside of their virtual environments

A natural extension to the preceding discussion on `sudo` is *how do I run a Python script from outside of its virtual environment?* The answer is the same as in the preceding section: just make sure you are using the absolute path to your virtual environment's Python interpreter.

Note: In the following two examples, we're not in a virtual environment—there is no `$ (venv)` on the prompt. If you still need to exit your Python virtual environment, type `deactivate`.

The following command will run a script as the currently *logged in* user (which, by default, is the `pi` user):

```
# Run script as logged-in user.
$ /home/pi/pyiot/chapter01/venv/bin/python gpio_pkg_check.py
```

Or to run the script as root, prefix `sudo`:

```
# Run script as root user by prefixing sudo
$ sudo /home/pi/pyiot/chapter01/venv/bin/python gpio_pkg_check.py
```

Since we are using the virtual environment's Python interpreter, we are still sandboxed to our virtual environment and any Python packages we installed are available.

Next, we will learn how to make a Python script run whenever you boot your Raspberry Pi.

Running a Python script at boot

There will come a time when you have developed an awesome IoT project and you want it to run automatically every time you start your Raspberry Pi. Here is one simple way to achieve this using a feature of `cron`, the Unix scheduler. If you are not familiar with the basics of `cron`, search the web for cron tutorial—you'll find heaps of them. I've provided curated links in the *Further reading* section.

Here are the steps to configure cron and make a script run on boot:

1. In your project folder, create a bash script. I've named it `run_on_boot.sh`:

    ```bash
    #!/bin/bash

    # Absolute path to virtual environment python interpreter
    PYTHON=/home/pi/pyiot/chapter01/venv/bin/python

    # Absolute path to Python script
    SCRIPT=/home/pi/pyiot/chapter01/gpio_pkg_check.py

    # Absolute path to output log file
    LOG=/home/pi/pyiot/chapter01/gpio_pkg_check.log

    echo -e "\n###### STARTUP $(date) ######\n" >> $LOG
    $PYTHON $SCRIPT >> $LOG 2>&1
    ```

    This bash script will run a Python script using the absolute paths for both the script and its Python interpreter. Also, it captures any script output and stores it in a log file. For this example, we're simply going to run and log the output of `gpio_pkg_check.py` on boot. It's the last line that ties everything together and runs and logs our Python script. The `2>&1` part at the end is necessary to ensure that errors, in addition to standard output, are also logged.

2. Mark the `run_on_boot.sh` file as an executable file:

    ```
    $ chmod u+x run_on_boot.sh
    ```

    If you are not familiar with the `chmod` command (*chmod* means change mode), what we are doing is giving the operating system permission to execute the `run_on_boot.sh` file. The `u+x` parameters mean *for the current **U**ser, make the file e**X**ecutable*. To learn more about `chmod`, you can type `chmod --help` or `man chmod` in the Terminal.

3. Edit your `crontab` file, which is the file where cron scheduling rules are stored:

```
$ crontab -e
```

4. Add the following entry to your `crontab` file, using the absolute path to the `run_on_boot.sh` bash script we created in *step 1*:

```
@reboot /home/pi/pyiot/chapter01/run_on_boot.sh &
```

Do not forget the `&` character at the end of the line. This makes sure the script runs in the background.

5. Run the `run_on_boot.sh` file manually in a Terminal to make sure it works. The `gpio_pkg_check.log` file should be created and contains the output of the Python script:

```
$ ./run_on_boot.sh
$ cat gpio_pkg_check.log
###### STARTUP Fri 13 Sep 2019 03:59:58 PM AEST ######
GPIOZero Available
PiGPIO Available
```

6. Reboot your Raspberry Pi:

```
$ sudo reboot
```

7. Once your Raspberry Pi has finished restarting, the `gpio_pkg_check.log` file should now contain additional lines, indicating that the script did indeed run at boot:

```
$ cd ~/pyiot/chapter01
$ cat gpio_pkg_check.log

###### STARTUP Fri 13 Sep 2019 03:59:58 PM AEST ######

GPIOZero Available
PiGPIO Available

###### STARTUP Fri 13 Sep 2019 04:06:12 PM AEST ######

GPIOZero Available
PiGPIO Available
```

If you are not seeing the additional output in the `gpio_pkg_check.log` file after a reboot, double-check that the absolute path you entered in `crontab` is correct and that it works manually as per *step 5*. Also, review the system log file, `/var/log/syslog`, and search for the text, `run_on_boot.sh`.

 Our cron-based example of running a script on boot is one of many options that are available in Unix-based operating systems such as Raspbian. Another common and more advanced option using `systemd` can be found on the Raspberry Pi website at `https://www.raspberrypi.org/documentation/linux/usage/systemd.md`. Irrespective of the option you prefer, the key point to remember is to ensure your Python scripts run from within their virtual environment.

We have now learned alternative methods to run a Python script, which will help you in the future to correctly run your Python-based IoT projects after they are developed or start them when your Raspberry Pi boots if required.

Next, we will now move on to making sure your Raspberry Pi is set up and configured correctly for the GPIO and electronic interfacing that we'll be diving into in the next chapter, `Chapter 2`, *Getting Started with Python and IoT*, and subsequent chapters.

Configuring the GPIO interface on our Raspberry Pi

Before we can start working with Python GPIO libraries and controlling electronics, one task we need to perform is to enable the GPIO interfaces on your Raspberry Pi. Even though we have installed Python packages for GPIO control, we have not told Raspbian OS that we want to use the Raspberry Pi's GPIO Pins for specific cases. Let's do that now.

Here are the steps to follow:

1. From your Raspbian desktop, navigate to the **Raspberry** menu | **Preferences** | **Raspberry Pi Configuration**, as shown here in *Figure 1.2*:

Figure 1.2 – Location of the Raspberry Pi Configuration menu item

Alternatively, interfaces can be managed at the command line with the `sudo raspi-config` command and navigating to the **Interfacing Options** menu.

2. Enable all of the interfaces as shown in the following screenshot:

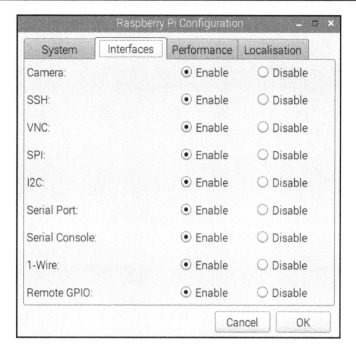

Figure 1.3 - Raspberry Pi Configuration Dialog

3. Click the **OK** button.

After you click the **OK** button, you may be prompted to reboot your Raspberry Pi; however, *do not* confirm the reboot just yet because there is one more task we need to perform first. We'll look at that next.

Configuring the PiGPIO daemon

We also need to start the PiGPIO daemon, which is a system service that needs to be running so that we can use the PiGPIO GPIO client library, which we will start using next in `Chapter 2`, *Getting Started with Python and IoT*.

 Architecturally, the PiGPIO library comprises two parts—a server service and a client that communicates over local pipes or sockets to the service. We will cover more about this basic architecture in `Chapter 5`, *Connecting Your Raspberry Pi to the Physical World*.

Execute the following in a Terminal. This will start the PiGPIO daemon and will ensure that the PiGPIO daemon is started automatically when your Raspberry Pi boots:

```
$ sudo systemctl enable pigpiod
$ sudo systemctl start pigpiod
```

Now, it's time to reboot your Raspberry Pi! So, take a break while your Raspberry Pi restarts. You deserve it because we have covered a lot!

Summary

In this chapter, we explored the Python ecosystem that is part of a typical Unix-based operating system such as Raspbian OS and learned that Python is a core element of the operating system tooling. We then covered how to create and navigate a Python virtual environment so that we can *sandbox* our Python projects so they will not interfere with one another or the system-level Python ecosystem.

Next, we learned how to use the Python package management tool, `pip`, to install and manage Python library dependencies from within a virtual environment, and we did this by installing the GPIOZero and PiGPIO libraries. And since there will be times that we need to execute a Python script as the root user, from outside its virtual environment or during boot up, we also covered these various techniques.

By default, Raspbian does not have all of its GPIO interfaces enabled, so we performed the configuration needed to enable these features so that they are readily available for use in later chapters. We also started and learned how to set up the PiGPIO daemon service so that it starts every time your Raspberry Pi is booted.

The core knowledge you have gained in this chapter will help you to correctly set up and navigate sandboxed Python development environments for your own IoT (and non-IoT) projects and safely install library dependencies so they do not interfere with your other Python projects or the system-level installation of Python. Your understanding of different ways of executing a Python program will also help you to run your projects with elevated user permissions (that is, as the root user), or at boot, should your project have these requirements.

Next, in `Chapter 2`, *Getting Started with Python and IoT*, we will jump straight into Python and electronics and create an end-to-end internet-enabled program that can control an LED over the internet. We will take a look at two alternative ways of flashing an LED using the GPIOZero and PiGPIO GPIO libraries before connecting our LED to the internet by using an online service, *dweet.io*, as our networking layer.

Questions

As we conclude, here is a list of questions for you to test your knowledge regarding this chapter's material. You will find the answers in the *Assessments* section of the book:

1. What is the main reason why you should always use a virtual environment for your Python projects?
2. Do you need to or should you place the virtual environment folder (that is, `venv`) under version control?
3. Why create a `requirements.txt` file?
4. You need to run a Python script as the root user. What step must you take to ensure that the script executes in its intended virtual environment context?
5. What does the `source venv/bin/activate` command do?
6. You are in an activated virtual environment. What is the command to leave the virtual environment and return to the host shell?
7. You created a Python project and virtual environment in PyCharm. Can you work on and run the project's Python scripts in a Terminal?
8. You want a GUI tool to edit and test Python code on your Raspberry Pi but do not have PyCharm installed. What pre-installed tool that comes with Python and Raspbian could you use?
9. You've advanced in your Python and electronics knowledge and are trying to hook up a device using I2C to your Raspberry Pi but you cannot get it to work. What might be the problem and how do you address it?

Further reading

We covered the `venv` virtual environment tool in this chapter. Here are links to its official documentation:

- venv documentation: `https://docs.python.org/3/library/venv.html`
- venv tutorial: `https://docs.python.org/3/tutorial/venv.html`

If you would like to learn about the `virtualenv` and `pipenv` alternative virtual environment tools, here is their official documentation:

- `virtualenv` home page: `https://virtualenv.pypa.io/en/latest`
- `pipenv` home page: `https://docs.pipenv.org/en/latest`

The following is a link to the *Python Packaging Guide*. Here you will find a comprehensive guide regarding Python package management, including `pip` and the easy-install/setup tools alternatives:

- Python Packaging User Guide: `https://packaging.python.org`

If you wish to learn more about scheduling and cron, here are two resources to get you started:

- An overview of cron syntax (and a GUI tool): `https://www.raspberrypi.org/documentation/linux/usage/cron.md`
- A detailed tutorial on cron syntax: `https://opensource.com/article/17/11/how-use-cron-linux`

Getting Started with Python and IoT

2

In `Chapter 1`, *Setting Up Your Development Environment*, we went through the essentials of the Python ecosystem, virtual environments, and package management and set up your Raspberry Pi for development and GPIO interfacing. In this chapter, we will begin our journey in Python and IoT.

What we cover in this chapter will lay the foundations and give us a working point of reference for the more advanced content that we'll cover in later chapters. We will learn to create a simple electrical circuit with a button, resistor, and LED (or light-emitting diode) and explore alternative ways to interact with the button and LED with Python. We will then proceed to create and discuss a complete end-to-end IoT program to control the LED over the internet and complete this chapter by looking at ways that you can extend the program.

In this chapter, we will cover the following topics:

- Creating a breadboard prototype circuit
- Reading an electronic schematic diagram
- Exploring two ways to flash a LED in Python
- Exploring two ways to integrate a push button in Python
- Creating your first IoT program
- Extending your IoT program

Technical requirements

To perform the exercises in this chapter and throughout this book, you will need the following:

- Raspberry Pi 4 Model B. A 1 GB RAM version will be adequate to run our examples. If you are working directly on your Raspberry Pi versus a **Secure Shell** (**SSH**) session; for example, more RAM is recommended to improve the Raspbian Desktop experience and responsiveness.
- You will need Raspbian OS Buster (with desktop and recommended software).
- You will need a minimum of Python version 3.5.

These requirements are what the code examples in this book are based on. It's reasonable to expect that the code examples should work without modification on a Raspberry Pi 3 Model B, Raspberry Pi Zero W, or a different version of Raspbian OS as long as your Python version is 3.5 or higher.

You will find this chapter's source code in the `chapter02` folder in the GitHub repository available at the following URL: `https://github.com/PacktPublishing/Practical-Python-Programming-for-IoT`.

You will need to execute the following commands in a Terminal to set up a virtual environment and install the Python libraries required for the code in this chapter:

```
$ cd chapter02            # Change into this chapter's folder
$ python3 -m venv venv    # Create Python Virtual Environment
$ source venv/bin/activate # Activate Python Virtual Environment
(venv) $ pip install pip --upgrade      # Upgrade pip
(venv) $ pip install -r requirements.txt # Install dependent
packages
```

The following dependencies are installed from `requirements.txt`:

- **GPIOZero**: The GPIOZero GPIO library (`https://pypi.org/project/gpiozero`)
- **PiGPIO**: The PiGPIO GPIO library (`https://pypi.org/project/pigpio`)
- **Requests**: A high-level Python library for making HTTP requests (`https://pypi.org/project/requests`)

We are going to require a few physical electronic components:

- 1 x 5 mm red LED
- 1 x 200 Ω resistor: Its color bands will be red, black, brown, and then gold or silver

- Momentary push button (**Single Pole Single Throw—SPST**)
- A breadboard
- Male-to-female and male-to-male jumper cables (sometimes called Dupont cables)

 You will find a complete parts list cataloging all of the electrical components required for every chapter in the *Preface*.

When you have your electronic components ready, we can proceed and arrange them on your breadboard.

Creating a breadboard prototype circuit

Throughout this book, we will be building many electrical circuits, and we will do this using an electronic breadboard. In the initial chapters, I will present many of the circuits with both a breadboard layout similar to that illustrated toward the end of this section in *Figure 2.7* and with a schematic diagram as shown in *Figure 2.8*.

As we progress through this book and you gain more experience building breadboard circuits, I will cease with the breadboard layouts for the simpler circuits; however, I will still present them for the more complex circuits so you have something to compare your builds against.

 Please note that the proceeding circuit examples and discussions are only brief. At this stage of this book, we intend to build a simple electronic circuit that will be the basis for our Python examples in this chapter and Chapter 3, *Networking with RESTful APIs and Web Sockets Using Flask*, and Chapter 4, *Networking with MQTT, Python, and the Mosquitto MQTT Broker*.

We will discuss the Raspberry Pi and its pin numbering in detail in Chapter 5, *Connecting Your Raspberry Pi to the Physical World*. Furthermore, we will cover in detail circuits and electronics fundamentals in Chapter 6, *Electronics 101 for the Software Engineer*, where among other topics we will learn the *why* behind how the button interacts electrically with your Raspberry Pi and why a 200 Ω resistor accompanies our LEDs.

Let's get started with building our first circuit. I'll walk you through the breadboard build step by step and talk briefly about each component as we work with them. We will start by discussing what a breadboard is and how it works.

Understanding the breadboard

An electronic *breadboard,* as illustrated in *Figure 2.1,* is a prototyping board that helps you to electrically connect components and wires quickly and easily. In this section, we will discuss the general properties of a breadboard in preparation for connecting components and wires together in the following sections:

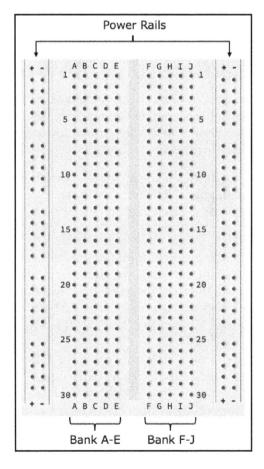

Figure 2.1 – Breadboard

Breadboards come in many different sizes, and our illustrated breadboard is a half-sized breadboard. Irrespective of their size, however, their basic layout and electrical connectivity are similar—with one small exception that I'll mention later.

Real breadboards may, or may not, have the row and column numbers markings on them. They have been included in the illustration to assist with the following discussion and explanations.

The *holes* in the breadboard are where you place electrical components and wires to electrically connect them. The holes are electrically connected in the following ways:

- The two outer columns of holes are commonly referred to as *power rails*. There is a positive (+) column and a negative (-) column on either side of the breadboard. Each column of holes is electrically connected and run for the full length of the breadboard. Hence, there are four independent power rails on this breadboard: a + and - rail on the left-hand side of the breadboard and a + and - rail on the right-hand side.

  The power rails are frequently used to help to distribute power around the breadboard to components. Please note that they do not provide power themselves! They need a power source such as a power supply or battery connected to them to provide power.

- The center of the breadboard has two banks of holes, which I have labeled *Bank A-E* and *Bank F-J*. Each *row* of holes in a bank is electrically connected. For example, holes A1 through to E1 are electrically connected, as are holes F1 through to J1. However, to be clear in our understanding, A1-E1 are *not* electrically connected to F1-J1 because they are on a separate bank.

We straddle **Integrated Circuits (ICs)**—commonly called *chips*—across the gap between the two banks when we connect them into a breadboard. We will see an example of this in `Chapter 10`, *Movement with Servos, Motors, and Steppers*, when we use an IC to control motors.

Here are a few more examples of how the holes are connected that you can work through to help with your understanding:

- B5 is electrically connected to C5 (they share the same row).
- H25 is electrically connected to J25 (they share the same row).
- A2 is *not* electrically connected to B2 (they don't share the same row).
- E30 is *not* electrically connected to F30 (they are on different banks).
- The third + hole (from the top of the breadboard) on the left-hand side power rail is electrically connected to the last + hole on the left-hand side power rail (they are in the same vertical column).
- The third + hole (from the top of the breadboard) on the left-hand side power rail is *not* electrically connected to the third + hole on the right-hand side power rail (they are on different power rails).

I mentioned at the start of this section that all breadboards are basically the same, with one minor exception. This exception relates to the power rails. Some full-size breadboards may split their power rails into two separate vertical banks (so, electrically, the vertical holes in a rail do not run the full length of the breadboard). It is not always visually obvious that the power rails are split, so discovery needs to happen on a breadboard-by-breadboard basis. I mention this just in case you are using a full-size breadboard and experience connectivity issues when using the power rails.

Now that we have introduced breadboards, and we understand how the holes are electrically related to one another, let's start plugging components and wires into our breadboards to create our first circuit. We'll start with the push button.

Positioning and connecting the push button

We are using a simple on/off button, also commonly known as an **Single Pole, Single Throw** (**SPST**) momentary switch. An example is shown in *Figure 2.2*:

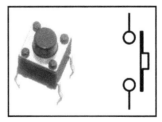

Figure 2.2 – A push button and schematic symbol

On the left-hand side of *Figure 2.2* is a photograph of a momentary push button, while the right-hand side shows the schematic symbol for a momentary push button. We'll see this symbol and discuss schematic diagrams where these types of symbols appear in the next section.

Push buttons come in many shapes and sizes; however, their general operation is the same. This specific push button pictured on the left-hand side is known as a *tactile* push button. They are small and well suited for use with a breadboard.

Figure 2.3 illustrates the push button connection we need to create on our breadboard. Please refer to this as you follow the forthcoming steps:

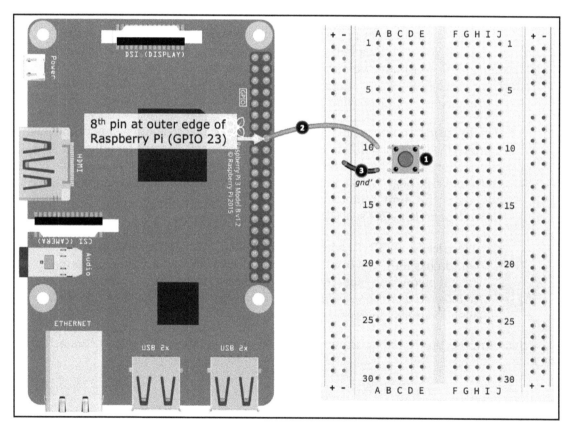

Figure 2.3 – Connecting the push button

Here is how to connect the push button into your breadboard and connect it to your Raspberry Pi. The following step numbers match the numbered black circles in *Figure 2.3*:

1. Position the button on the breadboard as shown. It does not matter exactly which row of holes the button goes into, however, *Figure 2.3* shows the button positioned (top-left leg) at hole **B10**.

2. Next, connect a jumper wire into the same row as the push button's top-most leg (our illustration uses hole **A10**). Connect the other end of this wire to the eighth pin counted down from the outer edge of your Raspberry Pi's GPIO header. This pin is known as GPIO 23.

> You can get header pin labels and breadboard compatible modules to assist you with Raspberry Pi pin connections and identification. Here is a link to a printable version to get you started: `https://github.com/splitbrain/rpibplusleaf`. We will cover GPIO pins and their numbering in `Chapter 5`, *Connecting Your Raspberry Pi to the Physical World*.

3. Finally, using another wire (labeled *gnd'*), we connect the other side of the push button (the leg in hole B2) to the negative power rail on your breadboard. Our illustration shows the *gnd'* wire connection from hole A12 to a nearby hole on the left-hand side negative (-) power rail. The abbreviation *gnd* means ground. We will cover this term in more detail in the forthcoming section, *Understanding ground connections and symbols*.

> Electrically, an SPST switch can be installed any way around. If your button has four legs (two sets will be electrically connected) and your circuit below does not work when we test it later in the *Exploring two ways to integrate a push button in Python* section try rotating the button in your breadboard 90 degrees.

Now that our push button is in position and wired, we will next position and connect our LED.

Positioning and connecting the LED

An LED is a small, yet bright, light made of a tiny crystal that emits a color when electricity is connected to it.

A typical LED is shown in *Figure 2.4.* The left-hand side of the diagram shows a physical representation of a LED, while the right-hand side shows the schematic symbol for a LED:

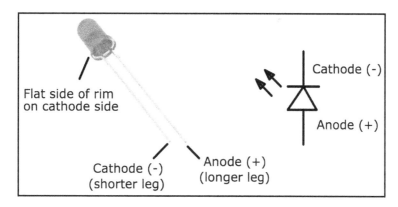

Figure 2.4 – LED and schematic symbol

LEDs need to be connected the correct way around into a circuit, otherwise, they will not work. If you look closely at your LED, you will notice a flat side on the LED casing. The leg on this side is the *cathode,* which connects to the negative or ground side of a power source. The cathode leg will also be the shorter of the LED's legs. The other leg is known as the *anode* and connects to the positive side of a power source. If you examine the LED symbol, you will notice that the cathode side of the LED has a line drawn across the tip of the triangle—if you think of this line as being like a big negative sign, it'll help you to remember which side of the symbol is the cathode leg.

Figure 2.5 the LED connection we are about to create. Please refer to this diagram as you follow the forthcoming steps:

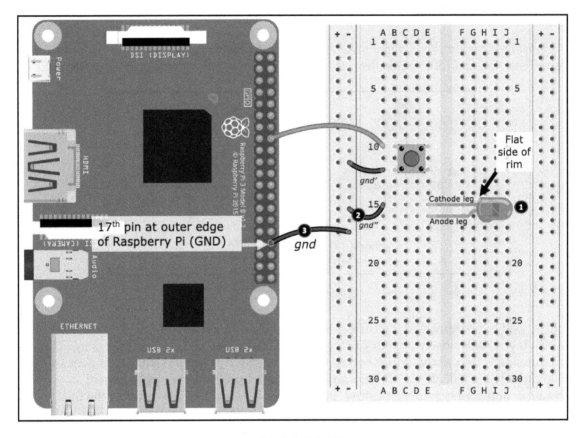

Figure 2.5 – Connecting the LED

Here is how to connect the LED into your breadboard and connect it to your Raspberry Pi. The following step numbers match the numbered black circles in *Figure 2.5* :

1. Connect the LED into your breadboard as illustrated, taking care to ensure that the LED is installed the correct way around. Our illustration shows the cathode leg in hole E15 and the anode leg in hole E16.

 You may need to bend the legs on your LED to get it into position. As you position your LED, make sure the two legs are not touching one another! If they are touching, this will cause what is known as an *electrical short*, and the LED part of the circuit will not work.

2. Next, using a jumper wire (labeled *gnd"*), connect the cathode leg of the LED into the same power rail shared by the push button. We have shown this connection with one end of the *gnd"* wire connected in hole **A15**, while the other end of the wire connected to a nearby hole on the left-hand side negative (-) power rail.

3. Finally, using another jumper wire (labeled *gnd),* connect the negative (-) power rail to the 17th outer edge pin on your Raspberry Pi's GPIO header. This pin is a ground (GND) pin on your Raspberry Pi.

Well done! That's our LED connected. Next, we add the resistor, which will complete our circuit.

Positioning and connecting the resistor

A resistor is an electronic component used to limit (that is, resist) current flow and divide voltage and they are a very common electrical component.

Shown in *Figure 2.6* are a physical resistor (left-hand side) and two schematic symbols (right-hand side). There is no practical difference between the schematic symbols pictured. They represent different documentation standards, and you will find that the author of a schematic diagram will choose and stick with one type of symbol. We'll be using the zig-zag symbol throughout this book:

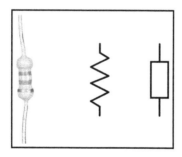

Figure 2.6 – Resistor and schematic symbols

Resistors come in many shapes, sizes, and colors. As a general guide, their physical shape and size relate to their physical properties and capabilities, while the color of their casing is usually insignificant, at least as far as their properties are concerned. The colored bands on a resistor, however, are very significant as they identify the resistor's value. It's worth mentioning that small general-purpose resistors (which are what we will be using) use color bands for specifying their value, while physically larger resistors used in high power applications frequently have their resistance value printed on their casing.

Resistors are an unbiased electrical component, meaning that they can be installed in an electrical circuit either way around. Their values, however, need to be chosen correctly, otherwise a circuit may not work as intended, or worse, the resistor and/or other components (including your Raspberry Pi) can be damaged.

When starting out and learning about circuits, it is highly recommended and safest to always use the intended resistor values that are listed for a circuit. Avoid any temptation to substitute different values when you do not have the correct value on hand as this can result in damage to components and even your Raspberry Pi.

Our use of resistors through this book will be pragmatic. although I will be explaining how and why we arrive at the certain values we use from Chapter 6, *Electronics 101 for the Software Engineer,* onward. If you are new to resistors, you will find two links in the *Further reading* section where you can learn more about them, including how to read their values.

Figure 2.7 demonstrates the resistor connection we need to create. Please refer to this as you follow the forthcoming steps:

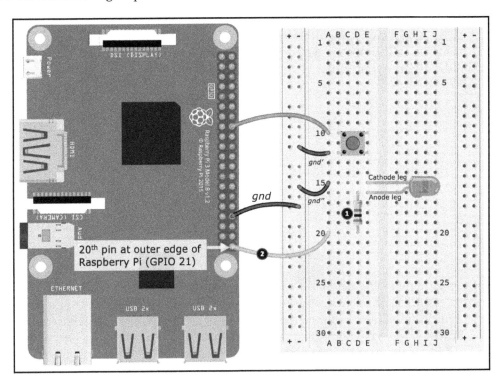

Figure 2.7 – Completed button and LED circuit on the breadboard

Here is how to connect the resistor into your breadboard. The following step numbers match the numbered black circles in *Figure 2.7*:

1. Place one leg (is does not matter which one) of the resistor into a hole that shares the same row as the LED's anode leg. This connection is shown at hole **D16**. Insert the other leg inserted into a vacant row, shown at **D20** (it'll be a vacant row on your breadboard until we connect the wire next).

2. Using a jumper wire (illustrated starting at hole **A20**), we connect the other leg of our resistor to the 20th pin on the outer edge of your Raspberry Pi's GPIO header. This pin is known as GPIO 21.

Well done! With that last connection, we have created our first circuit. We'll be using this base circuit throughout the rest of this chapter and in the next two chapters, Chapter 3, *Networking with RESTful APIs and Web Sockets Using Flask*, and Chapter 4, *Networking with MQTT, Python, and the Mosquitto MQTT Broker*. We will start to explore a range of other circuits from Chapter 5, *Connecting Your Raspberry Pi to the Physical World*, onward.

Now that we have completed our breadboard circuit and learned how components and wires are connected on our breadboard, we are ready to explore a diagramming technique that is used to describe electrical circuits.

Reading an electronic schematic diagram

In the last section, we built our first circuit on a breadboard by following a series of illustrated steps. In this section, we will learn about *schematic diagrams*, which is a formal way of documenting and describing an electrical circuit. These are the diagrams you find in electronic texts and datasheets.

We will learn how to read a simple schematic diagram and how it relates back to the breadboard layout we just created. Understanding how the two relate, and especially being able to create a breadboard layout from a schematic diagram, is an important skill you will need to develop as you continue your electronics and IoT journey.

The electronic circuits and schematic diagrams we will be seeing and working with throughout this book will be relatively simple as far as schematic diagrams are concerned. We will address important concepts and component symbols as we encounter them on a case-by-case basis. For our journey, a full and detailed explanation of the ins and outs of schematic diagramming is unnecessary and beyond the practical scope of this book. However, I encourage you to read through the Spark Fun tutorial that's mentioned in the *Further reading* section. It provides a brief, yet comprehensive overview of reading schematic diagrams and will provide you with a good foundational understanding of this diagramming technique and its semantics.

Let's start by looking at a schematic diagram that represents the breadboard circuit we just created as shown in *Figure 2.7*. Our semantic diagram is illustrated here:

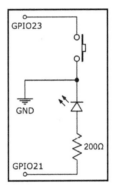

Figure 2.8 – Schematic diagram of the breadboard circuit from Figure 2.7

A schematic diagram can be correctly drawn in a multitude of ways; however, I've purposely drawn this diagram (and will do so where appropriate in this book) to closely resemble its equivalent breadboard layout to help with its interpretation and understanding.

We'll learn to read this schematic diagram by first explaining the push button connection and wiring.

Reading the push button schematic connection

I've combined the breadboard layout and schematic diagram (with a few additional labels) as follows:

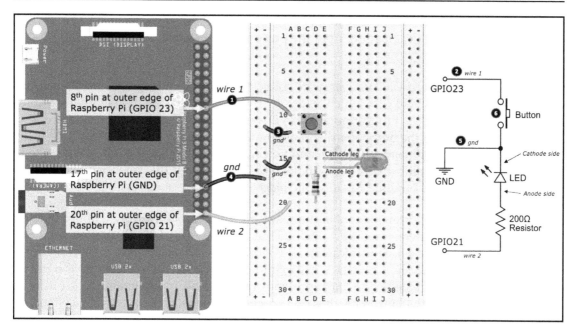

Figure 2.9 – Combined breadboard and schematic diagram, part 1 of 2

Here is how to read the pushbutton connection. The following step numbers match the numbered black circles in *Figure 2.9*:

1. Start at the breadboard with the wire labeled *wire 1*. If we look at the ends of this wire, we see that one end is connected to GPIO 23 on the Raspberry Pi, while the other end (at hole **A10**) connects to a row shared by the push button.

2. Looking at the schematic diagram, this breadboard connection is depicted diagrammatically by the line labeled *wire 1*. You will notice one end of the line is labeled GPIO23, while the other end leads into one side of the button symbol.

The color of a wire's casing has no inherent meaning. The color is simply a visual aid to help to distinguish different wires and connections. However, there are some common conventions such as using a red wire for a positive power connection and a black wire for the negative or ground wire

3. Next, starting at the other side of the push button on the breadboard (hole **A12**), notice the wire labeled *gnd'*. This wire connects the push button to the outer power rail on the breadboard.

4. Five holes down from this first power rail connection, we see a second ground wire (labeled *gnd)* leading from the breadboard back to a GND pin on the Raspberry Pi.

5. The breadboard *gnd* and *gnd'* wire connections are seen in the schematic diagram as the line labeled *gnd,* which leads out of the button and ends at a downward pointing *arrow* symbol annotated *GND* (remember *gnd* and *gnd'* are electrically connected on the breadboard and are therefore logically a single wire). This is the symbol for a *ground connection,* and you will frequently see this symbol repeated a lot in schematic diagrams. I'll have more to say about this symbol when we reach the section titled *Reading and understanding the ground symbol.*

6. Examine the button symbol in the schematic diagram and you will notice that the *wire 1* and *gnd* lines are not joined but rather terminate in the button symbol (the small circles). This is known as a *normally open connection* or, in our specific case, *a normally open* switch. You can think of *normally open* as meaning the line is broken (and remember a *line* represents a *wire).* Now, if you imagine the button *pressed,* then the button touches each circle and connects the *blue* and *gnd* lines, resulting in a *closed* connection that completes the circuit between GPIO 23 and GND. We'll discuss this idea more in `Chapter 6`, *Electronics 101 for the Software Engineer.*

When you are comfortable that you understand how the push button connections on the breadboard match the push button section of the schematic diagram, we will proceed and discuss LED and resistor connections.

Reading the LED and resistor schematic connection

Continuing from the previous section, where we learned how to read and understand the push button part of the schematic diagram, next we complete our explanation by covering the LED and resistor connections, as shown here:

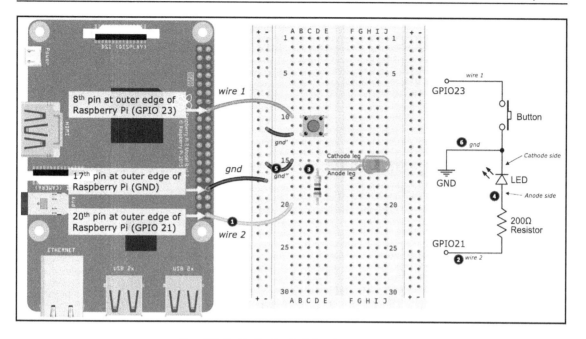

Figure 2.10 – Combined breadboard and schematic diagram, part 2 of 2

Here is how to read the LED and resistor connection. The following step numbers match the numbered black circles in *Figure 2.10*:

1. Start at the wire labeled *wire 2* on the breadboard. This wire connects GPIO 21 on the Raspberry Pi into the row shared by one end of the resistor (hole **A25**).

2. The *wire 2* connection is depicted by the line also labeled *wire 2* on the schematic diagram.

3. On the breadboard, the other end of the resistor is connected to the anode leg of the LED (hole **E15**). Remember, the resistor and anode leg of the LED are electrically connected because they share the same row of holes in the same bank on the breadboard.

4. We see the resistor/LED connection in the schematic diagram where the resistor symbol meets the LED symbol. We know the resistor connects to the anode side of the LED in the diagram by the way the LED symbol is orientated.

5. Next, on the breadboard, the other leg of the LED (hole **E15**)—the cathode leg—connects to the *gnd"* wire (hole **A15**), which then connects back to the outer power rail that is also shared by the push button's *gnd'* wire (which is then connected back to the Raspberry Pi's GND pin with the *gnd* wire.)

6. Finally, on the schematic diagram, this connection from the LED cathode leg to GND is depicted by the line labeled *gnd* (the same one used by the push button).

We have now completed our schematic diagram explanation. How did you do? I hope you were able to trace around the diagram and see how it relates back to the circuit we built on the breadboard.

Our last step illustrates an important concept in electronics—a *common ground*. We'll discuss this concept in more detail next.

Introducing ground connections and symbols

Electrical circuits all require a common electrical point of reference, and we call this point *ground*. This is why we see the push button and LED sharing a common connection on both the breadboard and schematic diagram (as a reminder, refer to *Figure 2.10*.

For the simple circuits presented throughout this book and when working with your Raspberry Pi's GPIO pins, it will be practical to consider the terms *negative* and *ground* as interchangeable. This is because the *negative* side of a power source will be our common point of electrical reference (and yes, GPIO pins are a source of power, which we will explore more in Chapter 6, *Electronics 101 for the Software Engineer*).

As mentioned previously in the *Reading the push button schematic connection* section, in *step 4*, we diagrammed the ground point using an arrow symbol. Our ground symbol (made out of line segments) is one common variation of a ground symbol. You'll see another variation in *Figure 2.11*:

Figure 2.11 – Common schematic diagram ground symbols

All ground points are electrically connected, and we may repeat the symbol many times in a schematic diagram to help to simplify the diagram. By using the ground symbol to indicate a common ground connection, we remove the need to draw many interconnecting lines to join all ground connections together (which would get rather messy for large or more complex circuits).

Our simple circuit certainly does not come under the banners of *large* or *complex*, however, to illustrate the concept of common ground, I have redrawn the schematic diagram shown originally in *Figure 2.8* here, only this time using multiple ground symbols:

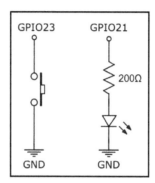

Figure 2.12 – Alternative schematic diagrams of the breadboard circuit in Figure 2.7

Although our alternative schematic diagram looks like two separate circuits, they are electrically connected exactly the same as our original schematic diagram in *Figure 2.8.*

Please take a moment now to examine both *Figure 2.8* and *Figure 2.12* and see whether you can work out how the two diagrams are electrically the same.

All I have done here is broken the line (labeled *gnd* in *Figure 2.8*) and redrawn the push button subcircuit and LED/resistor subcircuit in a different orientation and used separate ground symbol for each subcircuit.

As mentioned previously, at this stage of this book, we do not go into how or why this circuit works electronically or how it interacts electrically with the GPIO pins on your Raspberry Pi. We'll cover these topics and many more with practical and illustrative exercises when we reach Chapter 6, *Electronics 101 for the Software Engineer.*

Now that you have seen the schematic diagram that documents our breadboard circuit and see how they relate to one another, we're finally ready to dive into code and learn two ways to make our LED flash in Python!

Exploring two ways to flash an LED in Python

In this section, we will investigate two alternative GPIO libraries and ways to make an LED flash in Python, including the following:

- The GPIOZero library: An entry-level GPIO library
- The PiGPIO library: An advanced GPIO library

As we learn to use these two libraries, we will see how they approach GPIO control differently and discover their relative strengths and weaknesses.

After completing this section (and the following section, *Exploring two ways to integrate a push button in Python*), you will have explored and compared two very different approaches to GPIO control—the high-level (using GPIOZero) and a lower-level (using PiGPIO)—and have a good introductory grasp of when and how you would choose between the alternative when building an electronic interfacing program.

Let's start our practical exercises by making the LED blink using GPIOZero.

Blinking with GPIOZero

We are now ready to investigate our first blinking method using the GPIOZero library. You will find the code we are about to cover in the `chapter02/led_gpiozero.py` file. Please review this file before proceeding.

 In the *Further reading* section, you will find relevant links to the GPIOZero API documentation for the specific features of this library that we use in this section.

We will start by running our example code.

Run the program using the following command, remembering that you need to be in the *activated* virtual environment (if you need a refresher on how to activate a Python virtual environment, see Chapter 1, *Setting Up Your Development Environment*):

```
(venv) $ python led_gpiozero.py
```

If the LED is connected correctly, it should blink.

 If you receive an error about PiGPIO when you run the program, make sure you have enabled the pigpio daemon as outlined in Chapter 1, *Setting Up Your Development Environment*. We'll talk more about PiGPIO and the PiGPIO daemon in Chapter 5, *Connecting Your Raspberry Pi to the Physical World*.

Now that we have run the code and seen the LED blink, it's time to look through the code that makes this happen.

Imports

We will start our code exploration by looking at the external libraries we are importing in our Python program. They appear near the top of the source file, as shown here:

```
from gpiozero import Device, LED          # (1)
from gpiozero.pins.pigpio import PiGPIOFactory  # (2)
from time import sleep
```

 The imports of interest are the following:

- At line (1), we import the Device and LED classes from the GPIOZero package.
- At line (2), we are importing a GPIOZero *Pin Factory*. This is used together with the Device class, which we'll see next.

Next, we see how to set the GPIOZero Pin Factory implementation.

Pin Factory configuration

A *Pin Factory* is used in GPIOZero specify which concrete GPIO library GPIOZero will use to perform the actual GPIO work. We will discuss Pin Factories in more detail when we compare the GPIOZero and PiGPIO examples later in this chapter in the *Comparing the GPIOZero and PiGPIO examples* section:

```
Device.pin_factory = PiGPIOFactory()   # (3)
```

On line (3), we are telling GPIOZero to use PiGPIO as its *Pin Factory* using the `Device` and `PiGPIOFactory` imports.

Now that we've seen how a Pin Factory is set up, let's look at the code that makes our LED blink.

Blinking the LED

Here, we see the `LED` class at line (4) in the following is created and assigned to the `led` variable. The parameter to `LED` is the GPIO pin that the physical LED is connected to, as per the breadboard in *Figure 2.1*:

```
GPIO_PIN = 21
led = LED(GPIO_PIN)            # (4)
led.blink(background=False) # (5)
```

On line (5), we start the LED blinking. The `background=False` parameter to `blink()` is needed to run the LED on the main thread so the program does not exit (an alternative of `background=True` would be to use `signal.pause()`. We'll see an example of this in the next section).

GPIOZero makes it very easy to interface with common electronic components such as an LED. Next, we will perform the same exercise, only this time using the PiGPIO library.

Blinking with PiGPIO

Now that we have seen how to blink our LED using the GPIOZero library, let's look at an alternative method using the PiGPIO library.

The code we are about to walk through is contained in the `chapter02/led_pigpio.py` file. Terminate the previous example if it is still running, and run `led_pigpio.py`. The LED should blink again.

In the *Further reading* section, you will find relevant links to the PiGPIO API documentation for the specific features of this library that we are using in this section.

Let's walk through the PiGPIO version of our LED blinking code.

Imports

Starting at the top of the file, we have the `import` section of the source file:

```
import pigpio              # (1)
from time import sleep
```

This time around, on line (1), we only need to import the PiGPIO module.

Next, we will see how to configure PiGPIO and set the I/O mode on the GPIO pin that is connected to our LED.

PiGPIO and pin configuration

Let's look at the code that configures PiGPIO and the LED's GPIO pin:

```
GPIO_PIN = 21
pi = pigpio.pi()                       # (2)
pi.set_mode(GPIO_PIN, pigpio.OUTPUT)   # (3)
```

We create an instance of PiGPIO on line (2) and assign it to the `pi` variable. We use this variable to interact with the PiGPIO library from this point forward in the code.

On line (3), we configure GPIO pin 21 to be an *output* pin. Configuring a pin as *output* means we want to use that pin to control something connected to it from our Python code. In this example, we want to control the LED. Later in this chapter, we'll see an example of an input pin used to respond to button presses.

Now that we have imported our required libraries and configured PiGPIO and the out GPIO pin, let's now see how we are making the LED blink.

Blinking the LED

Finally, we make our LED blink:

```
while True:
    pi.write(GPIO_PIN, 1) # 1 = High = On      # (4)
    sleep(1) # 1 second
    pi.write(GPIO_PIN, 0) # 0 = Low = Off       # (5)
    sleep(1) # 1 second
```

We achieve the blinking with PiGPIO using a `while` loop. As the loop executes, we are toggling GPIO pin 21— our *output* pin—on and off (lines (4) and (5)), with a short `sleep()` function in between, hence making the LED appear to blink.

Next, we will compare our two libraries and their different approaches to blinking the LED.

Comparing the GPIOZero and PiGPIO examples

If you look at the code for the GPIOZero example, it's pretty obvious we're making an LED blink—it's pretty explicit in the code. But what about the PiGPIO example? There is no mention of LEDs or blinking. In truth, it could be doing anything—it's just we know an LED is connected to GPIO 21.

Our two blinking examples reveal important aspects of GPIOZero and PiGPIO:

- **GPIOZero** is a higher-level wrapper library. On the surface, it abstracts common electronic components such as LEDs into simple-to-use classes while, underneath, it is delegating the actual interfacing work to a concrete GPIO library.

- **PiGPIO** is a lower-level GPIO library where you work with, control, and access GPIO pins directly.

 The "zero" in GPIOZero refers to a naming convention for zero boilerplate code libraries where all of the complex internals are abstracted away to make it easier for beginners to get started.

GPIOZero performs its delegation to an external GPIO library using a *Pin Factory*. In our example, we delegated to PiGPIO using the line, `Device.pin_factory = PiGPIOFactory()`. We'll pick up the topic of GPIOZero and delegation again in Chapter 5, *Connecting your Raspberry Pi to the Physical World*.

As we proceed through this book, we will be using both GPIOZero and PiGPIO. We'll use GPIOZero to simplify and condense code where appropriate, while we will be using PiGPIO for more advanced code examples and to teach core GPIO concepts that are otherwise abstracted away by GPIOZero.

Next, we will continue building on our LED blinking examples by integrating the push button.

Exploring two ways to integrate a push button in Python

In the previous section, we explored two different approaches to making our LED blink—one using the GPIOZero library and the other with the PiGPIO library. In this section, we will integrate the push button from the circuit in *Figure 2.1* with Python and see how we can integrate the button using both the GPIOZero and PiGPIO libraries.

We will start by making our LED turn on and off with a button that is integrated using the GPIOZero library.

Responding to a button press with GPIOZero

The code we are about to cover is included in the `chapter02/button_gpiozero.py` file. Please review and run this file. The LED should turn on and off as you press the button. As per the circuit in *Figure 2.1*, the LED is still connected to GPIO 21, while our button is connected to GPIO 23.

 As mentioned previously in the *Creating a breadboard circuit* section, if your button has four legs (two sets will be electrically joined) and your circuit does not work, try rotating the button in the breadboard 90 degrees.

Let's walk through the significant parts of the code, noting that we are skipping sections of code that we've already covered.

Imports

Starting at the top of the source file, you will find the section of code where we import external libraries, as shown here:

```
from gpiozero import Device, LED, Button        # (1)
from gpiozero.pins.pigpio import PiGPIOFactory
import signal                                    # (2)
```

For this example, we have also imported the GPIOZero `Button` class (1) and the Python `signal` module (2).

Now that you have seen that we are importing the `Button` class, let's look at the handler function that will be called when the button is pressed.

Button pressed handler

We are using a callback handler to respond to button presses, defined in the `pressed()` function:

```
def pressed():
    led.toggle()                                    # (3)
    state = 'on' if led.value == 1 else 'off'       # (4)
    print("Button pressed: LED is " + state)        # (5)
```

On line (3), our LED is turned on and off each time `pressed()` is invoked using the `toggle()` method of `led`. On line (4), we query the `value` property of `led` to determine whether the LED is on (`value == 1`) or off (`value == 0`) and store it in the `state` variable, which we print to the Terminal on line (5).

 You can also control the LED with the `led.on()`, `led.off()`, and `led.blink()` methods. You can also directly set the LED on/off state by setting `led.value`, for example, `led.value = 1` will turn the LED on.

Let's continue and see how to create and configure a `Button` class instance and register the `pressed()` function so it is called when you press the physical button.

Button configuration

Following are the lines used to configure the push button. On line (6), the class we use is `Button`. In GPIOZero, we use a `Button` class for any *input* device that can be either on or off, such as buttons and switches:

```
button = Button(BUTTON_GPIO_PIN,
                pull_up=True, bounce_time=0.1)  # (6)
button.when_pressed = pressed                   # (7)
```

On line (7), we register the `pressed()` callback handler with our `button` instance.

Here are the meanings of the parameters to the `Button` constructor on line (6):

- The first parameter is the button's GPIO pin (`BUTTON_GPIO_PIN == 23`).
- The second parameter, `pull_up=True`, enables an internal pull-up resistor for GPIO 23. Pull-up and pull-down resistors are an important concept in digital electronics. We're are going to skip over this concept for now because we will be covering the importance and use of pull-up and pull-down resistors in greater detail in `Chapter 6`, *Electronics 101 for the Software Engineers*.
- The third parameter `bounce_time=0.1` (0.1 seconds), is used to compensate for an occurrence known as switch or contact *bounce*.

Bounce is a type of electrical noise that occurs as the metal contacts within a physical button or switch come together. The result of this noise is seen as a rapid succession of on-off (or high-low) states changes on a digital input pin. This is undesirable because we want *one* physical press of a button (or toggle of a switch) to be seen as *one* state change on the input pin. This is commonly achieved in code using a **debounce threshold** or **timeout**, which in our case is the amount of time that our Raspberry Pi ignores successive pin stage changes following an initial state change.

Try setting `bounce_time=0` (no debouncing). You should find that the button behaves very erratically. Then, use a higher number such as `bounce_time=5` (5 seconds), and you will find that after the first press the button is non-responsive until the duration expires.

 When it comes to push buttons, selecting an appropriate debounce threshold is a matter of balancing how rapidly a user needs to press the button (this demands lower thresholds) versus how much bounce is inherent in your button (this demands higher thresholds). About 0.1 seconds is a good suggested starting value.

Finally, let's cover a common technique that is used to prevent an electronic-interfacing Python program from exiting.

Preventing the main thread from terminating

It's common to see the use of `signal.pause()` or an equivalent construct in GPIO examples and programs:

```
signal.pause() # Stops program from exiting.   # (8)
```

Line (8) prevents the main program thread from reaching its natural end, which under normal circumstances is where the program terminates.

 Forgetting to add `signal.pause()` to the end of a GPIO-interfacing Python program is a common and often confusing mistake when starting out. If your program exits immediately after it's started, try adding `signal.pause()` at the end of your program as a first step.

We didn't need `signal.pause()` with our previous LED flashing examples. Here is why:

- Our GPIOZero example (`chapter02/led_gpiozero.py`) used `background=False` in the LED constructor. This prevented our program from exiting by keeping the LED's thread in the foreground.
- In the PiGPIO example (`chapter02/led_pigpio.py`), it's the `while` loop that prevents the program from exiting.

If this seems confusing, don't worry! Knowing how to prevent a program from existing abnormally all comes down to experience, practice, and understanding how Python and GPIO libraries work.

Next, let's see how to integrate the button using PiGPIO.

Responding to a button press with PiGPIO

We will now replicate the same functionality as our previous GPIOZero example to turn our LED on and off with a button press, only this time using the PiGPIO library. The code for our PiGPIO example can be found in the `chapter02/button_pigpio.py` file. Please review and run this file now, and confirm that the LED responds to your button presses.

Let's unravel the interesting parts of the code, starting with the GPIO pin configuration for the push button (again, noting that we're skipping sections of code that we've already covered).

Button pin configuration

Starting on line (1), we configure GPIO pin 23 (`BUTTON_GPIO_PIN == 23`) as an *input* pin:

```
pi.set_mode(BUTTON_GPIO_PIN, pigpio.INPUT)              # (1)
pi.set_pull_up_down(BUTTON_GPIO_PIN, pigpio.PUD_UP)     # (2)
pi.set_glitch_filter(BUTTON_GPIO_PIN, 10000)           # (3)
```

Next, on line (2), we enable an internal pull-up resistor for pin 23. In PiGPIO, we debounce the push button on line (3) using the `pi.set_glitch_filter()` method. This method takes the parameter in milliseconds.

Notice, in PiGPIO, we needed to configure each property for our button (pin input mode, a pull-up resistor, and debouncing) as a discrete method call, whereas in the previous GPIOZero example this all occurred on a single line when we created an instance of the GPIOZero LED class.

Button pressed handler

Our button callback handler is defined at starting on line (4) and is more involved than the previous GPIOZero handler:

```
def pressed(gpio_pin, level, tick):                    # (4)
    # Get current pin state for LED.
    led_state = pi.read(LED_GPIO_PIN)                  # (5)

    if led_state == 1:                                 # (6)
        # LED is on, so turn it off.
        pi.write(LED_GPIO_PIN, 0) # 0 = Pin Low = Led Off
        print("Button pressed: Led is off")
    else: # 0
        # LED is off, so turn it on.
        pi.write(LED_GPIO_PIN, 1) # 1 = Pin High = Led On
        print("Button pressed: Led is on")

# Register button handler.
pi.callback(BUTTON_GPIO_PIN, pigpio.FALLING_EDGE, pressed)  # (7)
```

Notice the signature of `pressed(gpio_pin, level, tick)`. Our previous GPIOZero version has no parameters while PiGPIO has three mandatory parameters. Our simple one-button example does not use these parameters; however, for completeness they are as follows:

- `gpio_pin`: This is the pin responsible for invoking the callback. This will be 23 in our example.
- `level`: This the state of the pin. For us, this will be `pigpio.FALLING_EDGE` (we'll see why shortly).
- `tick`: This is the number of microseconds since boot.

On line (5), we read the current state of GPIO 21 (our LED) into a variable with `led_state = pi.read()`. Then, starting on line (6), depending on whether the LED is currently on (`led_state == 1`) or off (`led_state == 0`), we set the GPIO 21 high or low using `pi.write()` to toggle the LED to its inverse on or off state.

Finally, the callback handler is registered on line (7). The parameter value, `pigpio.FALLING_EDGE`, means the call handler is `pressed()` whenever the GPIO pin, `BUTTON_GPIO_PIN`, (that is, 23) starts to transition from a digital high to a digital low. This is a lot more explicit than simply testing whether a pin is *high* or *low*; however, for simplicity, consider the following level parameter options to `pi.callback()`. Try changing the parameter and see what happens when you press the button:

- `pigpio.FALLING_EDGE`: This is low (think *falling* toward low). `pressed()` is called when you *press* the button.
- `pigpio.RAISING_EDGE`: This is high (think *raising* toward high). `pressed()` is called when you *release* the button.
- `pigpio.EITHER_EDGE`: This can be high or low. `pressed()` is called when you both *press* and *release* the button, effectively meaning the LED will only illuminate when you hold down the button.

Did you notice or think at any stage in the PiGPIO example that when the button is pressed—that is, you *activated* the button—GPIO pin 23 becomes low (that is, the `pigpio.FALLING_EDGE` parameter on line (7)), and this results in `pressed()` begin called? Did this seem a bit back-to-front or false from a programming perspective? We'll revisit this idea and discuss the reasons behind it in Chapter 6, *Electronics 101 for the Software Engineer*.

That's enough on GPIO libraries and electronics for now. We've seen how to respond to button presses with both the GPIOZero and PiGPIO libraries. In particular, we saw that the GPIOZero approach was rather simple and straightforward compared to the PiGPIO approach, which involved more code and more configuration. This is the same outcome we discovered in the previous section, *Exploring two ways to flash an LED in Python*—that is, the GPIOZero approach was simpler.

Is one approach better than the other? The answer to that all depends on what goal you are trying to achieve and how much lower-level control you require over your electronic interfacing to achieve that goal. At this stage of this book, I just wanted to give you contrasting options regarding GPIO libraries and how we interface them with electronics. We'll be picking this topic up again in greater detail when we revisit popular GPIO libraries for Python in `Chapter 5`, *Connecting Your Raspberry Pi to the Physical World*.

Let's move on and create an IoT program to control our LED over the internet.

Creating your first IoT program

We are about to create a Python program to integrate with a service called `dweet.io`. This is how their website describes the service: *"it's like Twitter for social machines."*

We will create simple *dweets,* which are the dweet.io equivalent of a *tweet,* by pasting a URL into a web browser.

Our program will monitor and receive our dweets by polling a dweet.io RESTful API endpoint for data. As data is received, it will be parsed to find an instruction specifying whether our LED should be turned on or off or made to blink. Based on this instruction, our LED state will be changed using the GPIOZero library. We'll have a look at data format received from dweet.io when we discuss the program's code in a subsequent section titled *Understanding the server code.*

 We're using the free public `dweet.io` service where all information is publicly accessible, so do not publish any sensitive data. There is a professional service available at `dweetpro.io` that provides data privacy, security, dweet retention, and other advanced features.

The code for this program is contained in the `chapter02/dweet_led.py` file. Read through the source code in this file to get a broad perspective about what's happening before continuing.

Running and testing the Python server

In this section, we will run and interact with a Python server program that will let us control our LED from a web browser by copying and pasting links. Once we have used the program to control our LED, we'll then delve into the mechanics of the code and how it works in the next section.

Here are the steps to follow:

1. Run the `chapter02/dweet_led.py` program. You should see output similar to the following:

   ```
   (venv) $ python dweet_led.py
   INFO:main:Created new thing name a8e38712                    # (1)
   LED Control URLs - Try them in your web browser:
    On    : https://dweet.io/dweet/for/a8e38712?state=on        # (2)
    Off   : https://dweet.io/dweet/for/a8e38712?state=off
    Blink : https://dweet.io/dweet/for/a8e38712?state=blink

   INFO:main:LED off
   Waiting for dweets. Press Control+C to exit.
   ```

   On line (1), the program has created a unique name for our *thing* to use with dweet.io. You'll notice this name in the URLs starting on line (2). The name created for your *thing* will be different from the preceding example.

   A *thing* name in dweet.io is analogous to an @handle on Twitter.

2. Copy and paste the URLs at starting on line (2) into a web browser (it could be a computer other than your Raspberry Pi). After a short delay, the LED should change its state (on, off, or blinking) depending on the URL used.

Once you have confirmed that the LED is controllable using the URLs, we will proceed and look at the program.

Understanding the server code

In this section, we will step through the major parts of the `dweet_led.py` program and discover how it works, starting with the imports.

Imports

First, at the start of the source code file, we see the Python imports:

```
...truncated...
import requests      # (1)
```

There is one specific import I want to draw your attention to. On line (1), we are importing the `request` module (this was installed earlier in this chapter when you ran `pip install -r requirements.txt`). `requests` is a high-level library for making HTTP requests in Python. Our program uses this module to communicate with the dweet.io APIs, which we'll see shortly.

Now that we understand that we are importing and will later use the `requests` library, let's cover the global variables used in our program.

Variable definitions

Next, we define several global variables. For now, review the following comments for their purposes. You'll see them being used as we progress through the code:

```
LED_GPIO_PIN = 21                        # LED GPIO Pin
THING_NAME_FILE = 'thing_name.txt'       # Thing name file
URL = 'https://dweet.io'                 # Dweet.io service API
last_led_state = None                    # "on", "off", "blinking"
thing_name = None                        # Thing name
led = None                               # GPIOZero LED instance
```

As you read through the master source file, following these variable definitions, you'll also notice that we are using the Python logging system instead of `print()` statements:

```
logging.basicConfig(level=logging.WARNING)
logger = logging.getLogger('main') # Logger for this module
logger.setLevel(logging.INFO) # Debugging for this file.    # (2)
```

If you need to turn on debugging for the program to diagnose a problem or to see the raw JSON data exchanged between our program and the dweet.io service, change line (2) to `logger.setLevel(logging.DEBUG)`.

Next, we will step through the significant methods in the program and see what they do.

The resolve_thing_name() method

The `resolve_thing_name()` method is responsible for loading or creating a unique name for our *thing* for use with dweet.io.

Our intention when using this method is to always reuse a name so that our dweet URLs for controlling our LED remain the same between the program restarts:

```
def resolve_thing_name(thing_file):
    """Get existing, or create a new thing name"""
    if os.path.exists(thing_file):                   # (3)
        with open(thing_file, 'r') as file_handle:
            name = file_handle.read()
            logger.info('Thing name ' + name +
                        ' loaded from ' + thing_file)
            return name.strip()
    else:
        name = str(uuid1())[:8]                       # (4)
        logger.info('Created new thing name ' + name)

        with open(thing_file, 'w') as f:              # (5)
            f.write(name)

    return name
```

On line (3), we load a name stored previously in `thing_file` if the file exists; otherwise, we use the Python UUID module method `uuid1()` on line (4) to create an 8-character unique identifier and use that as the thing name. We store this newly created identifier-cum-name in `thing_file` on line (5).

Next, we will look at the function that retrieves the last dweet made to our *thing*.

The get_lastest_dweet() method

`get_lastest_dweet()` queries the dweet.io service to retrieve the latest dweet (if any) made for our *thing*. Following is an example of the JSON response we expect to receive. It is the `content.state` property on line (1) that we are ultimately interested in:

```
{
  this: "succeeded",
  by: "getting",
  the: "dweets",
  with: [
    {
      thing: "a8e38712-9886-11e9-a545-68a3c4974cd4",
```

```
        created: "2019-09-16T05:16:59.676Z",
        content: {
          state: "on"                                    # (1)
        }
      }
    ]
  }
```

Looking at the following code, we see, on line (6), the creation of the resource URL used to query the dweet.io service. A call to this URL will return us a JSON similar to that shown in the preceding. You will find a link in the *Further reading* section to the complete dweet.io API reference.

Next, on line (7), the requests module use used to make an HTTP GET request to retrieve the latest dweet:

```
def get_lastest_dweet():
    """Get the last dweet made by our thing."""
    resource = URL + '/get/latest/dweet/for/' + thing_name    # (6)
    logger.debug('Getting last dweet from url %s', resource)

    r = requests.get(resource)                                # (7)
```

Starting on line (8) in the following, we check whether the request succeeded at the HTTP protocol level. If successful on line (9), we then proceed to parse the JSON response and extract and return the content property starting on line (10):

```
    if r.status_code == 200:                                  # (8)
        dweet = r.json() # return a Python dict.
        logger.debug('Last dweet for thing was %s', dweet)

        dweet_content = None

        if dweet['this'] == 'succeeded':                      # (9)
            # Interested in the dweet content property.
            dweet_content = dweet['with'][0]['content']       # (10)

        return dweet_content
    else:
        logger.error('Getting last dweet failed
                     with http status %s', r.status_code)
        return {}
```

Our next method to cover is poll_dweets_forever(), which will use get_lastest_dwcet().

The poll_dweets_forever() method

`poll_dweets_forever()` is a long-running function that periodically calls on line (11) the `get_lastest_dweet()` method we just covered. When a dweet is available, it is handled on line (12) by `process_dweet()`, which we will discuss shortly:

```python
def poll_dweets_forever(delay_secs=2):
    """Poll dweet.io for dweets about our thing."""
    while True:
        dweet = get_last_dweet()                  # (11)
        if dweet is not None:
            process_dweet(dweet)                  # (12)

        sleep(delay_secs)                         # (13)
```

We sleep for a default delay of 2 seconds on line (13) before continuing the loop. Practically, this means there will be up to an approximate 2-second delay between using one of the dweeting URLs to request a LED state change and the LED altering its state.

At this point in the master source file, you will come across a function named `stream_dweets_forever()`. This is an alternative and more efficient stream-based method of accessing dweets in real time using HTTP streaming.

The polling-based approach of `poll_dweets_forever()` was chosen here for discussion for simplicity. It will become clear as you read on where you can switch approaches.

Our next stop is the method we use to control the LED.

The process_dweet() method

As we saw previously when `poll_dweets_forever()` (similar to `stream_dweets_forever()`) gets a dweet, it parses out the `content` property from the dweet's JSON. This is then passed to `process_dweet()` for handling, where we extract the `state` child property from the `content` property:

```python
def process_dweet(dweet):
    """Inspect the dweet and set LED state accordingly"""
    global last_led_state

    if not 'state' in dweet:
        return
```

```
led_state = dweet['state']                    # (14)

if led_state == last_led_state:               # (15)
    return; # LED is already in requested state.
```

On line (15) (and (17) in the subsequent code block), we test for and maintain the LED's last known state and avoid interacting with the LED if it's already in the requested state. This will avoid potential visual glitching of the LED that can occur if it's repeatedly put into a blinking state when already blinking.

The core of `process_dweet()` is to access the `state` property of the dweet and change the LED's state, which starts on line (16):

```
if led_state == 'on':                   # (16)
    led_state = 'on'
    led.on()
elif led_state == 'blink':
    led_state = 'blink'
    led.blink()
else: # Off, including any unhanded state.
    led_state = 'off'
    led.off()

last_led_state = led_state              # (17)
logger.info('LED ' + led_state)
```

Following line (16), we set the LED state based on the dweet (remember the `led` variable is a GPIOZero LED instance) before keeping track of the new state on line (17), as mentioned, for subsequent testing when `process_dweet()` is called on line (15).

Thanks to the simplicity of GPIOZero, our LED controlling code only makes a fleeting appearance in the code!

We will conclude by covering the program's main entry point.

The main program entry point

At the end of the source file, we have the following code:

```
# Main entry point
if __name__ == '__main__':
    signal.signal(signal.SIGINT, signal_handler) # Capture CTRL + C
    print_instructions()                         # (18)

    # Initialize LED from last dweet.
    latest_dweet = get_latest_dweet()            # (19)
```

```
if (latest_dweet):
    process_dweet(latest_dweet)

print('Waiting for dweets. Press Control+C to exit.')

#Only use one of the following.
#stream_dweets_forever() # Stream dweets real-time.
poll_dweets_forever() # Get dweets by polling.      # (20)
```

On line (8), `print_instructions()` is responsible for printing the sweet URLs to the Terminal, while on line (19), we see a call to `get_latest_dweet()`. This call initializes our LED to the last dweeted state when the program starts. Finally, on line (20), we start polling the dweet.io service to access the latest dweets. It's here you swap the dweet polling method to the streaming method.

This now completes our walk-through of `dweet_led.py`. Through this discussion, we have now seen how to leverage the dweet.io service to create a simple and functional IoT program. Before we complete this chapter, I want to leave you with two bonus source code files that you can use to extend your IoT program.

Extending your IoT program

The following two files in the `chapter02` folder complement what we have covered in this chapter by combining the concepts we have learned. As the overall code and approach are similar to what we have already covered, we will not go through the code in detail:

- `dweet_button.py` provides an implementation showing how to use a push button to create a dweet with the dweet.io service. This will let you change your LED state with the press of a button.
- `pigpio_led_class.py` provides a code-level example of how a low-level library like PiGPIO relates to a high-level library like GPIOZero.

We'll start by discussing `dweet_button.py`.

Implementing a dweeting button

This program in `dweet_button.py` integrates the GPIOZero push button example with dweet.io. Earlier in this chapter, in the section titled *Running and testing the Python server*, we copied and pasted URLs into a web browser to control our LED.

When you run `dweet_button.py`, each time you press the button, this program cycles through the dweet.io URLs to change the LED's state. To configure this program, find and update the following line with the thing name you are using with `dweet_led.py`:

```
thing_name = '**** ADD YOUR THING NAME HERE ****'
```

Remember, that you'll also need the `dweet_led.py` program to be running in a Terminal, otherwise, the LED will not respond to your button presses.

Next, we see how to mimic GPIOZero using PiGPIO and a Python class.

PiGPIO LED as a class

In the `pigpio_led_class.py` file, we have a Python class that is a re-engineering of the PiGPIO LED example to wrap it as a class that mimics the GPIOZero `LED` class. It demonstrates the basic principle of how GPIOZero abstracts away lower-level GPIO complexity. This re-engineered class can be used as a drop-in replacement for the GPIOZero `LED` examples in this chapter, as shown here. See the header comments in `pigpio_led_class.py` for more information:

```
""" chapter02/dweet_led.py """
...
# from gpiozero import LED                      # Comment out import
from pigpio_led_class import PiGPIOLED as LED # Add new import
```

I hope you find these two bonus files interesting, and that by exploring the PiGPIO LED as a class example, you can better appreciate how the higher-level GPIOZero library and lower-level PiGPIO library relate to one another.

At this stage of your journey, if you are a little unclear about what's happening with `pigpio_led_class.py`, do not get worried. I wanted to simply set out a brief example of GPIO library interactions for you to ponder in the context of an end-to-end application, as this will serve as a point of reference as you continue reading. We'll be covering the GPIOPZero and PiGPIO libraries (plus others) in greater detail in Chapter 5, *Connecting Your Raspberry Pi to the Physical World*, plus we'll be covering more advanced concepts such as threading in electronic interfacing programs (similar to the use of threads in `pigpio_led_class.py`) in Chapter 12, *Advanced IoT Programming Concepts – Threads, AsyncIO, and Event Loops*.

Summary

Through this chapter, you've just created a real functional IoT application using a Raspberry Pi and Python. We saw two alternative ways to flash a LED and read a button press in Python using both the GPIOZero and PiGPIO GPIO libraries. We also compared the use of these libraries and saw that GPIOZero takes a higher-level and more abstract approach to coding and GPIO control than does the lower-level PiGPIO library. We also connected the LED to the internet using the online dweet.io service. Using simple URLs, we were able to turn on and off and blink the LED by simply visiting the URLs in a web browser.

As you proceed through the subsequent chapters in this book, we'll be building on and going deeper into the core knowledge you have learned in this chapter about GPIO interfacing, electronic circuits, and controlling a circuit over the internet. We will learn alternative approaches to building an application to those we have covered in this chapter and discover the core principles related to GPIO control and electronic interfacing. Equipped with this deepening knowledge, you'll be able to create even more powerful and grand IoT solutions by the time you complete this book!

In `Chapter 3`, *Networking with RESTful APIs and Web Sockets Using Flask*, we will be looking at the popular Flask microservices framework, and we will create two Python-based web servers and accompanying web pages to control the LED over a local network or the internet.

Questions

Here is a list of questions for you to test your knowledge regarding this chapter's material. You will find the answers in the *Assessments* section of the book:

1. You don't have the correct resistor value. Can you just substitute another value resistor that you have lying around?
2. The GPIOZero package is a compete GPIO library. Is it all you'll ever need?
3. Should you always use the built-in Python packages for networking wherever possible?
4. True or false: an LED is unbiased, meaning it can be plugged into a circuit any way around and still work.
5. You are building an IoT application that interacts with other existing networked devices and it times out. What could be the problem?
6. What Python module and function can be used to stop a program exiting?

Further reading

We connected our LED to the internet using the dweet.io service and called its RESTful APIs, which are documented at the following:

- Dweet.io API documentation: `https://dweet.io`

You may wish to familiarize yourself with the GPIOZero library briefly to get an idea about what it can do. It's well documented with heaps of examples. Here are a couple of useful links to relevant parts of the API documentation that we've covered so far:

- GPIOZero home page: `https://gpiozero.readthedocs.io`
- Output Devices (LED): `https://gpiozero.readthedocs.io/en/stable/api_output.html`
- Input Devices (Button): `https://gpiozero.readthedocs.io/en/stable/api_input.html`

Regarding PiGPIO, here are the relevant parts of its API documentation. You'll notice that PiGPIO is a more advanced GPIO library with less verbose documentation.

- The PiGPIO Python home page: `http://abyz.me.uk/rpi/pigpio/python.html`
- The `read()` method: `http://abyz.me.uk/rpi/pigpio/python.html#read`
- The `write()` method: `http://abyz.me.uk/rpi/pigpio/python.html#write`
- The `callback()` method: `http://abyz.me.uk/rpi/pigpio/python.html#callback`
- `set_glitch_filter()`: `https://abyz.me.uk/rpi/pigpio/python.html#set_glitch_filter`

Resistors are a very common electronic component. The following resources provide an overview of resistors and how to read their color bands to determine their resistance value in Ohms:

- Resistor overview: `https://www.electronics-tutorials.ws/resistor/res_1.html`
- Reading color bands: `https://www.electronics-tutorials.ws/resistor/res_2.html`

The following Spark Fun tutorial provides an excellent introduction to reading schematic diagrams:

- *How to Read a Schematic Diagram*: `https://learn.sparkfun.com/tutorials/how-to-read-a-schematic/all`

3
Networking with RESTful APIs and Web Sockets Using Flask

In Chapter 2, *Getting Started with Python and IoT*, we created a networked IoT application based on dweet.io where you controlled an LED connected to your Raspberry Pi over the internet. Our first IoT application was driven purely by making API requests.

In this chapter, we will turn our attention to alternative approaches to creating networked services in Python that can be accessed by both Python and non-Python clients. We will be looking at how to build a RESTful API server and a Web Socket server in Python and applying the electronic interfacing techniques we learned in the previous chapter to make them interact with our LED.

After completing this chapter, you will have an understanding of two different approaches to building servers with Python, complete with accompanying web pages that interact with the servers. These two servers will provide you with an end-to-end reference implementation that you can use as a starting point for your own network-connected IoT projects.

Since this chapter is about networking techniques, we will continue with our GPIOZero-based LED from the preceding chapter merely for simplicity and abstraction so that our examples are to-the-point and network-focused and not cluttered by GPIO-related code.

In this chapter, we will cover the following topics:

- Introducing the Flask microservices framework
- Creating a RESTful API service with Flask
- Adding a RESTful API client web page
- Creating a Web Socket service with Flask-SocketIO
- Adding Web Socket client web page
- Comparing the RESTful API and Web Socket servers

Technical requirements

To perform the exercises in this chapter, you will need the following:

- Raspberry Pi 4 Model B
- Raspbian OS Buster (with desktop and recommended software)
- A minimum of Python version 3.5

These requirements are what the code examples in this book are based on. It's reasonable to expect that the code examples should work without modification on a Raspberry Pi 3 Model B or a different version of Raspbian OS as long as your Python version is 3.5 or higher.

You will find this chapter's source code in the chapter03 folder in the GitHub repository available here: https://github.com/PacktPublishing/Practical-Python-Programming-for-IoT.

You will need to execute the following commands in a Terminal to set up a virtual environment and install Python libraries required for the code in this chapter:

```
$ cd chapter03            # Change into this chapter's folder
$ python3 -m venv venv    # Create Python Virtual Environment
$ source venv/bin/activate # Activate Python Virtual Environment
(venv) $ pip install pip --upgrade      # Upgrade pip
(venv) $ pip install -r requirements.txt # Install dependent packages
```

The following dependencies are installed from requirements.txt:

- **GPIOZero**: The GPIOZero GPIO library (https://pypi.org/project/gpiozero)
- **PiGPIO**: The PiGPIO GPIO library (https://pypi.org/project/pigpio)
- **Flask**: The core Flask microservices framework (https://pypi.org/project/Flask)
- **Flask-RESTful**: A Flask extension for creating RESTful API services (https://pypi.org/project/Flask-RESTful)
- **Flask-SocketIO**: A Flask extension for creating Web Socket services (https://pypi.org/project/Flask-SocketIO)

We will be working with the breadboard circuit we created in Chapter 2, *Getting Started with Python and IoT*, *Figure 2.7*.

Introducing the Flask microservices framework

Flask is a popular and mature microservices framework for Python that you can use for creating APIs, websites, and just about any other networked service you can imagine. Flask is certainly not the only option available for Python, even though its maturity, range of add-ons, and extensions plus the availability of quality documentation and tutorials make it an excellent choice.

We could conceivably do all of the following coding exercises in this chapter using just the core Flask framework; however, there are quality extensions that will make our life much easier. These extensions are **Flask-RESTful** for creating RESTful API services and **Flask-SocketIO** for building Web Socket services.

The official API documentation for Flask-RESTful and Flask-SocketIO (or any Flask extension for that matter) generally assume existing knowledge of the core Flask framework, classes, and terminology. If you can't seem to find answers to your questions in an extension's documentation, remember to check the core Flask API documentation also. You'll find a link to this documentation in the *Further reading* section.

Let's commence and create a RESTful API service in Python using Flask-RESTful.

Creating a RESTful API service with Flask-RESTful

In this section, we will explore our first Python-based server, which will be a RESTful API server implemented using the Flask-RESTful framework for Python.

A RESTful API (REST stands for Representational State Transfer) is a software design pattern used for building web service APIs. It's a flexible pattern that is both technology- and protocol-independent. Its technology independence helps to promote interoperability between different technologies and systems, including different programming languages. And although it does promote protocol independence, it's frequently and almost always by default (or, at the least, assumed to be) built on top of the HTTP protocol used by web servers and web browsers.

RESTful APIs are the most common technique used today for building web services and APIs. In fact, it's so common that many people learn about them and use the design pattern without ever understanding what they are! If you are new to RESTful APIs, you will a link in the *Further reading* section, which I encourage you to review as a primer before proceeding.

Our focus in this section will be on controlling an LED with a RESTful API and understanding how this is implemented using Python and the Flask-RESTful framework. After completing this section, you will be able to leverage this RESTful API server a starting point for your own IoT projects and integrate it with other electronics, especially as learn more about electronic actuators and sensors in part 3 of this book, *IoT Playground*.

 For the examples in this chapter, we will assume you are working and accessing the Flask-based servers locally on your Raspberry Pi. These servers will also be accessible from another device on your local network if you use the IP address or hostname of your Raspberry Pi. To make the servers directly accessible over the internet would require configuration of your specific firewall and/or router, which we cannot practically cover in this book. For prototyping ideas and creating demos, a simple alternative to configuring firewalls and routers is to use a service such as Local Tunnels (`https://localtunnel.github.io/www`) or Ngrok (`https://ngrok.com`), which will help you to make the Flask servers on your Raspberry Pi accessible over the internet.

We will start by running and using our RESTful API to interact with the LED before proceeding to review the server's source code.

Running and testing the Python server

You will find the code in the `chapter03/flask_api_server.py` file. Please review this file before proceeding to get an overall idea about what it contains before you proceed.

 We are running our Flask examples using Flask's built-in HTTP server. This is more than adequate for development purposes; however, it's not recommended for production usage. Consult the Flask documentation section titled *Deployment Options* for information on how to deploy a Flask application with production-quality web servers. You'll find a link in the *Further reading* section to the official Flask website and documentation.

To test the Python server perform the following steps:

1. Run our RESTful API server with the following command:

```
(venv) $ python flask_api_server.py
... truncated ...
NFO:werkzeug: * Running on http://0.0.0.0:5000/ (Press CTRL+C to
quit)
... truncated ...
```

The second to last line in the preceding code block indicates that our server has started successfully. Our server is running in debug mode by default, so its log output will be verbose and if you make any changes to flask_api_server.py or other resource files, the server will restart automatically.

 If flask_api_server.py raises an error when started in debug mode, clear the file's execute bit. This issue occurs on Unix-based systems and has to do with the development web server shipped with Flask. Here is the command to clear the execute bit:
$ chmod -x flask_api_server.py

2. We will create a web page to interact without API shortly; however, for now, browse to http://localhost:5000 in a web browser and verify that you can use the slider on the web page to change the brightness of the LED.

 Our example URL is http://localhost:5000, however, if you use your Raspberry Pi's IP address instead of localhost, you will be able to access the web page from another device on your local network.

The following screenshot is an example of the web page you will see:

Figure 3.1 – RESTful API client web page

3. We can also use the `curl` command-line tool to interact with the API. We will do this now to observe the input and output JSON from our API server requests.

Our first `curl` command in the following makes an HTTP GET request and we see the LED's brightness level (a number between 0 and 100) printed on the Terminal in JSON (line 1). The default LED brightness when the server is started is 50 (that is, 50% brightness):

```
$ curl -X GET http://localhost:5000/led
{
  "level": 50            # (1)
}
```

The options for `curl` are as follows:

- `-X GET`: The HTTP method used to make the request
- **<url>**: The URL to request

4. This next command performs an HTTP POST request, and we are setting the brightness level to its maximum of 100 (line 2), which is returned as JSON and printed back to the Terminal (line 3):

```
$ curl -X POST -d '{"level": 100}' \      # (2)
 -H "Content-Type: application/json" \
 http://localhost:5000/led
{
  "level": 100                            # (3)
}
```

The options for `curl` are as follows:

- `-X POST`: This is the HTTP method; this time, we're making a POST request.
- `-d` **<data>**: This is the data we want to POST to the server. We're posting a JSON string.
- `-H` **<HTTP headers>**: These are the HTTP headers to send with the request. Here, we're letting the server know that our data, (`-d`), is JSON.
- **<url>**: This is the URL to request.

An alternative to `curl` on the command line is Postman (`getpostman.com`). If you are not familiar with Postman, it's a free API development, querying, and testing tool that is invaluable when you are developing and testing RESTful API services.

Try altering the level value in the preceding `curl POST` example to a number outside of the range 0-100 and observe the error message you receive. We will see shortly how this validation logic is implemented with Flask-RESTful.

Let's now proceed to look at our server source code.

Understanding the server code

In this section, we will walk through our RESTful API server's source code and discuss the core parts to help you to understand how the server is coded and operates. Please keep in mind that we're about to cover many code-level artifacts that are specific to the Flask and Flask-RESTful frameworks, so don't get worried if, at first, some concepts do not make immediate sense.

Once you have an understanding of the foundations and an overall idea of how our sever works, you'll be in an excellent position to deepen your understanding of Flask and Flask-RESTful by consulting their respective websites (you will find links in the *Further reading* section). Furthermore, you will have a solid reference RESTful API server that you can rework and use as a starting point for your own future projects.

Please note that as we discuss the code, we will skip over any code and concepts that we covered in earlier chapters, such as **GPIOZero**.

We will start by looking at the imports.

Imports

At the top of the source code file, we see the following imports:

```
import logging
from flask import Flask, request, render_template          # (1)
from flask_restful import Resource, Api, reqparse, inputs  # (2)
from gpiozero import PWMLED, Device                         # (3)
from gpiozero.pins.pigpio import PiGPIOFactory
```

The Flask-related imports we see on lines (1) and (2) are all of the classes and functions of Flask and Flask-RESTful that we will require in our server. You will notice on line (3), we're importing PWMLED not LED as we have done in previous chapters. In this example, we're going to change the brightness of our LED rather than just turning it on and off. We'll cover more about PWM and PWMLED as we proceed with this chapter.

Next, in our source code, we start to work with Flask and the Flask-RESTful extension.

Flask and Flask-RESTful API instance variables

In the following, on line (4), we create an instance of our core Flask app and assign it to the app variable. The parameter is the name of our Flask application, and it's a common convention to use __name__ for the *root* Flask app (we only have a root Flask app in our example). Anytime we need to work with the core Flask framework, we will use the app variable:

```
app = Flask(__name__) # Core Flask app.              # (4)
api = Api(app) # Flask-RESTful extension wrapper     # (5)
```

On line (5), we wrap the core Flask app with the Flask-RESTful extension and assign it to the api variable, and as we will see shortly, we use this variable anytime we are working with the Flask-RESTful extension. Following our app and api variables, we define additional global variables.

Global variables

The following global variables are used throughout our server. First, we have the GPIO pin and an led variable, which will later be assigned a GPIOZero PWMLED instance for controlling our LED:

```
# Global variables
LED_GPIO_PIN = 21
led = None # PWMLED Instance. See init_led()
state = {                                        # (6)
    'level': 50 # % brightness of LED.
}
```

On line (6), we have a state dictionary structure that we will use to track the brightness level of our LED. We could have used a simple variable instead but have opted for a dictionary structure since it's a more versatile option because it will be marshaled into JSON to send back to a client, as we will see later on.

Next, we create and initialize our `led` instance.

The init_led() method

The `init_led()` method simply creates a GPIOZero `PWMLED` instance and assigns it to the global `led` variable that we saw previously:

```
def init_led():
    """Create and initialize an PWMLED Object"""
    global led
    led = PWMLED(LED_GPIO_PIN)
    led.value = state['level'] / 100        # (7)
```

We explicitly set the LED's brightness to match the value of our server's brightness state on line (7) to ensure the server's managed state and the LED are in sync when the server starts. We are dividing by 100 because `led.value` expects a float value in the range of 0-1, while our API will be using an integer in the range 0-100.

Next, we start to see the code that defines our server and its service endpoints, starting with the code that serves the web page we visited earlier.

Serving a web page

Starting on line (8), we use the Flask `@app.route()` decorator to define a callback method that is invoked when the server receives an HTTP GET request from a client to the root URL /, that is, a request to `http://localhost:5000`:

```
# @app.route applies to the core Flask instance (app).
# Here we are serving a simple web page.
@app.route('/', methods=['GET'])                        # (8)
def index():
    """Make sure index_api_client.html is in the templates folder
    relative to this Python file."""
    return render_template('index_api_client.html',
                    pin=LED_GPIO_PIN)                    # (9)
```

On line (9), `render_template('index_api_client.html', pin=LED_GPIO_PIN)` is a Flask method use to return a templated page to the requesting client.

The `pin=LED_GPIO_PIN` parameter is an example of how to pass a variable from Python to the HTML page template for rendering. We will cover the contents of this HTML file later in this chapter.

Notice, in the preceding code block on line (8), we have `@app.route(...)`. The presence of the `app` variable means we are using and configuring the *core* Flask framework here.

Returning an HTML page to the client is the only core Flask feature that we will cover in this book, however, there will be additional resources listed in the *Further reading* section for you to explore the core concepts of Flask further.

Our next stop in code is the `LEDController` class. It's here that we are interacting with the LED and GPIOZero.

The LEDControl class

In Flask-RESTful, API resources are modeled as Python classes that extend the `Resource` class, and on line (10) in the following snippet, we see the `LEDControl(Resource)` class defined that will contain the logic used to control our LED. Later on, we will see how we register this class with Flask-RESTful so that it responds to client requests:

```
class LEDControl(Resource):                                        # (10)
    def __init__(self):
        self.args_parser = reqparse.RequestParser()                # (11)
        self.args_parser.add_argument(
            name='level',                     # Name of arguement
            required=True,                    # Mandatory arguement
            type=inputs.int_range(0, 100),    # Allowed 0..100    # (12)
            help='Set LED brightness level {error_msg}',
            default=None)
```

On line (11), we create an instance of `RequestParser()` and assign it to the `args_parser` variable before configuring the parser with `add_argument()`. We use an instance of `RequestParser()` in Flask-RESTful to define validation rules for the arguments we expect our `LEDControl` resource to handle.

Here, we are defining a mandatory parameter named `level`, which must be an integer in the range 0 to 100, as shown on line (12). We've also provided a custom help message for when the `level` parameter is missing or out of range.

We will see the use of `args_parser` when we cover the `post()` method shortly, but first, let's discuss the `get()` method.

The get() class method

The get() class method handles HTTP GET requests for our LEDControl resource. It's what handled our URL request when we tested the API previously with the following command:

```
$ curl -X GET http://localhost:5000/led
```

get() simply returns, on line (13), the global state variable:

```
def get(self):
    """ Handles HTTP GET requests to return current LED state."""
    return state          # (13)
```

Flask-RESTful returns JSON responses to clients, and that's why we return the state variable. In Python, state is a dictionary structure that can be mapped directly into a JSON format. We saw the following JSON example previously when we make a GET request using curl:

```
{ "level": 50 }
```

This class-as-a-resource (for example, LEDControl) and method-to-HTTP-method mapping (for example, LEDControl.get()) is an example of how the Flask-RESTful extension makes RESTful API development easy.

There are also method names reserved for other HTTP request methods, including POST, which we cover next.

The post() class method

The post() class method handles HTTP POST requests made to the LEDControl resource. It is this post() method that received and processed our curl POST request when we made the following request earlier when we tested our server:

```
curl -X POST -d '{"level": 100}' \
    -H "Content-Type: application/json" \
    http://localhost:5000/led
```

post() is more complex than our get() method. It is here where we change the brightness of our LED in response to a requesting client's input:

```
def post(self):
    """Handles HTTP POST requests to set LED brightness level."""
    global state                                        # (14)
```

```
args = self.args_parser.parse_args()              # (15)

# Set PWM duty cycle to adjust brightness level.
state['level'] = args.level                        # (16)
led.value = state['level'] / 100                   # (17)
logger.info("LED brightness level is " + str(state['level']))

return state                                       # (18)
```

On line (14), we use the Python `global` keyword to indicate that we will be altering the `state` global variable.

On line (15), we see the use of `args_parser` that we discussed previously. It's this call to `args_parser.parse_args()` that will parse and validate the caller's input (remember `level` was a required argument and it must be in the range 0-100). If our predefined validation rules fail, the user will be issued with an error message, and `post()` will terminate here.

If the arguments are valid, their values are stored in the `args` variable, and the code continues to line (16) where we update the global `state` variable with the newly requested brightness level. On line (17), we alter the physical LED's brightness using the GPIOZero PWMLED instance, `led`, which expects a value between 0.0 (off) and 1.0 (full brightness), so we're mapping our `level` input range of 0-100 back to 0-1. The value of `state` is returned to the client on line (18).

Our final task is to register `LEDController` with Flask-RESTful and start the server.

LEDController registration and starting the server

After calling the `init_led()` method to initiate and default out GPIOZero `led` instance, we then see how to register our `LEDControl` resource with `api.add_resource()` on line (19). Here, we are mapping the URL endpoint, `/led`, with our controller.

 Notice, in the code block on line (19), we have `api.add_resource(...)`. The presence of the `api` variable means we are using and configuring the *Flask-RESTful extension* here.

Finally, on line (20), our server is started (in debug mode) and is ready to receive client requests. Notice that we use the *core* Flask instance in the `app` variable to start the server:

```
# Initialize Module.
init_led()
```

```
api.add_resource(LEDControl, '/led')          # (19)

if __name__ == '__main__':
    app.run(host="0.0.0.0", debug=True)        # (20)
```

Well done! We've just covered the build of a simple, yet, functional RESTful API server in Python. You'll find links in the *Further reading* section to the official Flask-RESTful documentation so you can take your knowledge further.

As mentioned, we've used `PWMLED` in our server. Let's briefly introduce the term *PWM* before we proceed and review the web page that accompanies our RESTful API server.

Introduction to PWM

In the proceeding example, we used `PWMLED`, not `LED`, from GPIOZero. `PWMLED` allows us to control the brightness of the LED using a technique known as **Pulse Width Modulation**, commonly abbreviated as **PWM**.

PWM is a technique used to create a lower the average voltage from a source signal, which can be a 3.3-volt GPIO pin. We will be covering PWM and GPIO pin voltages in detail in Chapter 6, *Electronics 101 for the Software Engineer*.

For our current example, briefly (and somewhat oversimplified), PWM pulses the LED on and off really, really fast, and our eyes observe different pulse durations (that are creating different voltages) manifesting as different brightness levels of the LED. We changed this pulse duration (known as the *duty-cycle*) using the `value` property of a `PWMLED` instance, that is, `led.value = state["level"]` in `LEDControl.post()`. In Chapter 5, *Connecting Your Raspberry Pi to the Physical World*, we will explore PWM in greater detail.

We've now covered our Python-based Flask-RESTful API server and learned how to implement a simple and functional RESTful API server that is capable of handling both GET and POST requests, the two most popular ways of interacting with RESTful API servers. Plus, we also saw how to achieve data validation with Flask-RESTful as a simple and effective way to guard our server against invalid input data.

We also learned to use the `curl` command-line tool to interact with and test our server. As you build, test, and debug RESTful API servers, you will find `curl` a useful addition to your development toolkit.

Next, we will take a look at the code behind the web page that interacts with our API.

Adding a RESTful API client web page

The web page we are about to discuss is the one you interacted with previously to change the brightness of your LED when you visited `http://localhost:5000` in your web browser. A screenshot of the web page is shown in *Figure 3.1*.

As we proceed through this section, we will be learning how to build this basic web page using HTML and JavaScript. We will discover how to make the HTML range component interact with the Flask-RESTful API server that we created in the previous section, so that when we change the range control (that is, slide the slider), our LED's brightness also changes.

You will find the page's code in the `chapter03/templates/index_api_client.html` file. Please review this file before proceeding to get an overall idea about what it contains.

The `templates` folder is a special Flask folder where template files are kept. An HTML page is considered a template in the Flask ecosystem. You will also find a folder named `static`. This folder is where static files are stored. For our example, this is where a copy of the jQuery JavaScript library file is found.

 All files and resources referenced in a web page served from Flask are relative to the server's root folder. For us, this is the `chapter03` folder.

Let's walk through the web page code.

Understanding the client-side code

This section's code is JavaScript, and we will be using the jQuery JavaScript library. An understanding of basic JavaScript and jQuery will be essential to understanding the code examples that follow. If you are not familiar with jQuery, you can find learning resources at jQuery.com.

JavaScript imports

We see in the following, on line (1), that we import the jQuery library that is contained in the `static` folder:

```
<!-- chapter03/templates/index_api_client.html -->
<!DOCTYPE html>
<html>
<head>
    <title>Flask Restful API Example</title>
    <script src="/static/jquery.min.js"></script>    <!--(1)-->
    <script type="text/javascript">
```

Next, we will start to cover the JavaScript functions in the file.

The getState() function

The primary purpose of `getState()` is to retrieve the LED's current state from the server. It uses the JQuery `get()` method to make an HTTP GET request to our API server's `/led` resource. We saw, in the previous section, that the URL path, `/led`, is mapped to the `LEDControl` Python class, and because we're making a GET request, it's `LEDControl.get()` that will receive and handle our request:

```
// GET request to server to retrieve LED state.
function getState() {
    $.get("/led", function(serverResponse, status) { // (2)
        console.log(serverResponse)
        updateControls(serverResponse)                // (3)
    });
}
```

The server's response is contained in the `serverResponse` parameter on line (2), which is passed to the `updateControls()` function on line (3) to update the web page controls. We'll cover this method shortly.

While `getState()` gets data from our Python server, our next method, `postUpdate()`, sends (that is, *posts)* data to the server.

The postUpdate() function

`postUpdate()` changes the LED's brightness by performing an HTTP POST to the server. This time, it's the `LEDControl.post()` method in our API server that handled the request:

```
// POST Request to server to set LED state.
function postUpdate(payload) {                              // (4)
    $.post("/led", payload, function(serverResponse, status) {
        console.log(serverResponse)
        updateControls(serverResponse);                    // (5)
    });
}
```

On line (4), it receives and parses (remember `arg_parser` from `LEDControl`) the data in the `payload` parameter. `payload` is a JavaScript object with a `state` child property. We'll see this object constructed later in the web page slider's change event handler.

For consistency, we also update the controls on line (5) even though, in our case, the `serverResponse` variable will contain the same level value as the `payload` parameter.

Next, we will see what the call to `updateControls()` on line (5) does.

The updateControls() function

`updateControls()` changes the visual appearance of the web page controls. This function receives JSON input as the `data` parameter, which is in the form: `{"level":50}`. Starting on line (6) and using jQuery selectors, we update the slider control and text on the web page to reflect the new level value:

```
function updateControls(data) {
    $("input[type=range].brightnessLevel").val(data.level);  // (6)
    $("#brightnessLevel").html(data.level);
}
```

Next, we'll see how we use JQuery to create an event handler that responds when we or another user changes to the web page's slider component.

Registering event handlers with jQuery

We are following jQuery best practice and using the jQuery *document ready function* (that is, $(document).ready(...)) to register the event handlers for our web page's slider control and initialize our web page elements:

```
$(document).ready(function() {
    // Event listener for Slider value changes.
    $("input[type=range].brightnessLevel")
        .on('input', function() {                       // (7)
            brightness_level = $(this).val();           // (8)
            payload = { "level": brightness_level }     // (9)
            postUpdate(payload);
        });

    // Initialize slider value form state on server.
    getState()                                          // (10)
});
</script>
</head>
```

On line (7), we register an event handler for the slider controls *input* event. This handler function will be called when a user interacts with the slider on the web page.

Starting on line (8), after a user moves the slider, we extract the slider's new value of the slider using val() (which will be between 0 and 100—we'll see why shortly when we review the page's HTML).

On line (9), we create a JSON object containing our new brightness level before passing it to postUpdate(), which calls our RESTful API to change the brightness of our physical LED.

Finally, on line (10), we call our getState() function, which makes an HTTP request to our server to get the current brightness level for the LED. As we saw previously, getState() then delegates to updateControls(), which then updates the slider and page text to reflect the LED's brightness value.

We'll conclude this section by looking at the HTML that makes up the web page.

The web page HTML

Previously in our Python server, we had the
line `render_template('index_rest_api.html', pin=LED_GPIO_PIN)`. It's the `pin`
parameter in this method call that is rendered on our web page on line (11), represented by
the template variable, `{{pin}}`:

```
<body>
    <h1>Flask RESTful API Example</h1>
    LED is connected to GPIO {{pin}}<br>            <!-- (11) -->
    Brightness: <span id="brightnessLevel"></span>%<br>
    <input type="range" min="0" max="100"          <!-- (12) -->
        value="0" class="brightnessLevel">
</body>
</html>
```

Finally, we see, on line (12), our HTML slider component is restricted to the range of 0-100.
As we saw previously, it's the call to `getState()` in the document ready handler that
updates the slider's value attribute to match the brightness level stored on the server after
the web page has finished loading.

Congratulations! We've reached a milestone now, having completed a full end-to-end
server and client example based on RESTful APIs. Our learning about Flask and Flask-
RESTful means we have learned to use one of the most popular and feature-
rich Python libraries for building web services. Plus, learning to build a RESTful API server
and matching client means we have practically implemented the most common approach
used today for client-server communication.

We have barely scratched the surface of what can be achieved with Flask, Flask-RESTful,
and RESTful APIs in general, and there is much more that can be explored. You'll find links
in the *Further reading* section if you wish to take your understanding of these topics further.

Next, we will create the same client and server scenario we built in this section, only this
time using Web Sockets as our transport layer.

Creating a Web Socket service with Flask-SocketIO

We will now implement our second Python-based server. Our overall outcome in this section will be similar to our RESTful API server and client that we created in the previous section—that is, we will be able to control our LED from a web browser. Our objective this time around, however, will be to create our program using a different technological approach using Web Sockets as our transport layer.

Web Sockets are a full-duplex communication protocol and are a common technology choice where real-time client/server interaction is required. Web Sockets are a technology that—in my opinion and experience—is best learned through doing rather than reading, especially if you are new to server development. A deep discussion of Web Sockets is beyond the scope of this chapter; however, you'll find two links in the *Further reading* section covering the basics.

If you are new to Web Sockets, I highly recommend reading those two resources as a primer before proceeding. And don't worry if the content does not sink in initially because I'm confident that, once you have used and understood how our Python Web Socket server and the accompanying Web Socket-enabled web page is implemented, the pieces of the larger Web Socket puzzle will start to come together.

For our Web Socket sever build, we will use the Flask-SocketIO library, which is modeled after and compatible with the popular Socket.IO library for JavaScript (`https://socket.io`).

We will start by running and using our Web Socket server to interact with the LED before proceeding to review the server's source code.

Running and testing the Python server

Let's start by having a quick look at our Python Web Socket server code and running the server to see it in operation. This will give us a broad idea of the code and a first-hand demonstration of how the code works before we discuss it in detail.

You will find the Web Socket server's code in the `chapter03/flask_ws_server.py` file. Please review this file before proceeding.

When you have looked through the code, we will run our server. Here are the steps to follow:

1. Run the Web Socket server with the following command:

```
(venv) $ python flask_ws_server.py
... truncated ...
NFO:werkzeug: * Running on http://0.0.0.0:5000/ (Press CTRL+C to
quit)
... truncated ...
```

The preceding output is similar to what we saw when we ran the RESTful API server; however, you can expect more output messages on your Terminal for this server. The additional output you will see has been truncated from the preceding example.

If `flask_ws_server.py` raises an error when started in debug mode, clear the file's execute bit. This issue occurs on Unix-based systems and has to do with the development web server shipped with Flask. Here the is command to clear the execute bit:
`$ chmod -x flask_ws_server.py`

2. Visit the `http://localhost:5000` URL in a web browser. You will get a web page with a slider as shown in *Figure 3.2*. While the visual appearance of the web page is similar to the RESTful API server's web page, the underlying JavaScipt is different:

Figure 3.2 – Web Socket client web page

Verify that you can use the slider on the web page to change the brightness of the LED.

Open a second web browser and visit `http://localhost:5000` (so now you have two pages open). Change the slider, and you will see that both pages stay in sync and in real time! And presto, you have discovered a unique advantage offered by Web Sockets compared to a RESTful API.

3. Find on the web page, the line **Connected to server: Yes**, then perform the following:

    - Terminate the server by pressing *Ctrl + C* in the Terminal, and you will notice the line changes to **Connected to server: No**.
    - Restart the server again and it changes back to **Connected to server: Yes**.

This illustrates the bi-directional nature of Web Sockets. We'll see how this is implemented on the web page when we review it's JavaScript but first, we will review the Python code that makes up our Web Socket server.

Server code walkthrough

In this section, we will walk through our Python server's source code and discuss the core parts. Again, we'll skip over any code and concepts that we covered in earlier chapters. First, let's see what we're importing.

Imports

Near the top of the source file, we have the following imports:

```
from flask import Flask, request, render_template
from flask_socketio import SocketIO, send, emit            # (1)
```

The main difference concerning our preceding imports compared to the RESTful API imports are on line (1), where we now import classes and functions from Flask-SocketIO.

Next, in our source code, we start to work with Flask and the Flask-SocketIO extension.

Flask and Flask-RESTful API instance variables

On line (2), we create an instance of `SocketIO` and the Flask-SocketIO extension and assign it to the `socketio` variable. It's this variable that we will use throughout our server to access and configure our Web Socket service:

```
# Flask & Flask Restful Global Variables.
app = Flask(__name__) # Core Flask app.
socketio = SocketIO(app) # Flask-SocketIO extension wrapper  # (2)
```

Following the creation of our SocketIO instance, we once again will server a web page from the default URL endpoint, `/`.

Serving a web page

Similarly to the RESTful API example, we configure the core Flask framework to serve a web page from the root URL using the `@app.route()` decorator:

```
@app.route('/', methods=['GET'])
def index():
    """Make sure index_web_sockets.html is in the templates folder
    relative to this Python file."""
    return render_template('index_web_sockets.html',         # (3)
                           pin=LED_GPIO_PIN)
```

For our Web Socket server, this time, we are serving the HTML file, `index_web_sockets.html`, which we will be covering shortly in the next section, *Adding a Web Socket client web page*.

Next, we start to see the code that sets up and handles Web Socket event messages.

Connecting and disconnecting handlers

From this point in code forward, we start to see the major differences between the RESTful API server and this Web Socket server:

```
# Flask-SocketIO Callback Handlers
@socketio.on('connect')                                      # (4)
def handle_connect():
    logger.info("Client {} connected.".format(request.sid)) # (5)

    # Send initializating data to newly connected client.
    emit("led", state)                                       # (6)
```

We see, on line (4), how to register a *message* or *event* handler using the Python decorator notation. The parameter to each `@socketio.on(<event_name>)` is the name of an event our server will listen for. The `connect` and `disconnect` events (in the following) are two reserved events. These handlers are called whenever a client *connects* to or *disconnects* from the server.

You will notice, on line (5), we are logging whenever a client connects, along with a unique identifier for the client accessed via `request.sid`. Each client session with the server receives a unique SID. When you visit `http://localhost:5000`, you will see this connected message logged by the server. If you open two or more web browsers (or tabs) to this URL, you will notice that each session receives a unique SID.

On line (6), we *emit* the current LED state back to the connecting client so it can initialize itself as required:

```
@socketio.on('disconnect')                              # (7)
def handle_disconnect():
    """Called with a client disconnects from this server"""
    logger.info("Client {} disconnected.".format(request.sid))
```

Our disconnect handler on line (7) is simply logging the fact that a client disconnects. As you browse away from `http://localhost:5000`, you will notice the server logging this message, along with the disconnecting client's `sid`.

Next, we come across the event handler that controls our LED.

LED handler

On line (8) in the following, we have another message handler—this time using a custom event named `led`. Also notice on line (9) that this event handler has a `data` parameter, whereas the connect and disconnect handlers in the preceding section had no parameters. The `data` parameter contains data sent from the client, and we see, on line (10), the `level` child property of `data`. All data form clients are strings, so here we validate the data and cast it to an integer on the following line. There is no equivalent built-in argument validating and parsing utility with Flask-SocketIO, so we must perform validation checks manually, as shown starting on line (11):

```
@socketio.on('led')                                     # (8)
def handle_state(data):                                 # (9)
    """Handle 'led' messages to control the LED."""
    global state
    logger.info("Update LED from client {}: {} "
                .format(request.sid, data))
```

```
if 'level' in data and data['level'].isdigit(): # (10)
    new_level = int(data['level'])

    # Range validation and bounding.            # (11)
    if new_level < 0:
        new_level = 0
    elif new_level > 100:
        new_level = 100
```

In the following code block, on line (12), we set the LED's brightness. On line (13), we see the server-side use of the `emit()` method. This method call *emits* a message to one or more clients. The `"led"` parameter is the name of the event that will be consumed by a client. We've called both the client-side and server-side events related to LED control the same name, `led`. The `state` parameter is the data to pass to the client. Similar to the RESTful API server, it's a Python dictionary object.

The `broadcast=True` parameter means that this *led* message will be emitted to *all* connected clients, not just the client that originated the *led* message on the server. The broadcasting of this event is why, when you opened multiple web pages and changed the slider on one, the others also stayed in sync:

```
led.value = new_level / 100                  # (12)
logger.info("LED brightness level is " + str(new_level))

state['level'] = new_level

# Broadcast new state to *every*
# connected connected (so they remain in sync)
emit("led", state, broadcast=True)           # (13)
```

Our final task is to cover how to start our Web Socket server.

Starting the server

Finally, we start the server on line (14). This time, we are using the Flask-SocketIO instance, `socketio`, rather than the core Flask `app` instance, as we did for the RESTful API server:

```
if __name__ == '__main__':
    socketio.run(app, host="0.0.0.0", debug=True)   # (14)
```

Well done! That's our Web Socket server complete.

We have now seen how we can build a Web Socket server using Python together with Flask-SocketIO. While the overall outcome of our Web Socket server implementation controls our LED similarly to our RESTful API server, what we have learned is a different approach to achieving the same end result. However, in addition to this, we demonstrated a feature provided by a Web Socket approach, which is how we can keep multiple web pages in sync!

 You will find links in the *Further reading* section to the Flask-SocketIO documentation so you can further your knowledge even more.

Now that we have seen the Python server implementation of a Web Socket server, we'll next turn our attention to the Web Socket version of the web page.

Adding a Web Socket client web page

In this section, we will review the HTML web page we used to control our LED from our Web Socket server. An example of this page as seen in *Figure 3.2*.

We will learn how to use the Socket.IO JavaScript library with our web page so we can send and receive *messages* (when we work in a Web Socket environment, we tend to refer to data as *messages)* to and from our Python Flask-SocketIO Web Socket server. Plus, as we explore the JavaScript and Socket.IO-related code, we'll discover how our client-side JavaScript code relates to our Python server-side code.

You will find the following web page's code in the `chapter03/templates/index_ws_client.html` file. Please review the contents of this file to get a broad overview of what it contains.

When you have reviewed our HTML file, we will continue and discuss the important parts of this file.

Understanding the client-side code

Now that you had a look through the `chapter03/templates/index_ws_client.html` file, it's time to discuss how this file is constructed and what it does. We will start our code walk-through with the additional JavaScript import we need for Web Socket support.

Imports

Our Web Socket client requires the Socket.IO JavaScript library, and we see this imported on line (1). You will find a link to the Socket.IO JavaScript library in the *Further reading* section if you want to learn more about this library and how it works:

```html
<!-- chapter03/templates/index_ws_client.html -->
<!DOCTYPE html>
<html>
<head>
    <title>Flask Web Socket Example</title>
    <script src="/static/jquery.min.js"></script>
    <script src="/static/socket.io.js"></script>   <!-- (1) -->
    <script type="text/javascript">
```

Following the imports, we will see next the JavaScript that integrates with our Python Web Socket server.

Socket.IO connect and disconnect handlers

In the `<script>` section of the file, on line (2), we create an instance of the `io()` class from the `socket.io` JavaScript library and assign it to the `socket` variable:

```javascript
var socket = io();                          // (2)

socket.on('connect', function() {           // (3)
    console.log("Connected to Server");
    $("#connected").html("Yes");
});

socket.on('disconnect', function() {        // (4)
    console.log("Disconnected from the Server");
    $("#connected").html("No");
});
```

On line (3), with `socket.on('connect', ...)`, we register a *connect* event listener. This handler is called every time our web page client connects successfully to our Python server. This is the client-side equivalent of the Python server's on connect handler we defined with `@socketio.on('connect')`.

On line (4), we see the `disconnect` handler that is called every time the client web page loses its connection to the server. This is the client-side equivalent of the Python server-side `@socketio.on('disconnect')` handler.

Notice, in both handlers, we update our web page to indicate whether it has a connection back to the server. We saw this in operation previously when we terminated and restarted the server.

Next, we have a handler related to our LED.

The on LED handler

On line (5), we have our `led` message handler, which is responsible for updating the HTML controls with the current brightness level of our LED:

```
socket.on('led', function(dataFromServer) {          // (5)
    console.log(dataFromServer)
    if (dataFromServer.level !== undefined) {
$("input[type=range].brightnessLevel").val(dataFromServer.level);
        $("#brightnessLevel").html(dataFromServer.level);
    }
});
```

If you review the Python server's `@socketio.on('connect')` handler, you will notice it contains the line `emit("led", state)`. When a new client connects to the server, it *emits* back to the connecting client a message containing the current state of our LED. It's the JavaScript `socket.on('led', ...)` part on line (5) that consumes this message.

Next, we have the jQuery document ready callback.

The document ready function

The jQuery document ready callback is where we set up the event handler for the HTML slider:

```
$(document).ready(function(){
    // Event listener for Slider value changes.
    $("input[type=range].brightnessLevel")
      .on('input', function(){
          level = $(this).val();
          payload = {"level": level};
          socket.emit('led', payload);          // (6)
      });
});
    </script>
</head>
```

On line (6), we see how to emit a message in JavaScript. The call to `socket.emit('led', payload)` emits a message to the Python server with the brightness level we want to apply to our LED.

It's the Python `@socketio.on('led')` handler that receives this message and changes the LED's brightness.

If you review this Python handler, you will notice the line: `emit("led", state, broadcast=True)`. This line broadcasts a message with the new LED state to all connected clients. Each client's `socket.on('led', ...)` handler will consume this message and synchronize their sliders accordingly.

Finally, we have the HTML that makes up our web page.

The web page HTML

The only difference to the RESTful API web page is the inclusion on line (7) of a message to indicate whether we have a connection to the Python server:

```
<body>
    <h1>Flask Web Socket Example</h1>
    LED is connected to GPIO {{pin}}<br>
    Connected to server: <span id="connected">No</span> <!-- (7) -->
    <br><br>
    Brightness <span id="brightnessLevel"></span>:<br>
    <input type="range" min="0" max="100"
            value="0" class="brightnessLevel">
</body>
</html>
```

Congratulations! That's two Python servers and web page clients using two different transport layers you have just completed.

We have seen how to implement the same project to control an LED's brightness using both a RESTful API-based approach and a Web Sockets-based approach. These are two very common options for implementing web services and integrating a web page (or any client for that matter) to a backend server, so an understanding and appreciation of both techniques are useful so you can choose the most suitable technique for your own applications or for those times when you are trying to understand how an existing application is implemented.

Let's recap what we have covered by comparing the approaches and learning a little more about which problem domains each approach is best suited for.

Comparing the RESTful API and Web Socket servers

A RESTful-based API is conceptually similar to design, develop, and test, and are more commonly found across the internet where a one-way request/response data exchange is needed.

Here are some defining characteristics of this approach:

- The communication protocol is built around HTTP methods with GET, POST, PUT, and DELETE being the most common.
- The protocol is half-duplex in the form of request-response. The client makes a request and the server responds. The server cannot initiate a request to a client.
- We have options including `curl` on the command line and GUI tools such as Postman to test and development RESTful APIs.
- We can use a common web browser to test HTTP GET API endpoints
- In Python, we can use the Flask-RESTful extension to help us to build a RESTful API server. We model endpoints as Python classes that have class methods such as `.get()` and `.post()` that match HTTP request methods.
- For a web page client, we can use a library such as jQuery to make HTTP requests to our Python server.

Web Sockets, on the other hand, are often found in chat applications and games where real-time two-way data exchange is needed, often with many simultaneous clients.

Here are some defining characteristics of this approach:

- The communication protocol is based on publishing and subscribing to messages.
- The protocol is full-duplex. Both the client and the server can initiate requests to one another.
- In Python, we can use the Flask-SocketIO extension to help us to create Web Socket services. We create methods and designate them as a callback handler for a message event.
- For a web page client, we use the `socket.io` JavaScript library. Similar to Python, we create common JavaScript functions and register them with `socket.io` as callback handlers for message events.

Is one approach better than the other? There is no single best or one-size-fits-all approach, so choosing a networking approach for your IoT applications is largely going to depend on what you are creating and how clients are going to connect to and use your application. If you are new to building networked applications and web services in general, RESTful APIs with Flask-RESTful is a great place to start while you learn the concepts and experiment. This is a very common and widely used approach, plus if you use a tool such as Postman (`getpostman.com`) as your API client while developing, then you'll have a powerful and fast way to play with and test the APIs that you create.

Summary

In this chapter, we have covered in two common methods for building networked services with Python—RESTful APIs and Web Socket services. We built these services in Python using the Flask microservices framework and the Flask-RESTful and Flask-SocketIO extensions. After we created each server, we also created web page clients. We learned how to use the JavaScript jQuery library to make a RESTful API request and the Socket.IO JavaScript library to perform Web Socket messaging and subscribing.

With this new knowledge, you now have the foundations and a simple end-to-end client-server framework built using Python, HTML, JavaScript, and jQuery that you can expand on and experiment with to create grander IoT applications. For example, as you proceed through Part 3 of this book, *IoT Playground,* and learn about different electronic sensors and actuators, you'll be in a position to expand and build upon this chapter's examples using different electronic components. We'll also see another example of Flask-RESTful and RESTful APIs when we reach `Chapter 14`, *Tying It All Together – An IoT Christmas Tree,* where we introduce a web page that interacts with a LED lighting strip and servo.

In `Chapter 4`, *Networking with MQTT, Python, and the Mosquitto MQTT Broker,* we will look at a more advanced and very versatile approach to building the networking layer of IoT applications, this time with MQTT, the Message Queue Telemetry Transport protocol.

Questions

As we conclude, here is a list of questions for you to test your knowledge regarding this chapter's material. You will find the answers in the *Assessments* section of the book:

1. What feature of the Flask-RESTful extension can we use to help to validate a client's input data?
2. What communication protocol can be used to provide real-time full-duplex communication between a client and a server?
3. How do we perform request data validation with Flask-SocketIO?
4. What is the Flask `templates` folder?
5. When using jQuery, where should we create component event listeners and initialize our web page content?
6. What command-line tool can be used to make requests to a RESTful API service?
7. What happens to the physical LED when we change the `value` property of a `PWMLED` instance?

Further reading

We have mentioned the word "RESTful" a lot in this chapter, without any deep discussion of what it means exactly. If you want all of the details, a great introductory tutorial can be found on SitePoint.com:

- REST on SitePoint.com: `https://www.sitepoint.com/developers-rest-api`

Our RESTful API example barely even touches the basics of Flask and Flask-RESTful but provides a working example that you can build upon. I encourage you to read at a minimum the Flask Quick Start Guide, followed by the Flask RESTful Quick Start Guide to get a good grounding and understanding of these two frameworks:

- Flask Quick Start: `https://flask.palletsprojects.com/en/1.1.x/quickstart`
- Flask-RESTful Quick Start: `https://flask-restful.readthedocs.io/en/latest/quickstart.html`

As mentioned during the chapter in the section titled *Introducing the Flask microservices framework*, if you experience difficulties with Flask-RESTful and cannot find answers in its documentation, you should also consult the official core Flask documentation:

- Flask documentation: `https://flask.palletsprojects.com`

We have also only scratched the surface of Web Sockets with Flask-SocketIO and Socket.IO. The following links point to the official Flask-SocketIO and Socket.IO libraries. I've also included two additional links that provide a generalized and simple introduction to Web Sockets. As a reminder, Web Sockets are a technology that is best learned through doing rather than reading, especially if you are new to server development. So, as you read introductory material on Web Sockets, expect core underlying concepts to be illustrated with a wide range of different code examples and libraries in addition to the Flask-SocketIO and Socket.IO libraries we used in this chapter:

- Flask-SocketIO: `https://flask-socketio.readthedocs.io`
- Socket.IO (JavaScript library): `https://socket.io`
- Web Socket basics: `https://www.html5rocks.com/en/tutorials/websockets/basics`
- Web Socket basics: `https://medium.com/@dominik.t/what-are-web-sockets-what-about-rest-apis-b9c15fd72aac`

Networking with MQTT, Python, and the Mosquitto MQTT Broker

4

In the previous chapter, we created two Python servers and accompanying web pages using both a RESTful API and Web Socket approach to networking. In this chapter, we will cover another networking topology that is common in the IoT world, known as **MQTT** or **Message Queue Telemetry Transport**.

We will commence by setting up your development environment and installing the Mosquitto MQTT broker service on your Raspberry Pi. Then, we will learn about MQTT features using command-line tools that come with Mosquitto to help you to understand the core concepts in isolation. After that, we'll proceed to a Python IoT application that uses MQTT for its messaging layer—and yes, it'll be all about controlling the LED!

We will cover the following topics in this chapter:

- Installing the Mosquitto MQTT broker
- Learning MQTT by example
- Introducing the Python Paho-MQTT client library
- Controlling an LED with Python and MQTT
- Building a web-based MQTT client

Technical requirements

To perform the exercises in this chapter, you will need the following:

- Raspberry Pi 4 Model B
- Raspbian OS Buster (with desktop and recommended software)
- A minimum of Python version 3.5

These requirements are what the code examples in this book are based on. It's reasonable to expect that the code examples should work without modification on a Raspberry Pi 3 Model B or a different version of Raspbian OS as long as your Python version is 3.5 or higher.

You will find this chapter's source code in the chapter04 folder in the GitHub repository available at the following URL: https://github.com/PacktPublishing/Practical-Python-Programming-for-IoT

You will need to execute the following commands in a Terminal to set up a virtual environment and install the Python libraries required for the code in this chapter:

```
$ cd chapter04            # Change into this chapter's folder
$ python3 -m venv venv    # Create Python Virtual Environment
$ source venv/bin/activate # Activate Python Virtual Environment
(venv) $ pip install pip --upgrade      # Upgrade pip
(venv) $ pip install -r requirements.txt  # Install dependent packages
```

The following dependencies are installed from requirements.txt:

- **GPIOZero**: The GPIOZero GPIO library (https://pypi.org/project/gpiozero)
- **PiGPIO**: The PiGPIO GPIO library (https://pypi.org/project/pigpio)
- **Paho-MQTT Client**: The Paho-MQTT client library (https://pypi.org/project/paho-mqtt)

We will be working with the breadboard circuit we created in Chapter 2, *Getting Started with Python and IoT, Figure 2.7.*

Installing the Mosquitto MQTT broker

MQTT, or **Message Queue Telemetry Transport**, is a lightweight and simple messaging protocol targeted specifically for IoT applications. While a Raspberry Pi is powerful enough to leverage more complex messaging protocols, if you are using it as part of a distributed IoT solution, chances are you are going to encounter MQTT; hence, learning it is very important. Besides, its simplicity and open nature make it easy to learn and use.

Our introduction to MQTT is going to be performed using a popular open source MQTT broker called *Mosquitto* that we will install on your Raspberry Pi.

 The examples we cover in this chapter were performed with the Mosquitto broker and client version 1.5.7, which are MQTT protocol version 3.1.1-complaint. A different version of the broker or client tools will be suitable as long as they are MQTT protocol version 3.1.x-compatible.

To install the Mosquitto MQTT broker service and client tools, follow these steps:

1. Open a new Terminal window and execute the following `apt-get` command. This must be performed using `sudo`:

   ```
   $ sudo apt-get --yes install mosquitto mosquitto-clients
   ... truncated ...
   ```

2. To ensure that the Mosquitto MQTT broker service has started, run the following command in the Terminal:

   ```
   $ sudo systemctl start mosquitto
   ```

3. Check that the Mosquitto service has started with the following `service` command. We expect to see the `active (running)` text printed to the Terminal:

   ```
   $ systemctl status mosquitto
   ... truncated ...
    Active: active (running)
   ... truncated ...
   ```

4. We can check the Mosquitto and MQTT protocol version with the `mosquitto -h` command. Here, we see that the Mosquitto broker is using MQTT version 3.1.1:

   ```
   $ mosquitto -h
   mosquitto version 1.5.7
   mosquitto is an MQTT v3.1.1 broker.
   ... truncated ...
   ```

5. Next, we will configure Mosquitto so that it can serve web pages and handle Web Socket requests. We will use these features when we come to build a web page client later in this chapter.

   In the `chapter4` folder, there is a file named `mosquitto_pyiot.conf`, which is partially replicated here. There is one line in this file that we need to check:

   ```
   # File: chapter04/mosquitto_pyiot.conf
   ... truncated...
   http_dir /home/pi/pyiot/chapter04/mosquitto_www
   ```

   For the exercises in this chapter, you need to update the `http_dir` setting on the last line so it's the absolute path to the `chapter04/mosquitto_www` folder on your Raspberry Pi. If you used the suggested folder, `/home/pi/pyiot`, when cloning the GitHub repository in `Chapter 1`, *Setting Up Your Development Environment*, then the path listed previously is correct.

6. Next, we copy the configuration in `mosquitto_pyiot.conf` using the following `cp` command into the appropriate folder so that it can be loaded by Mosquitto:

   ```
   $ sudo cp mosquitto_pyiot.conf /etc/mosquitto/conf.d/
   ```

7. Now we restart the Mosquitto service to load our configuration:

   ```
   $ sudo systemctl restart mosquitto
   ```

8. To check that the configuration has worked, visit the `http://localhost:8083` URL in a web browser on your Raspberry Pi, and you should see a page similar to the following screenshot:

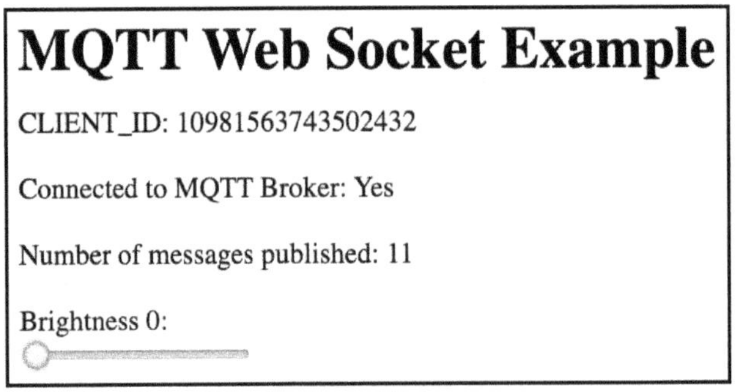

Figure 4.1 – Web page served by the Mosquitto MQTT broker

This is a giveaway to what we'll be doing later in this chapter! At the moment, while you can move the slider, it *will not* change the LED's brightness because we do not have the Python-side code running. We'll cover that in due course later in this chapter.

If you experience problems getting the Mosquitto MQTT Broker to start, try the following:

- Execute `sudo mosquitto -v -c /etc/mosquitto/mosquitto.conf` in a Terminal. This will start Mosquitto in the foreground and any start up or configurations errors will be shown on your Terminal.
- Read the troubleshooting comments in the `mosquitto_pyiot.conf` file for additional suggestions.

The default configuration of Mosquitto after installation creates an *unencrypted* and *unauthenticated* MQTT broker service. The Mosquitto documentation contains details regarding its configuration and how to enable authentication and encryption. You will find links in the *Further reading* section at the end of this chapter.

Now that we have Mosquitto installed and running, we can explore MQTT concepts and perform examples to see them in practice.

Learning MQTT by example

MQTT is a broker-based *publishing* and *subscription* messaging protocol (frequently paraphrased as *pub/sub*), while an MQTT *broker* (just like the Mosquitto MQTT broker we installed in the previous section) is a server that implements the MQTT protocol. By using an MQTT-based architecture, your applications can essentially hand off all complex messaging handling and routing logic to the broker so they can remain solution-focused.

MQTT clients (for example, your Python programs and the command-line tools we are about to use) create a subscription with the broker and *subscribe* to message topics they are interested in. Clients *publish* messages to a topic, and it is the broker that is then responsible for all message routing and delivery assurances. Any client may assume the role of a subscriber, a publisher, or both.

A simple conceptual MQTT-based system involving a pump, water tank, and controller application is illustrated in *Figure 4.2*:

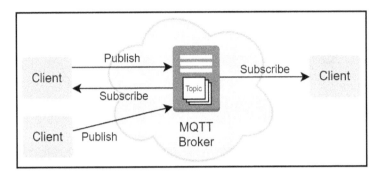

Figure 4.2 – MQTT example

Here is a high-level description of system components:

- Think of the *Water Level Sensor MQTT client* as the software connected to a water level sensor in a water tank. This client assumes the role of a *publisher* in our MQTT example. It periodically sends (that is, *publishes)* messages about how full the water tank is to the MQTT broker.
- Think of the *Pump MQTT client* as a software driver that is capable of switching a water pump on or off. This client assumes both the role of a *publisher* and *subscriber* in our example:
    - As a *subscriber,* it can receive a message (via a *subscription)* instructing it to switch the pump on or off.
    - As a *publisher,* it can send a message indicating whether the pump is on and pumping water or off.
- Think of the *Controller MQTT client* as the application where all of the control logic resides. This client also assumes both the roles of a *publisher* and *subscriber:*
    - As a *publisher,* this client can send a message that will tell the pump to switch on or off.
    - As a *subscriber,* this client can receive messages from both the water tank level sensor and the pump.

By way of example, the *Controller MQTT client* application could be configured to switch on the pump when the water level in the tank falls below 50% and switch off the pump when the level reaches 100%. This controller application may also include a dashboard user interface that displays the current water level in the tank and a status light indicating whether the pump is on or off.

An important point to note regarding our MQTT system is that each client is unaware of the other clients—a client only ever connects to and interacts with the MQTT broker, which then routes messages as appropriate to clients. This routing is achieved using message *topics*, which we will cover later in the section entitled *Exploring MQTT topics and wildcards*.

It's understandable why the pump would need to receive a message to tell it to turn on or off, but what about the pump's need to also send a message stating whether it is on or off? If you wondered about this, here is the reason. MQTT messages are send-and-forget, meaning that a client does not get an application-level response to a message that it publishes. So, in our example, while the controller client can publish a message asking the pump to turn on, without the pump publishing its status, the controller has no way of knowing whether the pump actually turned on.

In practice, the pump would publish its on/off status every time it turns on or off. This would allow the controller's dashboard to update the pump's status indicator in a timely manner. Furthermore, the pump would also periodically publish its status (just like the water level sensor) independent of any requests it receives to turn on or off. This way, the controller application can monitor the connection and availability of the pump and detect whether the pump goes offline.

For now, if you can grasp the basic ideas presented in the preceding example, then you are well on your way to understanding at a deeper level the core MQTT concepts that will be our focus for the remainder of this chapter. By the time we finish, you will have a fundamental end-to-end understanding of how to work with and design MQTT-based applications.

We will start by learning how to publish and subscribe to messages.

Publishing and subscribing MQTT messages

Let's work through the steps to send (that is, publish) and receive (that is, subscribe to) messages using MQTT:

1. In a Terminal, run the following command. `mosquitto_sub` (Mosquitto subscribe) is a command-line tool to *subscribe* to messages:

```
# Terminal #1 (Subscriber)
$ mosquitto_sub -v -h localhost -t 'pyiot'
```

The options are as follows:

- −v (--verbose): verbose is so we get both the message *topic* and *message* payload printed on the Terminal.
- −h (--host): localhost is the host of the broker we want to connect to; here it's the one we just installed. The default port used is 1883.
- −t (--topic): pyiot is the topic we want to subscribe to and listen to.

In this chapter, we will require two and sometimes three Terminal sessions for the examples. The first line of a code block will indicate which Terminal you need to run a command in; for example, **Terminal #1** in the preceding code block, and **Terminal #2** in the following code block.

2. Open a second Terminal and run the following command. mosquitto_pub (Mosquitto publish) is a command-line tool to *publish* messages:

```
# Terminal #2 (Publisher)
$ mosquitto_pub -h localhost -t 'pyiot' -m 'hello!'
```

Let's look at the options:

- −h and −t have the same meaning as in the preceding subscription command.
- −m 'hello!' (--message) is the message we want to publish. Messages in MQTT are simple strings— if you're wondering about JSON, it just needs to be serialized/deserialized to strings.

3. On **Terminal #1**, we see the topic and message, hello!, printed:

```
# Terminal #1 (Subscriber)
$ mosquitto_sub -v -h localhost -t 'pyiot'
pyiot hello!
```

The final line is in the format *<topic> <message payload>*.

The hello! message is preceded by the topic name, pyiot, because we have used the −v option to mosquitto_sub. Without the −v option, if we were subscribing to multiple topics, we could not identify which topic a message belonged to.

Now, we've learned how to publish and subscribe to messages with a simple topic. But is there any way we can organize these messages in a better way? Read on.

Exploring MQTT topics and wildcards

MQTT *topics* are used to categorize, or group, messages together in a hierarchical format. We have already been working with topics in our proceeding command-line examples, but in a non-hierarchical fashion. *Wildcards*, on the other hand, are special characters used by a *subscriber* to create flexible topic matching patterns.

Here are a few hierarchical topic examples from a hypothetical building with sensors. The hierarchy is delimited by the / character:

- `level1/lounge/temperature/sensor1`
- `level1/lounge/temperature/sensor2`
- `level1/lounge/lighting/sensor1`
- `level2/bedroom1/temperature/sensor1`
- `level2/bedroom1/lighting/sensor1`

There is no need to pre-create a topic on an MQTT broker. Using the *default* broker configuration (which we are), you just publish and subscribe to topics at will.

> When the Mosquitto broker is configured to use authentication, there is the possibility to restrict access to topics based on a client ID and/or username and password.

Messages *must* be published to a *specific* topic such as `pyiot`, while subscriptions can be made to a specific topic, or a range of topics, by using the wildcard characters, + and #:

- + is used to match a single element of the hierarchy.
- # is used to match *all* remaining elements in a hierarchy (it can only be at the end of a topic query).

Subscriptions to topics and wildcards are best explained by example. Using the aforementioned hypothetical building with sensors, consider the examples in the following table:

We want to subscribe to...	Wildcard topic	Topic matches
All **temperature** sensors everywhere	+/+/**temperature**/+	• level1/lounge/**temperature**/sensor1 • level1/lounge/**temperature**/sensor2 • level2/bedroom1/**temperature**/sensor1
All **light** sensors everywhere	+/+/**lighting**/+	• level1/lounge/**lighting**/sensor1 • level2/bedroom1/**lighting**/sensor1
Every sensor on **level 2**	**level2**/+/+/+	• **level2**/bedroom1/temperature/sensor1 • **level2**/bedroom1/lighting/sensor1
Every sensor on **level 2** (a simpler way where # matches every remaining child)	**level2**/#	• **level2**/bedroom1/temperature/sensor1 • **level2**/bedroom1/lighting/sensor1
Only **sensor1** everywhere	+/+/+/**sensor1**	• level1/lounge/temperature/**sensor1** • level1/lounge/lighting/**sensor1** • level2/bedroom1/temperature/**sensor1** • level2/bedroom1/lighting/**sensor1**
Only **sensor1** everywhere (a simpler way where # matches every remaining child)	#/**sensor1**	Invalid because # can only be at the end of the topic query
Every topic	#	Matches everything

We want to subscribe to...	Wildcard topic	Topic matches
Broker information	$SYS/#	This is a special reserved topic where the broker publishes information and runtime statistics.

Table 1 - MQTT wildcard topic examples

What may be evident from the preceding examples is that you need to take care when designing topic hierarchies for an application so that subscribing to multiple topics using wildcards is consistent, logical, and easy.

If you are subscribing using the + or # wildcards with `mosquitto_sub`, remember to use the -v (--verbose) option so that the topic name is printed in the output, for example, `mosquitto_sub -h localhost -v -t '#'`.

Try a few examples for yourself on the command line by mixing and matching the preceding topics and wildcards to get a feel for how topics and wildcards work. Following are the steps for one example where `mosquitto_sub` subscribes to all childtopics that have the parent *temperature* two levels down from the root topic:

1. In a Terminal, start a subscriber that subscribes to a wildcard topic:

```
# Terminal #1 (Subscriber)
mosquitto_sub -h localhost -v -t '+/+/temperature/+'
```

2. Using the topics from *Table 1 – MQTT wildcard topic examples,* here are two `mosquitto_pub` commands that will publish messages that will be received by the `mosquitto_sub` command in **Terminal** #1:

```
# Terminal #2 (Publisher)
$ mosquitto_pub -h localhost -t 'level1/lounge/temperature/sensor1' -m '20'
$ mosquitto_pub -h localhost -t 'level2/bedroom1/temperature/sensor1' -m '22'
```

We have just seen how to subscribe to topic hierarchies using the wildcard characters, + and *. Using topics and wildcards together is a design decision you'll need to make on a per-project level based on how your data needs to flow and how you envision it will be both published and subscribed by client applications. Time invested in designing a congruent yet flexible wildcard-based topic hierarchy will go a long way to helping you to build simpler and reusable client code and applications.

Next, we will learn all about message Quality of Service and how this impacts the messages you send through an MQTT Broker.

Applying Quality of Service to messages

MQTT provides three **Quality of Service (QoS)** levels for *individual message delivery*—I am emphasizing *individual message delivery* because QoS levels apply to the delivery of individual messages and not to a topic. This will become clearer as you work through the examples.

While you, as the developer, stipulate the QoS for your messages, it's the broker that is responsible for ensuring that the message delivery adheres to the QoS. Here is the QoS you can apply to a message and what they mean for delivery:

QoS level	Meaning	Number of messages delivered
Level 0	The message will be delivered at most once, but maybe not at all.	0 or 1
Level 1	The message will be delivered at least once, but perhaps more.	1 or more
Level 2	The message will be delivered exactly once.	1

Table 2 – Message QoS levels

You might be asking the question: Level 0 and 1 seem a bit random, so why not just always use Level 2? The answer is *resources*. Let's see why...

The broker and clients will consume more resources to process higher-level QoS messages than lower-level QoS messages—for example, the broker will need more time and memory to store and process messages, while both the broker and clients consume more time and network bandwidth with acknowledgment confirmations and connection handshaking.

For many use cases, including the examples that follow in this chapter, we will not notice a difference between QoS levels 1 and 2, nor will we be able to practically demonstrate them (Level 0 gets omitted for a good reason, which we'll see later on when we cover message retention and durable connections). However, set your mind to a distributed IoT system with thousands of sensors publishing thousands or more messages every minute, and now designing around QoS starts to make a little more sense.

QoS levels apply to both message *subscriptions* and message *publishing,* which may seem odd when you first think it through. For example, a client may publish a message with a QoS of 1 to a topic, while another client may subscribe to that topic with a QoS of 2 (I know I said QoS relates to messages, not topics, but here it's the messages flowing *through* the topic that the QoS relates to). What QoS is this message, 1 or 2? For the subscriber, it's 1—let's find out why.

It's the *subscribing* client that chooses the *highest* QoS of messages it wants to receive—but it may get lower. So, effectively, this means the delivery QoS received by a client is downgraded to the lowest QoS of the publication or subscription.

Here are a few examples for you to ponder:

Publisher sends message	Subscriber subscribing at	What subscriber gets
QoS 2	QoS 0	Delivery of message adhering to a QoS 0 (subscriber gets the message 0 or 1 time)
QoS 2	QoS 2	Delivery of message adhering to a QoS 2 (subscriber gets the message exactly once)
QoS 0	QoS 1	Delivery of message adhering to QoS 0 (subscriber gets the message 0 or 1 time)
QoS 1	QoS 2	Delivery of message adhering to QoS 1 (subscriber gets the message 1 or more times)
QoS 2	QoS 1	Delivery of message adhering to QoS 1 (subscriber gets the message 1 or more times)

Table 3 – Publisher and subscriber QoS examples

The takeaway from these examples is that, in practice, when designing or integrating IoT solutions, you need to be aware of the QoS used by both publishers and subscribers on either side of a topic—QoS cannot be interpreted on either side in isolation.

Following are the steps to play out QoS scenarios and see client-broker interactions in real time:

1. In a Terminal, run the following command to start a subscriber:

```
# Terminal 1 (Subscriber)
$ mosquitto_sub -d -v -q 2 -h localhost -t 'pyiot'
```

2. In a second Terminal, run the following command to publish a message:

```
# Terminal 2 (Publisher)
$ mosquitto_pub -d -q 1 -h localhost -t 'pyiot' -m 'hello!'
```

Here, we are again subscribing on **Terminal #1**, and publishing on **Terminal #2**. Here are the new options used with both `mosquitto_sub` and `mosquitto_pub`:

- `-d`: Turn on debugging messages
- `-q <level>`: QoS level

With debugging enabled (`-d`), try changing the `-q` parameter (to 0, 1, or 2) on either side and publishing new messages.

3. Observe the logged messages in **Terminal #1** and **Terminal #2**.

Among the debugging messages that will appear in **Terminal #1** and **Terminal #2**, you will obverse the QoS downgrade occurring at the subscription side (look for q0, q1, or q2) while, on both sides, you will also notice different debug messages depending on the QoS specified as the client and broker perform handshaking and exchange acknowledgments:

```
# Terminal 1 (Subscriber)
$ mosquitto_sub -d -v -q 2 -h localhost -t 'pyiot' # (1)
Client mosqsub|25112-rpi4 sending CONNECT
Client mosqsub|25112-rpi4 received CONNACK (0)
Client mosqsub|25112-rpi4 sending SUBSCRIBE (Mid: 1, Topic: pyiot,
QoS: 2) # (2)
Client mosqsub|25112-rpi4 received SUBACK
Subscribed (mid: 1): 2
Client mosqsub|25112-rpi4 received PUBLISH (d0, q1, r0, m1,
'pyiot', ... (6 bytes)) # (3)
Client mosqsub|25112-rpi4 sending PUBACK (Mid: 1)
pyiot hello!
```

Following is the debug output for the subscriber on **Terminal #1**. Notice the following:

- At line (1), we subscribed using QoS 2 (`-q 2`). This is reflected in the debug output, `QoS: 2`, on line (2).
- On line (3), we see the QoS downgrade. The message received is QoS 1 (`q1`), which is the QoS that the message was published in **Terminal #1**.

QoS is one of the more complex MQTT concepts to grasp. You will find links in the *Further reading* section if you want to go deeper into QoS levels and the lower level communications that take place between publishers, subscribers, and the broker.

Now that we have covered message QoS levels, we will next learn about two MQTT features that ensure offline clients can receive past messages when they come back online. We will also see how QoS levels impact these features.

Retaining messages for later delivery

An MQTT broker can be instructed to retain messages published to a topic. Message retention comes in two flavors, known as *retained messages* and *durable connections*:

- A **retained message** is where the broker retains the *last message* published on a topic. This is also commonly referred to as the *last known good message*, and any client subscribing to a topic automatically gets this message.
- **Durable connections** are also about retaining messages but in a different context. If a client tells the broker it wants a *durable connection*, then the broker retains QoS 1 and 2 messages for that client while it's offline.

 Unless configured specifically, Mosquitto *does not* retain messages or connections across server restarts. To persist this information across a restart, a Mosquitto configuration file must contain the entry `persistence true`. A default installation of Mosquitto on a Raspberry Pi should include this entry, however, to be sure it has also been included in `mosquitto_pyiot.conf` that we installed earlier. Please consult the official Mosquitto documentation for more information and configuration parameters regarding persistence. You will find a link in the *Further reading* section at the end of the chapter.

Next, we will learn about retained messages and cover durable connections in the subsequent section.

Publishing a retained message

A publisher can ask the broker to retain a message as the *last known good* message for a topic. Any newly connecting subscriber will immediately receive this last retained message.

Let's step through an example to demonstrate retained messages:

1. Run the following, noting that we're starting with **Terminal #2**, the publisher in this example:

```
# Terminal 2 (Publisher)
$ mosquitto_pub -r -q 2 -h localhost -t 'pyiot' -m 'hello, I have
been retained!'
```

A new option has been added, -r (--retain), to tell the broker that this message should be retained for the topic.

Only a single retained message can exist for a topic. If you publish another message using the -r option, the previous retained message will be replaced.

2. Start a subscriber in another Terminal, and immediately you will receive the retained message:

```
# Terminal 1 (Subscriber)
$ mosquitto_sub -v -q 2 -h localhost -t 'pyiot'
pyiot hello, I have been retained!
```

3. Press *Ctrl + C* in **Terminal #1** to terminate `mosquitto_sub`.

4. Start `mosquitto_sub` again using the same command from *step 2*, and you will see the retained message received again in **Terminal #1**.

You can still publish normal messages (that is, *not* using the -r option), however, it's the last retained message indicated by the use of the -r option that newly connecting subscribers will receive.

5. Our final command shows how to clear a previously retained message:

```
# Terminal 2 (Publisher)
$ mosquitto_pub -r -q 2 -h localhost -t 'pyiot' -m ''
```

Here, we are publishing (with -r) an empty message with -m ''. Note that we can use -n as an alternative to -m '' to indicate an empty message. The effect of retaining an empty message is to actually clear the retained message.

When you send an empty message to a topic to remove a retained message, any clients currently subscribed to the topic (including offline clients with durable connections—see the next section) will receive the empty message, so your application code must test for and handle empty messages appropriately.

Now that you understand and know how to use retained messages, we can now explore the other type of message retention available with MQTT, called *durable connections*.

Creating durable connections

A client subscribing to a topic can ask the broker to retain, or queue, messages for it while it's offline. This is known in MQTT terminology as a *durable connection*. For durable connections and delivery to work, the subscribing client needs to be configured and subscribe in a certain way, as follows:

- The client *must provide* a unique client ID to the broker when it connects.
- The client *must subscribe* with a QoS 1 or 2 (levels 1 and 2 guarantee delivery, but level 0 does not).
- The client is only guaranteed to get messages *published* with QoS 1 or 2.

The last two points concern an example where knowing QoS on both the publishing and subscribing sides of a topic is very important for IoT application design.

MQTT brokers can—and the default configuration of Mosquitto on the Raspberry Pi does—retain messages for durable connections between broker restarts.

Let's step through an example:

1. Start a subscriber, and then immediately terminate it with *Ctrl* + *C* so that it is offline:

```
# Terminal #1 (Subscriber)
$ mosquitto_sub -q 1 -h localhost -t 'pyiot' -c -i myClientId123
$ # MAKE SURE YOU PRESS CONTROL+C TO TERMINATE mosquitto_sub
```

The new options used are as follows:

- `-i <client id>` (–id <client id>) is a unique client ID (this is how the broker identifies the client).
- `-c` (--disable-clean-session) instructs the broker to keep any QoS 1 and 2 messages that arrive at subscribed topics even while the client is disconnected (that is, *retain* the messages).

It's worded a bit backward, but by starting the subscriber with the `-c` option, we've asked the broker to create a *durable connection* for our client by not clearing out any stored messages on connecting.

If you subscribe to a range of topics using wildcards (for example, `pyiot/#`) and request a durable connection, then all messages for all topics in the wildcard hierarchy will be retained for your client.

2. Publish a few messages (while the subscriber in **Terminal #1** is still offline):

```
# Terminal #2 (Publisher)
$ mosquitto_pub -q 2 -h localhost -t 'pyiot' -m 'hello 1'
$ mosquitto_pub -q 2 -h localhost -t 'pyiot' -m 'hello 2'
$ mosquitto_pub -q 2 -h localhost -t 'pyiot' -m 'hello 3'
```

3. Bring the subscriber in **Terminal #1** back online, and we will see that the messages published in *step 2* are delivered:

```
# Terminal 1 (Subscriber)
$ mosquitto_sub -v -q 1 -h localhost -t 'pyiot' -c -i myClientId123
pyiot hello 1
pyiot hello 2
pyiot hello 3
```

Try *steps 1* to *3* again, only this time omit the `-c` option from the subscriber in *steps 1* and *3* and you will notice that no messages are retained. Also, when you connect *without* the `-c` flag when there are retained messages waiting to be delivered, then all retained messages are purged (and is how you would clear retained messages for a client if you wanted to).

If you are using both *retained messages* (that is, last known good message) and *durable connections* together on a single topic and reconnect an offline subscriber, you will *receive the retained message twice*—one is the *retained message*, while the second is from the *durable connection*.

When building solutions around MQTT, your knowledge of retained messages and durable connections will be key to designing systems that are resilient and reliable, particularly where you need to handle offline clients. Retained (last known good) messages are ideal for initializing a client when they come back online, while durable connections will help you to retain and deliver messages in bulk for any offline client that must be able to consume every message for topics that it subscribes to.

Well done! We have covered a lot and you actually now know most of the core MQTT features you will use when building an MQTT-based IoT solution. Our last feature to learn about is known as a *Will*.

Saying goodbye with a Will

Our final MQTT feature for exploration is known as a Will. A client (publisher or subscriber) can register a special *Will* message with the broker so that if the client dies and disconnects from the broker abruptly (for example, it loses its network connection or its batteries go flat), the broker on the clients' behalf will send out the *Will* message notifying subscribers of the device's demise.

Wills are just a message and topic combination similar to what we have been using previously.

Let's see Wills in action, and for this, we're going to need three Terminals:

1. Open a Terminal and start a subscriber with the following command:

```
# Terminal #1 (Subscriber with Will)
$ mosquitto_sub -h localhost -t 'pyiot' --will-topic 'pyiot' --
will-payload 'Good Bye' --will-qos 2 --will-retain
```

The new options are as follows:

- `--will-payload`: This is the Will message.
- `--will-topic`: This is the topic the Will message will be published on. Here we are using the same topic that we are subscribing to, but it could be a different topic.
- `--will-qos`: This is the QoS for the Will message.
- `--will-retain`: If this option is present, then if the client disconnects abruptly, the Will message will be retained by the broker as the *retained (last known good) message* for the Will topic.

2. Start a subscriber in a second Terminal with the following command:

```
# Terminal #2 (Subscriber listening to Will topic).
$ mosquitto_sub -h localhost -t 'pyiot'
```

3. And in a third Terminal, publish a message using the following command:

```
# Terminal #3 (Publisher)
$ mosquitto_pub -h localhost -t 'pyiot' -m 'hello'
```

4. Once you execute the `mosquitto_pub` command in *step 3* on **Terminal #3**, you should see `hello` printed on *both* the subscribers in **Terminals #1** and **#2**.

5. In **Terminal #1**, press *Ctrl + C* to terminate the subscriber that registered the Will with the broker. *Ctrl + C* is seen as a non-graceful or abrupt disconnection from the broker.

6. In **Terminal #2**, we will see the Will's `Good Bye` message:

```
# Terminal #2 (Subscriber listening to Will topic).
$ mosquitto_sub -h localhost -t 'pyiot'
'Good Bye'
```

Okay, what about a graceful disconnection where the subscriber properly closes its connection with the broker? We can demonstrate this using the `-C` option with `mosquitto_sub`.

7. Restart the subscriber in **Terminal #1** with the following command:

```
# Terminal #1 (Subscriber with Will)
$ mosquitto_sub -h localhost -t 'pyiot' --will-topic 'pyiot' --
will-payload 'Good Bye, Again' --will-qos 2 --will-retain -C 2
```

The new `-C <count>` option tells `mosquitto_sub` to disconnect (gracefully) and exit after it has received the specified number of messages.

You will notice the `Good Bye` message printed immediately. This is because we specified the `--retain-will` option previously in **Terminal #1**. This option made the Will message become the retained or last known good message for the topic, so newly connecting clients will receive this message.

8. In **Terminal #3**, publish a new message, and the subscriber in **Terminal #1** will exit. Notice in **Terminal #3** that the Will message, `Good Bye, Again,` is *not* received. This is because our **Terminal #1** subscriber disconnected *gracefully* from the broker because of the `-C` option—and in case you are wondering about 2 in `-C 2`, the retained Will message counted as the first message.

Well done! If you have worked your way through each of the preceding MQTT examples, then you have covered the core concepts and use of MQTT and the Mosquitto broker. Do remember that all of these principles will apply to any MQTT broker or client since MQTT is an open standard.

So far, we've learned about message subscriptions and publication, how we segregate messages using topics, and how features including QoS, message retention, durable connections, and Wills can be leveraged to control how messages are managed and delivered. This knowledge alone provides you with the foundations to build complex and resilient distributed IoT systems using MQTT.

I'll leave you with one final tip (which caught me out a few times when I started with MQTT).

If your live, retained, or queued durable connection messages seem to be vanishing into a black hole, then check the QoS levels on both your subscribing and publishing clients. To monitor all messages, start a command-line subscriber with QoS 2, listening to the # topic, with both verbose and debug options enabled, for example, `mosquitto_sub -q 2 -v -d -h localhost -t '#'`.

We have now completed all of our examples from the MQTT-by-example section and learned how to interact with an MQTT broker from the command line. Next, I want to briefly make mention of public broker services. Following this, we'll get into code and see how we can leverage MQTT with Python.

Using MQTT broker services

There are several MQTT broker service providers on the internet that you can use to create MQTT-based messaging applications if you do not want to host your own MQTT broker. Many also offer free public MQTT brokers that you can use for testing and quick proofs-of-concept—but remember they are free and public, so do not publish any sensitive information!

If you experience frustration, disconnections, or unexpected behavior with a free public broker service, then test and verify your application with a local broker. You cannot reliably know or verify the traffic congestion, topic usage, or configuration details of an open public broker and how that may be impacting your application.

Here are a few free public brokers you can try. Just replace the −h *localhost* option in the preceding examples with the address of the broker. Visit the following pages for more information and instructions:

- `https://test.mosquitto.org`
- `http://broker.mqtt-dashboard.com`
- `https://ot.eclipse.org/getting-started`

In the following sections, we will move a level higher. Finally, we're up to the Python bit of MQTT! Rest assured that everything we just covered will be invaluable when you develop IoT applications that use MQTT because the command-line tools and examples we covered will become an important part of your MQTT development and debugging toolkit. We will be applying the core MQTT concepts we have learned already, only this time using Python and the Paho-MQTT client library.

Introducing the Python Paho-MQTT client library

Before we get into Python code, we first need an MQTT client library for Python. At the start of this chapter in the *Technical requirements* section, we installed the Paho-MQTT client library, which was part of `requirements.txt`.

 If you are new to MQTT and have not read the preceding section, *Learning MQTT by example*, I recommend stopping now and reading it first so you gain an understanding of MQTT concepts and terminology that will be used in the Python examples that follow.

The Paho-MQTT client library comes from the Eclipse Foundation, which also maintains the Mosquitto MQTT broker. In the *Further reading* section, you will find a link to the official *Paho-MQTT Client Library API* documentation. After completing this chapter, if you wish to deepen your understanding of this library and its capabilities, I recommend reading through the official documentation and the examples found therein.

The Python Paho-MQTT library has three core modules:

- **Client**: This gives you full life cycle management of MQTT in your Python application.
- **Publisher**: This is a helper module for message publishing.
- **Subscriber**: This is a helper module for message subscribing.

The client module is ideal if you are creating more complex and long-running IoT applications, whereas the publisher and subscriber helper modules are convenient for short-lived applications and situations where full life cycle management is not warranted.

 The following Python examples will connect to your local Mosquitto MQTT broker that we installed in the *Installing the Mosquitto MQTT broker* section previously.

We will be using the Paho client module so we can create a more complete MQTT example. However, once you can follow and understand the client module, creating alternatives using the helper modules will be a piece of cake.

 As a reminder, we will be working with the breadboard circuit we created in `Chapter 2`, *Getting Started with Python and IoT*, Figure 2.7.

Now that we have a basic familiarity with the Paho-MQTT library, we will next start by briefly reviewing what the Python program and the accompanying web page client do and see Paho-MQTT in action.

Controlling an LED with Python and MQTT

Previously, in the *Installing the Mosquitto MQTT broker* section, we tested the installation by visiting the `http://localhost:8083` URL, which gave us a web page with a slider. However, at the time, we could not change the LED's brightness. When you moved the slider, the web page was publishing MQTT messages to the Mosquitto broker, but no program was receiving the messages to change the LED's brightness.

In this section, we'll see the Python code that subscribes to a topic called `led` and processes the messages generated by the slider. We will start by running the Python code and making sure we can change the LED's brightness.

Running the LED MQTT example

You will find the code in the `chapter04/mqtt_led.py` file. Please review this file before proceeding to get an overall idea of what it contains and then follow these steps:

1. Run the program in a Terminal with the following command:

```
# Terminal #1
(venv) $ python mqtt_led.py
INFO:main:Listening for messages on topic 'led'. Press Control + C
to exit.
INFO:main:Connected to MQTT Broker
```

2. Now, open a second Terminal window and try the following, and the LED should turn on (be careful to make sure the JSON string is formed correctly):

```
# Terminal #2
$ mosquitto_pub -q 2 -h localhost -t 'led' -r -m '{"level": "100"}'
```

3. Did you notice the `-r` (`--retain`) option used in *step 2*? Terminate and restart `mqtt_led.py` and watch the log output in **Terminal #1** and the LED. You should notice on startup that `mqtt_led.py` receives the LED's brightness value from the topic's *retained message* and initializes the LED's brightness accordingly.

4. Next, visit the `http://localhost:8083` URL and make sure the LED changes its brightness as you move the slider.

Leave the web page open, and try the command in *step 2* again. Observe what happens to the slider—it will stay in sync with the new level value you specified.

5. Next, let's see durable connections in action. Terminate `mqtt_led.py` again and perform the following:
   - On the web page, move the slider around randomly for about 5 seconds. As you move the slider, messages are being published to the broker on the `led` topic. They will be queued for delivery to `mqtt_led.py` when it reconnects.
   - Restart `mqtt_led.py` and observe the Terminal and LED. You will notice a flood of messages on the Terminal, and the LED will flicker as the queued messages are delivered and processed by `mqtt_led.py`.

> By default, Mosquitto is configured to queue 100 messages per client that are using a durable connection. A client is identified by its client ID that you provide when connecting to the broker.

Now that we have interacted with and seen `mqtt_led.py` in action, let's take a look at its code.

Understanding the code

As we discuss the code found in `chapter04/mqtt_led.py`, pay particular attention to how the code connects to the MQTT broker and manages the connection life cycle. Furthermore, as we cover how the code receives and processes messages, try to relate the code workflow back to the command-line examples that we used to publish the message in the previous subsection, *Running the LED MQTT example*.

Once you have an understanding of our Python code and how it integrates with our MQTT broker, you'll have an end-to-end working reference solution built around MQTT messaging that you can adapt for your own needs and projects.

We will start by looking at the imports. As usual, we will skip over any common code that we have already covered in previous chapters, including logging setup and **GPIOZero**-related code.

Imports

The only new import we have in this example is for the Paho-MQTT client:

```
import paho.mqtt.client as mqtt   # (1)
```

At line (1), we are importing the Paho-MQTT `client` class and giving it the alias, `mqtt`. As mentioned previously, this is the client class that will allow us to create a full life cycle MQTT client in Python.

Next, we will consider global variables.

Global variables

The `BROKER_HOST` and `BROKER_POST` variables at line (2) are referring to our locally installed Mosquitto MQTT broker. Port `1883` is the standard default MQTT port:

```
# Global Variables
...
BROKER_HOST = "localhost"    # (2)
BROKER_PORT = 1883
CLIENT_ID = "LEDClient"      # (3)
TOPIC = "led"                # (4)
client = None # MQTT client instance. See init_mqtt()    # (5)
...
```

At line (3), we define `CLIENT_ID`, which will be the unique client identifier we use to identify our program with the Mosquitto MQTT broker. We *must* provide a unique ID to the broker so that we can use *durable connections*.

At line (4), we define the MQTT topic that our program will be subscribing to, while at line (5), the `client` variable is a placeholder that will be assigned the Paho-MQTT client instance, which we'll see shortly.

The set_led_level(data) method

`set_led_level(data)` at line (6) is where we integrate with GPIOZero to change the brightness of our LED and the method similar to the corresponding methods we covered in `Chapter 3`, *Networking with RESTful APIs and Web Sockets Using Flask*, so we will not cover the internals here again:

```
def set_led_level(data):  # (6)
    ...
```

The data parameter is expected to be a Python dictionary in the form of `{ "level": 50 }`, where the integer is between 0 and 100 to indicate the brightness percentage.

Next, we have the callback functions for MQTT. We'll start by reviewing `on_connect()` and `on_disconnect()`.

The on_connect() and on_disconnect() MQTT callback methods

The on_connect() and on_disconnect() callback handlers are examples of the full life cycle that is available using the Paho client class. We will see how to instantiate a Paho client instance and register these callbacks later when we cover the init_mqtt() method.

The parameters of interest to on_connect() at line (7) in the following code block are client, which is a reference to the Paho client class, and result_code, which is an integer describing the connection result. We see result_code used at line (8) to test the success of the connection. Notice the connack_string() method, which is used for a connection failure to translate result_code into a human-readable string.

When we speak of the MQTT *client* and see the client parameter at line (7) in the following code block, remember this is our Python code's client connection *to the broker*, NOT a reference to a client program such as the web page. This client parameter is very different in meaning to the client parameter we saw used in callback handlers for our Flask-SocketIO Web Socket server in *Chapter 3*, *Networking with RESTful APIs and Web Sockets Using Flask*.

For reference, the user_data parameter can be used to pass around private data between a Paho client's callback methods, while flags is a Python dictionary containing response and configuration hints from the MQTT broker:

```
def on_connect(client, user_data, flags, result_code): # (7)

    if connection_result_code == 0:                     # (8)
        logger.info("Connected to MQTT Broker")
    else:
        logger.error("Failed to connect to MQTT Broker: " +
                     mqtt.connack_string(result_code))

    client.subscribe(TOPIC, qos=2)                      # (9)
```

At line (9), we see the Paho client instance method, subscribe(), used to subscribe to the led topic using the TOPIC global variable, which we saw defined earlier. We also indicate to the broker that our subscription is a QoS level 2.

Always subscribe to topics in an `on_connect()` handler. This way, if the client ever loses the connection to the broker, it can re-establish subscriptions when it reconnects.

Next, at line (10) in the following, we have the `on_disconnect()` handler, where we are simply logging any disconnects. The method parameters have the same meanings as for the `on_connect()` handler:

```
def on_disconnect(client, user_data, result_code):  # (10)
    logger.error("Disconnected from MQTT Broker")
```

We will now move on to the callback method that handles incoming messages for the `led` topic that we subscribed to in `on_connect()` on line (9).

The on_message() MQTT callback method

It's the `on_message()` handler at line (11) that is called whenever a new message for a subscribed topic is received by our program. The message is available through the `msg` parameter, which is an instance of `MQTTMessage`.

At line (12), we access the `payload` property of `msg` and decode it into a string. We expect our data to be a JSON string (for example, `{ "level": 100 }`), so we parse the string into a Python dictionary using `json.loads()` and assign the result to `data`. If the message payload is not valid JSON, we catch the exception and log an error:

```
def on_message(client, userdata, msg):                       # (11)
    data = None
    try:
        data = json.loads(msg.payload.decode("UTF-8"))       # (12)
    except json.JSONDecodeError as e:
        logger.error("JSON Decode Error: "
                + msg.payload.decode("UTF-8"))

    if msg.topic == TOPIC:                                   # (13)
        set_led_level(data)                                  # (14)
    else:
        logger.error("Unhandled message topic {}
                with payload " + str(msg.topic, msg.payload)))
```

Using the `topic` property of `msg` on line (13), we check that it matches our expected `led` topic, which it will in our case since our program is only subscribing to this specific topic. However, this provides a point of reference regarding where and how you would perform conditional logic and routing for a program that subscribes to multiple topics.

Finally, at line (14), we pass our parsed message to the `set_led_level()` method, which, as discussed, changes the brightness of our LED.

Next, we will learn how the Paho client is created and configured.

The init_mqtt() method

We see the Paho-MQTT `client` instance created and assigned to the global `client` variable at line (15). A reference to this object is the `client` parameter we saw previously in the `on_connect()`, `on_disconnect()`, and `on_message()` methods.

The `client_id` parameter is set to be the client name we defined earlier in `CLIENT_ID`, while `clean_session=False` tells the broker that it *must not clear* any stored messages for our client when we connect. As we discussed earlier in the command-line examples, this is the back-to-front way of saying we want a durable connection so any messages published to the `led` topic are stored for our client when it's offline:

```
def init_mqtt():
    global client
    client = mqtt.Client(                              # (15)
        client_id=CLIENT_ID,
        clean_session=False)

    # Route Paho logging to Python logging.
    client.enable_logger()                             # (16)

    # Setup callbacks
    client.on_connect = on_connect                     # (17)
    client.on_disconnect = on_disconnect
    client.on_message = on_message

    # Connect to Broker.
    client.connect(BROKER_HOST, BROKER_PORT)           # (18)
```

An important point to note is on line (16). Our program is using the standard Python logging packages, so we need to make this call to `client.enable_logger()` to ensure that we get any Paho-MQTT client log message. Missing this call means helpful diagnostic information may not get logged.

Finally, at line (18), we connect to the Mosquitto MQTT broker. It's our `on_connect()` handler that will be called once the connection is established.

Next, we will see how our program is started.

Main entry point

After initializing our LED and client instances, we get to the program's main entry point.

We are registering a signal handler to capture *Ctrl + C* key combinations at line (19). The `signal_handler` method (not shown) simply turns off our LED and gracefully disconnects from the broker:

```
# Initialise Module
init_led()
init_mqtt()

if __name__ == "__main__":
    signal.signal(signal.SIGINT, signal_handler)     # (19)
    logger.info("Listening for messages on topic '"
        + TOPIC + "'. Press Control + C to exit.")

    client.loop_start()                              # (20)
    signal.pause()
```

At line (20), the call to `client.loop_start()` is what allows our client to start, connect to the broker, and receive messages.

Did you notice that the LED program is stateless? We are not storing or persisting any LED level in code or to disk. All our program does is subscribe to a topic on the broker and change the LED's brightness using GPIOZero. We effectively hand all state management over to the MQTT broker by relying on MQTT's retained message (also known as the *last known good message*) facility.

We have now finished exploring the Python code that interacts with both the LED and MQTT broker. We learned how to use the Python Paho-MQTT library to connect to an MQTT broker and subscribe to an MQTT topic. As we received messages on the subscribed topic, we saw how to process them and changed the brightness level of our LED according to the message payload.

The Python and Paho-MQTT framework and example we covered will provide you with a solid starting point for your own MQTT-based IoT projects.

Next, we will be looking at a web client that uses MQTT together with Web Sockets. This web client will connect to our Mosquitto MQTT broker and publish messages to control our LED.

Building a web-based MQTT client

In Chapter 3, *Networking with RESTful APIs and Web Sockets Using Flask*, we covered a code example using Web Sockets, which included an HTML file and JavaScript web client. In this section, we will also be looking at a Web Socket-based web client built using HTML and JavaScript. However, this time, we will be leveraging the built-in Web Socket features provided by the Mosquitto MQTT broker and the compatible JavaScript Paho-JavaScript Web Sockets library (you will find a link to this library in the *Further reading* section).

 For comparison, in Chapter 3, *Networking with RESTful APIs and Web Sockets Using Flask*, we created our Web Socket server ourselves in Python using Flask-SocketIO, while our web client used the Socket.io JavaScript Web socket library.

We interacted with the web client we are about to explore to control our LED previously in the *Installing the Mosquitto MQTT broker* at section *step 7*. You might like to quickly review *step 7* to refamiliarize yourself with the web client and how to access it in your web browser.

You will find the code for the web page client in the chapter04/mosquitto_www/index.html file. Please review this file before proceeding.

Understanding the code

While the JavaScript library we are using in this example is different, you will find that the general structure and use of the JavsScript code are similar to the code we saw for the socket.io-based web client in Chapter 3, *Networking with RESTful APIs and Web Sockets Using Flask*. As usual, we will start by looking at the imports.

Imports

Our web client imports the Paho-MQTT JavaScript client library at line (1):

```
<title>MQTT Web Socket Example</title>
<script src="./jquery.min.js"></script>
<script src="./paho-mqtt.js"></script>  <!-- (1) -->
```

paho-mqtt.js can be also found in the chapter04/mosquitto_www folder.

The official documentation page for the Paho-MQTT JavaScript library is available at `https://www.eclipse.org/paho/clients/js`, while its official GitHub page is found at `https://github.com/eclipse/paho.mqtt.javascript`.

 When you explore the Paho-MQTT JavaScript API further, start at its GitHub site and make note of any breaking changes that are mentioned. The documentation pages are known to contain code fragments that do not reflect the latest GitHub code base.

Next, we encounter the global variables.

Global variables

At line (2), we initialize a `Client_ID` constant that will identify our JavaScript client with the broker.

Each Paho JavaScript MQTT client *must* have a unique *hostname, port,* and *client ID* combination when it connects to the broker. To ensure we can run multiple web pages on a single computer for testing and demonstration, we use a random number to create a quasi-unique client ID for each web page:

```
<script type="text/javascript" charset="utf-8">
    messagePubCount = 0;
    const CLIENT_ID = String(Math.floor(Math.random() * 10e16)) // (2)
    const TOPIC    = "led";                                     // (3)
```

At line (3), we define the `TOPIC` constant with `led`, the name of the MQTT topic that we will be subscribing and publishing to shortly. Next, we create our client instance.

The Paho JavaScript MQTT client

At line (4), we create our Paho-MQTT Client instance and assign it to the `client` variable.

The parameters to `Paho.MQTT.Client()` are the broker's hostname and port. We are serving this web page via Mosquitto, so the broker's host and port will be the same as web pages:

```
const client = new Paho.Client(location.hostname,        // (4)
                               Number(location.port),
                               CLIENT_ID);
```

You may have noticed in the `http://localhost:8083` URL that the port is `8083`, while in Python we used port `1883`:

- Port `1883` is the MQTT protocol port on the broker. Our Python program connects directly to the broker on this port.
- We previously configured port `8083` as a Web Socket port on the Mosquitto broker. Web pages can speak HTTP and Web Socket protocols, not MQTT.

This raises an important point. While we're using the term MQTT in the context of our JavaScript code, we're really proxying the MQTT idea using Web Sockets back and forth to the broker.

 When we speak of the MQTT *client* and created the `client` instance at line (4), remember this is our JavaScript code's client connection *to the broker*.

Next, we see how to connect to the broker and register an `onConnect` handler function.

Connecting to the broker

We define our `onConnectionSuccess()` handler at line (5), which will be called after our `client` successfully connects to the broker. When we successfully connect, we then update the web page to reflect the successful connection and enable the slider control:

```
onConnectionSuccess = function(data) {        // (5)
    console.log("Connected to MQTT Broker");
    $("#connected").html("Yes");
    $("input[type=range].brightnessLevel")
        .attr("disabled", null);
    client.subscribe(TOPIC);                  // (6)
};

client.connect({                              // (7)
    onSuccess: onConnectionSuccess,
    reconnect: true
});
```

Next, at line (6), we subscribe to the `led` topic. It's at line (7) that we connect to the broker. Notice that we're registering the `onConnectionSuccess` function as the `onSuccess` option.

Remember, similar to the Python example, always subscribe to topics in an
onSuccess handler. This way, if the client ever loses the connection to the broker, it can re-establish subscriptions when it reconnects.

We also specify the `reconnect: true` option so that our client will automatically reconnect to the broker if it loses its connection.

It has been observed that it may take up to a minute for the JavaScript Paho-MQTT client to reconnect after losing a connection, so please be patient. This is in contrast to the Python Paho-MQTT client, which reconnects almost instantly.

Next, we have another two handlers to review.

The onConnectionLost and onMessageArrived handler methods

In the following code, at lines (8) and (9), we see how to register an `onConnectionLost` and `onMessageArrived` handler with our Paho-MQTT `client` instance:

```
client.onConnectionLost = function onConnectionLost(data) {    // (8)
    ...
}

client.onMessageArrived = function onMessageArrived(message) { // (9)
    ...
}
```

These two functions are similar in principle to their corresponding functions in the socket.io example from the previous Chapter 3, *Networking with RESTful APIs and Web Sockets Using Flask*, in that they update the slider and web page text based on the data found in their respective `data` and `message` parameters.

Next, we have our document ready function.

JQuery document ready function

Finally, we encounter the document ready function at line (1o) where we initialize our web page content and register the event listener for the slider:

```
$(document).ready(function() {                                    // (10)
    $("#clientId").html(CLIENT_ID);

    // Event listener for Slider value changes.
    $("input[type=range].brightnessLevel").on('input', function() {
        level = $(this).val();

        payload = {
            "level": level
          };

        // Publish LED brightness.
        var message = new Paho.Message(                           // (11)
            JSON.stringify(payload)
        );

        message.destinationName = TOPIC;                          // (12)
        message.qos = 2;
        message.retained = true;                                  // (13)
        client.send(message);
    });
});
```

Within the sliders event handler at line (11), we see how to create an MQTT message. Notice the use of JSON.stringify(payload). The Paho.Message constructor expects a String parameter, not an Object, so we must convert the payload variable (which is an Object) in to a string.

Starting at line (12), we set the message publication topic to led with message.destinationName = TOPIC before flagging its QoS level as 2.

Next, at line (13), with message.retained = true, we indicate that we want this message to be retained so that it is automatically delivered to new clients subscribing to the led topic. The retention of this message is what allows mqtt_led.py to reinitialize the LED's previous brightness between restarts.

Well Done! We have now covered both the Python and JavaScript sides of a simple MQTT-based application.

Summary

In this chapter, we have explored and practiced the core concepts of MQTT. After installing and configuring the Mosquitto MQTT broker on your Raspberry Pi, we moved straight into learning a range of examples on the command line. We learned how to publish and subscribe to MQTT messages, how to understand topic construction and name hierarchies, and how we can attach a QoS level to a message.

We also covered durable connections and retained messages, two mechanisms offered by MQTT brokers for storing messages for later delivery. We concluded our walk-through of MQTT concepts by exploring a special message and topic type known as a *Will*, whereby a client can register a message with a broker that gets automatically published to a topic in cases where the client abruptly loses its connection.

Next, we reviewed and walked through a Python program that used the Paho Python MQTT library to subscribe to an MQTT topic and control the brightness of our LED in response to the messages it received. We followed this with a walk-through of a web page built with the Paho JavaScript MQTT library that published the messages consumed by our Python program.

You now have a working knowledge of MQTT and a practical code framework you can now leverage for your own IoT applications. This is in addition to the other networking approaches and code frameworks that we've explored in earlier chapters, such as the dweet.io service, Flask-RESTful, and Flask-SocketIO. Which approach you use for your projects all depends on what you are trying to create and, of course, your own personal preference. For larger projects and projects where you need to integrate with external systems, you may find yourself needing to leverage multiple approaches in tandem and even find the need to research and explore additional techniques. I do not doubt that your learning and understanding of the alternative networking approaches we've covered so far will be of value and help with your understanding of other approaches you encounter.

In the next chapter, *Connecting Python to the Physical World*, we will be exploring a range of topics related to how you connect your Raspberry Pi to the world. We will run through popular Python GPIO library options in addition to GPIOZero and PiGPIO and look at the different types of electronic interfacing options and configurations that are available with a Raspberry Pi. We also have a comprehensive exercise where we will be adding an analog-to-digital converter to your Raspberry Pi and using it to create a program to explore PWM techniques and concepts.

Questions

As we conclude, here is a list of questions for you to test your knowledge regarding this chapter's material. You will find the answers in the *Assessments* section of the book:

1. What is MQTT?
2. Your retained MQTT messages never get delivered. What should you check?
3. Under what condition will an MQTT broker publish a *Will* message?
4. You choose to use MQTT as your IoT application's messaging layer and must ensure that messages are sent and received. What is the minimum QoS level required?
5. You develop an application using MQTT and use the Mosquitto broker, but now you need to use a different broker. What does this mean for your code base and deployment configuration?
6. Where in code (hint: which handler method) should you subscribe to MQTT topics and why?

Further reading

We covered the basics of MQTT from an operational level in this chapter. If you want to learn more about MQTT from a protocol and data level, HiveMQ (an MQTT broker and service provider) has an excellent 11-part series on the MQTT protocol available at `https://www.hivemq.com/blog/mqtt-essentials-part-1-introducing-mqtt`.

The home page of the Mosquitto MQTT broker and client tools are available at the following URL:

* Mosquitto MQTT broker: `https://mosquitto.org`

The documentation and API references for the Paho-MQTT libraries we used in this chapter are available at the following URLs:

* Paho-MQTT Python library: `https://www.eclipse.org/paho/clients/python`
* Paho-MQTT JavaSctipt library: `https://www.eclipse.org/paho/clients/js`

In addition to MQTT, HTTP RESTful APIs, and Web Sockets, there are complimentary communication protocols that are specially designed for constrained devices, known as CoRA and MQTT-NS. The Eclipse Foundation has a summary of these protocols available at `https://www.eclipse.org/community/eclipse_newsletter/2014/february/article2.php`.

Section 2: Practical Electronics for Interacting with the Physical World

2

In this section, we are going to explore concepts related to connecting your Raspberry Pi to the physical world with electronics using its *P1 header*, which is the large set of pins on the motherboard that we commonly just call the *GPIO pins.*

In essence, this section is the bridge between the software world and the electronics world. Our goal is to cover the core terminology and practical concepts that you need to know to start interfacing with both simple and complex electronics. By the end of this section, you will have the knowledge to further explore and investigate the challenges of interfacing electronics to a Raspberry Pi and make informed decisions and carry out directed research as your use cases and interests desire.

This section comprises the following chapters:

- Chapter 5, *Connecting Your Raspberry Pi to the Physical World*
- Chapter 6, *Electronics 101 for the Software Engineer*

Connecting Your Raspberry Pi to the Physical World

5

In this chapter, we will explore hardware and software concepts related to connecting your Raspberry Pi to the physical world. We will be covering popular numbering schemes that are used by GPIO libraries to refer to the GPIO header pins on your Raspberry Pi and provide an overview of popular GPIO libraries, in addition to the GPIOZero and PiGPIO libraries that we used in earlier chapters. As we will learn, understanding GPIO numbering schemes is crucial to ensure your understanding of how GPIO libraries work with GPIO pins.

Our journey will also include a conceptual overview and discussion of the many different ways in which electronics can be interfaced with our Raspberry Pi before we will finish with a detailed exercise and practical demonstration of two important electronic concepts—**Pulse-Width Modulation (PWM)** and analog-to-digital conversion.

We will cover the following topics in this chapter:

- Understanding Raspberry Pi pin numbering
- Exploring popular Python GPIO libraries
- Exploring Raspberry Pi electronic interfacing options
- Interfacing with an analog-to-digital converter

Technical requirements

To perform the exercises in this chapter, you will need the following:

- Raspberry Pi 4 Model B
- Raspbian OS Buster (with desktop and recommended software)
- A minimum of Python version 3.5

These requirements are what the code examples in this book are based on. It's reasonable to expect that the code examples should work without modification on a Raspberry Pi 3 Model B or a different version of Raspbian OS as long as your Python version is 3.5 or higher.

You will find this chapter's source code in the `chapter05` folder in the GitHub repository available at the following URL: `https://github.com/PacktPublishing/Practical-Python-Programming-for-IoT`

You will need to execute the following commands in a Terminal to set up a virtual environment and install Python libraries required for the code in this chapter:

```
$ cd chapter05              # Change into this chapter's folder
$ python3 -m venv venv      # Create Python Virtual Environment
$ source venv/bin/activate  # Activate Python Virtual Environment
(venv) $ pip install pip --upgrade       # Upgrade pip
(venv) $ pip install -r requirements.txt  # Install dependent packages
```

The following dependencies are installed from `requirements.txt`:

- **GPIOZero**: The GPIOZero GPIO library (`https://pypi.org/project/gpiozero`)
- **PiGPIO**: The PiGPIO GPIO library (`https://pypi.org/project/pigpio`)
- **RPi.GPIO**: The RPi.GPIO library (`https://sourceforge.net/p/raspberry-gpio-python/wiki/Home`)
- **ADS1X15**: The ADS11x5 ADC library (`https://pypi.org/project/adafruit-circuitpython-ads1x15`)

Besides the preceding installations, we require a few physical electronic components for the exercise in this chapter:

- 1 x 5 mm red LED
- 1 x 200 Ω resistor—its color bands will be red, black, brown, and then gold or silver
- 1 x ADS1115 ADC break-out module (for example, `https://www.adafruit.com/product/1085`)
- 2 x 10 kΩ potentiometers (any value in the range 10K to 100K will be suitable)
- A breadboard
- Male-to-female and male-to-male jumper cables (also called DuPont cables)

Understanding Raspberry Pi pin numbering

You will have noticed by now that your Raspberry Pi has a lot of pins sticking out of it! Since `Chapter 2`, *Getting Started with Python and IoT*, and all subsequent chapters, we have referenced these pins by referring to them, for example, as *GPIO Pin 23*, but what does this mean? It's time we understand this in more detail.

There are three common ways in which a Raspberry Pi's GPIO pins may be referenced, as illustrated in *Figure 5.1*:

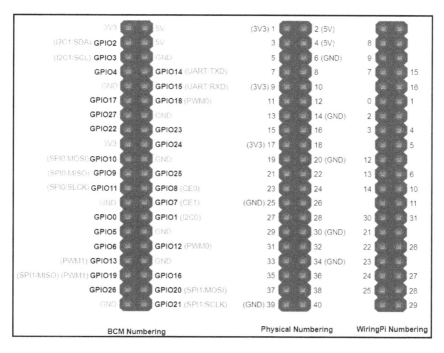

Figure 5.1 – GPIO pin numbering schemes

In all of the previous chapters, we've been talking about GPIO pins from the perspective of PiGPIO, which uses the **Broadcom** or **BCM** numbering scheme. BCM is the most common scheme used in Python-based GPIO libraries, and the GPIO libraries that we will discuss shortly all use BCM exclusively or by default. However, it is useful to know that other schemes exist because it will help when reading or debugging code fragments you come across on the internet and other resources.

The terms *GPIO* and pin can be rather loosely used when it comes to identifying pins. You need to interpret wording such as *GPIO 23* or *Pin 23* with consideration of the context and scheme in which it is being used.

Let's explore these alternatives as shown in *Figure 5.1*:

- **Broadcom/BCM Numbering**: This refers to the GPIO numbering of the Broadcom chip in your Raspberry Pi. With BCM numbering, when we say *GPIO 23*, we mean *GPIO 23* as labeled in a BCM pin-out diagram. This is the scheme we are using with the GPIOZero and PiGPIO examples presented in this book.
- **Physical/Board/P1 Header**: In this numbering scheme, the physical pin numbers of the P1 header are used, for instance, BCM GPIO 23 = Physical Pin 16.
- **WiringPi**: This is a popular C GPIO library called WiringPi that introduced its own pin mapping scheme. Due to the maturity of WiringPi (there is a Python port), you will come across this scheme from time to time—continuing our example, BCM GPIO 23 = Physical Pin 16 = WiringPi Pin 4.

There are also other methods and naming used to reference pins and interfaces to be aware of, and they include the following:

- **Virtual Filesystem**: There is a virtual filesystem mounted at /sys for general GPIO access, /dev/*i2c for I2C, /dev/*spi* for SPI, and /sys/bus/w1/devices/* for 1-wire devices.
- **Alternative Pin Functions**: The preceding BCM diagram in *Figure 5.1* lists GPIO pin numbers, together with alternative pin functions such as PWM0, I2C0, and SPI0 in parentheses. These represent alternative roles a pin can perform beyond basic digital I/O.
- **Bus/Channel Numbers**: For SPI and I2C interfacing and hardware PWM, it's common for a library to use the bus or channel number. For example, we can use BCM GPIO 18 as a general-purpose digital input and output, or we can use it in its alternate function mode as a hardware PWM output as PWM channel 0.

The pinout.xyz website is a great resource for exploring pin naming, alternative functions, and scheme mappings.

You now have an understanding of the different schemes that can be used to refer to GPIO pins on a Raspberry Pi. While the BCM scheme tends to be the most common and universal amongst Python-based GPIO libraries, it is imperative to never just assume that a GPIO library, code example, and even a breadboard layout or schematic diagram you are working with uses the BCM scheme to reference GPIO pins. A mismatch between the scheme used in code and the scheme used to physically wire electronics to the Raspberry Pi's GPIO pins is a common mistake that causes a circuit not to work.

I often see people (and I've done the same!) blame their wiring or believe an electronic component must be faulty when their circuit does not work with a code example they found somewhere online. As a first step toward diagnosis, check that the pin numbering scheme the code is using matches the scheme you used to wire the circuit to the Raspberry Pi's GPIO pins.

Now that we understand the use and importance of different GPIO numbering schemes, let's move on and review popular Python GPIO libraries.

Exploring popular Python GPIO libraries

If you are anything like me, when you first start with a Raspberry Pi, you probably just want to control *things*. Today, for many developers, their first point of contact with physical computing using a Raspberry Pi will be via the official Raspberry Pi website and with the GPIOZero library. However, after you've been tinkering with simple electronics such as buttons, LEDs, and motors for a while, you'll want to undertake more complex interfacing. If you've taken this step—or are about to—you may find yourself in the somewhat confusing world of GPIO libraries and options. This section is here to help you to navigate this path by presenting the more popular options.

I maintain a summary and comparison table of Python GPIO libraries (including additional libraries not listed in the following sections) at `https://10xiot.com/gpio-comp-table`.

We'll start our GPIO Library overview with GPIOZero.

Reviewing GPIOZero – simple interfacing for beginners

The focus of the GPIOZero library is on simplicity, making it a no-fuss library for beginners getting into physical computing and interfacing electronics. It achieves ease-of-use by abstracting away the underlying technical complexity and allows you to write code that deals with *devices* and *peripherals* such as LEDs, buttons, and common sensors, rather than writing lower-level code that directly manages pins.

Technically, GPIOZero is not actually a full-fledged GPIO library in terms of how it interacts with GPIO pin hardware. It is a simplifying wrapper around other GPIO libraries that are employed to do the actual GPIO grunt work. In Chapter 2, *Getting Started with Python and IoT*, we saw a push button and LED example in both GPIOZero and PiGPIO that illustrated this point.

Here are the key highlights of GPIOZero in a nutshell:

- **Description**: High-level GPIO Library designed for beginners
- **Pros**: Easy to learn and use with excellent documentation and many examples
- **Cons**: Limited in scope for use beyond simple electronic interfacing
- **Website**: https://gpiozero.readthedocs.io

Next, we will review RPi.GPIO, a popular low-level GPIO library.

Reviewing RPi.GPIO – a low-level GPIO for beginners

We mentioned previously that the essence of GPIOZero is writing code that deals with devices and components. Well, RPi.GPIO takes a different and more classical approach where we write code that works with and manages GPIO pins directly. RPi.GPIO is a popular low-level introduction to Raspberry Pi and electronics, so you will find many examples using it across the internet.

The GPIOZero documentation has a great section on RPi.GPIO, where it explains equivalent code examples in both GPIOZero and RPi.GPIO. This is a great resource to start learning lower-level pin level programming concepts.

There is also a library named RPIO that was created as a performance drop-in replacement for RPi.GPIO. RPIO is not currently maintained and does not work with the Raspberry Pi Model 3 or 4.

Here are the key highlights of RPI.GPIO in a nutshell:

- **Description:** Lightweight low-level GPIO
- **Pros**: Mature library with many code examples to be found on the internet
- **Cons**: Lightweight means that it is not a performance-orientated library and there's no hardware-assisted PWM
- **Website**: `https://pypi.python.org/pypi/RPi.GPIO`

Next, we will look at another high-level library designed for controlling complex devices.

Reviewing Circuit Python and Blinka – interfacing for complex devices

Blinka is a Python compatibility layer for Circuit Python (`circuitpython.org`), a version of Python designed for microcontrollers. It's created and championed by the electronics company Adafruit, which distributes many electronic breakout boards and gadgets. Adafruit provides quality high-level Circuit Python drivers for many of its product lines, essentially carrying forward the GPIOZero ease-of-use idea to more complex devices.

We are going to use Blinka and the Circuit Python driver library for an ADS1115 ADC breakout module later in this chapter to add analog-to-digital capabilities to our Raspberry Pi.

Here are the key highlights of Blinka in a nutshell:

- **Summary**: High-level library for controlling complex devices
- **Pros**: Makes using supported devices extremely easy irrespective of your level of experience
- **Cons**: For basic IO, it uses RPi.GPIO, so it has the same basic limitations
- **Website**: `https://pypi.org/project/Adafruit-Blinka`

Next, we will cover Pi.GPIO, a powerful low-level GPIO library.

Reviewing PiGPIO – a low-level GPIO library

PiGPIO is considered one of the most complete GPIO library options for the Raspberry Pi in terms of features and performance. Its core is implemented in C, and there is an official port available for Python.

Architecturally, PiGPIO is comprised of two parts:

- The **pigpiod daemon service** provides socket and pipe access to the underlying PiGPIO C library.
- The **PiGPIO client libraries** interact with the pigpiod service using sockets or pipes. It's this design that makes Remote GPIO features over a network possible with PiGPIO.

Here are the key highlights of PiGPIO in a nutshell:

- **Description**: An advanced low-level GPIO library
- **Pros**: Number of features available
- **Cons**: Additional setup necessary; simple documentation assumes knowledge of the underlying concepts
- **Website (Python Port)**: http://abyz.me.uk/rpi/pigpio/python.html

Before we move on to our next library, I want to draw your attention to a feature that is unique to this library and is very useful—remote GPIO.

Exploring remote GPIO with PiGPIO (and GPIOZero)

Once you have started the pigpiod service on a Raspberry Pi (covered in Chapter 1, *Setting Up Your Development Environment*), there are two ways to make your code remote, and by remote, I mean that your program code can be running on any computer (not just a Raspberry Pi) and control a remote Raspberry Pi's GPIOs.

Method 1: This method involves passing the remote Raspberry Pi's IP or host address to the PiGPIO constructor. Using this approach, you can also interface with multiple Raspberry Pi GPIOs by just creating additional instances of pigpio.pi(). For instance, in the following example, any methods called on the pi instance will be executed on the 192.168.0.4 host that has the pigpiod service running:

```
# Python Code.
pi = pigpio.pi('192.168.0.4', 8888) # Remote host and port (8888 is default
if omitted)
```

Method 2: A second method involves setting an environment variable on the computer and running your Python code (your Python code just needs to use the default PiGPIO constructor, `pi = pigpio.pi()`):

```
# In Terminal
(venv) $ PIGPIO_ADDR="192.168.0.4" PIGPIO_PORT=8888 python my_script.py
```

Remote GPIO can be a great development aid, but will add latency into your code's interaction with GPIO pins as data is transmitted over the network. This means it may not be desirable for non-development releases. Button presses, as an example, can feel less responsive, and for use cases where fast timing is important, remote GPIO may be impractical.

You may remember from `Chapter 2`, *Getting Started with Python and IoT*, that GPIOZero can use a PiGPIO *Pin Factory*, and when it does, GPIOZero automatically gets remote GPIO capabilities for free!

Finally, because it's a unique feature of the PiGPIO library, all of your code must use this library if we want remote GPIO features. If you install third-party Python libraries to drive an electronic device and it uses (for example) RPi.GPIO, this device is not remote GPO-enabled.

Next, we will look at two common lower-level libraries for I2C and SPI communication.

Reviewing SPIDev and SMBus – dedicated SPI and I2C libraries

When working with I2C and SPI-enabled devices, you will encounter the SPIDev and SMBus libraries (or comparable alternatives). SPIDev is a popular lower-level Python library for use with SPI communications, while SMBus2 is a popular lower-level Python library for use with I2C and SMBus communication. These two libraries are not general-purpose libraries—they cannot be used for basic digital I/O pin control.

When starting out, it is unlikely that you will want or need to use I2C or SPI libraries such as these directly. Instead, you will use higher-level Python libraries to work with an SPI- or I2C-enabled device that, underneath, would be using lower-level libraries like these to communicate with the physical device.

Here are the key highlights of SPIDev and SMBus2 in a nutshell:

- **Description**: These are lower-level libraries for SPI and I2C interfacing.
- **Pros**: Using a lower-level library gives you full control over an SPI or I2C device. Many high-level convenience wrappers only expose the most commonly needed features.
- **Cons**: Leveraging these lower-level libraries requires you to interpret and understand how to interface with electronics using low-level data protocols and bit manipulation techniques.
- **SPIDev website**: https://pypi.org/project/spidev
- **SMBus2 website**: https://pypi.org/project/smbus2

To complete this section on GPIO libraries, let me briefly discuss why this book is primarily based around the PiGPIO library.

Why PiGPIO?

You may have wondered why, of all of the options, I chose to use PiGPIO predominantly in this book. As a reader of this book, I'm assuming you have a good grounding in programming and technical concepts, and that working with and learning a library such as PiGPIO is not beyond your capabilities. PiGPIO is a comprehensive library if you are intending to extend your learning beyond the basics offered by libraries such as GPIOZero and RPi.GPIO and build more complex IoT projects in Python.

You will find the PiGPIO API and documentation is broken down into beginner, intermediate, and advanced sections, so in practice and while learning, you can mix and match how you use the library API depending on your experience level and needs.

We have now completed our exploration of several popular GPIO libraries and reviewed their basic architecture and design. Next, we will turn our attention to alternative methods through which we can connect and control electronics with our Raspberry Pi.

Exploring Raspberry Pi electronic interfacing options

We've just covered the software side of GPIO, so now we will turn our attention to the electronics side. The Raspberry Pi provides many standard ways to interface both simple and complex electronics. Often, your choice of electronic components and modules will dictate which interfacing technique you need to use, while sometimes you may get a choice.

Irrespective of whether you have a choice, your knowledge of the different options will help you to understand the how and why behind a circuit and its accompanying code and help you to diagnose and resolve any issues you may encounter.

In the following section, we will explore the concepts, followed by a practical exercise. We'll start with digital IO.

Understanding digital IO

Each of the Raspberry Pi GPIO pins can perform digital input and output. Digital simply means something is either fully on or fully off—there is no middle ground. We've been working with simple digital IO in previous chapters:

- Our LED was either on or off.
- Our button was either pressed (on) or non-pressed (off).

You will come across several interchangeable terms used to describe digital states, including the following:

- On = High = True = 1
- Off = Low = False = 0

Digital IO is a form of basic IO. Analog IO is another, so we will explore it next.

Understanding analog IO

Whereas digital deals with fully on and off states, analog deals with degrees—on, off, or somewhere in-between. Think of a window in your house. In a digital world, it could be fully open (digital high) or fully closed (digital low); however, in reality, it's analog in that we can open it somewhere between fully closed and fully open, for example, a quarter open.

Simple and common examples of analog electronic components include the following:

- **Potentiometers (also known as pots)**: This is a dial or slider that produces a range of resistance values. Real-world examples include volume controls and header thermostat controls.
- **Light-Dependent-Resistors (LDRs)**: These are electronic components to measure light levels, and you find these in automatic night lights.
- **Thermistors**: These are electronic components for measuring temperature that you might find in heaters, fridges, or anywhere where temperature is measured.

The Raspberry Pi does not come with analog IO capabilities, so we need to use external electronics known as an **Analog-to-Digital-Converter** (**ADC**) to read analog input, and this will be a core focus of a practical example later in this chapter in the section entitled *Interfacing with an analog-to-digital converter*.

To output an analog signal, we have two options—either use a **Digital-to-Analog Converter** (**DAC**) or use a digital technique known as PWM to produce an analog-style signal from a digital output. We will not be covering DACs in this book; however, we will be exploring PWM in depth, which we will do next.

Understanding Pulse-Width Modulation

Pulse-Width Modulation or **PWM** is a technique to produce an average voltage on a pin somewhere between fully on (high) and fully off (low) by rapidly pulsing the pin on and off. In this way, it's a little like providing a pseudo-analog output from a digital pin and is used for all sorts of control applications, such as altering the brightness of LEDs, motor speed control, and servo angle control.

PWM is defined by two main characteristics:

- **Duty cycle**: The percentage of time the pin is high
- **Frequency**: The time period during which the duty cycle repeats

As illustrated in *Figure 5.2* (and for a set frequency), a 50% duty cycle means the pin is high half of the time and low half of the time, while a 25% duty cycle means the pin is high only 25% of the time. And while not pictured, a 0% duty cycle would mean the pin is high 0% of the time (always low), so it's effectively off, while a 100% duty cycle is always high:

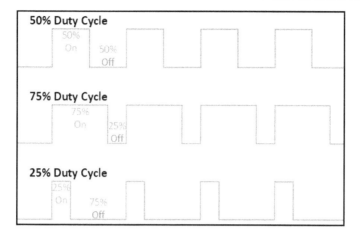

Figure 5.2 – PWM duty cycles

 The preceding diagram is taken from `https://en.wikipedia.org/wiki/File:Duty_Cycle_Examples.png`, author, Thewrightstuff. It falls under CC BY-SA 4.0: `https://creativecommons.org/licenses/by-sa/4.0/deed.en`.

Using PWM is easy on the Raspberry Pi, although there are alternative approaches for creating the PWM signal, which we will look at next.

Creating PWM signals

Different GPIO libraries approach PWM signal generation in different ways. Three common techniques are as follows:

- **Software PWM**: The frequency and duty cycle timing of a PWM signal are produced in code and can be made available on any GPIO pin. This is the least accurate method of creating PWM signals because the timing can be adversely affected by a busy Raspberry Pi CPU.
- **Hardware-timed PWM**: The PWM timing is performed using DMA and PWM/PCM hardware peripherals. It's highly accurate and is available on any GPIO pin.
- **Hardware PWM**: Hardware PWM is provided entirely via hardware and is the most accurate method of creating PWM signals. The Raspberry Pi has two dedicated hardware PWM channels, labeled PWM0 via GPIO pins 18 and 12 and PWM1 via GPIO pins 13 and 19 (refer to *Figure 5.1*).

It's not enough to just connect something to GPIOs 12, 13, 18, or 19 in order to get hardware PWM. These GPIOs are the BCM GPIOs that have PWM listed as their *alternative* functions. If you want to use hardware PWM, then two basic requirements must be met. Firstly, the GPIO library you are using must provide support for hardware PWM. Secondly, you must use the library and its hardware PWM functionality correctly, which would be detained in the library API documentation. Pins that share a common hardware PWM channel both get the same duty cycle and frequency applied to them, so while there are four hardware PWM pins, there are only two unique PWM signals.

Which PWM technique to use will always depend on what you are trying to build and how accurate the PWM signal needs to be. Sometimes, you will have direct control over which GPIO library (and hence PWM technique) you use for your projects, while other times—especially when using third-party higher-level Python libraries—you'll be forced to use whatever PWM techniques the library developer used.

As a general rule, when I am in control of the GPIO library choice, I avoid software PWM wherever possible. If I'm developing using PiGPIO, then I favor hardware-timed PWM simply because I can use it on any GPIO pin.

In relation to the GPIO libraries that we covered earlier, their support for PWM is as follows:

- **GPIOZero**: Inherits the PWM method available from its Pin Factory implementation
- **RPi.GPIO**: Software PWM only
- **PiGPIO**: Hardware-timed PWM and hardware PWM
- **Blinka**: Hardware PWM only

 You can attach external hardware PWM modules to your Raspberry Pi (usually by I2C) that will give you more hardware PWM outputs.

Now that we've seen three ways that PWM signals can be created, we will look next at SPI, I2C, and 1-wire interfaces.

Understanding SPI, I2C, and 1-wire interfaces

Serial Peripheral Interface Circuit (**SPI**), **Inter-Integrated Circuit** (**I2C**), and 1-wire are standardized communication interfaces and protocols that allow non-trivial electronics to communicate with each other. These protocols can be employed either directly at a low level through a bit of manipulation and math, or indirectly by using higher-level party Python driver modules to work with electronic peripherals, with the latter being more common for general use cases.

Examples of devices that work through these protocols include the following:

- Analog-to-digital converters (SPI or I2C)
- LED lighting strips and LCD displays (SPI or I2C)
- Environmental sensors such as temperature sensors (1-wire)

We will explore I2C in more detail later in this chapter when we connect an analog-to-digital converter to our Raspberry Pi.

Finally, we have serial communication and UART.

Understanding the serial / UART protocol

Universal Asynchronous Receiver/Transmitter (**UART**) is a serial communication protocol that has been around for a very long time and in common use before the prevalence of USB. UART actually refers to the electronic hardware used to implement the serial protocol, although it can be implemented in pure software.

Today, SPI or I2C tend to be used in preference to UART. GPS receivers are a common example where serial communication still prevails. If you have ever connected an Arduino to a PC for flashing or debugging, it's a serial communication protocol that the devices are using, with UART hardware being present in the Arduino.

We have now learned many of the standard ways that we can use to interface electronics with our Raspberry Pi, including analog and digital electronics, PWM, wire protocols such as I2C and SPI, and serial communication. We will start to see many of these interfacing options in practice and get a feel for what type of electronics use which type of interface as we proceed through this book.

Next, we will see some of the concepts we have covered so far in this chapter by adding an analog-to-digital converter to our Raspberry Pi.

Interfacing with an analog-to-digital converter

Congratulations on getting this far. I suspect you're itching to get into some code after all that reading!

We will change pace now and apply some of the knowledge we just covered to add an ADS1115 analog-to-digital converter to your Raspberry Pi. An example of a typical ADS1115 breakout module is pictured in *Figure 5.3*:

Figure 5.3 – ADS1115 breakout module

An ADC is a very handy addition because this alone opens you up to the world of analog components and gadgets that are otherwise not usable with the Raspberry Pi.

As part of this practical exercise, we are going to connect two potentiometers (also known as pots) to the ADS1115 and read in their values in Python. We will use these values to create a PWM signal by varying its duty cycle and frequency. We'll see the effects of varying these parameters by observing how it affects the LED and how the waveform changes in a program called PiScope, which is a part of the PiGPIO family of utilities.

We'll revisit potentiometers in more detail in `Chapter 6`, *Electronics 101 for the Software Engineer*.

To perform the following exercise, remember we need the electronic components listed in the *Technical requirements* section at the start of this chapter, including an ADS1115 breakout module. The ADS1115 is a common and powerful analog-to-digital converter that connects to its master (in our case, a Raspberry Pi) using I2C.

Here are the core specifications of the ADS1115 pulled from its datasheet that we require for our exercise:

- **Working voltage**: 2 to 5 volts (so we know it will work with the Raspberry Pi's 3.3-volt logic)
- **Interface**: I2C
- **Default I2C address**: 0x48

The terminals on the ADS1115 are as follows:

- **Vcc & GND**: Power for the device.
- **SCL**: Clock signal, used to synchronize communication between the master and slave.
- **SDA**: Data signal, used to send data between the Raspberry Pi and the ADS1115.
- **ADDR**: This terminal can be used to change the default address if required.
- **ALTR**: Alert signal for advanced usage (we won't be needing this).
- **A0 - A3**: Analog input channels (we will connect Pots to A0 and A1).

 Make sure you have the I2C interface enabled on your Raspberry Pi before proceeding. We covered the steps to enable interfaces, including I2C, in Chapter 1, *Setting Up Your Development Environment*.

First, let's start by building the circuit we require on our breadboard.

Building the ADS1115 ADC circuit

Let's build our breadboard circuit for this chapter's exercise. We will build our circuits in a series of steps, starting with placing the core components as illustrated in the following diagram:

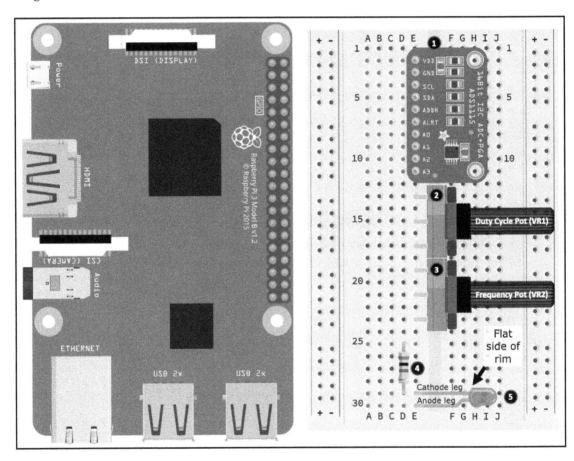

Figure 5.4 – Breadboard ADC circuit (part 1 of 3)

 The overall arrangement and placement of discrete components and wires on a breadboard are not overly important. However, the connections created between the components and wires are vitally important! If you need a refresher on breadboards, how they work, and, most importantly, how the holes are electrically connected, please refer back to Chapter 2, *Getting Started with Python and IoT*.

Here is how to lay out the component on your breadboard. The following step numbers match the numbered black circles in *Figure 5.4*:

1. Position the ADS1115 on your breadboard.
2. Position potentiometer **VR1** on your breadboard. The illustrated potentiometers are full-size potentiometers. If you have a different size, their leg configuration may span fewer breadboard holes.
3. Position the potentiometer **VR2** on your breadboard.
4. Position the **resistor** on your breadboard.
5. Position the **LED** on your breadboard, paying attention to ensure that its cathode leg shares the same row as the resistor (illustrated at holes **D29** and **E29**).

Next, we wire up the ADS1115 as illustrated here:

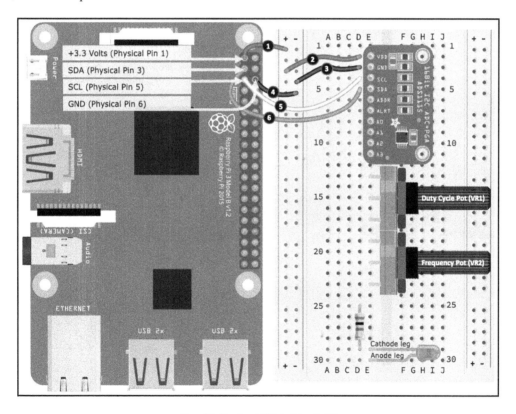

Figure 5.5 – Breadboard ADC circuit (part 2 of 3)

Here are the steps to follow. This time, the following step numbers match the numbered black circles in *Figure 5.5*:

1. Connect the Raspberry Pi **+3.3 volt pin** to the breadboard positive power rail.
2. Connect the **VDD** terminal on the ADS1115 to the breadboard positive power rail.
3. Connect the **GND** terminal on the ADS1115 to the breadboard negative power rail.
4. Connect the Raspberry Pi **GND** pin to the breadboard negative power rail.
5. Connect the **SCL** pin on your Raspberry Pi to the **SCL** terminal on the ADS1115.
6. Connect the **SDA** pin on your Raspberry Pi to the **SDA** terminal on the ADS1115.

Finally, we wire up the LED, resistor, and potentiometers, as illustrated in the following diagram:

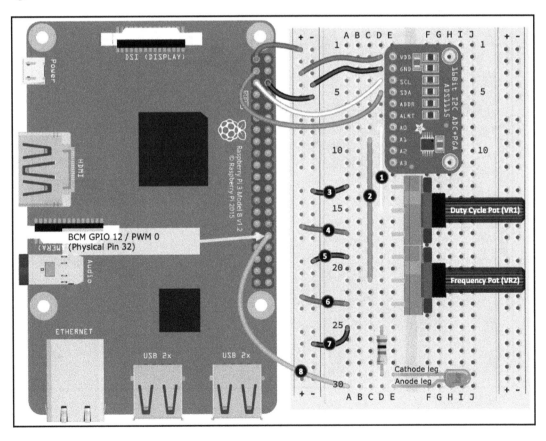

Figure 5.6 – Breadboard ADC circuit (part 3 of 3)

Here are the steps to follow. This time, the following step numbers match the numbered black circles in *Figure 5.6*:

1. Connect the **A0** terminal on the ADS1115 to the center leg of potentiometer **VR1**.
2. Connect the **A1** terminal on the ADS1115 to the center leg of potentiometer **VR2**.
3. Connect the upper leg of potentiometer **VR1** to the breadboard negative power rail.
4. Connect the lower leg of potentiometer **VR1** to the breadboard positive power rail.
5. Connect the upper leg of potentiometer **VR2** to the breadboard negative power rail.
6. Connect the lower leg of potentiometer **VR2** to the breadboard positive power rail.
7. Connect the upper leg of the **resistor** to the breadboard negative power rail.
8. Connect the anode leg of the **LED** to **BCM GPIO 12 / PWM 0** on your Raspberry Pi.

Well done! You have now completed this circuit. For your reference, a semantic diagram depicting the breadboard circuit is shown in *Figure 5.7*.

 As a reminder, we covered an example on how to read a semantic diagram back in Chapter 2, *Getting Started with Python and IoT*.

I encourage you to trace around this semantic diagram while referring back to the breadboard layout to understand how the lines and labels on the diagram relate back to the pictured components and wires on the breadboard. Investing the time to understand how paired schematic diagrams and breadboard circuits relate to one another will assist and increase your ability to create breadboard layouts directly from a schematic diagram:

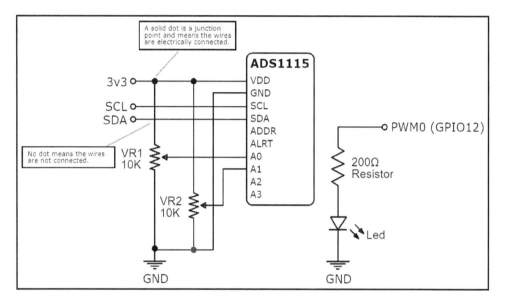

Figure 5.7 – ADC circuit semantic diagram

With the circuit complete, let's check that the ADS1115 can be seen by our Raspberry Pi.

Making sure the ADS1115 is connected to your Raspberry Pi

I2C devices are identified to their master (that is, our Raspberry Pi) by a unique address, and the default address for the ADS1115 is 0x48. Since I2C devices are addressed, multiple devices can share the same I2C channels (pins) on a Raspberry Pi.

You can change the I2C devices on most IC2 devices if you have multiple devices sharing the same address. This is the purpose of the ADDR terminal on the ADS1115, and you can find instructions for its use in the ADS1115 datasheet.

Raspbian OS contains the `i2cdetect` utility that queries the Raspberry Pi's I2C interface for connected devices. Run the following in a Terminal:

```
$ i2cdetect -y 1
```

The `-y` option assumes we answer yes to any prompts. `1` is the I2C bus number. It's always `1` on the Raspberry Pi 3 or 4. We expect to see the output like this:

```
     0  1  2  3  4  5  6  7  8  9  a  b  c  d  e  f
00:          -- -- -- -- -- -- -- -- -- -- -- -- --
10: -- -- -- -- -- -- -- -- -- -- -- -- -- -- -- --
20: -- -- -- -- -- -- -- -- -- -- -- -- -- -- -- --
30: -- -- -- -- -- -- -- -- -- -- -- -- -- -- -- --
40: -- -- -- -- -- -- -- -- 48 -- -- -- -- -- -- --
50: -- -- -- -- -- -- -- -- -- -- -- -- -- -- -- --
60: -- -- -- -- -- -- -- -- -- -- -- -- -- -- -- --
70: -- -- -- -- -- -- -- --
```

The fact that we see `48` (hex address) is indicative that our Raspberry Pi has detected the ADS1115. If you do not get this result, check your wiring and make sure I2C has been enabled as described in `Chapter 1`, *Setting Up Your Development Environment*.

Now that we have verified that our ADS1115 is visible to our Raspberry Pi, let's proceed and read the two potentiometers as analog input.

Reading analog input with the ADS1115

Now that we have our ADS1115 connected to our Raspberry Pi, it's time to learn how to use it to read in analog values, specifically the analog values created by our two potentiometers. We will use these analog values shortly to produce a PWM signal, which in turn will control the brightness of our LED.

The code we are about to cover can be found in the file `chapter05/analog_input_ads1115.py`. Please review this file before continuing.

1. Start by running the program in a Terminal:

   ```
   (venv) $ python analog_input_ads1115.py
   ```

2. You should receive a stream of output similar to the following (your **value** and **volts** numbers will be different):

   ```
   Frequency Pot (A0) value=3 volts=0.000 Duty Cycle Pot (A1) value=
   9286 volts=1.193
   Frequency Pot (A0) value=3 volts=0.000 Duty Cycle Pot (A1) value=
   9286 volts=1.193
   ...truncated...
   ```

3. Turn the two potentiometers and watch the output change—specifically, you will notice the numbers reported for value and volts change. The value and voltage will be in the following ranges:

   - **value** in the range 0 to 26294 (or thereabouts)
   - **voltage** in the range 0 to 3.3 volts (or thereabouts)

   The output will be as follows:

   ```
   Frequency Pot (A0) value=3 volts=0.000 Duty Cycle Pot (A1) value=
   9286 volts=1.193
   Frequency Pot (A0) value=4 volts=0.001 Duty Cycle Pot (A1)
   value=26299 volts=3.288
   ...truncated...
   ```

As we'll discuss more in Chapter 6, *Electronics 101 for the Software Engineer,* analog input is about reading voltages, in our case here, between 0 volts/GND (our reference voltage) and +3.3 volts. The integer value is the raw output of the ADS1115, and what its maximum value is will depend on how the ADS1115 IC is configured (we're using the defaults). The voltage value is derived from this raw value using math based on the ADS1115 configuration. All of the gooey details are in the ADS1115 datasheet and the library source code if you are interested.

Beneath the surface of a high-level ADC library, many low-level settings influence how the ADC chip works (just check its datasheet). Different library authors may implement these settings differently or use different default settings. What this means in practice is that two libraries for the same ADC might output different raw values (and some libraries might not even provide this value to the programmer). So, never make assumptions about what the expected raw output value will be, and instead rely on the voltage measurement, which is always the source of truth.

As you adjust the two potentiometers, do not get worried if the exact ends of these ranges do not marry up precisely to 0 and 3.3 volts, or if the values randomly twitch a little. This fuzzy result is expected when we deal with analog electronics.

Next, we will examine the code.

Understanding the code

Now that we have seen the basic operation of our ADS1115 ADC, it's time to have a look at the accompanying code to understand how we query the ADS1115 in Python to get analog readings. What we learn below will lay the foundations for the analog interfacing programs that we will see in *part 3* of this book.

We will commence our code walk-through with the imports.

Imports

There are two ways we can use the ADS1115 with our Raspberry Pi with Python:

- Read the ADS1115 datasheet and use a lower-level I2C such as SMBus to implement the data protocol used by the device.
- Find a ready-made Python library available through PyPi that we can install using `pip`.

There are several ready-made Python modules available to use with the ADS1115. We are using the Adafruit Binka ADS11x5 ADC library that we installed through `requirement.txt` at the start of this chapter:

```
import board                                          # (1)
import busio
import adafruit_ads1x15.ads1115 as ADS
from adafruit_ads1x15.analog_in import AnalogIn
```

Starting at line (1), we see the `board` and `busio` imports from Circuit Python (Blinka), while the last two imports starting with `adafruit` are from the Adafruit ADS11x5 ADC library and are used to configure the ADS1115 module and read its analog input, which we are going to look at next.

ADS1115 setup and configuration

At line (2) in the following code block, we use the `busio` import to create an I2C interface with Circuit Python/Blika. The `board.SLC` and `board.SDA` parameters indicate we are using the dedicated I2C channel (alternative functions of GPIO 2 and 3) on the Raspberry Pi:

```
# Create the I2C bus & ADS object.
i2c = busio.I2C(board.SCL, board.SDA)        # (2)
ads = ADS.ADS1115(i2c)
```

Next, we create an instance of `ADS.ADS1115` using the pre-configured I2C interface and assign it to the `ads` variable. From this point forward in the code, when we interact with our ADS1115 module, we will use this instance.

Next, let's consider the global variables.

Global variables

At line (3) in the following code snippet, we start with a few quasi-constants defining the maximum and minimum voltages we expect to receive through the analog input. When you ran the code previously, your end range voltages probably were not exactly 0 and 3.3 volts. This occurrence is expected, and it can make a program feel like the Pots do not reach the ends of their rotation. The value assigned to `A_IN_EDGE_ADJ` is used to compensate for this in code. We will revisit this variable in the next section:

```
A_IN_EDGE_ADJ = 0.002                        # (3)
MIN_A_IN_VOLTS = 0 + A_IN_EDGE_ADJ
MAX_A_IN_VOLTS = 3.3 - A_IN_EDGE_ADJ
```

Next, starting at line (4), we create two `AnalogIn` instances relating to the A0 and A1 inputs of the ADS1115 that are connected to our Pots. It's through these variables that we determine how much a user has rotated our frequency and duty cycle potentiometers:

```
frequency_ch = AnalogIn(ads, ADS.P0)  #ADS.P0 --> A0    # (4)
duty_cycle_ch = AnalogIn(ads, ADS.P1) #ADS.P1 --> A1
```

Next, we come to the program's entry point where we will read our analog inputs.

Program entry point

Our program continuously loops, reading our analog input values for each pot and prints formatted output to the Terminal.

At line (5), we see how to access the integer value from the frequency pot using `frequency_ch.value` and the voltage value using `frequency_ch.voltage`:

```
if __name__ == '__main__':
    try:
        while True:
            output = ("Frequency Pot (A0) value={:>5} volts={:>5.3f} "
                      "Duty Cycle Pot (A1) value={:>5} volts={:>5.3f}")
            output = output.format(frequency_ch.value,          # (5)
                                   frequency_ch.voltage,
                                   duty_cycle_ch.value,
                                   duty_cycle_ch.voltage)
            print(output)
            sleep(0.05)
    except KeyboardInterrupt:
        i2c.deinit()                                            # (6)
```

Finally, notice that the program is wrapped in a try/except block that will capture *Ctrl + C* so that we can perform a clean-up using `i2c.deinit()`.

Now that we have seen how to read analog input using our ADS1115, next, we will integrate the LED.

Using PWM to control an LED

Now we will add the LED into the code, only we'll be doing this differently to what we've done in previous chapters. The purpose of the LED for this exercise is to visually see the effects of changing the duty cycle and frequency characteristics of PWM. We will use the analog inputs of the two Pots to define the PWM duty cycle and frequency.

The code we discuss in this section extends the analog code example we just covered in `chapter05/analog_input_ads1115.py` to use PiGPIO to create a hardware PWM signal.

Two additional source code files are provided with this book that implement hardware-timed PWM using PiGPIO and software PWM using RPi.GPIO:

* `chapter05/pwm_hardware_timed.py`
* `chapter05/pwm_software.py`

Their overall code is similar, with the differences being the methods and input parameters used to invoke PWM. We will revisit these files again in the upcoming section, *Visualizing software and hardware-timed PWM*.

The code we are about to cover can be found in the `chapter05/pwm_hardware.py` file. Please review this file before continuing:

1. Run the program in a Terminal and observe the output:

```
(venv) $ python pwm_hardware.py
Frequency 0Hz Duty Cycle 0%
... truncated ...
Frequency 58Hz Duty Cycle 0%
Frequency 59Hz Duty Cycle 0%
... truncated ...
```

2. Adjust the Pots until the frequency reads 60 Hz and the duty cycle reads 0%. The LED should not be lit. The LED is unlit because the duty cycle is at 0%, so GPIO 12 (PWM0) is always low. Very slowly turn the duty cycle Pot to increase the duty cycle and observe the LED slowly increase in brightness. At a 100% duty cycle, GPIO 12 (PWM0) is always high 100% of the time and the LED is at its full brightness.

 If you are finding that the duty cycle printed on the Terminal does not reach 0% or 100% at either end of the Pot's movement range, try increasing the value of `A_IN_EDGE_ADJ` in your code (try +0.02 for starters). Also, tweak this adjustment if you experience a similar issue with the frequency range and dial.

3. Rotate the duty cycle dial until it reads less than 100% (for example, 98%), and then adjust the frequency dial. The LED blinks on and off at this frequency. As you lower the frequency toward zero, the LED blinks slower. For most people, at around 50-60 Hz, the LED will be blinking so fast that it appears to be just on. Remember that if the duty cycle is 0% or 100%, the frequency dial does not work! That's because at either end of the duty cycle, the PWM signal is fully off or on—it's not pulsing and hence frequency has no meaning.

Let's examine the code that makes this work.

Understanding the code

This example is using the hardware PWM features offered by PiGPIO. The ADS1115-related code is the same as our previous example, so we will not cover it again here. We'll start by looking at the additional global variables.

Global variables

At line (1) and (2) in the following code block, we define two variables for the minimum and maximum duty cycle and frequency values. These values come from the API documentation for the PiGPIO `hardware_PWM()` method, which we will see in use shortly:

```
MIN_DUTY_CYCLE = 0              # (1)
MAX_DUTY_CYCLE = 1000000
MIN_FREQ = 0                    # (2)
MAX_FREQ = 60 # max 125000000
```

We have capped `MAX_FREQ` to 60 Hz for our demonstration so our human eyes can observe the effects in the LED.

Next, we have a custom function to map value ranges.

Range mapping function

At line (3), we have a function named `map_value()`:

```
def map_value(in_v, in_min, in_max, out_min, out_max):          # (3)
    """Helper method to map an input value (v_in)
        between alternative max/min ranges."""
    v = (in_v - in_min) * (out_max - out_min) / (in_max - in_min) + out_min
    if v < out_min: v = out_min elif v > out_max: v = out_max
    return v
```

The purpose of this method is to map an input range of values into another range of values. For example, we use this function to map the analog input voltage range 0-3.3 volts into a frequency range 0-60. You will frequently use a value-mapping function like this when working with analog inputs to map raw analog input values into more meaningful values for your code.

Next, we are ready to create the PWM signal.

Generating the PWM signal

This next code fragment is found in the main `while` loop.

At lines (4) and (5), we are reading in the voltage values from the frequency and duty cycle Pots, before using the `map_value()` function to convert the voltage range of 0-3.3 volts into our desired frequency and duty cycle ranges we saw defined as global variables. Notice that we are also formatting the duty cycles as a percentage value for display purposes:

```
frequency = int(map_value(frequency_ch.voltage,                 # (4)
                          MIN_A_IN_VOLTS, MAX_A_IN_VOLTS,
                          MIN_FREQ, MAX_FREQ))

duty_cycle = int(map_value(duty_cycle_ch.voltage,               # (5)
                           MIN_A_IN_VOLTS, MAX_A_IN_VOLTS,
                           MIN_DUTY_CYCLE, MAX_DUTY_CYCLE))

duty_cycle_percent = int((duty_cycle/MAX_DUTY_CYCLE) * 100)

pi.hardware_PWM(LED_GPIO_PIN, frequency, duty_cycle)            # (6)
```

At line (6), we use `pi.hardware_PWM()` to use the Raspberry Pi's PWM hardware to generate a PWM signal on the LED's pin.

Now that we have seen the effects of varying the frequency and duty cycles on an LED, we will perform an exercise to visualize a PWM signal with a logic analyzer.

Visually exploring PWM with PiScope

Let's do an exercise and see the PWM waveform in a logic analyzer, which is a piece of equipment used to visualize electronic signals. While the general principles behind PWM are technically simple, to aid learning when starting out, it can be helpful to visualize what a PWM signal looks like and observe how it changes visually as its duty cycle and frequency change.

PiGPIO contains a software logic analyzer we can use for this purpose. Now, I need to point out that it's a basic software logic analyzer and in no way compares to professional-grade equipment, however, for our example and education, it will work a treat and cost us nothing.

Let's download, install, and run PiScope. Here are the steps to follow:

1. First, we must install PiScope. Run the following commands to download, compile, and install PiScope:

```
# Download and install piscope
$ cd ~
$ wget abyz.me.uk/rpi/pigpio/piscope.tar
$ tar xvf piscope.tar
$ cd PISCOPE
$ make hf
$ make install
```

2. Run PiScope with the following command:

```
$ piscope
```

I'd recommend shutting down any resource-heavy applications before starting PiScope and performing this exercise. The following screenshots do not show all GPIOs like yours would by default because I've turned some off via the menu **Misc | GPIOs.** If you, too, turn off GPIOs from the display, remember to leave on SDA (GPIO 2) and/or SCL (GPIO 3) for this exercise as this creates a continuous input signal for PiScope, which keeps the display moving in time. Without this continuous input, PiScope pauses the display when there is no signal input so our example will keep pausing the display at the duty cycle or frequencies of 0, which will make the demonstration feel clunky.

3. Make sure the `chapter05/pwm_hardware.py` program is running in a Terminal.

4. Slowly turn the duty cycle and frequency dials and observe how the PWM signal changes on row number 12. Keeping our frequency range very low (for example, 0 to 60 Hz) means we can observe the PWM signal easily in the PiScope logic analyzer:

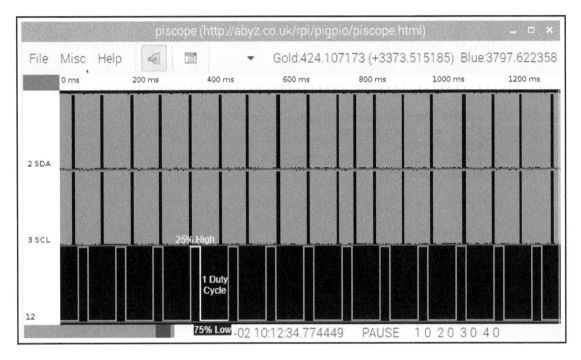

Figure 5.8 – 25% duty cycle at 10 Hz

The preceding screenshot shows a 25% duty cycle at 10 Hz. If you examine the last row in the screenshot, you will notice that GPIO 12 is high for 25% of a single cycle and low for 75%.

The following screenshot shows a 75% duty cycle at 10 Hz. If you examine the last row in the screenshot, you will notice that GPIO 12 is high for 75% of a single cycle and low for 25%:

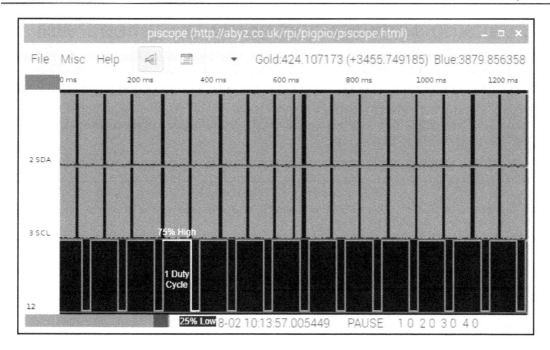

Figure 5.9 – 75% duty cycle at 10 Hz

We have now seen what a PWM signal waveform looks like visually using PiScope, which is a free and basic software logic analyzer provided by the developer of PiGPIO. Our primary purpose behind visualizing PWM signals as an exercise was to provide a visual aid to help you to understand PWM and its duty cycle and frequency properties.

In practice, when you are starting out and integrating with basic electronics, you probably won't need a logic analyzer or even the need to visualize signals. However, as you advance your knowledge and as you need to debug electronic integration problems at the electronics level, I hope this basic introduction to the use of logic analyzers proves useful and points you in the right direction for further inquiries.

Next, we'll point you toward the Python source files that demonstrate alternative PWM techniques.

Visualizing software and hardware-timed PWM

Our code examples from the previous sections, *Using PWM to control an LED*, and *Visually exploring PWM with PiScope*, both created a PWM signal using your Raspberry Pi's PWM hardware. Accompanying the code for this chapter and listed in the following table are alternative implementations that demonstrate the use of hardware-timed and software-generated PWM signals. You may recall that we discussed these alternatives back in the section entitled *Creating PWM signals*:

File	Details
`pwm_hardware.py`	This is hardware PWM using PiGPIO (this is the code we've seen in this chapter). You must use a PWM hardware GPIO pin 12, 13, 18, or 19.
`pwm_hardware_timed.py`	This is a hardware-timed PWM using PiGPIO. This will work with any GPIO pin.
`pwm_software.py`	This is software PWM using RPi.GPIO (PiGPIO does not provide software PWM). This will work with any GPIO pin.

Functionally, these examples are the same in that they will change your LED's brightness, and I predict that you will find that hardware and software PWM perform similarly. As you turn the frequency Pot's dial, the change to the LED and PiScope will feel smooth, while the hardware-timed PWM will feel a little chunky. This is because the hardware-timed frequencies (in PiGPIO) must be 1 of 18 predetermined values so the frequency progression as you adjust the pot is not incremental and linear, but instead jumps to/from the next predefined frequency. You'll see these predefined frequencies in an array in `pwm_hardware-timed.py`.

As mentioned previously, software PWM is the least reliable method of producing PWM signals because it is susceptible to distortion if your Raspberry Pi's CPU gets busy.

You can try to create and visualize PWM distortion with these steps:

1. Run `pwm_software.py` and set the duty cycle to high (for example, 98%) and the frequency to 60 Hz. Do not use a 100% duty cycle because this is a fully-on state and you would visually get a horizontal line, not repeating square waveforms.
2. Start a resource-intensive program on your Raspberry Pi—something that will put a load on the CPU. For example, try closing and relaunching the Chrome web browser.

3. If you closely observe the LED, it may flicker occasionally as the PWM signal is distorted. Alternatively, you may be able to observe the waveform distort in PiScope, as indicated by the arrows in the following screenshot. You will notice the width of the bars is not uniform when that the signal is distorting:

Figure 5.10 – Distortions in the PWM signal. 50% duty cycle at 50 Hz

Well done. You've just completed a detailed practical exercise using an ADS1115 to extend your Raspberry Pi so that you can also interface it with analog electronics. Along the way, you also learned how to produce a PWM signal with Python, saw the effects of varying this signal on an LED, and observed the signal visually with PiScope.

Summary

Well done on getting this far, as there has certainly been a lot to get our heads around! As a recap, we explored common numbering schemes for referencing GPIO pins and reviewed popular GPIO libraries for Python. We also looked at the various interfacing methods used to connect electronics to your Raspberry Pi and performed a practical exercise to add an ADC to your Raspberry Pi and use it to visually explore PWM concepts with an LED and the PiScope logic analyzer.

Your understanding of the fundamental concepts we explored and experimented with during this chapter will help you to understand how your Raspberry Pi interfaces to electronic components and devices and has provided you with a first-hand appreciation of how we interact with analog components (for instance, our potentiometers) and complex devices (that is, our ADS1115). We will be using and building on many of these fundamentals as we progress through the remainder of this book.

This chapter has been largely software library and code-focused. However, in the next chapter, *Electronics 101 for the Software Engineer*, we will turn our attention to electronic concepts and common circuits that are used to interface electronics to a Raspberry Pi.

Questions

As we conclude, here is a list of questions for you to test your knowledge regarding this chapter's material. You will find the answers in the *Assessments* section of the book:

1. What serial communication interface allows devices to be daisy-chained?
2. You have an I2C device but do not know its address. How can you find it?
3. You have started using a new GPIO Python library for the first time but can't seem to get any GPIO pins to work. What do you need to check?
4. You are using PiGPIO on Windows with Remote GPIO to drive a remote Raspberry Pi. Now, you try to install a third-party device driver library but it's failing to install under Windows However, you find it installed successfully on the Raspberry Pi. What is the likely problem?
5. True or false: The Raspberry Pi has pins for both 3.3 volts and 5 volts, so you can use either voltage when working with GPIO pins?
6. You have created a robot that uses servos. During simple testing, everything seemed fine. However, now that you have finished, you notice the servos randomly twitch. Why?
7. When the robot's servos move, you notice a lightning bolt icon on your monitor or display is going blank. Why could this be happening?

Further reading

The GPIOZero website has a range of examples showing functionally equivalent examples using both GPIOZero and RPi.GPIO. This is a great introductory resource for understanding lower-level GPIO programming concepts and techniques:

- https://gpiozero.readthedocs.io/en/stable/migrating_from_rpigpio.html

The following links contain additional material concerning the interfaces and concepts that we have discussed in this chapter:

- SPI interface: https://en.wikipedia.org/wiki/Serial_Peripheral_Interface
- I2C interface: https://en.wikipedia.org/wiki/I%C2%B2C
- 1-wire interface: https://en.wikipedia.org/wiki/1-Wire
- PWM: https://en.wikipedia.org/wiki/Pulse-width_modulation
- Potentiometers: https://en.wikipedia.org/wiki/Potentiometer
- ADS1115 datasheet: http://www.ti.com/lit/gpn/ads1115

Electronics 101 for the Software Engineer

6

So far in this book, we've focused mostly on software. In this chapter, we're about to flip that and focus on electronics. We'll do this by learning about the fundamental electronic concepts that are the basis for interfacing basic electronic sensors and actuators with your Raspberry Pi. What we'll learn about in this chapter will provide the foundation for many of the circuits we'll discuss in *Section 3, IoT Playground*.

We will begin by covering the essential workshop tools that you will require for working with electronics, and provide practical tips to help you purchase electronic components. Next, we'll provide you with guidelines to help keep your Raspberry Pi from being damaged as you work with its physical GPIO pins. We will also discuss common ways electronic components fail to help you diagnose circuits that do not work.

We will then get into the electronics! Here, we will look at two important electronic laws – Ohm's Law and Kirchoff's Law – and work through a practical example to explain why we used a 200Ω resistor to accompany our LED in the circuits we were using in earlier chapters (if you need a refresher about this LED circuit, please see `Chapter 2`, *Getting Started with Python and IoT*).

Next, we will explore both digital and analog electronics and discuss the core circuits and ideas that are used to integrate them with your Raspberry Pi. We will finish this chapter by learning about logic-level conversion, a practical technique that is used to interface electronics that operate at different voltages.

The following topics will be covered in this chapter:

- Fitting out your workshop
- Keeping your Raspberry Pi safe
- Three ways electronic components fail
- Electronic interfacing principles for GPIO control

- Exploring digital electronics
- Exploring analog electronics
- Understanding logic-level conversion

Technical requirements

To perform the exercises in this chapter, you will need the following:

- Raspberry Pi 4 Model B
- Raspbian OS Buster (with a desktop and recommended software)
- Minimum Python version 3.5

These requirements are what the code examples in this book are based on. The code examples should work without the need to modify a Raspberry Pi 3 Model B or use a different version of Raspbian OS, as long as your Python version is 3.5 or higher.

You can find this chapter's source code in the `chapter06` folder in this book's GitHub repository: `https://github.com/PacktPublishing/Practical-Python-Programming-for-IoT`.

You will need to execute the following commands in a Terminal to set up a virtual environment and install the Python libraries required for this chapter:

```
$ cd chapter06              # Change into this chapter's folder
$ python3 -m venv venv      # Create Python Virtual Environment
$ source venv/bin/activate  # Activate Python Virtual Environment
(venv) $ pip install pip --upgrade       # Upgrade pip
(venv) $ pip install -r requirements.txt  # Install dependent packages
```

The following dependency is installed from `requirements.txt`:

- **PiGPIO**: The PiGPIO GPIO library (`https://pypi.org/project/pigpio`)

The hardware components we will require for this chapter are as follows:

- A digital multimeter.
- A red LED (datasheet for reference – `https://www.alldatasheet.com/datasheet-pdf/pdf/41462/SANYO/SLP-9131C-81.html`; click on the **PDF** option).
- Momentary **Push Button Switch (SPST)**.

- 200 Ω, 1k Ω, 2k Ω, and 51k Ω resistors.
- 10k Ω potentiometer
- 4-channel MOSFET-based logic level shifter/converter module. See *Figure 6.12* (left-hand side module) for an example.

Fitting out your workshop

Having the right tools and equipment is important to help you put together, build, test, and diagnose problems in electronic circuits. Here are the bare essentials (besides electronic components) you're going to need as you journey deeper into electronics and create circuits like the ones shown in this book:

- **Soldering iron**: You will need a soldering iron (and solder) for odd jobs such as joining header pins to breakout boards or soldering wires to components so that they can be plugged into your breadboard.
- **Solder**: Look for a general-purpose 60/40 (60% tin and 40% lead) resin core solder with a diameter of around 0.5 mm to 0.7 mm.
- **Solder Sucker/Vacuum**: We all make mistakes, so this device helps you remove solder from a joint and undo your soldering work.
- **Wet Sponge or Rag**: Always keep your soldering iron tip clean by removing built-up solder – a clean tip promotes clean soldering.
- **Wire Stripper and Cutters**: Keep a set of wire cutters and strippers just for your electronics work. Chips and burrs in the cutter blades from other uses will degrade their performance.
- **Digital Multi Meter (DMM)**: An entry-level DMM will be suitable for general work and will include a range of standard features such as voltage, current, and resistance measurements.
- **Breadboard**: I highly recommend purchasing two full-size breadboards and joining them together to get more breadboard real-estate. It'll make working with the breadboard and components much easier.
- **Dupont (Jumper) Cables**: These are the wires used with a breadboard. They come in various types: male-male, male-female, and female-female. You will need a mixture of them all.
- **Loose Header Pins**: These are useful for joining Dupont cables together and for making non-breadboard-friendly components breadboard-friendly.
- **External Power Supply**: This is so you can power circuits externally from your Raspberry Pi. For the purposes of this book, at a minimum, you will need a breadboard power supply that can supply 3.3 and 5 volts.

- **Raspberry Pi Case**: Make sure you have a case for your Raspberry Pi. A caseless Raspberry Pi with all those exposed electronics underneath is an accident waiting to happen.
- **GPIO Breakout Header**: This makes working with a Raspberry Pi and breadboards much easier.

If you do not already have the aforementioned equipment, keep an eye out for a *soldering iron kit* and a *breadboard starter kit* on sites such as eBay and Banggood. These kits often come bundled with many of the items listed.

This list shows the basic tools that we require, but what about the actual electronics and gadgets to play with? We'll look at that next.

Buying electronic modules and components

A catalogue of all the components and modules used throughout this book is contained in the *Appendix*. In this section, I want to provide a few general tips and guidelines to help you out when purchasing electronic components in case you have not done much of this before. We will start with a few tips to help you when purchasing loose components.

Purchasing lose components

When it comes to purchasing loose components such as resistors, LEDs, push buttons, transistors, diodes, and other components (which we will be exploring in *Section 3, IoT Playground – Practical Examples to Interact with the Physical World*, of this book), there are some guidelines that will help you out, as follows:

- Source the specific component values and part numbers listed in the *Appendix*. Purchase many spares since it's possible that you will damage components while learning to use them.
- If you're purchasing from sites such as eBay or Banggood, carefully review the details of the item, and preferably zoom in on the images of the parts and check the part numbers shown. Never rely solely on the title of the listing. Many sellers add a variety of terms to their titles for search optimization purposes that do not necessarily relate to the actual item being sold.
- Search around sites such as eBay and Banggood for terms such as electronic starter kit. You may be able to pick up a mixed bundle of loose components in one transaction.

These points also apply when purchasing sensors and modules, which we will talk about next.

Purchasing open source hardware modules

I'm sure you are aware of open source software, but there is also open source hardware. This is where the maker of some electronic hardware publishes the design and schematics publicly so that anyone can make (and sell) the hardware. You will find many breakout modules (such as the ADS1115 modules we used in Chapter 5, *Connecting Your Raspberry Pi to the Physical World*) from various vendors with different (or no) branding. Different vendors may also make their modules in different colors and, while less common, different physical layouts.

The *core* or *heart* of a module – particularly the more simple ones – is often a single **integrated circuit** (**IC** or chip). As long as the core IC and I/O pins are similar, it's generally safe to assume that boards will operate the same way.

SparkFun (https://www.sparkfun.com/) and Adafruit (http://adafruit.com/) are two companies producing open source hardware that many others clone. A big advantage you will get when you purchase from these companies is that, often, their products include code examples, tutorials, and tips on using their products, and the products are of good quality. Yes, you may pay a little more, but when starting out and especially for more complex electronics, the investment can save you a lot of time. It's not uncommon to find that cheaper clones arrive faulty – so you'll need to purchase two or more to hedge your bets.

We have now covered some suggestions and tips to help you fit out your workshop and buy electronic components. Having the right tools available and learning how to use them (especially soldering, which will take practice if this is a new skill) is essential to help make your electronics journey a smooth and productive one. At times, purchasing loose components can be confusing and sometimes error-prone, especially where subtle differences in specifications or labeling can have dramatic practical implications, so be diligent and double-check what you are buying if you are unsure. Finally, as suggested in the *Appendex*, purchase spare components. It's no fun having to abruptly stop your learning midway through a circuit build because a component gets damaged and you need to source or wait for a replacement to arrive!

Next, we will discuss guidelines to help you keep your Raspberry Pi safe when interfacing electronics to it.

Keeping your Raspberry Pi safe

In this section, we will cover guidelines and suggestions to help keep your Raspberry Pi safe while you are interfacing electronics with it. By being careful and diligent in your approach, these guidelines will help you minimize any potential for damage to your Raspberry Pi or electronics components.

Don't worry if some of the electronic-orientated points such as voltages and currents do not make sense at the moment. We'll be touching on these concepts throughout this chapter, and during *Section 3, IoT Playground – Practical Examples to Interact with the Physical World*, of this book, so more context will be coming:

- *Never* apply more than 3.3 volts to any input GPIO pin. Higher voltages can cause damage.
- *Never* use more than 8 mA from any single output GPIO pin (they can handle up to ~16 mA, but by default, stick to 8 mA to ensure reliable GPIO operation). As a rule of thumb, do not power anything other than LEDs and breakout modules unless you know what you are doing. In Chapter 7, *Turning Things On and Off*, we'll look at circuits that can be used to switch higher current and voltage loads.
- *Never use* more than a combined 50 mA across multiple GPIO pins.
- *Never* use more than 0.5 mA with a GPIO pin configured for input.
- *Always* disconnect the power to your circuits before connecting or disconnecting them to your Raspberry Pi or making any changes.
- *Always* stop any running programs that are interacting with GPIO pins before connecting, disconnecting, or working on a circuit.
- *Always* double-check your wiring before applying power to your circuits.
- *Never* substitute random component values in a circuit – they don't have the correct and expected value shown in the schematic diagram.
- If you see a lightning bolt icon on your Raspberry Pi's monitor or the monitor goes blank when you run your program, that's the Pi telling you that your circuit is drawing too much power from the Raspberry Pi.
- *Never* directly connect and use inductive loads and mechanical devices such as motors, relays, or solenoids that use magnates from GPIO pins. They can draw too much current and cause a phenomenon known as *EMF flyback*, which can damage surrounding electronics, including your Raspberry Pi.

 The power supply you have for your Raspberry Pi should ideally be 3 amps (15 watts). Many phone chargers are rated less than this, and their use is a common reason for seeing the lightning bolt icon (or a blank display) when interfacing simple electronics.

When working with electronics, from time to time, components do get damaged or fail. Let's briefly look at ways this can occur.

Three ways electronic components fail

Working with electronics is different from software. In the software world, we can change code, break code, debug code, and fix code as many times as we want with no real harm. We can also freely back up and restore states and data. When working with electronics, we do not have this luxury. We're in the physical world, and if something gets damaged, it's final!

Components and circuits made of components, including a Raspberry Pi, can become damaged and fail in many different ways due to them being connected incorrectly, oversupplying too much voltage, supplying or sourcing too much current, overheating, and even mishandling delegate components to the point that they physically break or are damaged by static electricity from your body.

When a component fails, it can fail in a few different ways:

- It fails in a puff of smoke, melts, or otherwise displays a physical sign that it has been damaged.
- It fails silently, with no visual indication of the failure.
- It is damaged but continues to work more or less as expected, but then sometime in the future, it just silently fails without warning.

Failing with a physical sign is the outcome we want because it's obvious what failed and what needs to be replaced. It also gives us a starting point where we can start diagnosing our circuits. Silent failures and delayed failures are painful and time-consuming, especially when starting.

Here are some tips to help you build and debug faulty circuits when you're starting:

- Always double-check your circuits before applying power.
- Have spare parts at hand. It's much easier to diagnose and test circuits if you have known good parts you can substitute into the circuit.
- If you deem something damaged, then bin it immediately. You don't need faulty parts getting mixed up with good parts, especially when there is no obvious sign of damage.

Next, we will discuss core electronic principles that govern why and how components are chosen in a circuit and illustrate the concepts with our LED circuit.

Electronics interfacing principles for GPIO control

While this book is not a book on electronic theory, there are a few core principles that are important to have an appreciation for because they impact circuit design and how they interface with your Raspberry Pi. The goal of this section is to present you with a basic understanding of why circuits are designed in certain ways and how this relates to GPIO interfacing. Armed with this basic knowledge, I hope it provides you with the incentive to explore the core ideas and principles in more depth. You'll find suggested resources in the *Further reading* section, at the end of this chapter.

We will start our coverage of electronic principles with what is arguably two of the most fundamental electrical principles of them all – *Ohm's Law* and *power*.

Ohm's Law and power

Ohm's Law is a fundamental electronics principle that explains how *voltage, resistance,* and *current* relate to each other. Together with the principle of *power*, these are core underlying principles that explain why certain value components are chosen in circuits.

Ohm's Law is expressed as the following equation:

$$V = I \times R$$

Here, V is voltage measured in volts, I (capital i) is the current measured in amps, and R is resistance measured in Ohms, commonly prefixed with Ω, the Greek symbol for Omega.

On the other hand, power is expressed as the following equation:

$$P = I \times V$$

Here, P is power measured in Watts, I (capital i) is the current measured in amps (same as in Ohm's Law), and R is resistance measured in Ohms (same as in Ohm's Law).

The take-home principle regarding these equations is that you cannot change a single parameter in an electronic circuit without affecting another. This means that components are selected and arranged in a circuit to ensure that the voltage, current, and power is proportioned appropriately for individual components and the overall operation of the circuit.

If you are new to this world of electronics and this does not sink in straight away, do not get disheartened! It does take time and practice. In addition to Ohm's Law, we also have Kirchhoff's Law, which we will be talking about next.

Kirchhoff's circuit laws

Kirchhoff's voltage and current laws are two laws that circuits abide by. They are two laws essential to electrical engineering, and are stated as follows:

- The algebraic sum of all voltages in a loop must equal zero.
- The algebraic sum of all currents entering and exiting a node must equal zero.

That's about as deep as we're going to go on these laws. I have mentioned these laws here because the voltage law is the one we will see in action in the next section, when we calculate why we've been using a 200 Ohm resistor in earlier chapters for our LED circuits.

With that, we have covered briefly three important electrical principles or laws – Ohm's Law, power, and Kirchhoff's circuit laws. It's now time to put these principles into practice. We will do this with an exercise to work out why we have been using a 200Ω series resistor in our LED circuits.

Why are we using a 200 Ohm resistor for the LED circuit?

So far in this book, our electronics have mostly evolved around LEDs. I have done this for good reason. LEDs (and resistors) are easy to use components and provide the basic building blocks for learning about concepts such as Ohm's Law, power, and Kirchhoff's voltage law. Master the basics of LED circuits and the calculations that lie behind them and you will be well on your way to undertaking more complex components and circuits.

Let's go a little deeper with our LED and explore its data properties and see the application of Ohm's Law, power, and Kirchhoff's voltage law. Through a series of examples, we will work through a process to explain why the LED circuits you've seen previously in this book are using a 200 Ohm resistor.

The following is a basic LED circuit, similar to what we have been using so far in this book. If you need a refresher on this circuit, please revisit `Chapter 2`, *Getting Started with Python and IoT*:

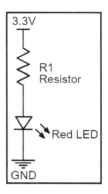

Figure 6.1 – LED and resistor circuit

We have been using a *typical* 5 mm *red* LED. I've extracted part of its *typical* technical specifications here. This distinction of *typical* and *red* is emphasized because LED specifications do vary, depending on their color, maximum luminosity, physical size, and manufacturer. Even LEDs from the same batch vary.

Here are some of the core specifications relating to our referenced red LED datasheet:

- **A Forward Voltage Drop (V_F) between 1.7 and 2.8 volts**, with the typical drop being 2.1 volts. This is the voltage the LED needs to illuminate. If there is not enough voltage in the circuit for the LED, it will not illuminate. If there is more than it requires, that's okay – the LED will just take what it needs.

- **A maximum continuous Forward Current (I_F) of 25 mA**. This is the safe current required to illuminate the LED to its maximum brightness when it's always on, which, for some LEDs, can be too bright for comfort. Providing less current means the LED will be dimmer, while providing more can damage the LED. For our LED and datasheet, when pulsing the LED (for example, using PWM), the maximum current can go up to (I_{FP}) 100 mA.

What about power? LEDs are components that work on voltage and current. If you look at the power equation ($P = I * V$), you'll see that power is a function of voltage (V) and current (I). As long as you are working within the current ratings of the LED, you will be within its power tolerances.

If you do not have a matching datasheet for an LED (which is common when pushing in small quantities), use a voltage drop of 2 volts and a reference amperage of 20 mA for your calculations. You can also use a digital multimeter set to the diode setting to measure the forward voltage for an LED.

Let's move on and see how we arrive at the value for the R1 resistor.

Calculating the resistor value

In the preceding circuit diagram, we have the following parameters:

- Supply voltage of 3.3 volts
- LED typical forward voltage of 2.1 volts
- LED current of 20 mA (test condition for mA is mentioned in the datasheet for voltage drops)

Here is the process to calculate the resistor value:

1. Our resistor (labelled R1) needs to drop 1.2 volts, which is a simple application of Kirchhoff's voltage law that we mentioned briefly previously; that is, *The algebraic sum of all voltages in a loop must equal zero*. So, if our source voltage is +3.3 volts and the LED drops 2.1 volts, then the resistor must drop 1.2 volts. This means we get the following equation:

$$+3.3V + -2.1V + -1.2V = 0V$$

2. We can arrange Ohm's Law algebraically so that we get the following:

$$R = \frac{V}{I}$$

3. Using this formula, we calculate our resistor's value:

$$R1 = \frac{1.2 \; volts}{0.02 \; amps}$$

$$= 60\Omega \text{ (hence, resistor R1 in the preceding circuit is } 60\Omega)$$

But this is not 200Ω. Our example so far is a simple LED and resistor circuit connected to a 3.3 volt supply, not a Raspberry Pi. There's more to consider because we need to respect the current limitations of the Raspberry Pi's GPIO pins, which we'll do next.

Factoring in the Raspberry Pi's current limits

The maximum current we can safely use with a GPIO pin configured for output is 16 mA. However, there is a configurable aspect of GPIO pins, which means that, by default, we should not use more than 8 mA per GPIO. This limit can be configured so that it goes up to 16 mA, but this is beyond our scope. Ideally, we want to be moving toward external circuits when more current is needed rather than pushing the pins higher and higher. We will learn how to do this in Chapter 7, *Turning Things On and Off*.

While we want to limit a single GPIO *output* pin to 8 mA, we should not exceed a combined total of ~50 mA over multiple GPIO pins. When it comes to GPIO *input* pins, we should limit the current to 0.5 mA for safe operation when connecting an external input device or component. Connecting an input GPIO pin directly to the Raspberry Pi's +3.3 V or GND pin is fine as the measured current is approximately 70 *micro*amps. (We'll learn how to measure current with a multimeter in Chapter 7, *Turning Things On and Off*.)

Let's modify our calculation and continue with this process:

1. If we cap the current to 8 mA, we can use our previous equation to arrive at the value for R1:

$$R1 = \frac{1.2\ volts}{0.008\ amps}$$

R1 = 150Ω

2. A resistor's rated value is never expected to be exact. They have a value tolerance, and if our physical resistor was less than 150Ω, according to Ohm's Law, we'd increase the current in the circuit and exceed the 8 milliamp limit.

Due to this, we will choose a slightly higher value. This might be as simple as using a rule of thumb, such as selecting a standard resistor value 2 values higher than 150Ω, or multiplying 150Ω by our resistor's tolerance and selecting the next highest standard value. Let's use the latter approach, assuming our resistor's tolerance is ±20% (which, by the way, would be a very poor quality resistor. 5% and 10% is more common):

$$150Ω \times 1.2 = 180Ω$$

180Ω just happens to be a standard resistor value, so we can use it, but I don't have one (and you'll often find that you don't have the exact resistor values you want after calculations either!). However, I do have a supply of 200Ω resistors, so I will just use one of these.

For prototyping and tinkering, any resistor from 180Ω up to about 1kΩ will be more than adequate for our circuit. Just remember that as you increase the resistor's value, you limit the current, so the LED will be dimmer.

But what about the power going through the resistor and its power rating? We'll calculate that next.

Calculating the resistor's power dissipation

General-purpose resistors like the ones we're using in our breadboards are commonly rated to be 1/8 Watt, 1/4 Watt, or 1/2 Watt. If you supply too much power to a resistor, it will burn out with a puff of smoke and give off a horrible smell.

Here is how we calculate the power dissipation of our 200Ω resistor when we have a 3.3-volt power source:

1. The power dissipated by a resistor can be calculated with the following formula. Note that the voltage V is the voltage drop across the resistor in volts, while R is the resistance in Ohms:

$$P = \frac{V^2}{R}$$

2. Therefore, when we substitute our resistor's voltage drop and resistance value in the formula, we get the following:

$$P = \frac{1.2^2}{200}$$

= 0.0072 Watts, or 7.2 milliwatts (or mW)

3. Our power value of 7.2 mW is below even a 0.25 Watt-rated resistor, so a 1/8 Watt or above resistor is safe in our circuits and will not burn out in a puff of smoke.

If you think the power equation looks different from the one you saw earlier, you're right. This is the power equation rewritten to use voltage and resistance. Here's a handy diagram that I'm sure you will see during your electronics journey that expresses Ohm's Law and power in different ways:

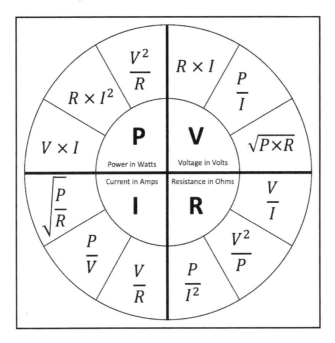

Figure 6.2 – Ohm's Law power wheel

I'll leave you with a final tip about LEDs, and something to think about.

It's the current that alters the LED's brightness. The 25 mA value from the datasheet is the maximum continuous safe current to drive the LED to its maximum brightness. Less current is fine; it just means the LED will be dimmer.

Hang on a minute – in `Chapter 5`, *Connecting Your Raspberry Pi to the Physical World*, we used PWM, which is a pseudo-analog *voltage* used to change the brightness of the LED. Pause and think about this for a minute…what's going on? It's simply an application of Ohm's Law. In our circuit, our resistor was fixed at 200Ω. Hence, by varying the voltage, we also vary the current and hence the brightness of the LED.

What do you think? Rest assured that's as complex as the math will get in this book. I do, however, encourage you to repeat these exercises until you are comfortable with the process. Understanding the basics of electronics (and the calculations that go with it) is the difference between a hobbyist who just guesses at components using trial and error until a circuit works and an engineer who can actually build what they need.

Next, we will explore core concepts related to digital electronics.

Exploring digital electronics

Digital I/O essentially means detecting or making a GPIO pin high or low. In this section, we will explore core concepts and see some examples of digital I/O in operation. We'll then talk about how this relates to your Raspberry Pi and any digital electronic components you will interface with it. We will start or digital I/O journey by looking at and playing with digital output.

Digital output

In simple electrical terms for our Raspberry Pi, when we drive a GPIO pin high, its voltage measures ~3.3 volts, and when we drive it low, it measures ~0 volts.

Let's observe this using a multimeter:

Different multimeters may have different connections and labeling than the multimeter illustrated here. Consult your multimeter's manual if you are unsure how to set it up for measuring voltage.

1. Set your multimeter to its voltage setting and attach it to GPIO 21 and GND, as shown in the following diagram:

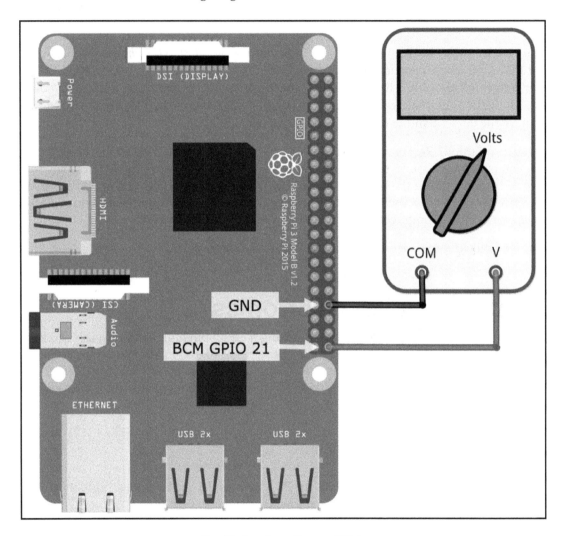

Figure 6.3 – Connecting a multimeter to a GPIO pin

2. Run the following code, which you can find in the
   `chapter06/digital_output_test.py` file. You will notice that the meter
   toggles between about 0 volts and about 3.3 volts. I say *about* because nothing is
   ever really perfect or precise in electronics; there are always tolerances. Here's a
   synopsis of the code:

```
# ... truncated ...
GPIO_PIN = 21
pi = pigpio.pi()
pi.set_mode(GPIO_PIN, pigpio.OUTPUT)           # (1)

try:
    while True:                                # (2)
        # Alternate between HIGH and LOW
        state = pi.read(GPIO_PIN); # 1 or 0
        new_state = (int)(not state) # 1 or 0
        pi.write(GPIO_PIN, new_state);
        print("GPIO {} is {}".format(GPIO_PIN, new_state))
        sleep(3)
# ... truncated ...
```

On line 1, we configured GPIO 21 as an output pin, while on line 2, we started a
`while` loop that alternates the state of GPIO 21 between high and low (that is, 0
and 1) with a 3-second delay in between each state transition.

As you may have noticed, digital output on our Raspberry Pi is that simple – high or low.
Now, let's consider digital input.

Digital input

Generally, when we think about digital input and voltages for a 3.3-volt device such as the
Raspberry Pi, we think of connecting a pin to the ground (0 volts) to drive it low or connect
it to 3.3 volts to make it high. In most applications, this is exactly what we will strive to do.
However, in truth, there is more to this story because GPIO pins don't just operate at two
discrete voltage levels. Instead, they work within a range of voltages that define an input
pin as being high and low. This applies to the Raspberry Pi and similar computers with
GPIOs, microcontrollers, ICs, and breakout boards.

Consider the following diagram, which shows a voltage continuum between 0 and 3.3 volts, as well as three highlighted areas labeled *low*, *floating*, and *high*:

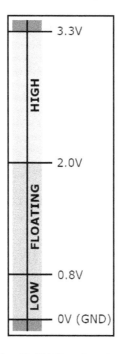

Figure 6.4 – Digital input trigger voltages

This illustration is telling us that if we apply a voltage between 2.0 volts and 3.3 volts, then the input pin will read as a digital high. Alternatively, if we apply a voltage between 0.8 volts and 0 volts, the pin will read as a digital low. Anything beyond these ranges is a danger zone and you'll likely damage your Raspberry Pi. While you probably won't be accidentally applying a negative voltage to a pin, there is a real risk of accidentally applying more than 3.3 volts to a pin since it is common to be working with 5-volt digital circuits.

So, what about that gray area in the middle? Are we digital high or digital low? The answer is that we do not know and can never reliably know. In this range, the pin is said to be *floating*.

Let's see the effects of a floating pin. We'll start by creating the following circuit on our breadboard:

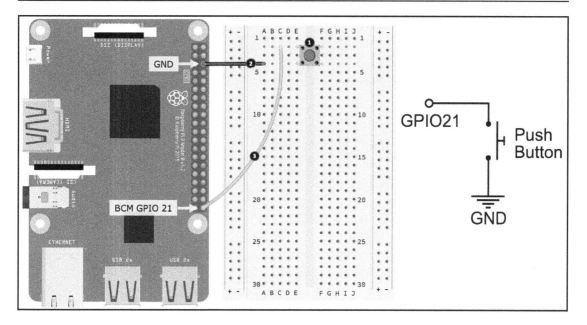

Figure 6.5 – Push button circuit

Here are the steps for this. The step numbers here match the numbered black circles shown in the preceding diagram:

1. Position the push button on your breadboard.
2. Connect one leg of the push button to a GND pin on your Raspberry Pi. In the diagram, we are connecting the lowermost leg of the push button (shown at hole **E4**).
3. Finally, connect the other leg of the push button (in the diagram, this is the uppermost leg, shown at hole **E2**) to GPIO 21 on your Rasberry Pi.

With your circuit build now complete, let's test the circuit and see what happens:

1. Run the following code, which can be found in the chapter06/digital_input_test.py file:

```
# ... truncated...
GPIO_PIN = 21
pi = pigpio.pi()
pi.set_mode(GPIO_PIN, pigpio.INPUT)    # (1)
# ... truncated...

try:
    while True:                        # (2)
```

```
        state = pi.read(GPIO_PIN)
        print("GPIO {} is {}".format(GPIO_PIN, state))
        sleep(0.02)

except KeyboardInterrupt:
    print("Bye")
    pi.stop() # PiGPIO cleanup.
```

This code configures GPIO21 as input on line (1). On line (2), using a `while` loop, we rapidly read in the GPIO pin's value (1 or 0) and print it to the Terminal.

2. Touch the wires on the breadboard with your fingers, as well as any exposed metal contacts surrounding the switches. The wires and contacts act like an antenna picking up electrical noise, and you should see the Terminal output fluctuating between high (1) and low (0) – this is a *floating* pin. This also illustrates a common misconception that a GPIO pin configured for input and connected to nothing is always low by default.

If your initial thoughts were along the lines of "*Wow! I can create a touch switch because of this,*" then sorry; you'll be disappointed – it's just not reliable, at least not without additional electronics.

Next, we will look at two common ways to avoid floating pins.

Using pull-up and pull-down resistors

When a pin is not connected to anything, it's said to be floating. As shown in the preceding example, it *floats* around, picking up electrical noise around it from other nearby components, wires connected to it, and charges coming from yourself.

Referring again to the preceding diagram, when the button is *pressed*, the circuit completes and GPIO 21 gets connected to the ground, and hence we can say for certain that the pin is low. And as we just saw when the button is *not* pressed, GPIO 21 is floating – it can fluctuate between high and low due to external noise.

This needs to be rectified, and we can do this two ways – with a resistor or in code.

The resistor solution

If we add an external resistor to the circuit, as shown in the following diagram, then we'll introduce what is called a *pull-up resistor*, which serves the purpose of *pulling* (meaning connecting) GPIO pin 21 *up* (meaning connected to a positive voltage) to 3.3 volts:

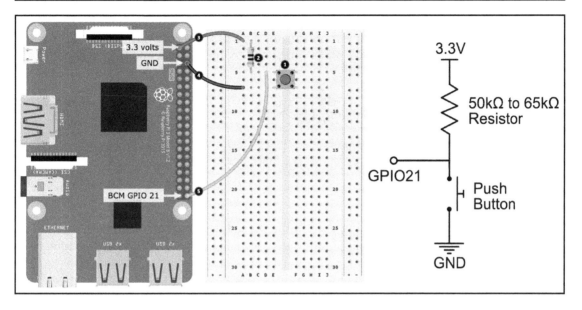

Figure 6.6 – Push button circuit with a pull-up resistor

Here are the steps to create this circuit on your breadboard. The step numbers here match the numbered black circles shown in the preceding diagram:

1. Place the push button on your breadboard.
2. Place the resistor (with a value between 50kΩ to 65kΩ) on your breadboard. One end of the resistor shares the same row (shown at hole **B5**) as the upper positioned leg of the push button. The other end of the resistor is placed on an empty row.
3. Connect the other end of the resistor to a 3.3-volt pin on your Raspberry Pi.
4. Connect the lower leg of the push button to a GND pin on your Raspberry Pi.
5. Finally, connect the row shared by the upper leg of the push button and lower leg of the resistor (shown at hold **D5**) to GPIO 21 on your Raspberry Pi.

Now that you have created the circuit, here is a brief description of how it works:

- When the button is *not pressed*, the resistor *pulls* GPIO 21 *up* to the 3.3-volt pin. Current flows along this path and the pin will read as a guaranteed digital high.

- When the button *is pressed*, the segment of the circuit connecting GPIO 21 to the ground is created. Because more current flows in this path since it has less (near-zero) resistance, the GPIO pin is connected to the ground, and thus will read as low.

Run the same code in `chapter06/digital_input_test.py`, only this time, when you touch the wires, the output *should not* fluctuate.

If your circuit does not work and your wiring is correct, try rotating your push button 90 degrees on the breadboard.

Why is a 50kΩ to 65kΩ resistor being used in the preceding diagram? Read on – we'll find out why when we look at a code-based alternative to using our own physical resistors.

The code solution

We can solve our floating pin situation in code by telling our Raspberry Pi to activate and connect an embedded pull-up resistor to GPIO 21, which, according to the Raspberry PI's documentation, will be within the range 50kΩ-65kΩ, hence why we stipulated that range in the circuit shown in the previous diagram.

The following diagram shows a circuit similar to the one shown in the preceding diagram, but without the physical resistor in the external circuit. I've added a resistor inside the Raspberry Pi diagram to illustrate the fact that there is a physical resistor hiding away somewhere in the Raspberry Pi's circuitry, even though we can't see it:

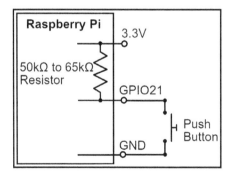

Figure 6.7 – Push button circuit using an embedded pull-up resistor

Let's enable a pull-up resistor in code and test this circuit. Here are the steps for you to follow:

1. This example uses the push button circuit shown previously in *Figure 6.5*. Please recreate this circuit on your breadboard before continuing.

2. Next, edit the `chapter06/digital_input_test.py` file to enable an internal pull-up resistor, as follows:

```
#pi.set_pull_up_down(GPIO_PIN, pigpio.PUD_OFF) <<< COMMENT OUT THIS
LINE
pi.set_pull_up_down(GPIO_PIN, pigpio.PUD_UP)   <<< ENABLE THIS LINE
```

3. Run the `chapter06/digital_input_test.py` file again. As you press the button, you should see the high/low (0/1) values changing on the Terminal; however, touching the wires or Terminals of the button should not cause any interference.

When reading through the preceding code and observing the Terminal output, if the fact that the Terminal prints 1 when the button is *not pressed* and 0 when it is *pressed* (that is, button pressed = pin low) seems a bit back to front in a programming sense, then you are right…and wrong. It's because you're looking at the circuit as a programmer. I've done this on purpose because it is a configuration you will see often. This is known as *active low*, which means the button is active (pressed) when the pin is low.

The opposite resistor setup is also possible and equally valid. That is, you can design the circuit with GPIO 21 pulled to the ground by default, in which case we are employing a *pull-down* resistor, whether it be a physical resistor or an embedded one activated in code. In this scenario, you will then see that when the button is pressed, the pin reads 1 (high), and it may feel more comfortable in code!

As an exercise, try to change the circuit and code so that it's pull-down by default.

 When reading a digital input circuit, you need to read the circuit in combination with the code that accompanies it, or in respect to the code you will write. Overlooking how pull-up or pull-down resistors are used can be the basis for seemingly simple digital input circuits not working.

Now that we understand we can have physical and code-activated pull-up and pull-down resistors, can we say that one approach is better than the other? The short answer is, yes, sometimes…external resistors do have an advantage.

The advantage of an external pull-up or pull-down resistor is that they are always present. Code-activated pull-up and pull-downs are only present if two conditions are met:

- Your Raspberry Pi is powered on.
- You have run the code that activates the pull-up or pull-down. Until this happens, the pin is floating! We will look at an application where we prefer an external pull-down resistor in `Chapter 7`, *Turning Things On and Off*.

This is not to say that code-activated pull-up and pull-down resistors are inferior, it just means you need to consider the impact of a floating pin for your circuit when your Raspberry Pi is off or you are not running code.

We have now covered the basics of digital input and output, which, in many ways, are the backbone of electronic interfacing. We also learned that there is more going on with digital input than simply a high/on or low/off state in that threshold voltage levels actually determine what voltage level is considered a digital high or a digital low for your Raspberry Pi. In addition to this, we also learned that it is necessary to appropriately employ a pull-up or pull-down resistor when dealing with digital input so that the input circuit is reliable and predictable – that is, it's not *floating*.

Your understanding of digital I/O will be beneficial to you when designing predictable digital input circuits (floating pins and missing or incorrectly used pull-up or down-down resistors are common sources of errors when starting out!). Furthermore, your understanding of threshold digital high/low voltage levels will be valuable when you are integrating with non-Raspberry Pi devices and electronics. We'll pick up on this digital voltage theme again later in this chapter, in the *Logic-level conversion* section.

Now, let's move on from digital and explore analog electronics.

Exploring analog electronics

As we saw in the previous section, digital I/O is all about discrete highs or lows, as determined by voltage. Analog I/O, on the other hand, is all about degrees of voltage. In this section, we will explore some core concepts and look at examples of analog I/O in operation.

Analog output

In Chapter 5, *Connecting Your Raspberry Pi to the Physical World*, we discussed that by using PWM on a digital output pin, we can create a pseudo-analog output or the appearance of a variable output voltage. Furthermore, we also saw PWM in use back in Chapter 3, *Networking with RESTful APIs and Web Sockets Using Flask*, when we used this concept to control the brightness of an LED.

In this section, we'll explore the idea underlying PWM just a little further with a short exercise. Our example is similar to the one we performed for digital output previously, only this time, we are using PWM to produce a varying voltage on a GPIO pin. Here are the steps we need to follow:

1. Connect your multimeter to your Raspberry Pi as we did for digital output in *Figure 6.3*.
2. Run the following code, which you can find in the chapter06/analog_pwm_output_test.py file.
3. As the code runs, your multimeter will step through a range of different voltages. They won't be exact, as per the Terminal screen output shown here, but should be reasonably close enough to illustrate the intent:

```
(venv) $ analog_pwm_output_test.py
Duty Cycle 0%, estimated voltage 0.0 volts
Duty Cycle 25%, estimated voltage 0.825 volts
Duty Cycle 50%, estimated voltage 1.65 volts
Duty Cycle 75%, estimated voltage 2.475 volts
Duty Cycle 100%, estimated voltage 3.3 volts
```

Let's have a look at the code, which is partly replicated here.

It is using PiGPIO's hardware-timed PWM, which is configured on line 1, while a set of duty cycle percentages are defined on line 2. These are the duty cycle values that our code will step through on line 3. It's on line 4 that we set the duty cycle for GPIO 21 before sleeping for 5 seconds so that you can read the value on the Terminal and your multimeter:

```
# ... truncated ...
pi.set_PWM_frequency(GPIO_PIN, 8000)                        # (1)

duty_cycle_percentages = [0, 25, 50, 75, 100]               # (2)
max_voltage = 3.3

try:
    while True:
        for duty_cycle_pc in duty_cycle_percentages:        # (3)
            duty_cycle = int(255 * duty_cycle_pc / 100)
```

```
            estimated_voltage = max_voltage * duty_cycle_pc / 100
            print("Duty Cycle {}%, estimated voltage {} volts"
                  .format(duty_cycle_pc, estimated_voltage))
            pi.set_PWM_dutycycle(GPIO_PIN, duty_cycle)      # (4)
            sleep(5)

    # ... truncated ...
```

If you ever need to provide a more true form analog output from your Raspberry Pi, then you might like to explore how you can use a **Digital-to-Analog Converter** (**DAC**). They will typically interface via I2C or SPI, and you will control them via a driver library similar to the ADS1115 ADC, only you'll be outputting a varying voltage rather than reading one.

Now that we've discussed analog output and seen a simple example of how to create one using PWM, next, we will look at the input side of analog electronics.

Analog input

In Chapter 5, *Connecting Your Raspberry Pi to the Physical World*, we learned how to use the ADS1115 ADC breakout module, and that analog input is all about measuring a voltage from within a predefined range, which, for our purposes, is between 0 volts and 3.3 volts. While in digital I/O, we'd say 0 volts measured on a pin means low and 3.3 means high, in analog I/O, there are no concepts of high or low in this regard.

Many simple analog components and sensors operate on the principle that their resistance changes in accordance with what they measure. For example, a **light dependent resistor**, or **LDR**, changes its resistance in proportion to the light it detects. However, analog input is all about measuring voltage. To turn a varying resistance into a varying voltage, we use a voltage divider circuit.

Voltage dividers

The following diagram shows a simple two-resistor voltage divider circuit. Our resistor values are fixed for this example to illustrate the basic principle. Notice that we've used 5 volts in this example. The reason for this will be revealed shortly when we cover logic-level conversion:

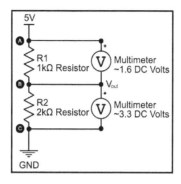

Figure 6.8 – Measuring voltages across a voltage divider

It's a principle of electronics and resistors that voltage is *dropped* across series resistors in proportion to their resistance. In the preceding circuit, R1 is twice as high as R2, so it drops twice as much voltage. Here is the basic formula, as applied to the preceding circuit (it's actually the application of Kirchhoff's Law and Ohm's Law again):

$$V_{out} = V_{in} \times \frac{R2}{R1 + R2}$$

V_{out} = 5 volts x 2000Ω / (1000Ω + 2000Ω)

V_{out} = 3.33333 volts

We'll see the application of voltage dividers in *Section 3, IoT Playground – Practical Examples to Interact with the Physical World*, but for now, to see this principle in practice and to help cement the concept, apply a digital multimeter across the points marked in the preceding diagram to verify that the measured voltages are close to what's indicated; that is ~1.6 volts across R1 (points A and B in the preceding diagram) and ~3.3 volts across R2 (points B and C). The measurement across R2 (points B and C) is the V_{out} in the preceding equation.

What about the choice of resistor values? For a voltage divider, the most important part of the resistor value's choices is their relative ratios to divide the voltage in a way we want. Beyond that, it comes down to current flow and resistor power ratings – again, these are applications of Ohm's Law and power.

Remember the potentiometers in `Chapter 5`, *Connecting Your Raspberry Pi to the Physical World*? They're actually voltage dividers! We had the middle wiper connected to AIN1 and AIN2 of the ADS1115 and when you turned the dial on the potentiometer, what you were doing was changing the resistance across Terminals A and B relative to the center wiper, thus creating the variable voltage that's read by the ADS1115.

The following diagram shows how a potentiometer relates to a semantic diagram. Points A, B, and C are comparable to those indicated in the preceding circuit:

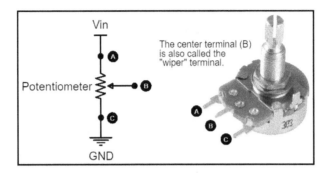

Figure 6.9 – A potentiometer is a voltage divider

Let's perform an experiment to see how a potentiometer acts as a voltage divider by creating the circuit shown here:

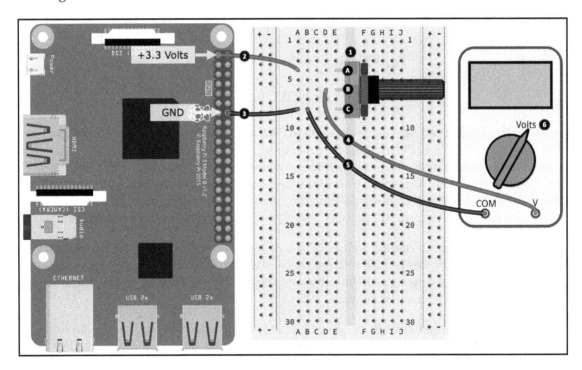

Figure 6.10 – A potentiometer circuit

Here are the first set of steps to follow. The step numbers here match the numbered black circles shown in the preceding diagram:

1. Place the 10kΩ potentiometer on your breadboard. You'll notice that I have marked Terminals A, B, and C so that they match the labeling shown in *Figure 6.9*.
2. Connect an outer Terminal (labeled **A**) of the potentiometer to a 3.3-volt pin on your Raspberry Pi. In this circuit, we are only using our Raspberry Pi as a power source. You could use an external power supply or a battery if you desired.
3. Connect the alternate outer Terminal (labeled **C**) of the potentiometer to a Raspberry Pi **GND** pin.
4. Connect the voltage measuring lead from your multimeter to the middle Terminal (labeled **B**) of the potentiometer.
5. Connect the *com* Terminal of your multimeter to **GND** (which, in our example, is shared by the potentiometer Terminal labeled **C**).
6. Turn your multimeter on and select its voltage mode.

Now, with your multimeter on, turn the potentiometer's dial and observe the voltage reading on your multimeter change within the range of ~0 volts and ~3.3 volts.

This now concludes our introduction to analog electronics. We performed a simple exercise to demonstrate and visualize, with a multimeter, how PWM produces a variable output voltage. We also learned about *voltage dividers*, how they work, and why they are a crucial part of any analog input circuit. We finished by revisiting *potentiometers* once more and looking at how they work as varying *voltage dividers*.

These analog concepts, while relatively short and simple, are two core principles underlying analog circuits that every electronic engineer – whether you are a professional or a hobbyist – needs to understand. These concepts – especially *voltage dividers* – will feature in many circuits in upcoming chapters (we will be using them in conjunction with an ADS1115 analog-to-digital converter), so please play around with the preceding examples and principles to ensure you grasp the basics!

Next, we will discuss logic-level conversion and look at another practical application of voltage dividers, only this time in the *digital input* space.

Understanding logic-level conversion

There will be occasions when you need to interface with 5-volt devices from your Raspberry Pi's 3.3-volt GPIO pins. This interfacing may be for the purpose of GPIO input, output, or bi-directional I/O. The technique used to convert between logic-level voltages is known as *logic-level conversion* or *logic-level shifting*.

There are a variety of techniques that can be used to shift voltages, and we will cover two of the more common ones in this section. One uses a voltage divider circuit, which we discussed under the previous heading, while the other uses a dedicated logic-level shifting module. Our first example of logic-level conversion will be to look at a resistor-based solution known as a *voltage divider*.

Voltage dividers as logic-level converters

A voltage divider circuit constructed of appropriately selected resistors can be used to *shift down* from 5 volts to 3.3 volts, allowing you to use a 5-volt output from a device as the input to your 3.3-volt Raspberry Pi pin.

To be crystal clear in your understanding and learning, in this section, we are dealing with *digital* electronics, specifically digital input and the application of a *voltage divider* within a digital input circuit. For your own learning and understanding, please ensure that, after completing this chapter, you are comfortable with the basic practical differences and application of a *voltage divider* in both analog and digital circuits.

The following diagram is the same example we saw previously in *Figure 6.8,* only this time, it's been drawn within a different context; that is, showing how a 5-volt input can be *shifted down* to 3.3 volts:

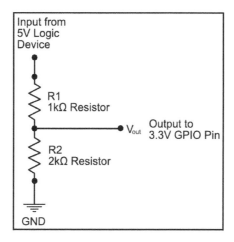

Figure 6.11 – Using a voltage divider as a logic-level shifter

A voltage divider cannot *shift up* a voltage from 3.3 volts to 5 volts. However, cast your mind back to our discussion on digital input and *Figure 6.4*, where we explained how an input pin reads a digital high as long as the voltage was >= ~2.0 volts. Well, the same often applies to 5-volt circuits – as long as the input voltage is >= ~2.0 volts (which 3.3 volts is), the 5-volt logic will register a logic high. The digital low works in the same manner too when a voltage of <= ~0.8 volts is applied.

This is often the case, though you will need to check the details and datasheet of the 5-volt device in question. It may mention the minimum voltage explicitly, or may simply mention that it will work with 3.3-volt logic. If there is no obvious indication of the device supporting 3.3-volt logic, you can always test it out yourself using 3.3 volts. This is safe to do because 3.3 volts is less than 5 volts, which means there is no risk of damage. At worst, it just will not work or work unreliably, in which case you can use a dedicated logic-level converter. We'll discuss this next.

Logic-level converter ICs and modules

An alternative to a voltage divider circuit is a dedicated logic-level shifter or converter. They come in IC (chip) form and breadboard-friendly breakout modules. There's no math involved because they are more or less plug and play, and they include multiple channels so that they can convert multiple I/O streams simultaneously.

The following image shows typical 4-channel (left) and 8-channel (right) logic-level conversion breakout modules. The 4-channel on the left is built using MOSFETs, while the 8-channel on the right uses a TXB0108 IC. Please note that while we will cover MOSFETs in Chapter 7, *Turning Things On and Off*, our focus will be using MOSFETs as switches, not logic-level conversion applications:

Figure 6.12 – Logic-level converter breakout modules

Logic-level shifter modules also have two halves – a *low voltage* side and a *high voltage* side. In relation to your Raspberry Pi, we connect its 3.3-volt pin and the GPIOs to the low-voltage side, and then connect another higher voltage circuit (for example, a 5-volt circuit) to the high-voltage side.

 The forthcoming example will be based around a module similar to the 4-channel MOSFET module pictured previously, which has an LV and HV Terminal, and two GND Terminals. If you are using a different module, you may need to consult its datasheet and adjust the wiring appropriately for use in the example.

Let's see level conversion in action. We will do this by building a circuit and measuring the voltage. Previously, in the *Digital output* section, we connected a multimeter directly to a Raspberry Pi GPIO pin and observed that when the GPIO was high, the multimeter read ~3.3 volts. This time, we will connect our multimeter to the HV side of a logic-level converter and observe that the multimeter reads ~5 volts when the GPIO pin is high.

We will start by building our circuit, which we will do in two parts:

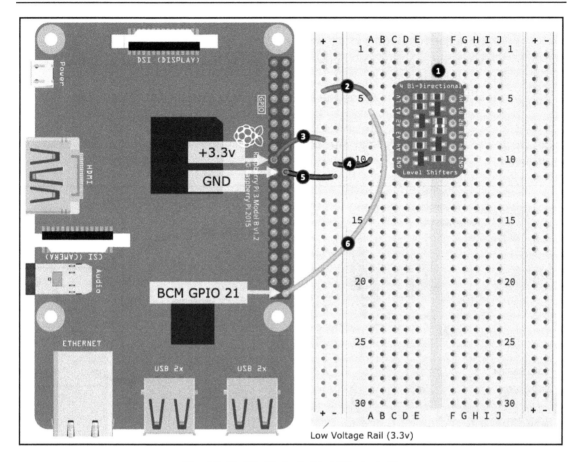

Figure 6.13 – Visualizing 3.3-volt to 5-volt level shifting (part 1 of 2)

Here are the first set of steps to follow, in which we place the components that wire up the low-voltage side of the logic-level converter. The step numbers here match the numbered black circles shown in the preceding diagram:

1. Place your logic-level converter on your breadboard.
2. Connect the **LV** (low voltage) Terminal of the logic-level converter to the positive side of the left-hand side power rail. We will call this rail the *low voltage rail* because it will be connected to the lower of our supply voltages (that is, 3.3 volts). The **LV** Terminal is the low voltage side power input Terminal for the logic-level converter.
3. Connect the positive side of the *low voltage rail* to a 3.3-volt power pin on your Raspberry Pi.

4. Connect the **GND** Terminal on the low voltage side of the logical-level converter to the negative rail on the *low voltage rail*.

5. Connect the negative rail on the *low voltage rail* to a **GND** pin on your Raspberry Pi.

6. Finally, connect port **A1** on the logic-level converter to **GPIO 21** on your Raspberry Pi.

Next, we'll wire up the high voltage side of the logic-level converter and connect our multimeter:

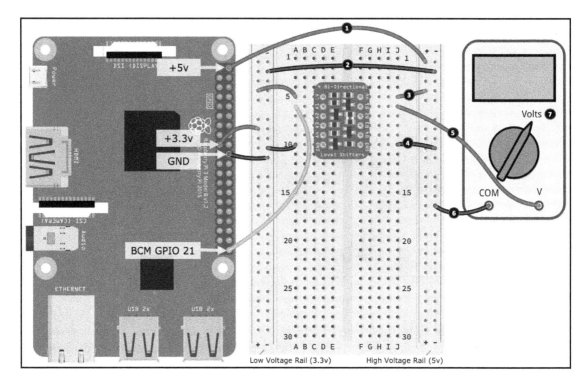

Figure 6.14 – Visualizing 3.3-volt to 5-volt level shifting (part 2 of 2)

Here are the second set of steps to follow. The step numbers here match the numbered black circles shown in the preceding diagram:

1. Connect the positive rail on the right-hand side power rail to a 5-volt pin on your Raspberry Pi. We will call this rail the *high voltage rail* because it will be connected to the higher of our supply voltages (that is, 5 volts). The **HV** Terminal is the high voltage side power input Terminal for the logic-level converter.

2. Connect the negative rail of the *high voltage rail* to the negative rail of the *low voltage rail.* You may recall that all **GND** connections are common across a circuit. If you need a refresher on this concept, please revisit the *Introducing ground connections and symbols* section in `Chapter 2`, *Getting Started with Python and IoT.*

3. Connect the **HV** Terminal of the logic-level converter to the positive side of the *high voltage rail.*

4. Connect the **GND** Terminal on the high voltage side of the logic-level converter to the negative rail of the *high voltage rail.*

5. Connect the *voltage*-measuring Terminal of your multimeter to port **B1** on the logic-level converter.

6. Connect the *com* Terminal of your multimeter to the negative rail of the *high voltage rail.*

7. Finally, set your multimeter to its voltage mode.

Now that we have built our circuit, let's run a Python program and confirm that our multimeter reads ~5 volts when GPIO 21 is high. Here is what we need to do:

1. Run the code in the `chapter06/digital_output_test.py` file – it's the same code we used previously for digital output in the section titled *Digital output.*

2. On the low voltage side, our Raspberry Pi is pulsing GPIO 21 between low (0 volts) and high (3.3 volts) on channel 1 port **A1**, while on the high voltage side, our multimeter, which is connected to channel 1 port **B1**, will alternate between 0 and ~5 volts, illustrating the shift of a 3.3-volt logic-level high to a 5-volt logic-level high.

The reverse scenario is also possible; that is, if you applied a 5-volt input to the high voltage side, it will be converted into 3.3 volts on the low voltage side, which can safely be read as input by a 3.3-volt Raspberry Pi GPIO pin.

Building this reverse scenario is an exercise that you might like to try on your own – you already have the core knowledge, code, and circuits to achieve this; you just need to wire it all up! I encourage you to try this, and to get you started, here are some tips:

- Place a push button and pull-up resistor on your breadboard, and wire it up to port **B1** on the high voltage side of the logic-level converter. This circuit (schematically) is identical to what you have seen previously in *Figure 6.6*, except that the source will now be 5 volts, and the GPIO pin is now port **B1.**

- To test your circuit, you can use the same digital input code we used previously, which can be found in the `chapter06/digital_input_test.py` file.

- If you get stuck, need a reference breadboard layout, or wish to check your circuit build, you can find a breadboard layout in the `chapter06/logic_level_input_breadboard.png` file.

 When using a logic-level converter IC, breakout module, or a voltage-divider as a level shifter, always test the input/output voltages with your multimeter before connecting them to an external circuit or your Raspberry Pi. This check will ensure you have wired the converter correctly and that the voltages have been shifted as you intended.

Let's conclude our discussion of level conversion by comparing the two approaches we have looked at.

Comparing voltage dividers and logic-level converters

Is one approach better than the other? It depends, though I will say that a dedicated converter will always outshine a basic voltage divider, and they are a lot less fiddly to use with a breadboard. A voltage divider is cheaper to build but only works in a direct direction (you'll need two voltage divider circuits to perform bi-directional I/O). They also have relatively high electrical impedance, meaning that there is a practical delay that occurs between the variable resistance changing and the measurable voltage changing. This delay is enough to make a simple voltage divider impractical for circuits where there is fast switching between high and low states. A dedicated logic-level converter overcomes these limitations, plus they are multi-channel, bi-directional, faster, and more efficient.

Summary

This chapter commenced with a quick overview of the basic tools and equipment that you will need as you get further into electronics and the circuits that we will cover in *Section 3* (which we'll be commencing in the next chapter). Then, we went through some suggestions to help keep your Raspberry Pi safe while you are connecting electronics to its GPIO pins, as well as a few tips when it comes to purchasing components.

Then, we explored Ohm's Law (and very briefly Kirchhoff's) before working through the reasons and calculations as to why our LED circuit was using a 200 Ohm resistor. We followed this example by looking at the electronic properties of digital circuits, where we explored logic voltage levels, floating pins, and pull-up and pull-down resistors. We then looked at analog circuits and worked through an example of a voltage divider circuit. We concluded this chapter by looking at logic-level conversion and how you can interface a 5-volt logic device with a 3.3-volt logic device such as your Raspberry Pi.

The goal of this chapter was to introduce you to fundamental electronic principles underpinning basic electronics and, in particular, electronic interfacing to devices such as a Raspberry Pi. I have endeavored to also explain the basic *why* behind these principles and how they influence what components are chosen for a circuit. Armed with this information, you should now be in a position to better understand how simple circuits are built to work with your Raspberry Pi.

Furthermore, you can leverage this understanding as your starting point to further develop and advance your electronic skills. You'll find links to useful electronic-based websites in the *Further reading* section, plus we'll see many of these principles in use as we proceed through *Section 3, IoT Playground*.

When you're ready to get started, I'll see you in the next chapter – which is also the start of *Section 3, IoT Playground* – where we will explore different methods of switching things on and off.

Questions

As we conclude, here is a list of questions for you to test your knowledge regarding this chapter's material. You will find the answers in the *Assessments* section of the book:

1. You have a circuit that requires a 200Ω resistor, but you only have a 330Ω resistor available. It is safe to use this value?

2. You substitute a higher value resistor in a circuit but the circuit does not work. With respect to Ohm's Law, what could be the problem?

3. You calculated a suitable resistor value for a circuit using Ohm's Law, but when you applied power to the circuit, the resistor started to discolor and let off smoke. Why?

4. Assuming GPIO 21 is configured via Python as an input pin and it is connected by a wire directly to the +3.3-volt pin, what value will `pi.read(21)` return?

5. You have a push button set up so that when it's pressed, it connects GPIO 21 to a GND pin. When the button is *not* pressed, you notice that your program is erratic and appears to receive a phantom button press. What could the problem be?

6. You want to connect a device that operates its output pins at 5 volts to a Raspberry Pi GPIO input pin. How can you do this safely?

7. True or false – A resistor voltage divider circuit can be used to convert a 3.3-volt input into 5 volts for use with a 5-volt logic input device.

Further reading

The following two sites are electronic manufacturers and they both feature a wide range of entry-to-mid-level tutorials. They focus on the practical aspects of electronics and don't bombard you with too much theory. Try a search for *Raspberry Pi* on their sites:

- `https://learn.adafruit.com`

- `https://learn.sparkfun.com`

In relation to the concepts that we have covered in this chapter, here are some specific links on the aforementioned sites:

- All About LEDs: `https://learn.sparkfun.com/tutorials/light-emitting-diodes-leds`

- Ohm's Law, Power, and Kirchhoff's Law Primer: `https://learn.sparkfun.com/tutorials/voltage-current-resistance-and-ohms-law`

- Voltage Dividers: `https://learn.sparkfun.com/tutorials/voltage-dividers`

- Pull-Up/Down Resistors: `https://learn.sparkfun.com/tutorials/pull-up-resistors/all`

- Resistors and Color Codes: `https://learn.sparkfun.com/tutorials/resistors`

If you want to go deeper, the following two websites are excellent (and free) resources that cover a diverse range of topics on electronic fundamentals and theory:

- `https://www.allaboutcircuits.com`

- `https://www.electronics-tutorials.ws`

I recommend spending a few moments just clicking around these sites to get an idea of what they include. That way, if you come across an electronic term, component, or concept in this book that you want to explore further, you'll have an idea where to start your investigation. Here are the two links to begin your exploration:

- `https://www.electronics-tutorials.ws/category/dccircuits` (DC Circuit Theory)

- `https://www.allaboutcircuits.com/textbook/direct-current` (DC Circuit Theory)

If you browse through the indexes on these sites, you will find sections including Ohm's Law, power, Kirchhoff's Laws, voltage dividers, and digital and analog electronics.

3
Section 3: IoT Playground - Practical Examples to Interact with the Physical World

This is the section where we cover the *Things* part of IoT. We will explore and experiment with a variety of common sensors, actuators, and electronic circuits, which we will use to interact with the physical world using Python. And along the way, we will see many practical applications of the core electronics principles that we learned in *Section 2*. In the latter part of this section, we will also combine our learning from *Section 1* (that is the *Internet* part of IoT) to create end-to-end IoT applications using a variety of different approaches.

This section comprises the following chapters:

- Chapter 7, *Turning Things On and Off*
- Chapter 8, *Lights, Indicators, and Displaying Information*
- Chapter 9, *Measuring Temperature, Humidity, and Light Levels*
- Chapter 10, *Movement with Servos, Motors, and Steppers*
- Chapter 11, *Measuring Distance and Detecting Movement*
- Chapter 12, *Advanced IoT Programming Concepts – Threads, AsyncIO, and Event Loops*
- Chapter 13, *IoT Visualization and Automation Platforms*
- Chapter 14, *Tying It All Together – An IoT Christmas Tree*

Turning Things On and Off

7

In the previous chapter, we looked at core electronic circuits and concepts that you will use when interfacing digital and analog circuits with your Raspberry Pi's GPIO pins.

In this chapter, we will cover how to switch *things* on and off that require more voltage and current than can be safely used with your Raspberry Pi. When it comes to electronics, hundreds of different components can be used for controlling and switching. And there are thousands of different ways they can be configured. We will be focusing on three common complements—optocouplers, transistors, and relays.

An understanding of how to control and switch electrical circuits on or off is a very important topic when interfacing with a Raspberry Pi. As we discussed in `Chapter 5`, *Connecting your Raspberry Pi to the Physical World*, Raspberry Pi GPIO pins are only capable of safely delivering a few milliamps of output current and a fixed 3.3-volts. After completing this chapter, your knowledge of optocouplers, transistors, and relays will mean you can start controlling devices that have different current and voltage requirements.

Here is what we will cover in this chapter:

- Exploring a relay driver circuit
- Determining a load's voltage and current
- Using an optocoupler as a switch
- Using a transistor as a switch
- Using a relay as a switch

Technical requirements

To perform the exercises in this chapter, you will need the following:

- Raspberry Pi 4 Model B
- Raspbian OS Buster (with desktop and recommended software)
- A minimum of Python version 3.5

These requirements are what the code examples in this book are based on. It's reasonable to expect that the code examples should work without modification on a Raspberry Pi 3 Model B or a different version of Raspbian OS as long as your Python version is 3.5 or higher.

You will find this chapter's source code in the `chapter07` folder in the GitHub repository available here: `https://github.com/PacktPublishing/Practical-Python-Programming-for-IoT`.

You will need to execute the following commands in a Terminal to set up a virtual environment and install the Python libraries required for the code in this chapter:

```
$ cd chapter07              # Change into this chapter's folder
$ python3 -m venv venv      # Create Python Virtual Environment
$ source venv/bin/activate  # Activate Python Virtual Environment
(venv) $ pip install pip --upgrade       # Upgrade pip
(venv) $ pip install -r requirements.txt  # Install dependent packages
```

The following dependencies are installed from `requirements.txt`:

- **PiGPIO**: The PiGPIO GPIO library (`https://pypi.org/project/pigpio`)

The electronic components we will need for this chapter's exercises are as follows:

- 1 x 2N7000 MOSFET (sample datasheet: `https://www.alldatasheet.com/datasheet-pdf/pdf/171823/ONSEMI/2N7000.html`)
- 1 x FQP30N06L MOSFET (optional—sample datasheet: `https://www.alldatasheet.com/datasheet-pdf/pdf/52370/FAIRCHILD/FQP30N06L.html`)
- 1 x PC817 optocoupler (sample datasheet `https://www.alldatasheet.com/datasheet-pdf/pdf/547581/SHARP/PC817X.html`)
- 1 x SDR-5VDC-SL-C relay (sample datasheet: `https://www.alldatasheet.com/datasheet-pdf/pdf/1131858/SONGLERELAY/SRD-5VDC-SL-C.html`)
- 1 x 1N4001 diode
- 2 x 1k Ω and 1 x 100k Ω resistors

- 1 x 5mm red LED
- 1 x Size 130 (R130) DC motor rated 3-6 volts (ideally with a stall current < 800mA) or alternate DC motor with compatible voltage and current ratings
- Digital multimeter capable of measuring current (it'll have an A or mA setting)
- 2 x External power sources—at a minimum, a 3.3V/5V breadboard-mountable power supply

Exploring a relay driver circuit

A common introduction to electronic switching is the mechanical relay—a device that operates like a common switch, only it's turned on and off by applying power to it. Unfortunately, connecting a relay directly to a Raspberry Pi is dangerous! Relays commonly require too much current and voltage and (if they do switch) can damage your Raspberry Pi. So, we need a driver circuit that sits between your Raspberry Pi and the relay. An example of this circuit is shown in *Figure 7.1*:

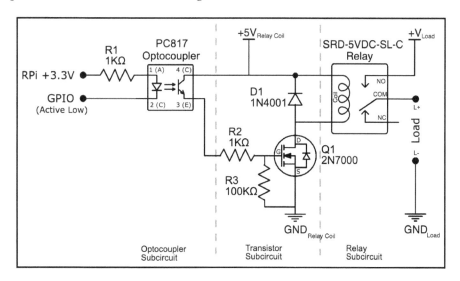

Figure 7.1 – Relay driver circuit

This is the circuit we will build, piece-by-piece during this chapter. This circuit is representative of the many relay control modules that you will find on eBay, Banggood, and similar web sites. These boards are certainly convenient to use—when you get them to work. Unfortunately, all too often, a lack of clear documentation can make getting them to work fiddly and difficult, especially if you are new to electronics.

We are about to build and explore the three sub-circuits depicted in *Figure 7.1*. This will help you to understand how optocouplers, transistors, and relays work as switches and why they are often chained together to control a relay. This knowledge will also help you to reverse-engineer a pre-made relay control module in case you can't get one working.

Before we look at the optocoupler sub-circuit, we need to first discuss load voltages and currents.

Determining a load's voltage and current

A *load* is something that you want to control, or for this chapter, switch on and off. LEDs, transistors, optocouplers, relays, lights, electric motors, heaters, pumps, automatic garage doors, and TVs are all examples of a load. If you refer back to *Figure 7.1*, you will notice the word **Load** on the right-hand side of the diagram. This is where you connect the thing you want to switch on or off.

The *transistors, optocouplers,* and *relays* components appear in this aforementioned load list. Referring back to *Figure 7.1*, the relay appears as the load to the transistor sub-circuit while the transistor sub-circuit appears as the load to the optocoupler sub-circuit.

It's important to know two properties about the load you want to control:

- What **voltage** does the load require?
- What **current** does the load require?

Sometimes, these properties can be found on the device itself or in its manual or datasheet. At other times, they need to be calculated or the load needs to be manually measured.

Knowing these properties is important because they influence which components are chosen for a circuit, including the specifications for a suitable power supply. We will make mention of load currents as we build circuits throughout this chapter, so a little more context is coming. For now, let's look at how to measure the current load of a DC motor.

Measuring the current requirement of a DC motor

Motors are a common item that people want to control, and they serve as an excellent example in current measurement. Let's perform an exercise to measure the current used by our DC motor:

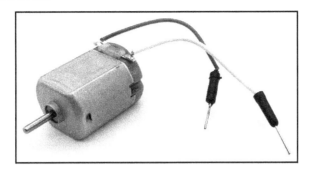

Figure 7.2 – R130 DC Motor

A typical size 130 (R130) DC motor is shown in the preceding photograph, together with a set of jumper leads soldered to the motor's terminals so it can be plugged easily into a breadboard. This motor has a red back, however, other colors are common—especially clear/white. The color has no bearing on the motor specifications.

 As you proceed with the following steps, please consult your multimeter manual if you are unsure how to place it into current measurement mode.

Here are the steps to follow:

1. Connect up a circuit as shown in *Figure 7.3*:

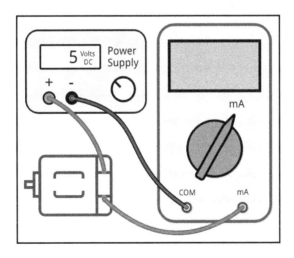

Figure 7.3 – Measuring current with a multimeter

We are assuming that the motor here is the one mentioned in the *Technical requirements* section at the start of the chapter. This motor is small enough to be powered from a breadboard power supply, which typically can supply between 500mA and 800mA. For larger motors (and other items where you do not know their ratings and want to measure them), you will require a more capable power supply.

 If you are powering a breadboard power supply from a USB phone charger, check your power supplies 5-volt output with a multimeter to make sure it is providing about 5 volts. Low wattage chargers and poor quality USB cables might not be able to deliver enough power for the power supply to operate correctly. Ideally, read the datasheet and use the suggested power adapter, which commonly are 7 to 12 volts and 1 amp.

2. Make sure your multimeter is set to measure **milliamps** (**mA**), and that its red lead is connected to the correct lead input (typically it will be labeled A or mA). If your DMM has a µA input, *do not use it* or you may blow your DMM's protection fuse (the fuse can be replaced).
3. Apply power to the circuit, and the motor will spin.
4. Your multimeter will display the current draw of the motor. Write down this value. This is known as the **continuous** or **free current** and is the current your motor uses while freely spinning with nothing connected to its shaft.
5. Disconnect power to the motor.
6. Using a pair of pliers, hold the motor's shaft so it cannot spin.
7. Reapply power to the motor, and quickly observe (and write down) the DMM's reading. This reading is called the **stall current**. A motor will use the most current when its shaft has been forcefully stopped from moving.
8. Disconnect the power to the motor.

We have now measured two currents. My readings on an R130 motor were as follows (and yours will be different):

- **Continuous or free current**: ~110mA to ~200mA—As the motor heats from use, it will use less; the ~200mA measurement was when the motor was cold. Over one minute, it dropped to ~110mA.
- **Stall current**: This was ~500mA to ~600mA.

What this means is that our motor will need between 200mA and 600mA milliamps for normal operation and that any circuit we wish to use with our motor must be able to realistically handle 600mA so that it will not get damaged if the motor stalls (or we need to design suitable protection, however, this is beyond our scope).

It is interesting to note that there's also a **start-up current**, which is a momentary peak current that occurs when the motor starts, but we won't be able to measure that on a generic DMM.

Now that we have the current draw for our R130 motor, let's collect more current data for a relay and an LED.

Measuring the current requirement of a relay and LED

We will also measure the current draw of an LED and the relay we will use in this chapter when we reach the section titled *Using a relay as a switch*. You can measure the current draw using *steps 1 to 4* from the preceding section. The setup to perform this measurement for an LED and resistor pair is illustrated here:

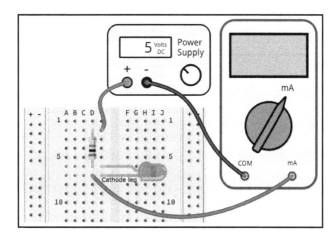

Figure 7.4 – Measuring current through a resistor/LED circuit

This is the basic process we follow:

1. We attach an LED and a 1kΩ resistor (or a relay) in place of the motor shown in *Figure 7.3*.
2. Set your multimeter to milliamps mode.
3. Apply power to the circuit.
4. Measure the amperage on your multimeter.

Once you have performed (and jotted down) the measurement you receive, remove the LED and resistor from the breadboard and wire in your relay and perform the same measurement.

The following diagram shows an SRD-05VDC-SL-C relay and which terminals on your relay you need to connect. Please note that you will need to solder header pins (pictured) or wires (a good option is to cut in half a DuPont cable) onto your relay's terminals as it will not fit directly into a breadboard:

Figure 7.5 – SRD-05VDC-SL-C relay

With a 5V source, you should obtain values similar to these on your multimeter:

- 5mm red LED in series with a 1000Ω resistor: 3mA (values from Ohms calculation and rounded up $I = (5V - 2.1V) / 1000Ω = 2.9mA$)
- Relay: 70mA to 90mA (values from the datasheet and confirmed by my own measurements)

The process for calculating the current for the LED was discussed in `Chapter 6`, *Electronics 101 for the Software Engineer*. The only difference is that here we are using a 5-volt source and a 1kΩ resistor, not 3.3 volts and a 200Ω resistor as we did in that chapter.

 Please note that the optocoupler and MOSFET component we will be using do have a voltage drop aspect to them that does affect current through the attached load. This impact of these voltage drops are immaterial for our purposes, so they are not taken into account for the calculations in this chapter for brevity.

You have now learned how to measure the current draw of a DC motor, LED/resistor pair, and a relay using a multimeter. Knowing the current limitations and expectations of a device you want to control, and even the sub-circuit you are connecting to, is a vital piece of information that is required so that you can select suitably rated components when designing a circuit and choosing a suitable power source.

We will be referencing the measurements you have performed in this section as we explore optocouplers, MOSFETs, and relays throughout this chapter. Specifically, we will compare the current ratings of these components (found in their respective datasheets) to our DC motor, LED/resistor, and relay measurements and consider what components can be used to directly control which load.

We will start by learning about optocouplers and how to use them as a switch.

Using an optocoupler as a switch

An optocoupler (or optoisolator) is a light-controlled component that is used to electrically isolate two circuits. An illustration and the schematic symbol of an optocoupler are shown here:

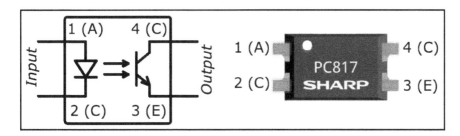

Figure 7.6 – Optocoupler symbol and component with pins labeled

The two sides of an optocoupler can be described as follows:

- An *input* side: The side we will connect to a Raspberry Pi GPIO pin
- An *output* side: The side we will connect to another circuit

Inside an optocoupler on the *input* side is an internal LED (you will notice the LED symbol within the optocoupler symbol in *Figure 7.6*) while on the *output* side there is a phototransistor that responds to the LED's light. What this means is that the transfer of control (that is, switching) from the *input* side to the *outside* side is performed by light, hence, there is no physical electrical connection between the two sides. For us, this means that any failures or accidents on the output side should not cause damage to our Raspberry Pi. The PC817 has its isolation rated as 5000 volts, which are well beyond any voltages we would expect to be used with IoT electronics and devices.

When the *input* side LED is off, the *output* side phototransistor is off. However, when the LED is illuminated (it's inside the optocoupler component, so you will not see it) by applying current to pins 1 (anode) and 2 (cathode), the phototransistor is activated (on) and allows current to flow between pins 4 (collector) and 3 (emitter).

Let's create a simple circuit to demonstrate a PC817 optocoupler, which has the following specifications:

- Input side (the LED): This has the following:
  - Typical **forward voltage (V_F)** is 1.2 volts DC
  - Maximum **forward current (I_F)** is 50mA DC
- Output side (the phototransistor): This has the following:
  - Maximum **collector-emitter voltage (V_{CEO})**: 80 volts DC
  - Maximum **collector current (I_C)**: 50mA DC
  - **Collector-Emitter Saturation Voltage $V_{CE(sat)}$** in the range 0.1 to 0.2 volts (basically the voltage drop)

Keeping these specifications in mind, let's begin our circuit build.

Building the optocoupler circuit

We're about to build the circuit illustrated in the following diagram. This circuit uses the PC817 optocoupler to electrically isolate our Raspberry Pi and the LED subcircuit:

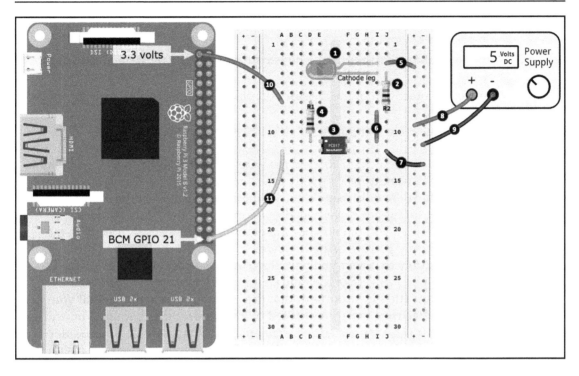

Figure 7.7 – Optocoupler circuit

The step numbers here match the numbered black circles in *Figure 7.7*:

1. Place the LED into your breadboard, taking care to orientate the LED as illustrated regarding its cathode leg.
2. Place a 1kΩ resistor into the breadboard. One end of this resistor connects inline with the cathode leg of the LED.
3. Place the PC817 Optocoupler IC into your breadboard. The white dot on the IC indicates pin number 1 of the IC. Your IC may have or not have the white dot, however, there should be a distinct marking on the IC to tell you the first pin. Please refer back to *Figure 7.6* for all pin numberings.
4. Place a 1kΩ resistor into your breadboard. One end of this resistor connects with pin 1 of the PC817.
5. Connect the anode leg of the LED to the positive rail of the right-hand side power rail.
6. Connect pin 4 of the PC817 to the other end of the resistor you placed at *step 2*.
7. Connect pin 3 of the PC817 to the negative rail of the right-hand side power rail.

8. Connect the positive output of a 5-volt power supply into the right-hand side positive power rail.

9. Connect the negative output of a power supply into the right-hand side negative power rail.

10. Connect the other end of the resistor you placed at *step 4* to a 3.3-volt pin on your Raspberry Pi.

11. Finally, connect pin 2 of the PC817 to GPIO 21 on your Raspberry Pi.

 In *Figure 7.7*, you could connect the wires at *steps 8* and *9* (which go to the External Power Supply) directly to your Raspberry Pi's +5-volt pin and a GND pin. We're only using a small amount of current for the red LED, however, for higher current loads, you must use an external power supply. The +5 volt pin on your Raspberry Pi is connected directly to the power supply you are using to power your Raspberry Pi. Using this power supply to power your circuits effectively robs current available to your Raspberry Pi. Take too much, and your Raspberry Pi will reset! **Please note (this is important) that the caveat of this action is that you lose the electrical isolation offered by the optocoupler** because you will have electrically connected the *input* and *output* sides of the optocoupler together (remember, the *input* and *output* sides are not electrically inside the optocoupler because control is achieved by light).

Now that you have completed the circuit build, we will test the circuit and explore the code that makes it work.

Controlling the optocoupler with Python

Start by running the code in the chapter07/optocoupler_test.py file, and observe the LED blink. Following is the part of the code responsible for the blinking:

```
# ... truncated ...
pi.write(GPIO_PIN, pigpio.LOW) # On.      # (1)
print("On")
sleep(2)
pi.write(GPIO_PIN, pigpio.HIGH) # Off.    # (2)
print("Off")
sleep(2)
# ... truncated ...
```

Here's what's happening:

- At line (1), GPIO 21 is low and the internal LED on the *input* side is on. The phototransistor on the *output* side detects this light and is activated, allowing current to flow between the output side's collector (pin 4) and emitter (pin 3), and hence our red LED illuminates.
- The input side of the PC817 circuit is wired as *active low*—that's why at line (1), GPIO 21 is made low to turn the circuit on, and at line (2), GPIO 21 is set to high to turn the circuit off. Alternative wiring would be *active high*. If you want to experiment and change the circuit to be active-high, you would attach the wire from *step 10* in *Figure 7.7* to a GND pin (rather than a 3.3-volt pin), and reverse the `pigpio.LOW` and `pigpio.HIGH` statements in the code.

We could have used a lower value resistor for R1 for the input-side LED, however, a 1kΩ resistor provides more than enough current (($3.3V - 1.2V)/1000\Omega = 2.1mA$) to the internal LED for the optocoupler circuit to work. You'll see 1kΩ, 10kΩ, and 100kΩ resistors used in a lot of circuits simply because these are nice round values. We've also used a 1kΩ resistor for R2 for the red LED for convenience.

Can you remember from the previous chapter, `Chapter 6`, *Electronics 101 for the Software Engineer*, when we discussed that we should not expect more than 8mA from a Raspberry Pi GPIO pin? Well, by using a PC817 optocoupler, we can now control up to 50mA by placing an optocoupler between a GPIO pin and a circuit. Furthermore, we are also not limited to the 3.3 volts of a GPIO pin since the PC817 can handle up to 80 volts.

Remember that a GPIO pin's primary role is to *control* something, not *power* it, so always think about *control* and *power* requirements independently.

In the previous section, we calculated (or measured) the current draw of our motor, relay, and an LED. Here is that data in the context of our PC817 optocoupler using a 5-volt power source on the output side:

- The LED and 1kΩ resistor needed a current of 3mA.
- The relay needed between 70mA and 90mA.
- The motor needed ~500mA to ~600mA (stall current).

The LED's 3mA is less than the optocouplers maximum output-side rating of 50mA, so it's fine to drive the LED directly on the output side. The relay and motor, however, require a current beyond the limits of the PC817, so using them on the output may result in damage to the optocoupler.

While we can and do use optoisolators as a digital switch, they are often used as an isolating barrier to drive other components, which in turn can drive loads requiring higher currents. We will see this later on when we build the full relay driver circuit from *Figure 7.1*, but for now, let's learn how to use a transistor as a digital switch.

Using a transistor as a switch

Transistors are a hands-down most significant electronic component in use today and the backbone of the digital revolution. They can be used in two basic ways—as an amplifier or as a digital switch. Our focus is going to be on digital switching, and we will be using a transistor type known as a **Metal-Oxide-Semiconductor-Field-Effect Transistor** (**MOSFET**), specifically, an N-Channel Enhancement Mode MOSFET—yes, it's a mouthful!

Don't get too caught up on the long technical name or the many forms of transistors that exist. The simple take-home here is that an N-Channel Enhancement Mode MOSFET works well as a digital switch that we can control using our Raspberry Pi, or as we will see later, from another source such as an optocoupler.

 FETs are *voltage*-controlled transistors. Another type of transistor known as a **Bipolar Junction Transistor** (**BJT**) is a *current*-controlled transistor. BJTs are perfectly fine to use with a Raspberry Pi but require additional considerations. You'll find a link in the *Further reading* section to further your learning on transistors.

The following exercise will be using a 2N7000, an N-Channel Enhancement Mode MOSFET, as illustrated in *Figure 7.8*. The leg names are Source, Gate, and Drain. Two different packaging styles are also illustrated, the TO92 and TO220. Notice that the arrangement of the Source, Gate, and Drain legs on the two styles are different:

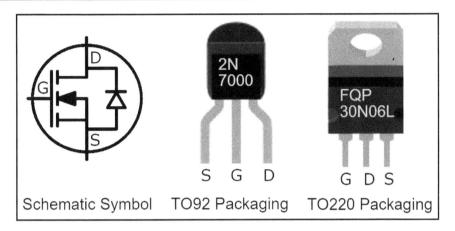

Figure 7.8 – N-Channel Enhancement MOSFET symbol and common package styles

The 2N7000 has the following specifications in its datasheet:

- Maximum **Drain Source Voltage (V$_{DSS}$)** of 60 volts DC
- Maximum **Continuous Drain Current (I$_D$)** of 200 mA DC
- Maximum **Pulsed Drain Current (I$_{DM}$)** of 500 mA DC
- **Gate Threshold Voltage (V$_{GS(th)}$)** in the range of 0.8 to 3 volts DC
- **Drain–Source On–Voltage (V$_{DS(on)}$)** in the range of 0.45 to 2.5 volts DC (voltage drop)

Here is how to interpret these parameters regarding the 2N7000:

- It can safely control a load not exceeding 60 volts (V$_{DSS}$) and a continuous 200mA (I$_D$), but a pulse of 500mA (I$_{DM}$) is OK.
- It will ideally require a voltage >= 3 volts to switch it on (V$_{GS(th)}$).
- It will consume, on the load-side circuit, a voltage in the range of 0.45 to 2.5 volts (V$_{DS(on)}$).

The 2N7000 (and the FQP30N06L that we will discuss shortly) are logic-level comparable MOSFETs. They are suitable for a Raspberry Pi because their maximum gate voltage V$_{GS(th)}$ is less than a GPIO pin's 3.3 volts.

Let's get started and build a circuit to use the 2N7000 with our Raspberry Pi.

Building the MOSFET circuit

We will build our circuit in two parts, starting with the placement of the components on our breadboard:

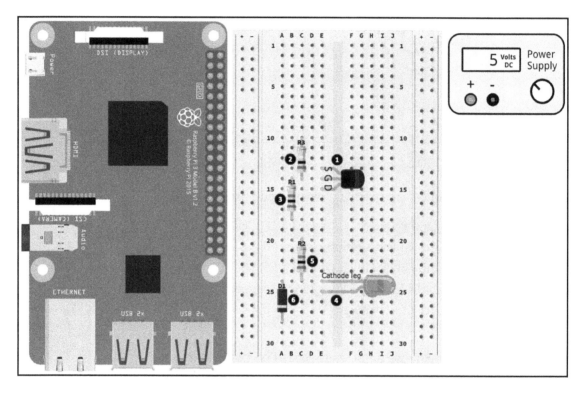

Figure 7.9 – MOSFET transistor circuit (part 1 of 2)

Following are the steps for the first part of our build. The step numbers match the numbered black circles in *Figure 7.9*:

1. Place the MOSFET into your breadboard, taking care to orientate the component the correct way around regarding the **Source**, **Gate**, and **Drain** legs. Our example layout assumes a 2N7000 MOSFET. Please see *Figure 7.8* if you need help to identify the legs.
2. Place a 100kΩ resistor into your breadboard. One end of this resistor connects to the **Gate** leg of the MOSFET.
3. Place a 1kΩ resistor into the breadboard. One end of this resistor also connects to the **Gate** leg of the MOSFET.

4. Place the LED into the breadboard, taking care to orientate the component as shown regarding its cathode leg.
5. Place a 1kΩ resistor into the breadboard. One end of this resistor connects with the cathode leg of the LED.
6. Place the diode into the breadboard, orientating the component so that the cathode leg (the end of the diode with the band on the casing) is facing toward the bottom of the breadboard. We will discuss the purpose of this diode shortly.

Now that we have placed the components into our breadboards, let's wire them all up:

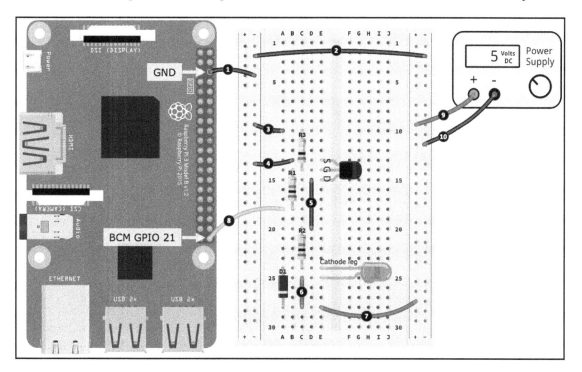

Figure 7.10 – MOSFET transistor circuit (part 2 of 2)

Following are the steps for the second part of the build. The step numbers match the numbered black circles in *Figure 7.10*:

1. Connect a GND pin from your Raspberry Pi into the negative rail of the right-hand side power rail.
2. Connect the negative rails of the right-hand side and left-hand side power rails.
3. Connect the 100kΩ resistor into the negative power rail.
4. Connect the **Source** leg of the MOSFET into the negative power rail.

5. Connect the **Drain** leg of the MOSFET to the 1kΩ resistor.

6. Connect the anode leg of the LED to the cathode leg of the diode.

7. Connect the anode leg of the LED (and cathode leg of the diode) to the positive power rail on the right-hand side power rail.

8. Connect the 1kΩ resistor to GPIO 21 on your Raspberry Pi.

9. Connect the positive output terminal on your power supply into the positive rail of the right-hand side power rail.

10. Connect the negative output terminal on your power supply into the negative rail of the right-hand side power rail.

Well done. That's our circuit build complete. Let's briefly discuss this circuit before we test it out.

Notice in *Figure 7.10* (and *Figure 7.1*) the 100kΩ resistor R3. This is an external pull-down resistor that ensures that the **Gate** leg of the MOSFET is tied to GND (0 volts) when it is not pulled up to +3.3 volts when GPIO 21 is high. MOSFETs have capacitive charge, so without a pull-down, the MOSFET may appear sticky and slow when it transitions from on (GPIO 21 is high) to off (GPIO 21 goes low) as it discharges (note that this circuit is active high). The pull-down resistor ensures a rapid discharge into the off state. We use an external pull-down resistor in preference to an in-code activated pull-down to ensures the MOSFET **Gate** is pulled down even when the Raspberry Pi is powered off or when code has not run.

You will also notice that R1 and R3 create a voltage divider. The ratio of 1kΩ and 100kΩ is suitable to ensure that >3 volts get to the gate leg of the MOSFET to switch it on. If you need a refresher on pull-down resistors and voltage dividers, we discussed them in `Chapter 6, Electronics 101 for the Software Engineer`.

When adding resistors into a circuit—like adding in a pull-down—always consider with the wider impact of the change. If, for example, the addition creates a voltage divider due to the presence of an existing resistor, you then need to access the impact of the change on the surrounding circuit. For our scenario, this is to ensure enough voltage is reaching the MOSFET gate leg to turn it on.

After running the code in the next section, try removing R3 and run the code again. I can't guarantee that you will see anything at your end, but you may observe that the red LED fizzles out slowly rather than turning off promptly when GPIO 21 goes low and that it behaves erratically instead of fading in and out smoothly.

As with the optocoupler example, you can connect the wire's external power supply to your Raspberry Pi's +5 pin and a GND pin for this LED example since its current requirements are low.

With this basic understanding of a MOSFET circuit, let's run and explore a simple Python program that interacts with our circuit.

Controlling the MOSFET with Python

Run the code in the chapter07/transistor_test.py file, and the red LED will turn on then off, then fade in and out. Once you have confirmed that your circuit works, let's continue and look at the code:

```
# ...truncated ...
pi.set_PWM_range(GPIO_PIN, 100)                    # (1)

try:
    pi.write(GPIO_PIN, pigpio.HIGH) # On.      # (2)
    print("On")
    sleep(2)
    pi.write(GPIO_PIN, pigpio.LOW) # Off.
    print("Off")
    sleep(2)
```

We are using PWM in this example. In line (1), we are telling PiGPIO that, for GPIO 21 (GPIO_PIN = 21), we want its duty cycle to be constrained to the value range 0 to 100 (rather than the default 0 to 255). This is an example of how we can change the granularity of duty cycle values in PiGPIO. We're using 0 to 100 just to make reporting easier because it maps into 0% to 100% for terminal output.

Next, in line (2), we simply turn the GPIO on and off for a duration to test the transistor circuit, and we will see the LED turn on then off after a 2-second delay.

In line (3) in the following code, we use PWM to fade in the LED, before fading it out again at line (4), both times using the duty cycle range set at line (1) in the preceding code block:

```
# Fade In.
for duty_cycle in range(0, 100):                    # (3)
    pi.set_PWM_dutycycle(GPIO_PIN, duty_cycle)
    print("Duty Cycle {}%".format(duty_cycle))
    sleep(0.01)

# Fade Out.
```

```
    for duty_cycle in range(100, 0, -1):                    # (4)
        pi.set_PWM_dutycycle(GPIO_PIN, duty_cycle)
        print("Dyty Cycle {}%".format(duty_cycle))
        sleep(0.01)
# ...truncated ...
```

Let's check whether our relay and motor are safe to use with this transistor circuit, given our 2N7000 is rated for 200 milliamps:

- The relay can be used in place of the LED because it only needs between 70mA and 90mA.
- The motor requires ~200mA to spin freely *(continuous* current), so it might be safe...or not? Let's see.

When we tested the motor earlier in this chapter, we anticipated it will need between ~200mA (the *continuous* current when cold) and ~500mA to ~600mA (the *stall* current)—*remember these are my measurements, so replace the values with your measurements.* So, in principle, our 2N7000 will be OK as long as the motor is not under load. Realistically, as soon as we place a load on the motor's shaft, it will require more than 200mA continuous current. In this respect, the 2N7000 is probably not an ideal transistor for driving this motor. We need to seek out a MOSFET that can comfortably handle 600mA of continuous current or more. We'll see the FQP30N06L MOSFET shortly, which can handle this current and much more.

While the LED faded in and out with the PWM-related code, if you connect the motor into the circuit in place of the LED/resistor pair, you will notice it revs up then down. You've just discovered how to use the duty cycle property of PWM to control the speed of a motor! We will be covering motors in more detail in Chapter 10, *Movement with Servos, Motors, and Steppers.*

 To use the motor or relay, you must use an external power supply and not the +5-volt pin on your Raspberry Pi. If you try and use the +5-volt pin, you may find your Raspberry Pi resets as you run the code.

We do not use PWM with relays because they're too slow to switch and if they do work (at a very low PWM frequency), it's only wearing them out—but try it anyway to see what happens; a short test will do no harm (try adjusting the frequency of 8000 in code down to 10, that is, pi.set_PWM_frequency(GPIO_PIN, 10)).

In our circuit, there is also the 1N4001 diode D1. This is known as a fly-back or suppression diode. Its role is to protect the circuit from reverse voltage spikes that can occur in electromagnetic components such as a relay or motor when they are powered down. Granted, our LED is not magnetic, however, it does not do any harm having the diode present.

 Anytime you are controlling a component that works on electromagnetism (also known as an inductive load), always correctly install a fly-back suppression diode.

In *Figure 7.8*, we also have an illustration of an FQP30N06L. This is a Power N-Channel Enhancement Mode MOSFET capable of driving high amperage loads. It has the following specifications in its datasheet:

- Maximum **Drain Source Voltage (V_{DSS})** of 60 volts DC
- Maximum **Continuous Drain Current (I_D)** of 32A DC (amps not milliamps!)
- Maximum **Pulsed Drain Current (I_{DM})** of 128A DC
- **Gate Threshold Voltage ($V_{GS(th)}$)** in the range of 1 to 2.5 volts DC (< 5 volts so it's logic-level compatible)
- **Drain–Source On–Voltage (V_{SD})** maximum of 1.5 volts DC

You can substitute an FQP30N06 (or another N-Channel Enhancement mode logic-level capable MOSFET) in the preceding circuit and it will work, but keep the following in mind:

- The G, D, and S legs of the FQP30N06L are in a different order to the 2N7000 so you will need to adjust the wiring.
- When dealing with higher voltages and currents, it's a good idea to electrically isolate the MOSFET from the Raspberry Pi using an optocoupler (we'll see this configuration when we discuss relays next).
- At high currents, Power MOSFETs can get very hot—the surrounding components and wires and even the breadboard can melt, so approach their use with caution and care.

 Higher power MOSFETs can get hot when controlling high power loads and can be fitted with a heatsink, for example, the FQP30N06L has a metal top with a hole where the heatsink is attached. The determining factors and calculations as to when a headsink is required are beyond our scope, however, if your MOSFET is getting too hot (and you are using it within its datasheet parameters), then add a heatsink.

If you like the idea of controlling higher current loads using MOSFETs, you might like to research ready-made MOSFET modules on sites such as eBay. You now have the background after learning about optocouplers and MOSFETs to understand how these modules are constructed—some just use a MOSFET directly connected to the controlling device (that is, GPIO pin) as we have just done while others place an optocoupler in between the controlling device and the MOSFET.

You have learned the basics of using a MOSFET transistor as a digital switch. Next, we will put that learning together with our learning on optocouplers to build our relay driver circuit on a breadboard.

Using a relay as a switch

Classic relays are an electro-mechanical component that allows a smaller current device to switch a higher current device or load on and off. In principle, they are just like the MOSFET or optocoupler we used previously. So, why have relays? Here are a few reasons:

- For high voltage and current loads, they tend to be much cheaper compared to an equivalent MOSFET.
- At high currents, they do not get untouchably hot like a MOSFET.
- Similar to an optocoupler, relays also provide electrical isolation between the input and output circuits.
- They are simply electrically controlled switches so they are easy to understand and use for non-electrical engineers.
- They have stood the test of time and proven to be a simple and robust way to control high loads (even though they eventually will wear out—the SRD-05VDC-SL-C datasheet lists its rated life expectancy to be 100,000 operations).

 There is also a type of relay known as a **Solid State Relay** (**SSR**) that has no moving parts, however, they are typically more expensive than a comparable mechanical relay.

Our first task is to create our circuit, which we will do next.

Building the relay driver circuit

Let's build our relay driver circuit. We will do this in three parts, starting with the placements of the components:

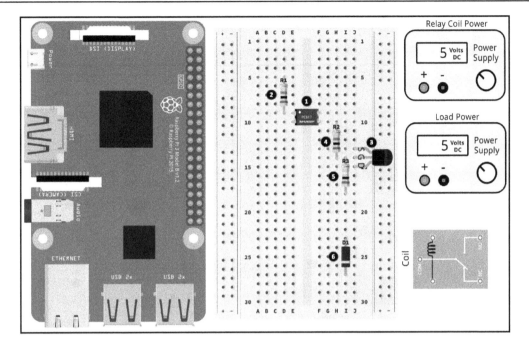

Figure 7.11 – Relay driver circuit (part 1 of 3)

Following are the steps for the first part of the build. The step numbers match the numbered black circles in *Figure 7.11*:

1. Place the PC817 into your breadboard, taking care that pin 1 of the IC is connected to the left-hand breadboard bank as illustrated.

2. Place a 1kΩ resistor into your breadboard. One end of the resistor connects to pin 1 of the PC817.

3. Place the MOSFET into your breadboard, taking care to orientate the component the correct way around regarding the **Source**, **Gate**, and **Drain** legs. Our example layout assumes a 2N7000 MOSFET. Please see *Figure 7.8* if you need help to identify the legs.

4. Place a 1kΩ resistor into your breadboard. One end of this resistor connects the **Gate** leg of the MOSFET.

5. Place a 100kΩ resistor into your breadboard. One end of this resistor also connects the **Gate** leg of the MOSFET.

6. Place the diode into your breadboard, taking care to orientate the component as illustrated with the cathode leg (the end of the component with the band) pointing toward the bottom of the breadboard.

Now that you have placed the individual components, next, we will wire up the components:

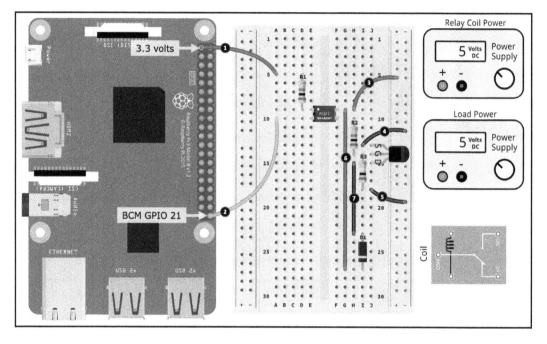

Figure 7.12 – Relay driver circuit (part 2 of 3)

Following are the steps for the second part of the build. The step numbers match the numbered black circles in *Figure 7.12*:

1. Connect the resistor you placed at the previous *step 2* to a 3.3-volt pin on your Raspberry Pi.
2. Connect pin 2 of the PC817 to GPIO 21 on your Raspberry Pi.
3. Connect pin 4 of the PC817 to the positive rail of the right-hand side power rail.
4. Connect the **Source** leg of the MOSFET into the negative rail of the right-hand side power rail.
5. Connect the 100kΩ resistor that connects into the **Drain** leg of the MOSFET to the negative rail of the right-hand side power rail.
6. Connect pin 4 of the PC817 to the cathode leg of the diode.
7. Connect the **Drain** leg of the MOSFET to the anode leg of the diode.

Finally, we will connect the power supplies and relay:

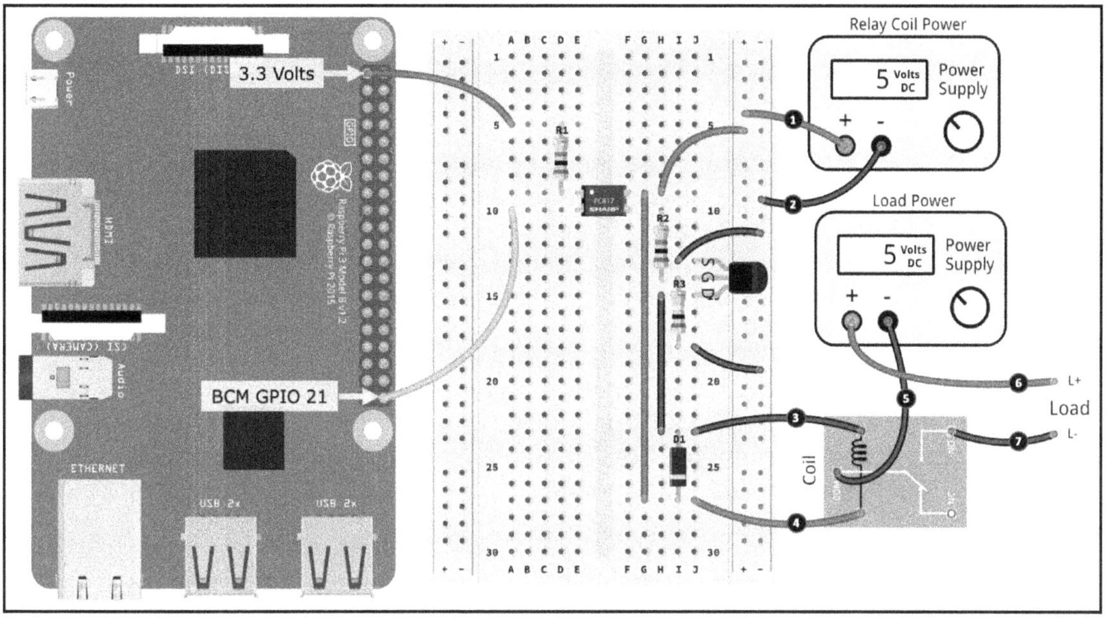

Figure 7.13 – Relay driver circuit (part 3 of 3)

Following are the steps for the third and last part of the build. The step numbers match the numbered black circles in *Figure 7.13*:

1. Connect the positive rail of the right-hand side power rail to the positive output terminal of a 5-volt power supply.
2. Connect the negative rail of the right-hand side power rail to the negative output terminal of a 5-volt power supply.
3. Connect the anode leg of the diode to one of the relay's coil terminal.
4. Connect the cathode leg of the diode to the relay's other coil terminal.
5. Connect the negative output of a *different* 5-volt power supply to the **com** terminal on your relay.

> At *step 5*, you must use two different external power sources for this circuit because the current requirements of the relay coil and potential relay load will very likely be too much to borrow (rob) from your Raspberry Pi's power supply.

6. Connect the positive output terminal of the *different* 5-volt power supply to the positive input terminal of your load (for example, one of the terminals on a motor).

7. Finally, connect the **NO (Normally Open)** terminal of the relay to the negative input terminal of your load.

> Using the NO terminal on the relay means the load will be off by default and only powered when the relay is engaged, which happens when GPIO 21 is low (remembering this circuit is *active-low*). If you connect your load to the **NC (Normally Closed)** terminal in the relay, the load will be powered by default, including when your Raspberry Pi is switched off.

Well done! Your completed breadboard circuit, as illustrated in *Figure 7.13*. This is the breadboard build that matches the schematic diagram shown at the commencement of this chapter in *Figure 7.1*. This breadboard circuit is shown with a 5-volt *relay coil power* source and a 5-volt *load power* source. This circuit, however, can be used with different power supplies subject to the following pointers:

- The choice of resistors and the 2N7000 MOSFET used in this circuit is capable of driving a 12-volt relay like an SRD-12VDC-SL-C. You'll just need to make sure the *relay coil power* source is 12 volts rather than 5 volts.
- The load power source is illustrated as 5 volts, however, if your load requires more voltage (that's within the relay's specifications), it can be increased.

Now that we have a finished circuit, let's run a Python program to control the relay.

Controlling the Relay Driver Circuit with Python

Run the following code, which is in the `chapter07/optocoupler_test.py` file. The relay should activate with a click sound, and deactivate after 2 seconds. This is the same code we used when we created and tested our optocoupler circuit since it's the optocoupler that our Raspberry Pi is connected to.

We saw earlier when we learned about MOSFETs that we could connect the MOSFET directly to a GPIO pin and control the relay, without needing an optoisolator. So, why does the preceding circuit have one?

The answer is that our circuit does not technically need one, and there are ready-made relay modules to be found (though rarer) that do not have an optoisolator. However, there is no harm in having one present since it does provide a level of electrical isolation protection just in case the relay control circuit fails or there is a mishap when wiring up the power supply.

Finally, what about relay modules you can find on sites such as eBay that have more than one relay? There is just a single relay circuit replicated multiple times—you will typically be able to count a transistor and optocoupler pair for each relay (although optocouplers and transistors can come in chip form, that is, multiple optocouplers or optocouplers in a single package, so on some modules you may just see the chips instead). Also, note that some modules will use a BJT rather than a MOSFET. If you can read the part numbers on the components, you can always perform a web search to determine what they are.

To conclude our exploration of turning things on and off, here is a table comparing the switching components we used in this chapter:

	Optocoupler	MOSFET	Relay
Construction	Solid state	Solid state	Mechanical
Current	AC or DC (depending on optocoupler)	DC only (start your research with TRIACS for AC)	AC and DC
Cost	$ - $$	$ (low capacity) to $$$ (high capacity)	$
Gets Really Hot (Can't touch)	No	Yes for high current power MOSFETs	No
Control Voltage / Current	Low (need to turn off and on the internal LED)	Low (need to apply voltage to the Gate)	High (need to energize the relay coil)
Load Voltage / Current	Low (for example, PC817 max 50mA)	Low (for example, 2N27000 at 200mA); High (for example, FQP30N06L at 32A)	High (for example, SRD-05VDC-SL-C 10A)
Electrical Isolation	Yes	No	Yes
Example application	Provides electrical isolation between a controlling circuit and the circuit to be controlled	Allows a low current/voltage circuit to control a higher voltage/current circuit	Allows a low current/voltage circuit to control a higher voltage/current circuit
Longevity	Long life	Long life	Short life (moving parts will wear out eventually)
Use PWM	Yes	Yes	No—a relay will not switch fast enough, plus you'll only wear out the relay faster!

Well done on completing this chapter! You now understand multiple ways to control loads that have voltage and current requirements beyond the 3.3 volt/8mA limits of your Raspberry Pi's GPIO pins.

Summary

In this chapter, we learned how to switch things on and off. We commenced by briefly reviewing a typical relay driver circuit, before learning how to measure the current requirements of a DC motor, LED, and relay using a multimeter. Next, we discussed the properties of an optocoupler and learned at low to use it as a digital switch. Then, we discussed MOSFETs and discovered how to use them as a switch and for motor speed control using PWM.

The information, circuits, and exercises you have learned in this chapter will help you to make informed decisions and make the necessary calculations and measurements to select suitable components and create circuits that can be used to switch devices on and off and other loads that demand more current and higher voltages that can be sourced safely from a Raspberry Pi pin.

Our approach to this chapter was to incrementally explore and build a relay driver circuit, which provides you with a practical example of how and why switching components are chained together to control higher power components and/or loads. Also, we learned that optocouplers can be used to electrically isolate circuits, which can be a useful and practical technique to help us to isolate and protect our Raspberry Pi from accidental damage should a circuit fail or be wired incorrectly.

In the next chapter, we turn our attention to different types of LEDs, buzzers, and visual components we can use to signal or display information to users.

Questions

As we conclude, here is a list of questions for you to test your knowledge regarding this chapter's material. You will find the answers in the *Assessments* section of the book:

1. When it comes to controlling a transistor, how do MOSFET and BJT differ?
2. You are controlling a motor using a MOSFET, however, you switch off the MOSFET (for example, making the GPIO pin low), but the motor does not turn off promptly but instead spins down. Why?
3. You have selected a random MOSFET that you want to control from a Raspberry Pi 3.3-volt GPIO but it does not work. What is some possible cause of the problem?
4. Other than switching, what common feature do optocouplers and relays share that transistors do not?

5. What is the difference between an active low and active high GPIO?
6. Why do we prefer a physical pull-down resistor for the MOSFET's Gate leg over an in-code activated pull-down?
7. For a DC motor, what does the stall current represent?
8. For a DC motor, what is the difference between continuous and free current?

Further reading

The following tutorial is a thorough introduction to transistors, their various types, and applications:

- https://www.electronics-tutorials.ws/category/transistor (start with the MOSFET sections)

8
Lights, Indicators, and Displaying Information

In the previous chapter, we explored and learned how to use an optocoupler, transistor, and relay circuit and how these three components work together to create a common relay control module. We also covered how to measure the current usage of a load using a multimeter so that you can make an informed decision on what method or component should be used to switch or control an external load.

In this chapter, we will cover two alternative ways of making color with RGB LEDs and create a simple application to monitor your Raspberry Pi's CPU temperature and display the result on an OLED display. We will conclude by seeing how we can combine PWM and buzzers to create sound.

After you complete this chapter, you will have the knowledge, experience, and code examples that you can adapt to your own projects for those situations you need to display information to users, make a noise, or simply dazzle them with lights! Furthermore, what you learn will be adaptable to other types of compatible displays and lighting devices if you wish to explore these topics further.

We will cover the following topics in this chapter:

- Making color with an RGB LED
- Controlling a multi-color APA102 LED strip with SPI
- Using an OLED display
- Making sound with buzzers and PWM

Technical requirements

To perform the exercises in this chapter, you will need the following:

- Raspberry Pi 4 Model B
- Raspbian OS Buster (with desktop and recommended software)
- A minimum of Python version 3.5

These requirements are what the code examples in this book are based on. It's reasonable to expect that the code examples should work without modification on a Raspberry Pi 3 Model B or a different version of Raspbian OS as long as your Python version is 3.5 or higher.

You will find this chapter's source code in the `chapter08` folder in the GitHub repository available here: `https://github.com/PacktPublishing/Practical-Python-Programming-for-IoT`.

You will need to execute the following commands in a Terminal to set up a virtual environment and install the Python libraries required for the code in this chapter:

```
$ cd chapter08              # Change into this chapter's folder
$ python3 -m venv venv      # Create Python Virtual Environment
$ source venv/bin/activate  # Activate Python Virtual Environment
(venv) $ pip install pip --upgrade      # Upgrade pip
(venv) $ pip install -r requirements.txt  # Install dependent packages
```

The following dependencies are installed from `requirements.txt`:

- **PiGPIO**: The PiGPIO GPIO library (`https://pypi.org/project/pigpio`)
- **Pillow**: Python Imaging Library (PIL) (`https://pypi.org/project/Pillow`)
- **Luma LED Matrix Library** (`https://pypi.org/project/luma.led_matrix`)
- **Luma OLED Library** (`https://pypi.org/project/luma.oled`)

The electronic components we will need for this chapter's exercises include the following:

- 1 x passive buzzer (rated for 5 volts)
- 1 x 1N4001 Diode
- 1 x 2N7000 MOSFET
- 2 x 15Ω, 200Ω, 1kΩ & 100kΩ Resistors
- 1 x RGB LED with a common cathode (datasheet: `https://pdf1.alldatasheet.com/datasheet-pdf/view/292386/P-TEC/PL16N-WDRGB190503.html`)

- 1 x SSD1306 OLED display (with an I2C interface) or another model compatible with the Luma OLED Python library (datasheet (Driver IC): `https://www.alldatasheet.com/datasheet-pdf/pdf/1179026/ETC2/SSD1306.html`)
- 1 x APA102 RGB LED strip (datasheet (Single APA102 Module): `https://www.alldatasheet.com/datasheet-pdf/pdf/1150589/ETC2/APA102.html`)
- 1 x logic level shifter/converter module
- 1 x external power supply (for example, a 3.3V/5V breadboard power supply)

Let's make a start by looking at how we can use PWM to set the color of an RGB LED.

Making color with an RGB LED and PWM

In this section, we will learn how to use **Pulse-Width Modulation** (**PWM**) together with an RGB LED to create different colors. As a reminder, PWM is a technique to create a variable voltage, which when applied to an LED and resistor pair can be used to change the brightness of an LED. We first discussed PWM and used it to change the brightness of an LED back in `Chapter 2`, *Getting Started with Python and IoT*. We then covered PWM in greater depth in `Chapter 5`, *Connecting your Raspberry Pi to the Physical World*.

An RGB LED is three single-color LEDs (red, green, and blue) in a single package, as illustrated in *Figure 8.1*:

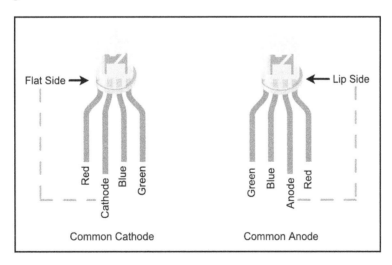

Figure 8.1 – RGB LED varieties

You will notice that two types are shown:

- **Common Cathode**: The red, green, and blue LEDs share a common *cathode* leg, meaning that the common leg is what connects to the negative or ground voltage source—cathode = negative.
- **Common Anode**: The red, green, and blue LEDs share a common *anode* leg, meaning that the common leg is what connects to the positive voltage source—anode = positive.

The common leg will be the longest of the four legs. If the longest leg is closest to the flat side of the LED's casing, it's a common cathode type. On the other hand, if the longest leg is nearer the lip (and hence furthest from the flat side), it's a common anode type.

We learned previously in Chapter 5, *Connecting Your Raspberry Pi to the Physical World*, how to set the brightness of a single LED using PWM, but what happens if we vary the brightness of the three individual colors in an RGB LED? We mix the individual colors to create new colors! Let's create a circuit and start mixing.

Creating the RGB LED circuit

In this section, we will create a simple circuit to control an RGB LED, and we will be using a *common cathode* RGB LED (that is, the three individual LEDs share a common GND connection).

We will start by building the circuit as shown in *Figure 8.2* on our breadboard:

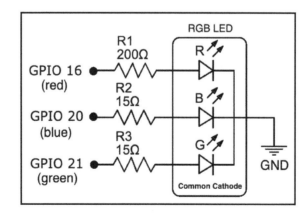

Figure 8.2 – Common cathode RGB LED schematic

Following is the accompanying breadboard layout for this schematic that we are about to build:

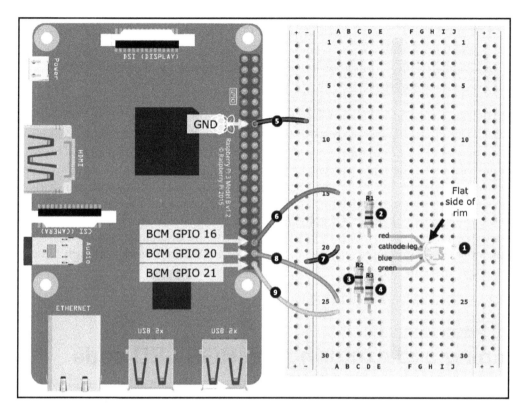

Figure 8.3 – Common cathode RGB LED circuit

Here are the steps to follow, which match the numbered black circles in *Figure 8.3*:

1. Start by placing the RGB LED into your breadboard, taking care to orientate the LED regarding the positioning of its cathode leg.
2. Position the 200Ω resistor (R1). One end of this resistor connects to the *red* leg of the LED.
3. Position the first 15Ω resistor (R2). One end of this resistor connects to the *blue* leg of the LED.
4. Position the second 15Ω resistor (R3). One end of this resistor connects to the *green* leg of the LED.
5. Connect a ground pin on your Raspberry Pi to the negative power rail.

6. Connect GPIO 16 on your Raspberry Pi to the other end of the 200Ω resistor (R1) you placed at *step 2*.
7. Connect the cathode leg of the RGB LED to the negative power rail.
8. Connect GPIO 20 on your Raspberry Pi to the other end of the 15Ω resistor (R2) you placed at *step 3*.
9. Connect GPIO 21 on your Raspberry Pi to the other end of the 15Ω resistor (R3) you placed at *step 4*.

Before we test our RGB LED circuit, let's briefly recap how we arrived at the 200Ω and 15Ω resistors in this circuit. The 200Ω resistor (R1) was derived using the same process we covered in `Chapter 6`, *Electronics 101 for the Software Engineer*. The 15Ω resistors for R2 and R3 are derived using the same process, with the difference being that the *typical forward voltage* used in the calculations for the blue and green LED was 3.2-volts. If you study the sample datasheet, you will notice that the forward voltage for the blue and green LEDs lists a maximum forward voltage of 4.0 volts. Even at the typical value of 3.2 volts, we are very close to the 3.3 volts of a Raspberry Pi GPIO pin. If you are unlucky to get an RGB LED needing more than 3.3 volts for its blue or green LED, it will not work—though I have never come across one...yet.

Now we are ready to test our RGB LED.

Running and exploring the RGB LED code

Now that you have your circuit ready, let's run our example code. Our example will light up the LED and make it alternate different colors. Here are the steps to follow:

1. Run the code in the `chapter08/rgbled_common_cathode.py` file and you should observe the RGB LED cycling colors. Take note of the first three colors, which should be red, green, and then blue.

 To use a **common anode** RGB LED, it needs to be wired differently than shown in *Figure 8.2*—the common anode leg must go to the +3.3V pin on your Raspberry Pi, while the GPIO connections remain the same. The other change is in code where we need to invert the PWM signals—you will find a file called `rgbled_common_anode.py` in the `chapter08` folder with the differences commented.

2. If your first three colors are not red, green, and then blue, your RGB LED may have its legs in a different order than the RGB LED's pictured in *Figure 8.1* and the circuit in *Figure 8.2*. What you will need to do is change the GPIO pin numbering in the code (see the following code snippets) and re-run the code until the color order is correct.

3. After the red, green, and then blue cycle, the RGB LED will animate a rainbow of colors before the program completes.

Let's discuss the interesting sections of the code and see how it works:

In line (1), we are importing `getrgb` from the `PIL.ImageColor` module. `getrgb` provides us with a convenient way to convert common color names such as red or hex values such as #FF0000 into their RGB component values such as (255, 0, 0):

```
from time import sleep
import pigpio
from PIL.ImageColor import getrgb      # (1)

GPIO_RED = 16
GPIO_GREEN = 20
GPIO_BLUE = 21

pi.set_PWM_range(GPIO_RED, 255)         # (2)
pi.set_PWM_frequency(GPIO_RED, 8000)
# ... truncated ...
```

Starting at line (2), we explicitly configure PWM for each of the GPIO pins (the duty cycle range of 255 and frequency of 8,000 are the PiGPIO defaults). The PWM duty cycle range of 0 to 255 maps perfectly into the RGB component color value range of 0...255, which we will see shortly is how we set the individual brightness of each color LED.

In the following code, in line (3), we have the `set_color()` definition, which is responsible for setting the color of our RGB LED. The `color` parameter can be either a common color name such as `yellow`, a HEX value such as #FFFF00, or one of the many formats that `getrgb()` can parse (see the `rgbled_common_cathode.py` source file for a list of common formats):

```
def set_color(color):                              # (3)
    rgb = getrgb(color)
    print("LED is {} ({})".format(color, rgb))
    pi.set_PWM_dutycycle(GPIO_RED,   rgb[0])       # (4)
    pi.set_PWM_dutycycle(GPIO_GREEN, rgb[1])
    pi.set_PWM_dutycycle(GPIO_BLUE,  rgb[2])
```

In line (4), we see how to use PWM with the individual GPIO pins to set the RBG LED's color. Continuing with yellow as our example, we see the following:

- GPIO_RED is set to a duty cycle of 0.
- GPIO_GREEN is set to a duty cycle of 255.
- GPIO_BLUE is set to a duty cycle of 255.

A duty cycle value for green and blue of 255 means that these LEDs are fully on and, as we know, mixing green and blue makes yellow.

As you browse the source file, you will encounter another two functions at lines (6) and (7):

```
def color_cycle(colors=("red", "green", "blue"), delay_secs=1):    # (6)
    # ...truncated...

def rainbow_example(loops=1, delay_secs=0.01):                     # (7)
    # ...truncated...
```

Both of these methods delegate to set_color(). color_cycle() loops through the list of colors provided as its color parameter, while rainbow_example() generates and loops through a range of colors to produce the rainbow sequence. These functions are what generated the light sequences when we ran the code in *step 1*.

Our RGB LED circuit comes with limitations and drawbacks:

- Firstly, we need three GPIO pins per RGB LED.
- Secondly, we're restricting the current to 8mA with the resistors so we cannot achieve maximum potential brightness of the individual LEDs (we would need ~20mA for full brightness).

While we could introduce transistors (or an appropriate multi-channel LED driver IC) to increase the current, our circuit would quickly become cumbersome! Luckily, there is another way we can create color with LEDs, and that is with addressable LEDs, which we'll look at next.

Controlling a multi-color APA102 LED strip with SPI

The APA102 is an addressable multi-color (RGB) LED that is controlled using a **Serial Peripheral Interface** (**SPI**). In simplistic terms, we *send instructions* to the LED asking it what color to display rather than individually controlling each of the three red-green-blue legs of the LED using PWM as we did in the previous example.

If you need a quick refresher on SPI, we covered it back in `Chapter 5`, *Connecting Your Raspberry Pi to the Physical World*. We will also discuss SPI further the context of the APA102, the Raspberry Pi, and Python after we explore APA102 specific code shortly.

APA102 LEDs can also be connected or chained together to create LED strips or LED matrices to create dynamic and multi-LED lighting and display solutions. Irrespective of how the LEDs are arranged, we control them using a common technique where we send multiple sets of instructions to a chain of APA102 LEDs. Each individual LED consumes one instruction and passes the rest on to be consumed by upstream LEDs. We will see this idea in action as we work with an APA102 LED strip shortly.

 APA102 LEDs also go by the name Super LEDs, DotStar LEDs, and sometimes Next Generation NeoPixels. There is also another addressable LED, the WS2812, also known as a NeoPixel. While similar in principle and operation, WS2812 RGB LEDs are not compatible with the APA102.

Let's create a circuit and run the code to control our APA102 LED strip.

Creating the APA102 circuit

In this section, we will create our APA102 circuit, as shown in the following diagram. We will do this on our breadboard in two parts:

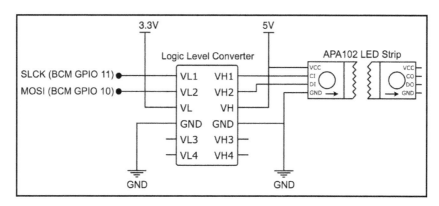

Figure 8.4 – APA102 LED strip circuit schematic

Let's get started on the first part, which will be to place the components and wire up the *low-voltage* side of a logic level converter:

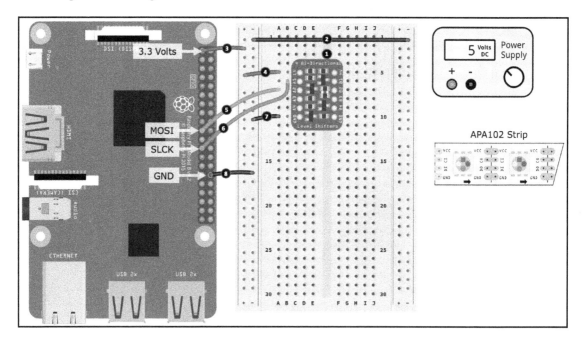

Figure 8.5 – APA102 LED circuit (part 1 of 2)

Here are the steps to follow. The step numbers match the numbered black circles in *Figure 8.5*:

1. Place the logic level converter (logic level shifter) into the breadboard, positioning the *low-voltage* side toward your Raspberry Pi. Different logic level converters may have different labeling, however, it should be clear which is the low-voltage side. In our illustration, one side has an **LV** (**Low Voltage**) terminal while the other has an **HV** (**High Voltage**) terminal, which distinguishes the sides.
2. Connect the negative rails on the left-hand side and right-hand side power rails.
3. Connect a 3.3-volt pin on your Raspberry Pi to the positive rail of the left-hand side power rail.
4. Connect the LV terminal on the logic level converter into the positive rail of the left-hand side power rail.
5. Connect the **MOSI** (**Master Out Slave In**) pin on your Raspberry Pi to the A2 terminal on the logic level converter.
6. Connect the **SLCK** (**Serial Clock**) pin on your Raspberry Pi to the A1 terminal on the logic level converter.
7. Connect the GND terminal on the logic level converter to the negative rail on the left-hand side power rail.
8. Connect the negative rail on the left-hand side power rail to a GND pin on your Raspberry Pi.

Now that we have wired the *low-voltage* side of the logic level converter to our Raspberry Pi, next we will wire the *high-voltage* side to the APA102 LED strip. As a reminder, Raspberry Pi GPIO pins operate at 3.3 volts (hence it's the *low* voltage) while the APA102 operates at 5 volts (hence it's the *high* voltage):

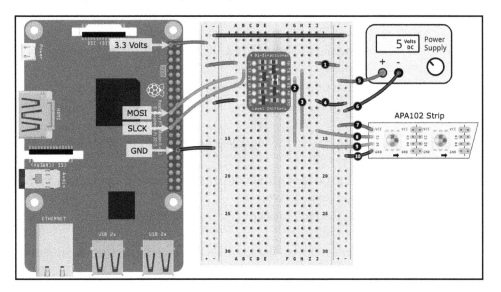

Figure 8.6 – APA102 LED circuit (part 2 of 2)

Here are the steps to follow for the second part of our build. The step numbers match the numbered black circles in *Figure 8.6*:

1. Connect the HV terminal of the logic level converter to the positive rail of the right-hand side power rail.
2. Place a jumper wire from terminal B2 to an unused row on your breadboard (in the illustration, this is shown at hole G16).
3. Place another jumper wire from terminal B1 to an unused row on your breadboard (in the illustration, this is shown at hole H14).
4. Connect the GND terminal on the high-voltage side of the logic level converter to the negative rail of the right-hand side power rail.
5. Connect the positive output of your power supply to the positive rail of the right-hand side power rail.
6. Connect the negative output of your power supply to the negative rail of the right-hand side power rail.
7. Connect the VCC terminal or wire of your APA102 LED strip to the positive rail of the right-hand side power rail.

Your APA102 must be connected the correct way around. You will notice the arrows on the APA102 LED strip shown in *Figure 8.4*. These arrows indicate the direction of the data flow. Make sure your APA102 LED strip arrows match the illustration (that is, the arrows are pointing away from the breadboard).

If your APA102 does not have the arrows, look at the naming of the terminals. One side of an LED strip may have CI/DI (I = Input), while the other side has DO/CO (O = Output). It's the *Input* side we need to connect to the logic level converter.

8. Connect the **CI** (**Clock Input**) terminal or wire of your APA102 LED strip to the wire you placed at *step 3* that connects back to the B1 terminal of the logic level converter.

9. Connect the **DI** (**Data Input**) terminal or wire of your APA102 LED strip to the wire you placed at *step 2* that connects back to the B2 terminal of the logic level converter.

10. Finally, connect the GND terminal or wire of your APA102 LED strip to the negative rail of the right-hand side power rail.

Well done! You have now completed your APA102 LED strip circuit. As you completed this circuit build, you will have noticed that we are using a logic level converter. This is because the APA102 requires 5-volt logic to operate *properly*. The APA102 datasheet explicitly mentions the minimum logic voltage to be 0.7 VDD, which is 0.7 x 5 volts = 3.5 volts, which is higher than the Raspberry Pi's 3.3-volt logic-level.

If you need a refresher on logic-levels and logic-level conversion, refer back to `Chapter 6`, *Electronics 101 for the Software Engineer*.

Let's consider the situation (in case you were wondering) that 3.3 volts is only slightly less than 3.5 volts—surely, that's close enough? You can try and control an APA102 with 3.3-volts, and it *may* give you some level of success. However, you *may* also experience some random effects and confusion—for example, random LEDs not turning on or off as expected, flickering LEDs, or LEDs displaying with the wrong color. Unfortunately, the APA102 is one of the 5-volt logic devices that are not 3.3-volt compatible, so we must take the extra step and use a logic level converter to meet its 3.5-volt minimum logic-level requirements.

Now that you have built your APA102 circuit, next we will discuss the considerations we need to think about to power this circuit.

Powering the APA102 circuit

In Chapter 7, *Turning Things On and Off,* we discussed the importance of knowing the current requirements of a "load" that you are using. Let's apply that learning to our APA102 LED strip so we can power it correctly. Our example is assuming a LED strip containing 60 LEDs, however, you will need to adjust the calculations based on the number of LEDs on your strip.

By the way of example, we have the following:

- An APA102 LED strip with 60 LEDs.
- Each LED uses (on average) a maximum of 25mA (from the datasheet and confirmed by measurement).
- The LED strip consumes approximately 15mA when idle (no LED is lit).

 A single RGB LED uses its maximum current when it is set to the color white, which is when each individual LED (red, green, and blue) are at their full brightness.

Using the preceding values, we can calculate our expected maximum current requirement for 60 LEDs, which is just over 1.5 amps:

$$(60 \times 25mA) + 15mA = 1515mA$$

If we work in the assumption that we are using a breadboard power supply, then if we conservatively assume that our breadboard power suppler can only supply around 700mA maximum, we cannot realistically turn on all LEDs on a 60 LED strip to full white. If we do, then (depending on the power supply) it could turn off if its internal overload protection kicks in, it might go up in a puff of smoke, or it might limit its output current, which we may observe as the LEDs looking reddish rather than white.

Let's work backward to work out the safe number of LEDs that we can power from a 700mA power supply:

$$\frac{(700mA - 15mA)}{25mA} = 27$$

If we then subtract 2 LEDs (50mA) as a small safety buffer, we get 25 LEDs. Remember this number (or the number you calculate) as we will need it next when we run our example code.

After calculating the number of safe LEDs you can use with your power supply, we are now ready to configure and run our Python example.

Configuring and running the APA102 LED strip code

Now that you have your circuit ready and our LED strip's expected current usage, let's configure and light up our LED strip:

1. Edit the `chapter08/apa102_led_strip.py` file and look for the following line near the top of the file. Adjust the number to be the number of safe LEDs you calculated previously, or the number of LEDs on your strip if it had a suitably capable power supply:

   ```
   NUM_LEDS = 60      # (2)
   ```

2. Save your edits and run the code. If everything is connected correctly, you should observe the LEDs on the strip cycle through the colors red, green, and blue and then perform a few different light sequences.

If your LED strip is not working, check out the *APA102 LED strip troubleshooting tips* later in the section.

If your strip does not show red, green, and blue in that order, then you would need to adjust code to set the correct order—I'll show you where in the code you can adjust the LED ordering when we come to that section of code shortly.

With our safe number of LEDs now configured in code, let's walk through the code to see how it works.

APA102 LED strip code walkthrough

Starting at line (1) in the following code, we have the imports. We will be using a Python `deque` collection instance (I'll just refer to is as an array for simplicity) to model in-memory the APA102 LED strip—we will build up and manipulate the order of colors we want each individual LED on to display in this array before applying it to the LED strip. We then import the `getrgb` function from the PIL library for working with color formats (as we did in the preceding RGB LED example):

```
# ...truncated...
from collections import deque                                      # (1)
```

```
from PIL.ImageColor import getrgb
from luma.core.render import canvas
from luma.led_matrix.device import apa102
from luma.core.interface.serial import spi, bitbang
```

Lastly, the three `luma` imports are for the APA102 LED strip control. Luma is a mature high-level library for working with a range of common display devices using Python. It has support for LCDs, LED strips and matrices, and much more, including OLED displays, which we will cover later in this chapter.

We can only scratch the surface of what can be done with the Luma library in this chapter, so I encourage you to explore its documentation and range of examples—you'll find links in the *Further reading* section at the end of this chapter.

Next, we come to line (3) in the following code, where we assign `color_buffer` to an instance of `deque` that is initialized with the same number of elements as there are LEDs in our strip. Each element defaults to black (that is, the LED is off):

```
# ...truncated...
color_buffer = deque(['black']*NUM_LEDS, maxlen=NUM_LEDS)        # (3)
```

In line (4) in the following code, we start to create our software interface to the APA102. Here, we are creating a `spi()` instance representing the default hardware SPI0 interface on the Raspberry Pi. To use this interface, your APA102 must be connected to the SPI pins on your Raspberry Pi, which are as follows:

- DI connected to MOSI
- CI connected to SCLK

In the following code snippet `port=0` and `device=0` relate to the SPI0 interface:

```
# ...truncated...
serial = spi(port=0, device=0, bus_speed_hz=2000000)              # (4)
```

The `bus_speed_hz` parameter sets the speed of the SPI interface and, for our examples, we lower it from its default value of 8,000,000 to 2,000,000 just to ensure that your logic level converter will work. Not all logic level converters are the same, and they will have a maximum speed at which they can convert logic levels. If the SPI interface operates faster than the logic level converter can convert, our circuit will not work.

In line (5) in the following code—which is commented out—we have a software alternative to hardware SPI known as big-banging, which will work on any GPIO pins at the expense of speed. It's similar to the software versus hardware PWM trade-off we discussed back in Chapter 5, *Connecting Your Raspberry Pi to the Physical World*:

```
# ...truncated...
# serial = bitbang(SCLK=13, SDA=6)                              # (5)

# ...truncated...
device = apa102(serial_interface=serial, cascaded=NUM_LEDS)    # (6)
```

In line (6) in the preceding code, we created an instance of the `apa102` class specifying the `serial` instance we just created, and the number of LEDs in our strip. From this point forward in code, to interact with our APA102 LED strip, we use the `device` instance.

To initialize our LED strip, in line (7) in the following code, we call `device.clear()` and set the default global contrast to 128 (so, half brightness). You can adjust this level to find a brightness that you are comfortable with, remembering that more contrast/brightness means more current usage. Note that previously when we calculated the number of safe LEDs, the 25mA per LED used in the calculations assumed maximum brightness (that is, 255):

```
device.clear()                                                 # (7)
contrast_level = 128 # 0 (off) to 255 (maximum brightness)
device.contrast(contrast_level)
```

In line (8) in the following code, we have the `set_color()` function. We use this function to set individual or all elements to a specified color in the `color_buffer` array. This is how we build up in-memory the color arrangements we want our APA102 LED strip to display:

```
def set_color(color='black', index=-1):                        # (8)
    if index == -1:
        global color_buffer
        color_buffer = deque([color]*NUM_LEDS, maxlen=NUM_LEDS)
    else:
        color_buffer[index] = color
```

Now, we will jump to line (12) in the following code block to the `update()` function. This function loops through `color_buffer` and, using the Luma `device` instance representing our APA102, it feeds the device the colors to display using `draw.point((led_pos, 0), fill=color)`. This is the magic of the Luma library—it shields us from the lower level APA102 and SPI data and hardware protocols by giving us a very simple software interface to use.

If you want to learn more about lower level SPI use and protocols, then APA102 is a good place to start. Start by reading the APA102 datasheet for its data protocol, then find a simple APA102 module on `pypi.org` or GitHub and review its code. There is also an APA102 example that can be found on the PiGPIO website—a link is included in the *Further reading* section.

It's important to remember that `update()` needs to be called after you make changes to `color_buffer`:

```
def update():                                               # (12)
    with canvas(device) as draw:
        for led_pos in range(0, len(color_buffer)):
            color = color_buffer[led_pos]

            ## If your LED strip's colors are are not in the expected
            ## order, uncomment the following lines and adjust the indexes
            ## in the line color = (rgb[0], rgb[1], rgb[2])
            # rgb = getrgb(color)
            # color = (rgb[0], rgb[1], rgb[2])
            # if len(rgb) == 4:
            #     color += (rgb[3],)   # Add in Alpha

            draw.point((led_pos, 0), fill=color)
```

If, for some reason, you find your LED strip colors are not in the standard red, green, and blue order then the preceding commented-out section of code can be used to change the color order. I've never encountered a non-standard APA102, but I have read about addressable RGB LEDs having non-standard ordering, so I thought I'd just drop that bit of code in, just in case.

Moving on to lines (9), (10), and (11), we have three functions that simply manipulate `color_buffer`:

```
def push_color(color):                                      # (9)
    color_buffer.appendleft(color)

def set_pattern(colors=('green', 'blue', 'red')):           # (10)
    range(0, int(ceil(float(NUM_LEDS)/float(len(colors))))):
        for color in colors:
            push_color(color)

def rotate_colors(count=1):                                 # (11)
    color_buffer.rotate(count)
```

push_color(color) in line (9) pushes a new color into color_buffer at index 0 while set_pattern() in line (10) fills color_buffer with a repeating color pattern sequence. rotate_colors() in line (11) rotates the colors in color_buffer (and wraps them around—the last one becomes for the first one). You can rotate backward by using a count value < 0.

Finally, toward the end of the source code, we have the following functions that provide the examples you saw when you run the file. These functions use combinations of the functions discussed previously to control the LED strip:

- cycle_colors(colors=("red", "green", "blue"), delay_secs=1)
- pattern_example()
- rotate_example(colors=("red", "green", "blue"), rounds=2, delay_secs=0.02)
- rainbow_example(rounds=1, delay_secs=0.01)

We will complete our coverage of the APA102 with a few concluding notes on its use of the SPI interface.

Discussion of APA102 and the SPI interface

If you cast your mind back to Chapter 5, *Connecting Your Raspberry Pi to the Physical World*, where we discussed **Serial Peripheral Interface** (**SPI**), you may remember that we mentioned it uses four wires for data transfer. However, if you consider our circuit in *Figure 8.6*, we're only using two wires (DI and CI), not four. What's going on?

Here is the SPI mapping for the APA102:

- **Master-Out-Slave-In** (**MOSI**) on your Raspberry Pi connects to **Data In** (**DI**) on the APA102. Here, your Raspberry Pi is the *master* sending data to the *slave* APA102 LEDs on the strip.
- **Master-In-Slave-Out** (**MISO**) is not connected because the APA102 does not need to send data back to the Raspberry Pi.
- SCLK on your Raspberry Pi connect to the **Clock In** (**CI**) on the APA102.
- **Client Enable/Slave Select** (**CE/SS**) is not connected.

The last line CE/SS of importance and worthy of further discussion. A CE/SS channel is used by a master device to tell a specific slave device that it's about to receive data. It's this mechanism that allows a single SPI master to control multiple SPI slaves.

But, we're not (and cannot) use CE/SS it with the APA102 because we have nowhere to connect the CE/SS pins to. The implication of this is that the APA102 is always listing for instructions from a master, effectively hogging the SPI channel.

If we are using an APA102 (or any device that has no CE/SS), then we cannot connect more than one SPI device to a master's hardware SPI, unless we take extra steps. Some of the options are as follows:

- Use big-banging on generic GPIO pins if the performance reduction does not have adverse effects.
- Enable hardware SPI1 on your Raspberry Pi. It's not enabled by default and requires editing /boot/config.txt. You'll find instructions and tips if you search the web for *Raspberry Pi enable SPI1*.
- Find a logic level converter that includes an enable pin and write code to manually control this pin as a proxy CE/SS.

We will conclude this section on the APA102 with a few troubleshooting tips.

APA102 LED strip troubleshooting tips

If you cannot get your APA102 to light up or if you find that random LEDs are not turning on or off or they are displaying unexpected colors or random flickers, try the following:

- The APA102 needs 5-volt logic: Make sure you are using a logic level converter and that is connected the correct way around—HV to 5 volts and LV to 3.3 volts.
- Ensure that the DI/CI side of the APA102 is connected to the logic level converter.
- Make sure your power source can supply enough current. As an example, under-supply of current or voltage can make white look more like red.
- Make sure the ground of your power supply is connected to a ground pin on your Raspberry Pi.
- If you are using big banging, move to hardware SPI.
- If using the hardware SPI (that is, creating an instance of the spi() class), try the following:
    - If you are receiving the error *SPI device not found*, make sure SPI has been enabled in the Raspbian OS. We covered this in Chapter 1, *Setting Up Your Development Environment*.

- If you have been using GPIO 8,9, 10, or 11 previously for general I/O, then either disable and re-enable the SPI interface as per the preceding point or reboot your Raspberry Pi to reset the hardware SPI interface.
- Try lowering the SPI bus speed in case your logic level converter cannot keep up—that is, it cannot convert 3.3-volt to 5-volt signals as fast as the SPI interface is producing them (hint: lower the `bus_speed_hz` parameter in `serial = spi(port=0, device=0, bus_speed_hz=2000000)` to 1,000,000 or 500,000).
- Connect the APA102's DI and CI directly to SDA and SCLK on the Raspberry Pi. The goal here is to bypass the logic level converter to rule it out as the problem.

Well done! This was a lengthy and detailed section on the APA102. We covered a lot of concepts in addition to the APA102 itself, including how to calculate the power requirements of a LED strip and an introduction to the Luma library, which can be used to control a host of different lighting and display devices besides the APA102. Then, we concluded with practical troubleshooting tips in case your APA102 circuit, setup, or code did not work on the first go.

All of this knowledge and experience will be adaptable to similar lighting projects you undertake and SPI-based projects in general. In particular, it will be a helpful reference to calculate the power requirements of lighting projects and troubleshoot circuits and code when they do not work. It also provides the basic foundations that we will be building on in the next section where we look at how to interface an OLED display with our Raspberry Pi.

Using an OLED display

An **OLED** or **Organic LED** display is a type of technology used to make screens. Our example will be using an SSD1306, which is a monochrome 128x64 pixel display, however, the information will apply to other OLED displays too.

Our sample program will read your Raspberry Pi's CPU temperature and display it on the OLED display together with a thermometer icon. We will be assuming the OLED will connect using an I2C interface, however, an SPI interface device should also be compatible if you use an `spi()` instance (like in the APA102 example) for the `serial` object. The ability to change the interacting method used by the Luma library means you can reuse existing code with compatible display devices with minimal code changes.

We will commence by connecting the OLED display to the Raspberry Pi and verifying that it is connected.

Connecting the OLED display

Let's connect your OLED display to your Raspberry Pi, as shown in *Figure 8.7*:

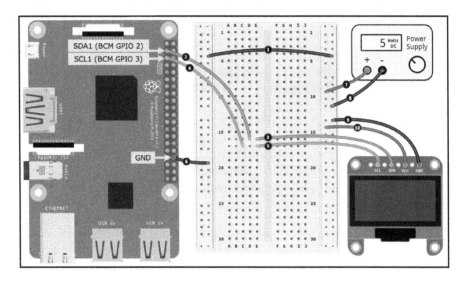

Figure 8.7 – I2C OLED display circuit

 IMPORTANT NOTE ON POWERING YOUR OLED: Our circuit, shown in *Figure 8.6*, and the associated discussion uses a 5-volt power supply. If you consult the SSD1306 OLED datasheet mentioned at the beginning of this chapter, you will discover that it mentions a minimum supply voltage of 7 volts. Furthermore, you will find other sources and SSD1306 OLED modules that indicate different voltage requirements. **Please consult the documentation or place of purchase to obtain the correct operating voltage for your OLED and adjust the supply voltage as required (*steps 7 and 8* in the following list).**

You can connect the OLED with the following steps, which correspond to the numbered black circles in *Figure 8.7*:

1. Connect the negative rails on the left-hand side and right-hand side power rails.

2. Connect the SDA1 (Data) pin of your Raspberry Pi into a vacant row on your breadboard.

3. Connect the SDA (Data) terminal or wire of your OLED display into the same row use used for *step 2*.

4. Connect the SCL1 (Clock) pin of your Raspberry Pi into a vacant row on your breadboard.

5. Connect the SCL (Clock) terminal or wire of your OLED display into the same row use used for *step 4*.

6. Connect a GND Pin on your Raspberry Pi to the negative rail of the left-hand side power rail.

7. Connect the positive output of a 5-volt power supply to the positive rail of the right-hand side power rail.

8. Connect the negative output of a 5-volt power supply to the negative rail of the right-hand side power rail.

9. Connect the GND terminal or wire of your OLED display to the negative rail of the right-hand side power rail.

10. Connect the VCC terminal or wire of your OLED display (it might also be named VDD, Vin, V+, or something similar indicating a voltage input) to the positive rail of the right-hand side power rail.

Good job! This completes our OLED circuit. As you can see, we are powering the OLED from a 5-volt power supply, however, the SDA (Data)/SLC (Clock) channels are connected directly to your Raspberry Pi. Unlike the APA102 LED strip we used in the previous section, the SSD1306 OLED is 3.3-volt logic compatible, hence, we do not need a logic level converter to convert logic level voltages on the clock and data channels.

Let's briefly consider the current requirements for the SSD1306 OLED. My testing resulted in the following current measurements:

- Black screen: ~3mA
- White screen (every pixel on): ~27mA

At a maximum current usage of ~27mA, you can try connecting the +5V to the Raspberry Pi's 5-volt pin, but remember this will take reserve current away from your Raspberry Pi (and it may reset when you run the code if your Raspberry Pi's power supply is not adequate).

 If you need a recap on current measurement using a digital multimeter, please refer to Chapter 7, *Turning Things On and Off*.

With your OLED connected to your Raspberry Pi's SDA and SCL pins next, we will verify that it has been detected by your Raspberry Pi using the `i2cdetect` utility.

Verifying whether the OLED display is connected

Previously, in Chapter 5, *Connecting Your Raspberry Pi to the Physical World,* we used the `i2cdetect` command-line tool to check whether an I2C device was connected and to verify its I2C address. Check that your Raspberry Pi can see your OLED display by running the following in a Terminal:

```
$ i2cdetect -y 1
```

If your OLED is connected, you will see the following output, which tells us that the OLED was detected and has the hex address, `0x3C`:

```
# ...truncated...
30: -- -- -- -- -- -- -- -- -- -- -- -- 3c -- -- --
# ...truncated...
```

If your address is different, that's okay, we just need to adjust the address in code which we will do next.

Configuring and running the OLED example

The code we are about to explore is contained in the `chapter08/oled_cpu_temp.py` file. Please review this file to get an overall view of what it contains before continuing:

1. If the OLED I2C address you obtained in the preceding was different to `0x3C`, find the following line in the source code and update the address parameter to match your OLED I2C address:

   ```
   serial = i2c(port=1, address=0x3C)
   ```

2. Run the program, and you should observe the CPU temperature and a thermometer icon drawn on the OLED display.

Once you have configured your OLED display address in code and confirmed the example works on your OLED, we are ready to review the code and learn how it works.

OLED code walkthrough

Commencing with the imports, in line (1), we import classes from the **PIL (Pillow)** module, which we use to create the image we want to render on the OLED display. We also import several other classes from the Luma module related to our SSD1306 OLED and its I2C interface (SPI is also imported for reference).

We see how to create an I2C instance in line (2) representing the interface that our OLED is connected to. Commented out is an SPI alternative. In line (3), we create an instance of ssd1306 that represents our OLED display and assign it to the device variable. If you are using a different OLED display than the SSD1306, you will need to identify and adjust the ssd1306 import line, and the device instance created in line (3):

```
from PIL import Image, ImageDraw, ImageFont          # (1)
from luma.core.interface.serial import i2c, spi
from luma.core.render import canvas
from luma.oled.device import ssd1306
#...truncated...

# OLED display is using I2C at address 0x3C
serial = i2c(port=1, address=0x3C)                   # (2)
#serial = spi(port=0, device=0)

device = ssd1306(serial)                             # (3)
device.clear()
print("Screen Dimensions (WxH):", device.size)
```

In line (4), we encounter the get_cpu_temp() function, which calls a command-line utility to retrieve your Raspberry Pi's CPU temperature before parsing and returning the result that we will use shortly to construct our display image:

```
def get_cpu_temp():      # (4)
    temp = os.popen("vcgencmd measure_temp").readline() # Eg 62.5'C
    data = temp.strip().upper().replace("TEMP=", "").split("'")
    data[0] = float(data[0])

    if data[1] == 'F':  # To Celsius just in case it ever returns
Fahrenheit
        data[0] = (data[0] - 32) * 5/9
        data[1] = 'C'

    return (data[0], data[1])  # Eg (62.5, 'C')
```

In the following code in line (5), we define temperature thresholds that influence the icon we show on our OLED display. We will also use the high threshold to make the OLED display blink to help to create a visual attention-grabber.

In line (6), we load in three thermometer images and scale them down starting at line (7) to a size that is workable with the 128x64 pixel dimensions of our SSD1306 OLED:

```
# Temperature thresholds used to switch thermometer icons
temp_low_threshold = 60    # degrees Celsius                          # (5)
temp_high_threshold = 85   # degrees Celsius

# Thermometer icons
image_high = Image.open("temp_high.png")                             # (6)
image_med  = Image.open("temp_med.png")
image_low  = Image.open("temp_low.png")

# Scale thermometer icons (WxH)
aspect_ratio = image_low.size[0] / image_low.size[1]                 # (7)
height = 50
width = int(height * aspect_ratio)
image_high = image_high.resize((width, height))
image_med  = image_med.resize((width, height))
image_low  = image_low.resize((width, height))
```

Next, we define two variables starting at line (8) in the following. `refresh_secs` is the rate at which we check the CPU temperature and update the OLED display while `high_alert` is used to flag a breach of the maximum temperature threshold and start the screen blinking:

```
refresh_secs = 0.5   # Display refresh rate                           #(8)
high_alert = False # Used for screen blinking when high temperature

try:
    while True:
        current_temp = get_cpu_temp()
        temp_image = None

        canvas = Image.new("RGB", device.size, "black")              # (9)
        draw = ImageDraw.Draw(canvas)                                # (10)
        draw.rectangle(((0,0),
                (device.size[0]-1, device.size[1]-1)),
                outline="white")
```

In the `while` loop, in line (9), we see the use of the PIL module. Here, we are creating a blank image using the same dimensions as the OLED device (that is, 128x64 for the SSD1306) and storing it in the `canvas` variable. In subsequent code, we manipulate this in-memory canvas image before sending it to the SSD1306 for rendering.

The draw instance created in line (10) is a PIL helper class that we use for drawing on the canvas. We use this instance for placing a bounding rectangle around the canvas and will use it later to add text to the canvas. The `draw` instance can also be used to draw many other shapes including lines, arcs, and circles. A link to the PIL API documentation can be found in the *Further reading* section.

The block of code starting at line (11) in the following is what will make our OLED display blink when `high_alert` is `True`:

```
if high_alert:                                   # (11)
    device.display(canvas.convert(device.mode))
    high_alert = False
    sleep(refresh_secs)
    continue
```

Starting at line (12), we compare the temperature reading we obtained from `get_cpu_temp()` to the threshold values defined earlier. Depending on the result, we change the thermometer image that will be shown, and for a high threshold breach, we set `high_alert = True`. Setting `high_alert` to `True` will cause the OLED display to blink on the next loop iteration:

```
if current_temp[0] < temp_low_threshold:        # (12)
    temp_image = image_low
    high_alert = False

elif current_temp[0] > temp_high_threshold:
    temp_image = image_high
    high_alert = True

else:
    temp_image = image_med
    high_alert = False
```

We start constructing our display starting at line (13) in the following. We calculate `image_xy` to be a point at which our thermometer image would be centered on the display and then offset that point using the `image_x_offset` and `image_x_offset` variables to move the image into the position we want it rendered.

In line (14), we then paste our thermometer image onto the canvas:

```
# Temperature Icon
image_x_offset = -40                              # (13)
image_y_offset = +7
image_xy = (((device.width - temp_image.size[0]) // 2) +
        image_x_offset, ((device.height - temp_image.size[1]) // 2)
        + image_y_offset)
canvas.paste(temp_image, image_xy)        # (14)
```

Moving on to line (15) in the following code block, we create the text we want to display on our OLED screen and use the same technique as for the image to position the text on the canvas in line (17). Notice the use of `draw.textsize()` to obtain the pixel dimensions of the text.

In line (16), we set `font = None` to use a default system font for the example because I cannot be entirely sure what fonts you have available on your Raspberry Pi. The line after line (16) that is commented out shows an example of using a custom font.

Run the `fc-list` command in a Terminal to see a list of fonts installed on your Raspberry Pi.

Finally, in line (18), we draw the text on the canvas:

```
# Temperature Text (\u00b0 is a 'degree' symbol)            # (15)
text = "{}\u00b0{}".format(current_temp[0], current_temp[1]) # Eg 43'C

font = None # Use a default font.                          # (16)
# font = ImageFont.truetype(font="Lato-Semibold.ttf", size=20)

text_size = draw.textsize(text, font=font)                 # (17)
text_x_offset = +15
text_y_offset = 0
text_xy = (((device.width - text_size[0]) // 2) + text_x_offset,
((device.height -  text_size[1]) // 2) + text_y_offset)
draw.text(text_xy, text, fill="white", font=font)          # (18)
```

We have now reached the tail-end of the while loop. In line (19) in the following code, we use the `device` instance that represents the SSD1306 OLED display to display `canvas`. The `canvas.convert(device.mode)` call converts the canvas image that we created into a format usable by the SSD1306:

```
# Render display with canvas
device.display(canvas.convert(device.mode))          # (19)
sleep(refresh_secs)
```

Before we complete our exploration of OLEDs, I want to point you to more examples. The Luma library contains an extensive range of examples covering many aspects of using an OLED display. A link to the examples can be found in *Further reading*.

OLED displays are low cost, small in size, and light on power consumption, so you frequently find them used in battery-operated devices. If you want to explore other display options for your Raspberry Pi, you might like to investigate the range of Raspberry Pi TFT displays that are available (just search for that term on sites such as eBay.com or Banggood.com). These are full-color mini-monitors for your Raspberry Pi, and there are even touch-screen options available.

This now concludes our coverage of lighting and displays with our Raspberry Pi and Python. The knowledge you have learned so far will enable you to use and correctly power your own simple LED lighting projects and leverage a range of OLED displays for those projects where you wish to display textual and graphical information to users.

To conclude the exercises for this chapter, next, we will revisit **Pulse-Width-Modulation (PWM)** briefly and see how we can use it to generate sound.

Making sound with buzzers and PWM

In the final section of this chapter, we will walk through an example of how to make simple sound and music with PWM. Our sample program is going to play a musical scale on the buzzer, and we will be using a music score format called **Ring Tone Text Transfer Language (RTTTL)**, which was developed by Nokia in the pre-smartphone era for creating ringtones. As we learn, we can use a simple Python library to parse an RTTTL music score and turn its notes into a PWM frequency and duration that can then be used to associate a buzzer to create an auditable tune.

To make a sound with PWM, we need a form of a speaker, and we will be using what is known as a *passive* buzzer. Buzzers come in two basic forms:

- **Active buzzers**: These buzzers contain an internal oscillator that generates a single set tone. All you need to do us apply a DC voltage to an active buzzer and it will make a noise.
- **Passive buzzers**: These do not contain any internal smarts to make them work, so the oscillating must be done by the controlling device. The upside of this is that we can set and change the tone as we wish, and we can achieve this using PWM.

Now that we understand a little about how to make sound with buzzers, let's continue and create our sound-making circuit.

Building the RTTTL circuit

In this section, we will be building a circuit to drive a passive buzzer. This circuit, shown in *Figure 8.8* is very similar to the MOSFET circuit that we covered in `Chapter 7`, *Turning Things On and Off*, only this time with a buzzer connected as the load:

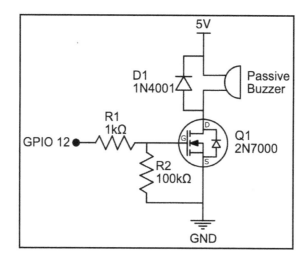

Figure 8.8 – Buzzer driver circuit Schematic

We will start our circuit build by placing the components onto our breadboard:

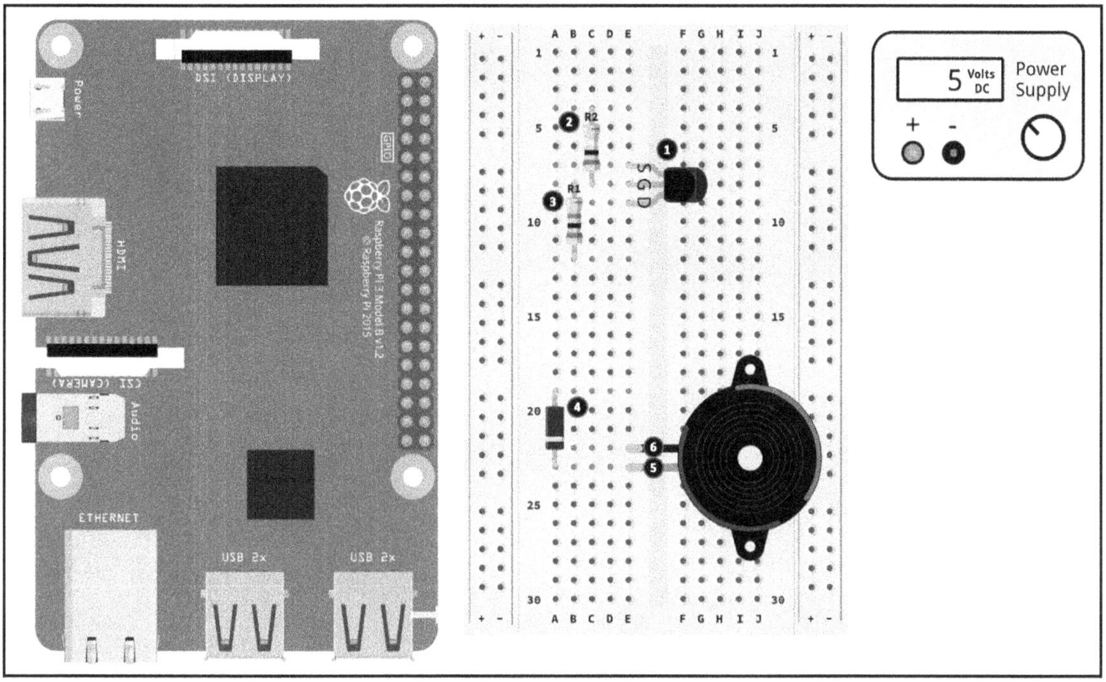

Figure 8.9 – Buzzer driver circuit (part 1 of 2)

The following step numbers match the numbered black circles in *Figure 8.9*:

1. Place the MOSFET onto the breadboard, paying attention to the orientation of the component with regards to the legs. Please see *Figure 7.7* in Chapter 7, *Turning Things On and Off*, if you need help to identify the MOSFET's legs.
2. Place the 100kΩ resistor (R2) into your breadboard. One end of this resistor shares the same row as the MOSFET's Gate (G) leg.
3. Place the 1kΩ resistor (R1) into your breadboard. One end of this resistor also shares the same row as the MOSFET's Gate (G) leg.
4. Place the diode into your breadboard, with the cathode leg (the leg at the end with the band) pointing toward the end of the breadboard.
5. Connect the positive wire of your buzzer into the same row shared by the diode's cathode leg.
6. Connect the negative wire of your buzzer into a vacant breadboard row.

Now that we have laid the components, let's wire them up:

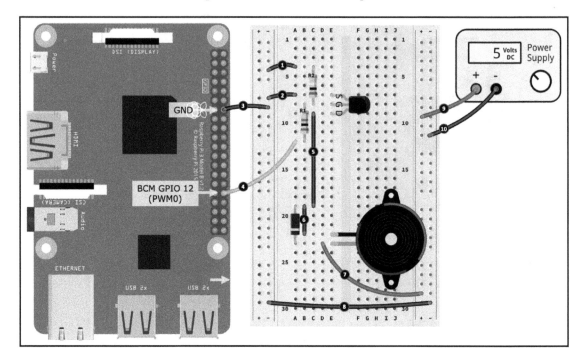

Figure 8.10 – Buzzer driver circuit (part 2 of 2)

The following step numbers match the numbered black circles in *Figure 8.10*:

1. Connect the negative rail of the left-hand side power rail to the 1kΩ resistor (R2).
2. Connect the Source leg (S) of the MOSFET to the negative rail of the left-hand side power rail.
3. Connect the negative rail of the left-hand side power rail to a GND pin on your Raspberry Pi.
4. Connect the end of the 100kΩ resistor (R1) to GPIO 12/PWM0 on your Raspberry Pi. As a reminder, GPIO 12 in its alternative function is channel PWM0, a hardware PWM pin.
5. Connect the Drain leg (D) of the MOSFET to the anode leg of the diode.
6. Connect the anode leg of the diode to the negative wire of your buzzer.
7. Connect the buzzer's positive wire/diode's cathode leg into the positive rail of the right-hand side power rail.
8. Connect the negative rails of the left-hand side and right-hand side power rails.

9. Connect the positive output of the power supply to the positive rail of the right-hand side power rail.

10. Connect the negative output of the power supply to the negative rail of the right-hand side power rail.

Now that you have completed this circuit build, we will proceed and run our Python example, which will make some music!

Running the RTTTL music example

Run the code in the chapter08/passive_buzzer_rtttl.py file, and your buzzer will play a simple musical scale.

The code to perform this is quite simple. In line (1) in the following code, we are using the rtttl module to parse an RTTTL music score into a series of notes defined by frequency and duration. Our score is stored in the rtttl_score variable:

```
from rtttl import parse_rtttl
rtttl_score = parse_rtttl("Scale:d=4,o=4,b=125:8a,8b,       # (1)
    8c#,8d,8e,8f#,8g#,8f#,8e,8d,8c#,8b,8a")
```

Next, in line (2), we loop through the parsed notes in rtttl_score and extract the frequency and duration:

```
for note in rtttl_score['notes']:                    # (2)
    frequency = int(note['frequency'])
    duration = note['duration'] # Milliseconds
    pi.hardware_PWM(BUZZER_GPIO, frequency, duty_cycle)  # (3)
    sleep(duration/1000)                             # (4)
```

In line (3), we set the frequency on the buzzer's GPIO pin using PWM, and hold the note for its duration at line (4) before continuing to the next note.

In line (3), note that we are using PiGPIO's hardware_PWM() and that BUZZER_GPIO *must* be a hardware compatible PWM pin. PiGPIO's hardware-timed PWM (which is available on any GPIO pin) is not suitable for music creation because it is restricted to a discrete range of frequencies. If you need a refresher on PWM techniques, revisit Chapter 5, *Connecting Your Raspberry Pi to the Physical World*.

Making music with RTTTL is very electronic-sounding, so to speak, and is a popular technique with resource-limited microcontrollers. However, remember that, with our Raspberry Pi, we have more than enough resources and the built-in hardware to play rich media such as MP3s.

 Try a web search for *RTTTL Songs* and you'll find many scores for songs, retro computer games, and TV and movie themes.

If you want to explore playing and controlling MP3s via Python, you'll find many resources, tutorials, and examples across the web. Unfortunately, there are many ways to achieve this task (including changes across different versions of Raspbian OS), so it can be a bit finicky at times getting your Raspberry Pi and Raspbian OS set up and configured reliably. If you go down this route, my recommendation is to explore playing MP3s and controlling audio (that is, changing volume) on the command line first. Once you have a stable and reliable setup, then proceed to explore a Python-based way.

Summary

In this chapter, we learned how to use PWM to set the color of an RGB LED and that a standalone single RGB LED requires three dedicated GPIO pins to work—one for each of the colors, red, green, and blue. We then explored another type of RGB LED, the APA102, which is a 2-wire SPI controllable device that can be chained together to create LED lighting strips. Next, we learned how to use an OLED display by creating an example application that displayed your Raspberry Pi's CPU temperature. We concluded with an example of using PWM together with a passive buzzer to make sound by parsing an RTTTL music score.

What you have learned in this chapter will allow you to add visual and auditable feedback to your own projects. You will also be able to extend your learning to other types of displays with relative ease, as the Luma library we have used is capable of working with a range of other display types and models in addition to the APA102 LED strip and SSD1306 OLED devices we used in this chapter.

In the next chapter, we will be looking at components and techniques to measure environmental conditions including temperature, humidity, and light.

Questions

As we conclude, here is a list of questions for you to test your knowledge regarding this chapter's material. You will find the answers in the *Assessments* section of the book:

1. Your APA102 LED strip is set to show all LEDs as white, but instead, all of the LEDs look reddish. What could be the problem?
2. What limitation does the APA102 place on SPI?
3. Your APA102 does not work when you use a logic level converter but appears to work when you connect it directly to the MOSI and SCK pins on your Raspberry Pi (hence bypassing the logic level converter). What are some possible causes of the problem?
4. What is the basic process for creating and displaying an image on an OLED display using the Luma OLED library?
5. What is RTTTL?

Further reading

An APA102 is a good choice to commence your learning on lower level data protocol and communication. After reviewing the APA102 datasheet for its data protocol (see the link under *Technical requirements* at the start of this chapter), the next logical step is to review some lower-level code. The APA102 example for PiGPIO is a one such starting point, but you'll find others on PyPi.org:

* `http://abyz.me.uk/rpi/pigpio/examples.html#Python_test-APA102_py`

The Luma suite of libraries offers many high-level modules for integrating common display with a Raspberry Pi beyond the APA102 and SSD1306 OLED we covered in this chapter. Furthermore, Luma contains an extensive range of examples:

* Luma: `https://pypi.org/project/luma.core` (follow the links for different display types)
* Luma examples on GitHub: `https://github.com/rm-hull/luma.examples`

Luma uses a PIL (Python Imaging Library)/Pillow comparable API for drawing and manipulating displays. We specifically used `ImageDraw` in our OLED example. You will find the PIL API documentation at the following link:

- `https://pillow.readthedocs.io`

If you would like to explore the RTTTL format further, its Wikipedia site is an excellent starting point:

- RTTTL `https://en.wikipedia.org/wiki/Ring_Tone_Transfer_Language`

9
Measuring Temperature, Humidity, and Light Levels

In the previous chapter, we explored two methods of making color with RGB LEDs – using a common RGB LED and with an addressable APA102 RGB LED strip. We also learned how to use a simple OLED display and how PWM can be used to play music using a passive buzzer.

In this chapter, we will be looking at some common components and circuits for collecting environmental data, including temperature, humidity, whether it's dark or light, and how to detect moisture.

The circuits and code examples we will learn will be useful for building and experimenting with your own environmental monitoring projects. These circuits can be considered input or sensor circuits that measure environmental conditions. By way of example, you could combine the circuit ideas and examples from Chapter 7, *Turning Things On and Off*, to switch on a pump to water a plant when the soil is dry, or switch on a low-voltage LED lamp when it gets dark. In fact, we have an example of a visualization platform in Chapter 13, *IoT Visualization and Automation Platforms*, where we will capture, record, and visualize historical temperature and humidity data using one of the circuits from this chapter!

Furthermore, throughout this chapter, we will see practical examples of analog electronics and associated concepts such as a voltage divider, which we learned about in Chapter 6, *Electronics 101 for the Software Engineer*.

Here is what we will cover in this chapter:

- Measuring temperature and humidity
- Detecting light
- Detecting moisture

Technical requirements

To perform the exercises in this chapter, you will need the following:

- Raspberry Pi 4 Model B
- Raspbian OS Buster (with desktop and recommended software)
- Minimum Python version 3.5

These requirements are what the code examples in this book are based on. It's reasonable to expect that the code examples should work without modification on Raspberry Pi 3 Model B or a different version of Raspbian OS as long as your Python version is 3.5 or higher.

You will find this chapter's source code in the `chapter09` folder in the GitHub repository available at `https://github.com/PacktPublishing/Practical-Python-Programming-for-IoT`.

You will need to execute the following commands in a terminal to set up a virtual environment and install the Python libraries required for the code in this chapter:

```
$ cd chapter09            # Change into this chapter's folder
$ python3 -m venv venv    # Create Python Virtual Environment
$ source venv/bin/activate # Activate Python Virtual Environment
(venv) $ pip install pip --upgrade        # Upgrade pip
(venv) $ pip install -r requirements.txt  # Install dependent packages
```

The following dependencies are installed from `requirements.txt`:

- **PiGPIO**: The PiGPIO GPIO Library (`https://pypi.org/project/pigpio`)
- **PiGPIO DHT**: DHT11 and DHT22 sensor library (`https://pypi.org/project/pigpio-dht`)
- **Adafruit ADS1115**: ADS1115 ADC library (`https://pypi.org/project/Adafruit-ADS1x15`)

The electronic components we will need for this chapter's exercises are as follows:

- 1 x DHT11 (lower accuracy) or a DHT22 (higher accuracy) temperature and humidity sensor
- 1 x **LDR** (**Light Dependent Resistor**, also known as a photocell or photoresistor)
- Resistors:
    - 1 x 200 Ω resistor
    - 1 x 10kΩ resistor

- 1 x 1kΩ resistor
- 1 x 100kΩ resistor

- 1 x red LED
- 1 x ADS1115 analog-to-digital converter module
- External power sources – at a minimum, a 3.3 V/5 V breadboard-mountable power supply.

Measuring temperature and humidity

The measurement of temperature and related environmental properties is a common task, and there are many different types of sensors available for measuring these properties, including thermistors (a temperature-dependent resistor), sophisticated breakout modules that connect via SPI and I2C, and sensor varieties such as the DHT11 or DHT22 sensors, which we will be using for our example.

All sensors have their relative strengths and weaknesses when it comes to accuracy, response times (how fast we can rapidly get data from them), and cost.

DHT sensors, as illustrated in *Figure 9.1*, are inexpensive, durable, and easy to use:

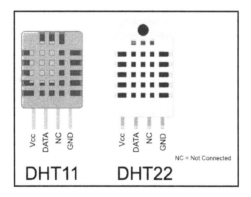

Figure 9.1 – DHT11 and DHT22 temperature and humidity sensors

The DHT11 is a very common low-cost sensor. The DHT22 is its higher-accuracy cousin. Both are pin-compatible and will be suitable for our example. The pinouts of these sensors as illustrated in the preceding figure are as follows:

- **Vcc**: 3- to 5-volt power source
- **Data**: Data pin that connects to a GPIO pin

- **NC**: Not connected, meaning that this pin is not used
- **GND**: Connects to ground

Here are the core similarities and differences between the DHT11 and DHT22:

	DHT 11	DHT 22
Operating Voltage	3 to 5 volts	3 to 5 volts
Operating Current	µA (microamps)	µA (microamps)
Temperature Range	0 to 50° Celsius	- 40 to 125° Celsius
Temperature Accuracy	±2%	±0.5%
Humidity Range	20 - 80%	0 - 100%
Humidity Accuracy	±5%	±2% to 5%
Maximum Sampling Rate	Faster – once every 1 second (1Hz)	Slower – once every 2 seconds (0.5Hz)

As mentioned, the DHT11 and DHT22 sensors are pin-compatible. They differ only in their measurement accuracy and range. Either sensor will be suitable for the circuit we are about to create for measuring temperature and humidity.

Creating the DHT11/DHT22 circuit

We will begin by creating the circuit illustrated in *Figure 9.2* on our breadboard:

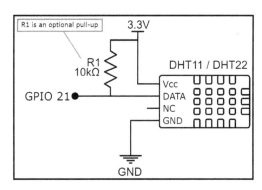

Figure 9.2 – DHT sensor schematic

The following is the breadboard layout for this circuit that we are about to build:

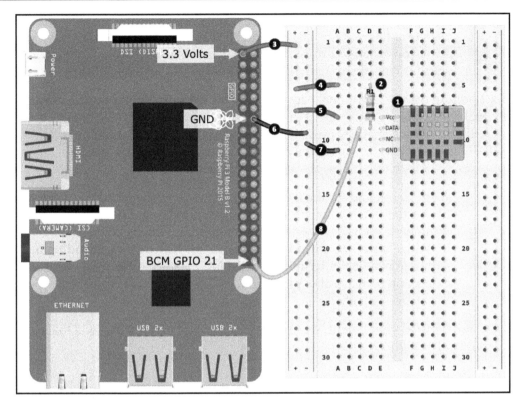

Figure 9.3 – DHT sensor circuit

Here are the steps to follow, which match the numbered black circles in *Figure 9.3*:

1. Place your DHT11 or DHT22 sensor into your breadboard.
2. Place the 10kΩ resistor (R1) into the breadboard. One end of the resistor shares the same row as the DHT sensor's DATA pin. We will discuss this resistor and why it's marked as optional in *Figure 9.2* after we complete the circuit build.
3. Connect a 3.3-volt pin on your Raspberry Pi to the positive rail of the power rail.
4. Connect the 10kΩ resistor (R1) to the positive power rail.
5. Connect the DHT Vcc pin to the positive power rail.
6. Connect a GND pin on your Raspberry Pi to the negative power rail.
7. Connect the GND pin on the DHT sensor to the negative power rail.
8. Finally, connect the DHT sensor's DATA pin to the GPIO 21 on your Raspberry Pi.

This now completes our DHT sensor circuit build.

In our circuit, Vcc is connected to 3.3 volts, which makes the DHT data pin operate at this voltage. DHT11 and DHT22 are rated for 5 volts; however, if you connected Vcc to 5 volts, the data pin becomes a 5-volt logic pin, which is not safe for use with the Raspberry Pi's 3.3-volt GPIO pin.

The 10kΩ pull-up resistor is optional because the DHT software library we are using already enables Raspberry Pi's internal pull-up resistor by default. I've included the pull-up resistor in the circuit schematic because it's included in the circuit examples in many DHT11/DHT22 datasheets. If you need a refresher on pull-up resistors, please revisit Chapter 6, *Electronics 101 for the Software Engineer*.

 In our circuit and for the DHT11/DHT22, the leg labeled **NC** means **Not Connected**. NC is a common abbreviation used to indicate that a leg or terminal of a sensor, IC, or component is not internally connected to anything. However, when we are dealing with switches – including relays – a component leg or terminal labeled NC means the **Normally Closed** connection path...so always interpret NC in the context of the component you are looking at.

Once you have created your circuit, we are ready to run and explore the code to measure temperature and humidity.

Running and exploring the DHT11/DHT22 code

Run the code found in the chapter09/dht_measure.py file, and the measured temperature and humidity will be printed to your terminal, similar to the following:

```
(venv) python DHT_Measure.py
{'temp_c': 21, 'temp_f': 69.8, 'humidity': 31, 'valid': True}
```

Here, we have the following:

- temp_c is the temperature in degrees Celsius.
- temp_f is the temperature in degrees Fahrenheit.
- humidity is the relative humidity percentage.
- valid indicates whether the reading is considered valid by way of an internal sensor checksum check. Readings where value == False must be abandoned.

The code in the source file is concise and is fully replicated here.

In line 1, we import the DHT sensor library and instantiate it in line 2. Update the line to match the DHT11 or DHT22 sensor you are using:

```
from pigpio_dht import DHT11, DHT22    # (1)

SENSOR_GPIO = 21
sensor = DHT11(SENSOR_GPIO)             # (2)
#sensor = DHT22(SENSOR_GPIO)

result = sensor.read(retries=2)         # (3)
print(result)

result = sensor.sample(samples=5)       # (4)
print(result)
```

In lines 3 and 4, we use the `pigpio-dht` library to request a temperature and humidity measurement from the sensor. A call to `read()` will query the sensor for measurement and will keep retrying for `retries` times if the measurements come back as `valid == False`. An alternative method for measurement is the `sample()` method, which will take many individual samples of the temperature and humidity and return a normalized measurement.

The advantage of `sample()`, especially for the less-accurate DHT11 sensor, is a more consistent temperature and humidity readings since outlier readings (random spikes) are removed; however, it does significantly increase the time it takes to read measurements – refer back to the *Maximum Sampling Rate* row in the table at the start of this section.

As an example, for a DHT11 with a maximum sampling rate of 1 second, for 5 samples, the `sample(samples=5)` call will take approximately *1 second x 5 samples = 5 seconds* to return, while a DHT22 with a 2-second sample rate will take about 10 seconds.

 DHT11 and DHT22 are pin-compatible; however, they are not software-compatible due to the way each sensor encodes its data while mixing up the software driver and sensor. For example, while a DHT22 sensor using a DHT11 library will generate results, they will be inaccurate (and it'll be pretty obvious – for example, saying your room is 650+ degrees Celsius!)

How easy was that! The DHT series are popular low-cost sensors that measure both temperature and humidity. For those cases where you need to perform more rapid readings, or you need to mount a sensor in hostile environments, such as in water or outside, directly exposed to the elements, you will certainly be able to find a sensor for your needs.

Here is a quick rundown of the other ways temperature (and similar environmental) sensors can connect to your Raspberry Pi:

- **Thermistors** are temperature-sensitive resistors that are very small and ideal for tight spaces, and you can get them in sealed packages for outside and in-liquid use. You can use them with a voltage-divider circuit (similarly to the **Light-Dependent-Resistor** (**LDR**) we will cover in the next section).
- There are many varieties of I2C and SPI sensors available that can be queried fast and may also have other additional on-board sensors, such as air pressure. These modules are typically larger and are probably best not exposed directly to the elements.
- **1-wire** temperature sensors are also compact and easily sealable and have the advantage that they can have long wires (100 meters plus).

With this, we come to the end of this section on measuring temperature and humidity. Many environmental monitoring projects require you to measure temperature and humidity, and using a DHT11 or DHT22 with Raspberry Pi is an easy and cost-effective way to achieve this. We will revisit our DHT11/22 circuit again in `Chapter 13`, *IoT Visualization and Automation Platforms*, where we will integrate this sensor with an IoT platform to collect and monitor the temperature and humidity.

Now that we have explored temperature sensors, let's learn how to detect light.

Detecting light

Detecting the presence or absence of light is easily achieved with a special type of resistor known as an **LDR**. LDRs are a low-cost light sensor, and we find them in many applications, from light-activated switches and lamps or as part of the circuit that dims your alarm clock display when it's dark, to part of alarm circuits on cash boxes and safes.

 You may also find LDRs referred to as photoresistors or photocells.

The following figure shows a typical LDR component, together with a few varieties of LDR schematic symbols. If you examine the symbols, you will notice that they are a resistor symbol with inward-pointing arrows. You can think of these arrows as representing light falling on the resistor:

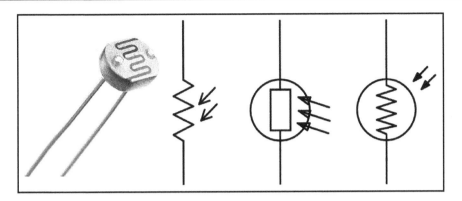

Figure 9.4 – A physical LDR component and a variety of schematic symbols

An LDR varies its resistance with the relative light it detects. If you placed the terminals of your multimeter in Ohms mode across an LDR, you will find (roughly after a few seconds) the following:

- When the LDR is in the dark (for example, if you cover it up), its resistance will typically measure many mega-ohms.
- In a normally lit room (for example, on the table with the ceiling lights on), the LDR's resistance will measure in kilo-ohms.
- When an LDR is in bright light (direct sunlight or shining a torch on it), its resistance will measure a few hundred-ohms or less.

This gives us distinct regions where it becomes possible to work out the presence or absence of light. With calibration and a little tuning, we can easily identify a point between dark and light that we can use to trigger an event. For example, you could use an LDR circuit such as the one we will create next to programmatically control the switching circuits we created in Chapter 7, *Turning Things On and Off*.

 LDRs are only good at measuring relative light levels – the presence or absence of light. If you want absolute measurements such as lux levels, or even to detect color, there is a range of ICs in the I2C or SPI breakout module form that can achieve this.

Using this basic understanding, we will build our LDR circuit to detect light.

Creating an LDR light-detecting circuit

As discussed, an LDR varies its resistance in relation to the relative light it detects. To detect varying resistance with our Raspberry Pi, we need to take a few steps that were covered in previous chapters:

- We need to turn the varying resistance into a varying voltage because our Raspberry Pi GPIO pins work on voltage, not resistance. This is an application of Ohms law and a voltage-divider circuit, which we learned about in `Chapter 6`, *Electronics 101 for the Software Engineer*.
- Our Raspberry Pi GPIO pins can only read digital signals – for example, a high (~3.3 volts) or low (~0 volts) signal. To measure a varying voltage, we can attach an **Analog-to-Digital Converter** (**ADC**) such as an ADS1115. We covered the ADS1115 and accompanying Python code in `Chapter 5`, *Connecting Your Raspberry Pi to the Physical World*.

We are about to create the circuit illustrated in *Figure 9.5* on your breadboard. This circuit and the accompanying code will illuminate the LED when it detects a certain level of darkness:

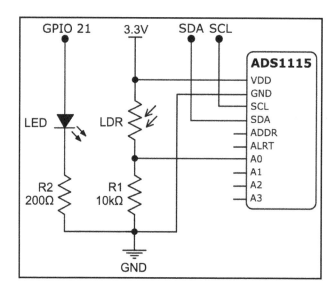

Figure 9.5 – LDR circuit with the ADS1115 ADC schematic

We will build our circuit in two parts. For the first part, we will place the components onto our breadboard, as shown:

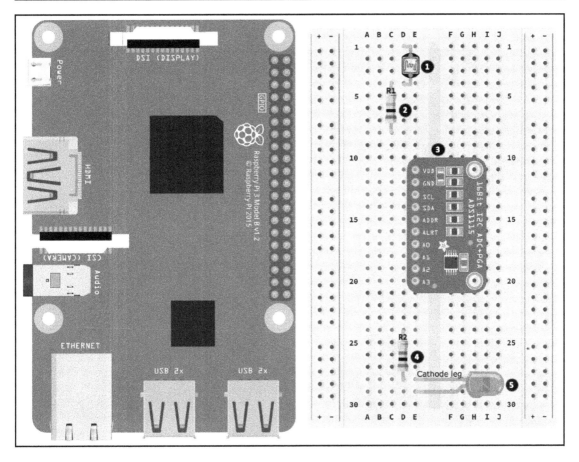

Figure 9.6 – LDR circuit with ADS1115 ADC circuit (part 1 of 2)

Here are the steps to follow, which match the numbered black circles in *Figure 9.6*:

1. Place the LDR onto the breadboard.
2. Place a 10kΩ resistor (R1) onto the breadboard. One end of this resistor shares the same row as one of the LDR.
3. Place the ADS1115 ADC onto the breadboard.
4. Place a 200kΩ resistor (R2) onto the breadboard.
5. Place an LED onto the breadboard, paying careful attention to connect the LED's cathode leg to the same row shared by one of the legs of the 200kΩ resistor.

Now that we have placed our components, we will wire them up:

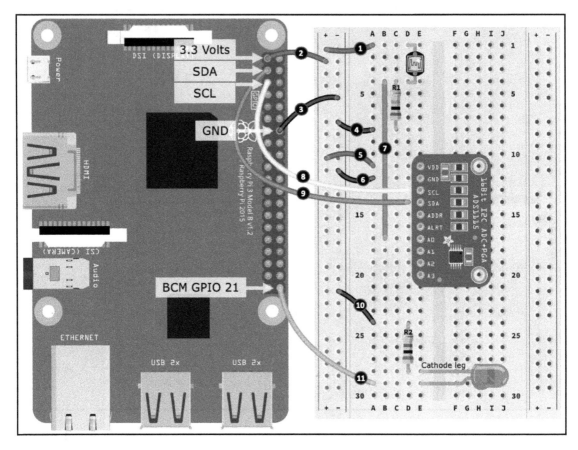

Figure 9.7 – LDR circuit with ADS1115 ADC circuit (part 2 of 2)

Here are the steps to follow; this time they match the numbered black circles in *Figure 9.7*:

1. Connect the positive rail of the power rail to the LDR.
2. Connect a 3.3-volt pin from your Raspberry Pi to the positive rail of the power rail.
3. Connect a GND pin from your Raspberry Pi to the negative tail of the power rail.
4. Connect the negative power rail to the 10kΩ resistor (R1).
5. Connect the Vdd terminal of the ADS1115 to the positive power rail.
6. Connect the GND terminal of the ADS1115 to the negative power rail.

7. Connect the junction of the LDR and 10kΩ resistor (R1) to port A0 on the ADS1115 (can you see how the LDR and resistor are creating a voltage divider, with the varying voltage output now attached to A0?).
8. Connect the Raspberry Pi's SDA pin to the ADS1115 SDA terminal.
9. Connect the Raspberry Pi's SCL pin to the ADS1115 SCL terminal.
10. Connect the negative power rail to the 200kΩ resistor.
11. Connect the anode leg of the LED to your Raspberry Pi's GPIO 21 pin.

I hope you were able to see the voltage divider that was formed by the LDR and the 10kΩ resistor R1. We will cover the reasoning behind the 10kΩ resistor later in the chapter in the section titled *LDR configuration summary*.

As the light detected by the LDR varies, its resistance varies. The effect of this is to alter the relative ratios of R1 (fixed resistor) and the LDR's resistance (varying resistance), which in turn changes the voltage measured at the interception of the LDR and R1 (that's where A (analog-in) of our ADS1115 is attached to measure this varying voltage).

 Don't place your LED too close to your LDR. When it illuminates, the LED is a source of light that is detectable by the LDR, and it could interfere with your LDR readings in the code.

Now that you have created the LDR circuit, we will calibrate and run our example code.

Running the LDR example code

We are about to run two programs:

- chapter09/ldr_ads1115_calibrate.py, which will help us calibrate our LDR readings
- chapter09/ldr_ads1115.py, which monitors the light level and switches on the LED when the light falls below a configurable level

First, we should check that the ADS1115 is connected correctly and can be seen by your Raspberry Pi. Run the `i2cdetect` command in a Terminal. If your output does not include a number (for example `48`), then please verify your wiring:

```
$ i2cdetect -y 1
# ... truncated ...
30: -- -- -- -- -- -- -- -- -- -- -- -- -- -- -- --
40: -- -- -- -- -- -- -- -- 48 -- -- -- -- -- -- --
50: -- -- -- -- -- -- -- -- -- -- -- -- -- -- -- --
# ... truncated ...
```

We first covered the ADS1115 analog-to-digital converter and the `i2cdetect` utility in Chapter 5, *Connecting Your Raspberry Pi to the Physical World*.

Let's run the examples, starting with the calibration program:

1. Run the code found in the `chapter09/ldr_ads1115_calibrate.py` file, and follow the instructions that appear on your terminal, which are as follows:

    1. `Place the LDR in the light and press Enter:` Use the ambient room light for this exercise, and be careful that you are not casting a shadow over the LDR. When you are building your application, you will want to use the source of light that makes sense for your purposes, be it direct sunlight, room light, or shining a bright torch into the LDR, for example.

    2. `Place the LDR in the dark and press Enter:` I'd suggest completely covering the LDR with a dark cloth or cup. Using your finger is not always ideal as a sensitive LDR may still detect a level of light through your finger:

    ```
    (venv) python ldr_ads1115_calibrate.py
    Place LDR in the light and press Enter
    Please wait...

    Place LDR in dark and press Enter
    Please wait...

    File ldr_calibration_config.py created with:
    # This file was automatically created by
    ldr_ads1115_calibrate.py
    # Number of samples: 100
    MIN_VOLTS = 0.6313
    MAX_VOLTS = 3.2356
    ```

The calibration program takes a number of samples (by default, `100`) from the ADS1115 in both the dark and light conditions and calculates the average reading. Next, the program writes the results (also shown in the terminal) into the `ldr_calibration_config.py` file. This is a Python source file for our example, imported into our actual LDR and LED example, as we will see in the next step.

2. Run the program found in the `chapter09/ldr_ads1115.py` file, and observe the output on the terminal, which displays the voltage read by the ADS1115:

```
LDR Reading volts=0.502, trigger at 0.9061 +/- 0.25,
triggered=False
```

Hopefully, the output should read `triggered = False`, and the LED should be off. If this is not the case, try repeating the calibration process in *step 1*, or read on and you'll discover how to adjust the trigger point in code.

3. Gradually move your hand nearer and nearer to the LDR restrict the amount of light reaching it. As you move your hand, you will notice the `voltage` reading on the terminal change, and at a certain voltage level, the trigger point will be reached and the LED will illuminate:

```
LDR Reading volts=1.116, trigger at 0.9061 +/- 0.25,
triggered=False
LDR Reading volts=1.569, trigger at 0.9061 +/- 0.25, triggered=True
```

What you are witnessing is the function of the voltage divider varying the voltage as the LDR's resistance changes in response to the light it detects. This voltage is then read by the ADS1115.

You may have noticed that the voltage produced is not the full range of ~0 volts to ~3.3 volts as it was when we used a potentiometer with our ADS1115 back in Chapter 5, *Connecting Your Raspberry Pi to the Physical World.* Our restricted range is a side-effect and limitation of our fixed resistor (R1) and varying-resistance (LDR) circuit, which cannot vary resistance to the extremes necessary to reach ~0 or ~3.3 volts. You will encounter this restriction in voltage divider circuits since they will by design include a fixed resistor value. By contrast, our potentiometers are *two* variable resistors creating a voltage divider, and we can effectively zero-out (get close to 0 Ω) one side of the divider, depending on which direction we turn the potentiometer's dial, allowing us to get near to both 0 volts and 3.3 volts.

Now that we have seen this code running, let's see how it works.

LDR code walkthrough

A bulk of the code in both `chapter09/ldr_ads1115_calibrate.py`
and `chapter09/ldr_ads1115_calibrate.py` is the boilerplate code to set up and
configure the ADS1115 and set up the LED using PiGPIO. We will not recover the common
code here. If you need a refresher on the ADS1115-related code, please review the exercise
found in `Chapter 5`, *Connecting Your Raspberry Pi to the Physical World*.

Let's look at the Python code that makes our LDR work.

In line 1, we see that we are importing the `ldr_calibration_config.py` file that we
created with our calibration program previously.

Next, in line 2, we are assigning the calibration values to the `LIGHT_VOLTS` (the voltage
detected by the ADS1115 when the LDR was in the light) and `DARK_VOLTS` (the voltage
detected when you covered up the LDR) variables:

```
import ldr_calibration_config as calibration          # (1)

# ... truncated ...

LIGHT_VOLTS = calibration.MAX_VOLTS                    # (2)
DARK_VOLTS = calibration.MIN_VOLTS

TRIGGER_VOLTS = LIGHT_VOLTS - ((LIGHT_VOLTS - DARK_VOLTS) / 2) # (3)
TRIGGER_BUFFER = 0.25                                  # (4)
```

In line 3, we create a trigger point. This is a voltage point we will use later in code to switch
on and off the LED.

> You can adjust and experiment with the formula or value of
> `TRIGGER_VOLTS` to change the lighting condition that causes the code to
> trigger.

The `TRIGGER_BUFFER` variable at line 4 is used to create a buffer or lag in our trigger, better
known in electronic terms as *hysteresis*. This value creates a small window range where the
detected voltage can vary without causing a trigger or un-trigger event. Without
this *hysteresis*, the trigger (and LED) would turn on and off rapidly as the detected voltage
oscillates around the `TRIGGER_VOLTS` trigger voltage.

To experience this effect practically, set `TRIGGER_BUFFER = 0` and you will find that as you move your hand above the LDR, the LED is very sensitive to on and off, and at a certain point may even appear to blink. As you increase the value of `TRIGGER_BUFFER`, you will notice that the hand movement required to switch the LED becomes on and off greater.

Moving on, in line 5, we come to the code that determines whether our trigger point has been reached. The `update_trigger()` function compares the voltage detected by the ADS1115 to the `TRIGGER_VOLTS` value adjusted for `TRIGGER_BUFFER`, and updates the `triggered` global variable if the triggering point is breached:

```
triggered = False # (5)
def update_trigger(volts):
    global triggered

    if triggered and volts > TRIGGER_VOLTS + TRIGGER_BUFFER:
        triggered = False
    elif not triggered and volts < TRIGGER_VOLTS - TRIGGER_BUFFER:
        triggered = True
```

Near the end of the source file, we have a `while` loop in line 6. We are reading in the ADS1115 detected voltage, updating the global `triggered` variable, before printing the results to the terminal:

```
trigger_text = "{:0.4f} +/- {}".format(TRIGGER_VOLTS, TRIGGER_BUFFER)

  try:
      while True:                                           # (6)
          volts = analog_channel.voltage

          update_trigger(volts)

          output = "LDR Reading volts={:>5.3f}, trigger at {},
triggered={}"
                      .format(volts, trigger_text, triggered)
          print(output)

          pi.write(LED_GPIO, triggered)                     # (7)
          sleep(0.05)
```

Finally, in line 7, we toggle the LED on or off depending on the value of `triggered`.

Now that we have seen how we detect light with our LDR circuit and Python code, I want to briefly cover how the series resistor is chosen for the LDR circuit.

LDR configuration summary

You may have realized while working with the LDR circuit and code that there are a few tunable parameters that influence how the circuit and code work, and did you wonder why we used a 10kΩ resistor?

No two LDRs will give the same resistance-to-light measurement and their resistance-to-light range is not linear. The implication of this is that your LDR, plus the lighting conditions you plan to use it in, can influence a suitable fixed resistor value.

Here is a rough guide to selecting an appropriate fixed resistor:

- If you want the LDR to be more sensitive in **darker conditions**, use a **higher value** resistor (for example, try 100kΩ).
- If you want your LDR to be more sensitive in **brighter conditions**, use a **lower value** resistor (for example, try 1kΩ).

Remember that these are just suggestions, so feel free to try different resistances for your own needs. Plus, whenever you change the value of the fixed resistor, rerun the calibration code.

There is also a formula known as Axel Benz that can be used to calculate a reference resistance value for an analog component such as an LDR. The formula is expressed as follows:

$$R_{ref} = \sqrt{R_{max} \times R_{min}}$$

The parameters in the formula are as follows:

- R_{ref} is the value of the fixed resistor, R1.
- R_{max} is the maximum resistance of the LDR (when in dark). A typical value might be 10 Ω.
- R_{min} is the minimum resistance of the LDR (when in bright light). A typical value might be 10M Ω.

So, if we use the typical values, we get the 10kΩ value we used for R1:

$$\sqrt{10^6 \times 100} = 10k\Omega$$

Measure the extremes on your LDR with a multimeter and see what value you calculate. Do not be surprised if your measurements vary widely from the typical 10kΩ. When you consider we are working with an LDR ohmic range of ~10 Ω to ~10,000,000 Ω, the difference may still only be a fraction of a percent!

We also saw previously in the code that two variables influence how our code triggers:

- Change the value of TRIGGER_VOLTS to change the point at which the code triggers – for example, turns on or off the LED.
- Change the value of TRIGGER_BUFFER to alter how sensitive the trigger is to changing light conditions.

Finally, remember that an LDR detects light logarithmically, not linearly – for example, as you gradually lower your hand or an object over the LDR to restrict light, the voltages reported by the LDR will not necessarily change in proportion to the amount of light you are restricting. This is a reason why we need to change the fixed resistor value if we want the LDR to be more sensitive in darker or brighter conditions.

You can experiment with replacing the fixed resistor, R1, with a variable resistor (for example, replace the fixed 10kΩ with a 20kΩ variable resistor set to 10kΩ. We choose 20kΩ because we can adjust it above and below 10kΩ. A 10kΩ variable resistor would only let us adjust down resistance). After code calibration at 10kΩ and defining a trigger point in code, you can then fine-tune the trigger point by adjusting the variable resistor.

This concludes our discussion of LDRs. We have seen how to build a simple LDR circuit together with an ADS1115 ADC, and how to detect light with Python. You could use this simple circuit and accompanying code for any project where the detection of light or darkness is the desired input trigger – for example, a light-activated switch.

Next, we will learn how to detect moisture.

Detecting moisture

Guess what...we have already done the grunt work to detect moisture! It's just another application of the LDR circuit and code, only we replace the LDR with probes.

For this exercise, you can create a set of probes using two pieces of wire (with the ends stripped), and attach them in place of the LDR, as shown in *Figure 9.8*. This is the same circuit we built in the previous section and showed in *Figure 9.7*, only this time, we have replaced the LDR with two wires. Let's make this slight change now:

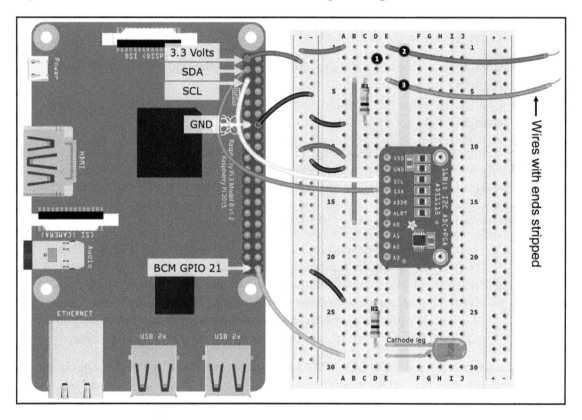

Figure 9.8 – Moisture detection circuit

Here are the steps to follow, which match the numbered black circles in *Figure 9.8*:

1. Remove the LDR from the breadboard.
2. Place a wire (with both ends stripped) into a breadboard row that previously connected to one of the LDR's legs (in the illustration, this new wire connects back to 3.3 volts on your Raspberry Pi).
3. Place another wire (with both ends stripped) into a breadboard row that previously connected the LDR's other leg (in the illustration, this new wire connects to the row shared by the 10kΩ resistor (R1)).

This small change – replacing the LDR with bare wires – turns our circuit into a basic moisture-detecting circuit. Let's try the circuit out!

In the `chapter09` folder, you will find two files, named `moisture_calibrate.py` and `moisture_ads1115.py`. These files are almost identical to the LDR file set we used in the previous section, except I've changed the wording and variable names from `Light`/`Dark` to `Wet`/`Dry`. The core differences are marked by comments in the respective files.

Given the similarity, we will not cover these source files and the moisture circuit in detail; however, for reference, these are the steps to follow:

1. Ensure the probe is dry.
2. Run `moisture_calibrate.py` and follow the instructions to perform a voltage calibration.
3. Run `moisture_ads1115.py`.
4. Check that the terminal output indicates `trigger=False` (the code triggers on the wet condition).
5. Place the probe in a cup of water (yes, it's safe to do this) and observe the voltage reading on the terminal change (It's also OK if the probes get shorted accidentally as it will not cause any damage).
6. With the probes immersed in water, check whether the terminal output reads `trigger=True` (probe wet condition).
7. If the trigger is still `True`, you will need to adjust the value of `TRIGGER_VOLTS` in the code.

You can also place the probe in dry dirt and observe the voltage readings. Slowly wet the dirt and the voltage reading should change. We now have the basis of a program to tell you when your plant needs watering!

So, why does this work? Simple – water is a conductor of electricity and is behaving like a resistor between our two probes.

Different water in different parts of the world and from different sources – for example, tap versus bottle – may conduct electricity differently. This means you might need to play with the value of the R1 resistor if your circuit is not responding well with the 10kΩ resistor. In addition, you can also experiment with the distance between the probe wires and their size.

We will conclude our discussion on moisture detection by comparing what we have just created with an off-the-shelf moisture detector that you can purchase.

Comparing detection options

How do our simple circuit and wire probes compare to a *water/moisture detection module* that you can find on retail sites such as eBay? These products typically contain a probe of some sort, plus a small electronic module. A picture of one of these modules, plus a few probes, are shown here:

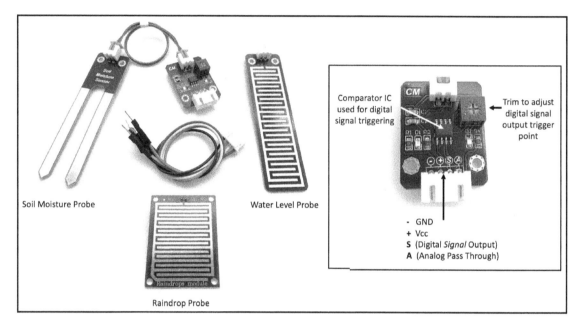

Figure 9.9 – Moisture detection module and probes

The three probes pictured each have two terminals and are simply an exposed copper trace on a circuit board, analogous to the exposed wires we saw in our circuit in *Figure 9.8*. A key difference is that these probes expose a larger surface area and are therefore more sensitive. Furthermore, they are also likely to be less prone to corrosion (at least in the short-to-medium term) than two stripped wires.

 You can connect these probes directly to the exposed wires in our circuit shown in *Figure 9.8* to expand and enhance the detection capabilities of the circuit!

Let's discuss the electronic module (zoomed in and labeled in *Figure 9.9* on the right-hand side).

In addition to a Vcc/Vin and a GND terminal, these modules *often* (not always, but often) have two output terminals or pins, which are as follows:

- An *analog* output (in our example, this is labeled **A**)
- A *digital* output (labeled **S**)

 Please note that I am not providing instructions on how to connect the previously pictured module to your Raspberry Pi, but rather, I will keep the discussion general. There are many variations of these modules available and while their operation is similar, there can be differences in how they need to be wired. At this stage of the book, if you are comfortable with the basic principles of analog versus digital, voltage dividers, and ADC, you have all you need to understand and make an informed decision on how to interface these modules to a device such as a Raspberry Pi. A good starting place will be your modules' datasheet or any information provided at the place of purchase.

The *analog output* is a pass-through to the probe. You connect it directly into a voltage divider circuit and measure a varying voltage with an ADC such as the ADS1115 – the exact scenario we created in *Figure 9.8*. If you use the analog pass-through, you are bypassing all the other circuitry on the module (hence why you can just connect the probes directly into our example circuit).

The *digital output* is what uses the module circuitry. A typical module circuit includes, at a minimum, an integrated circuit known as a voltage comparator, a fixed resistor, and a variable resistor, which is a trigger-point trim adjustment. The fixed resistor together with the probe creates a voltage divider. The voltage comparator is responsible for monitoring the voltage across the voltage divider and triggering the digital output (for example, transition from LOW to HIGH) at a point determined by trim adjustment. An example of a trim adjustment variable resistor can be seen in *Figure 9.9*.

If this voltage comparison and triggering sounds a little familiar, you are correct. This module with its voltage comparator and configurable trigger point is, in principle, a purely electronic version of the LDR and moisture circuits and Python code we have created. And yes, you could use the LDR in one of these modules instead of a probe!

So, to conclude, what's better – using an ADS1115 and voltage divider type circuit such as that shown in *Figure 9.8*, or using a module such as that pictured in *Figure 9.9*? There is no one best answer; however, the following points will help you make your own decision:

- Using a circuit such as that in *Figure 9.8* is an analog approach. The raw voltage detected by the sensor is passed directly to your Raspberry Pi. One simple advantage of this approach is that you have full control over a *trigger* point in code. You could, as an example, remotely adjust the trigger point from a web page. The downside of this approach is that you need a more complex circuit that involves an ADS1115 and a voltage divider.
- Using a module such as that pictured in *Figure 9.9* as a digital approach promotes a simpler interfacing circuit to your Raspberry Pi in that you can connect the digital output terminal directly to a GPIO pin (as long as the digital output of the module 3.3-volts). The caveat is that you must have physical access to the module and the adjustment trim to change the trigger point.

Summary

In this chapter, we learned how to measure temperature and humidity using the common DHT11 and/or DHT22 sensors. We also looked at how to use an LDR to detect light, and this allowed us to explore voltage divider circuits and ADCs in greater detail. We concluded by retrofitting our LDR circuit so that we could detect moisture.

The example circuits and code we covered in this chapter provide practical examples of measuring environmental conditions with readily available sensors and simple circuits. Your understanding of these sensors and circuits now means you can adapt the examples for your own environmental monitoring projects, including using them as input triggers together with Python to control other circuits.

We also saw new practical applications of voltage divider circuits and how they are used in analog circuits to turn variable resistance into a variable voltage for use with an ADC. These examples and your understanding of them represent an important skill that you can adapt and use with other analog-based sensors.

In the next chapter, we will learn how to go deeper into DC motor control and learn how to control a servo.

Questions

As we conclude, here is a list of questions for you to test your knowledge of this chapter's material. You will find the answers in the *Assessments* section of the book:

1. Can you list two differences between a DHT11 and DHT22 temperature and humidity sensor?
2. Why is the external 10kΩ pull-up resistor optional in our DHT11/22 circuit?
3. Describe the basic electronic principle used with an LDR to measure light.
4. How can you make an LDR more or less sensitive to certain lighting conditions?
5. You have created an LDR circuit and calibrated the Python code. Now, you change the LDR and find that the voltages readings and in-code trigger point behave slightly differently. Why?
6. Why does placing two wires in water work as a basic moisture detector when used with a voltage divider and ADS1115 circuit?

Movement with Servos, Motors, and Steppers

10

In the previous chapter, we covered how to measure temperature, humidity, light, and moisture. In this chapter, we will turn our attention to the control of motors and servos, which are common devices for creating physical movement and motion. The core concepts, circuits, and code you will learn in this chapter will open up a world of physical automation and robotics using your Raspberry Pi.

We will be learning how **Pulse Width Modulation** (**PWM**) is used to set the angle of a servo, and how we use an H-Bridge IC to control the direction and speed of a DC motor. We will look at stepper motors and how they can be controlled for precise movement.

Here is what we will cover in this chapter:

- Using PWM to rotate a servo
- Using an H-Bridge IC to control a motor
- Introduction to stepper motor control

Technical requirements

To perform the exercises in this chapter, you will need the following:

- Raspberry Pi 4 Model B
- Raspbian OS Buster (with desktop and recommended software)
- Minimum Python version 3.5

These requirements are what the code examples in this book are based on. It's reasonable to expect that the code examples should work without modification on Raspberry Pi 3 Model B or a different version of Raspbian OS as long as your Python version is 3.5 or higher.

You will find this chapter's source code in the `chapter10` folder in the GitHub repository available at `https://github.com/PacktPublishing/Practical-Python-Programming-for-IoT`.

You will need to execute the following commands in a terminal to set up a virtual environment and install the Python libraries required for the code in this chapter:

```
$ cd chapter10            # Change into this chapter's folder
$ python3 -m venv venv    # Create Python Virtual Environment
$ source venv/bin/activate # Activate Python Virtual Environment
(venv) $ pip install pip --upgrade    # Upgrade pip
(venv) $ pip install -r requirements.txt  # Install dependent packages
```

The following dependency is installed from `requirements.txt`:

- **PiGPIO**: The PiGPIO GPIO library (`https://pypi.org/project/pigpio`)

The electronic components we will need for this chapter's exercises are as follows:

- 1 x MG90S hobby servo (or an equivalent 3-wire 5-volt hobby servo). Reference datasheet: `https://www.alldatasheet.com/datasheet-pdf/pdf/1132104/ETC2/MG90S.html`
- 1 x L293D **integrated circuit** (**IC**) (make sure it has the D – that is, L293**D**, not L293). Reference datasheet: `https://www.alldatasheet.com/datasheet-pdf/pdf/89353/TI/L293D.html`
- 1 x 28BYJ-48 stepper motor (5 volts, 64 steps, 1:64 gearing). Note: 28BYJ-48 comes in 5-volt and 12-volt varieties and different configuration steps and gearings. Reference datasheet: `https://www.alldatasheet.com/datasheet-pdf/pdf/1132391/ETC1/28BYJ-48.html`
- 2 x size 130 (R130) DC motor rated 3-6 volts (ideally with a stall current < 800 mA), or alternate DC motor with compatible voltage and current ratings
- External power source – at a minimum, a 3.3 V/5 V breadboard-mountable power supply

Let's commence by learning how to use a servo with our Raspberry Pi, Python, and PiGPIO.

Using PWM to rotate a servo

Common servomotors, or servos, are internally geared motors that allow you to rotate its shaft to a precise angle within a 180-degree arc. They are a core component of industrial robots, and toys alike, and we're all familiar with hobby servos found in toys such as radio-controlled cars, planes, and drones.

Pictured in *Figure 10.1* are a full-size hobby-style servo, a micro servo, and a set of header pins, which are useful to help connect a servo to a breadboard, which we will need to do later in this section as we build our circuit:

Figure 10.1 – Servos

The great feature of servos is that they are essentially a Plug'n'Play style device – after we connect them to the power supply, we just need to send them a PWM signal that encodes the angle we want the servo to rotate to, and presto! We're done. No ICs, no transistors, or any other external circuitry. What's even better is that servo control is so common that many GPIO libraries – including PiGPIO – include convenience methods for their control.

Let's start our servo exploration by connecting one to our Raspberry Pi.

Connecting a servo to your Raspberry Pi

Our first task for our servo example is to wire it up to a power source and our Raspberry Pi. A schematic representing this wiring is shown here:

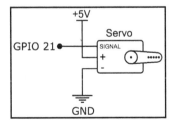

Figure 10.2 – Servo wiring schematic

Let's get started wiring our servo using a breadboard, as shown:

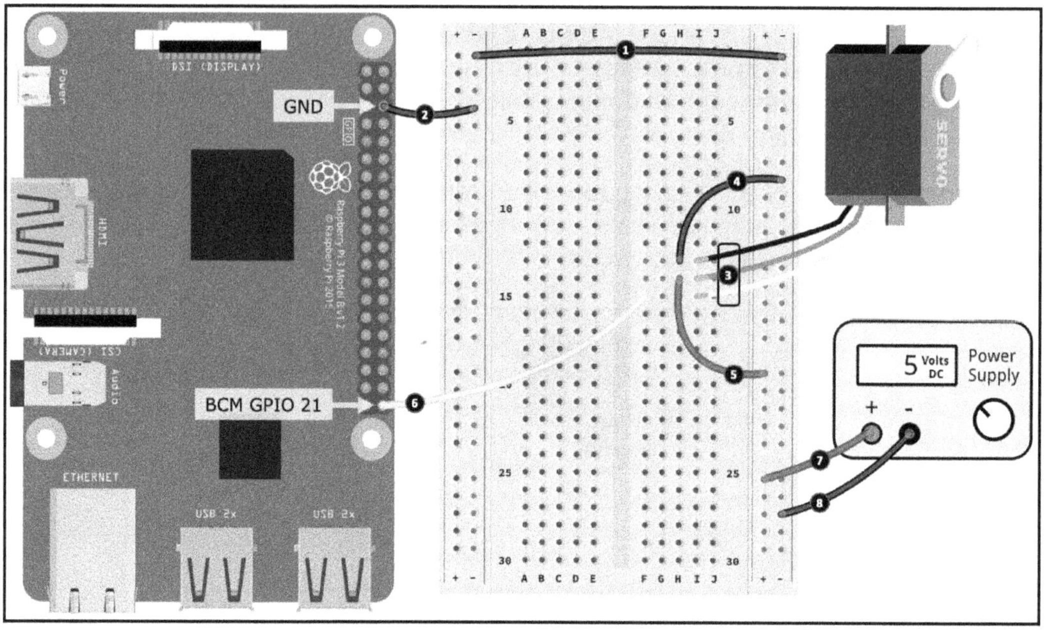

Figure 10.3 – Servo breadboard layout

Before we step through the wiring procedure, first I want to briefly discuss the wire colors coming out of a servo. While servo wire colors are somewhat standard, they can vary between different manufacturers and servos. Use the following pointers when connecting your servo at *steps 4, 5,* and *6.* If your servo has colored wires that I do not list in the following list, you will need to consult the datasheet for your servo.

Common servo wire colors are as follows:

- The brown or black wire connects to GND
- The red wire connects to +5-volts
- The orange, yellow, white, or blue wire is the signal/PWM input wire that connects to a GPIO pin

Here are the steps to follow to create your breadboard build. The step numbers match the numbers in the black circles in *Figure 10.3*:

1. Connect the left-hand side and right-hand side negative power rails together.
2. Connect a GND pin on your Raspberry Pi to the left-hand side negative power rail.
3. Connect the servo into the breadboard. As mentioned previously and shown in *Figure 10.1*, you will need a set of header pins (or alternatively, male-to-male jumper cables) to connect your servo to your breadboard.
4. Connect the black wire (negative/GND) from the servo to the negative rail of the right-hand side power rail.
5. Connect the red wire (5-volt power) from the servo to the positive rail of the right-hand side power rail.
6. Connect the signal wire from the servo to GPIO 21 on your Raspberry Pi.
7. Connect the positive output terminal of a 5-volt power supply to the positive rail of the right-hand side power rail.
8. Connect the negative output terminal of the power supply to the negative rail of the right-hand side power rail.

You will need to use an external 5-volt power source (*steps 7* and *8*) to power your servo. A small servo such as an MG90S uses ~200mA as it rotates with no load on the shaft/horn (the horn is the arm connected to the shaft of the servo), and ~400+mA maximum current if you attach a heavy load to the horn or you forcefully stop a rotation. Drawing this current directly from your Raspberry Pi's 5-volt pin may be enough to cause it to reset.

Many cheap car-like toys have a hard left/right mock servo for their steering mechanisms. It might look like a servo on the outside, but in truth, it's just a basic DC motor with some gears and a spring that create the hard left/right steering angle. It's the spring that returns the servo to center when the motor is not engaged. If you do not have granular control over the angle, it's not a true servo.

Before we get into some code, we'll take a quick look at how PWM is used to control a servo. This will give you some background on what's happening when we get to the code.

How a servo is controlled using PWM

Servos typically require around a 50 Hz PWM signal (some variation around 50 Hz is okay, but we'll stick with 50 Hz as this is the common reference point), and a pulse width between 1.0 milliseconds and 2.0 milliseconds that determines the angle of rotation. The relation between pulse widths, duty cycles, and angle is illustrated in *Figure 10.4*. Don't worry if all this does not sink in just yet. It should become more clear as we see our servo in action and review our servo-related code in the next section:

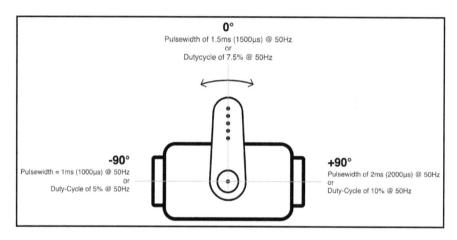

Figure 10.4 – Servo's pulse width, duty cycle, and angles

We have not covered pulse width in relation to our earlier coverage of PWM; however, it's just another way of describing the duty cycle.

Here is an example:

- If we have a PWM signal at 50 Hz (that is, 50 cycles per second), then this means that 1 PWM cycle takes *1 / 50 = 0.02* seconds, or 20 ms.
- Thus, a pulse width of 1.5 ms expressed as a duty cycle is *1.5 ms / 20 ms = 0.075*, multiplied by 100 gives us a duty cycle of 7.5%.

To work backward, we have the following:

- A duty cycle of 7.5% divided by 100 is 0.075. Then, *0.075 x 20 ms = 1.5 ms* – that is, a 1.5 ms pulse width.

If you'd prefer a formula to relate *pulse width*, *frequency*, and *duty cycle*, here it is:

$$duty\ cycle\ \% = \frac{pulse\ width\ in\ seconds}{\frac{1}{frequency\ in\ hertz}} \times 100$$

To convert back, we have the following:

$$pulse\ width\ in\ seconds = \frac{duty\ cycle\ \%}{100} \times \frac{1}{frequency\ in\ hertz}$$

Okay, enough with the math. Let's run and review the Python code to make our servo move.

Running and exploring the servo code

The code we are about to run can be found in the `chapter10/servo.py` file. I recommend reviewing the source code before proceeding so that you have an overall idea about what the file contains.

When you run the code found in the `chapter10/servo.py` file, your servo should rotate left and then right several times.

Let's look at the code, starting with some pulse width variables defined at line 1:

```
LEFT_PULSE  = 1000   # Nano seconds              # (1)
RIGHT_PULSE = 2000
CENTER_PULSE = ((LEFT_PULSE - RIGHT_PULSE) // 2) + RIGHT_PULSE  # Eg 1500
```

These pulse widths represent our servo's extreme left and right rotation.

 Note that the `LEFT_PULSE` and `RIGHT_PULSE` values are in nanoseconds, as this is the unit used by the PiGPIO servo functions.

These values of `LEFT_PULSE = 1000` and `RIGHT_PULSE = 2000` are the perfect world values that you will see sighted often. In reality, you may need to make slight adjustments to these variables to get the full rotation out of your servo. For example, my test servo needed the `LEFT_PULSE = 600` and `RIGHT_PULSE = 2450` values to achieve full rotation. You'll know if you have adjusted too far if your servo motor stays engaged and makes a groaning noise when it is at full left or right rotation. If this happens, disconnect power immediately to prevent damage to the servo and readjust your values.

If your serve rotates backward – for example, it rotates to the left when you expect it to rotate to the right – swap the values for `LEFT_PULSE` and `RIGHT_PULSE`. Or, just turn your servo upside down.

At line 2, we define the `MOVEMENT_DELAY_SECS= 0.5` variable, which we need later to add a delay between servo movements:

```
# Delay to give servo time to move
MOVEMENT_DELAY_SECS = 0.5                    # (2)
```

As you work with servos and send them a PWM rotation signal, you will find that they behave asynchronously. That is, the code does not block until the servo finishes its rotation. If we intend to make many rapid servo movements that you want to complete in full, we must add a short delay to ensure the servo has time to complete the rotation. An example of this is found in the `sweep()` function we will cover shortly. The delay of 0.5 seconds is only a suggestion, so feel free to experiment with different numbers.

Starting at line 3, we define three basic functions to control our servo:

```
def left():                                          # (3)
    pi.set_servo_pulsewidth(SERVO_GPIO, LEFT_PULSE)

def center():
    pi.set_servo_pulsewidth(SERVO_GPIO, CENTER_PULSE)

def right():
    pi.set_servo_pulsewidth(SERVO_GPIO, RIGHT_PULSE)
```

The `left()` function simply sets the PWM pulse width to `LEFT_PULSE` on the servo's GPIO pin using the PiGPIO `set_servo_pulsewidth()` method. This is a convenience function for servo control offered by PiGPIO as a practical alternative to using the `set_PWM_dutycycle()` and `set_PWM_frequency()` methods that we have seen in many previous chapters. We'll say more about these methods after we've reviewed the code.

The `center()` and `right()` functions perform their respective equivalent action to `left()`.

If you rotate your servo to a specified angle and try to move the horn with your hand, you will notice that the servo resists the change. This is because the servo is continuously receiving (at a rate of 50 Hz) the last pulse set via `set_servo_pulsewidth()`, so it resists any attempt to change its set position.

In the previous section, when we wired the servo to your Raspberry Pi, we mentioned the servo's maximum current of ~400+mA. The preceding paragraph is an example where this maximum current is drawn by the servo. When the servo is receiving its pulse width instruction, it resists any force to change its position, resulting in more current usage. It is similar in principle to the stall current of a DC motor we discussed back in `Chapter 7`, *Turning Things On and Off*.

If you set the servo's pulse width to zero, as we do in the `idle()` function shown at line 4, you will now find that you can freely rotate the servo by hand with little force. When my test servo was idle (or at rest), it used approximately 6.5 mA:

```
def idle():                                        # (4)
    pi.set_servo_pulsewidth(SERVO_GPIO, 0)
```

So far, we've seen how to make the servo rotate to the left, center, and right, but what if we want to rotate it to a particular angle? Easy(-ish), we just need a little math, as shown in the `angle()` function at line 5:

```
def angle(to_angle):                               # (5)
    # Restrict to -90..+90 degrees
    to_angle = int(min(max(to_angle, -90), 90))

    ratio = (to_angle + 90) / 180.0                # (6)
    pulse_range = LEFT_PULSE - RIGHT_PULSE
    pulse = LEFT_PULSE - round(ratio * pulse_range)    # (7)

    pi.set_servo_pulsewidth(SERVO_GPIO, pulse)
```

The `angle()` function takes an angle in the range -90 to +90 degrees (0 degrees being center), works out the ratio of our input angle relative to the 180-degree range of our servo at line 6, before deriving the corresponding pulse width at line 7. This pulse width is then sent to the servo and it will adjust its angle accordingly.

Finally, we encounter the `sweep()` function at line 10. This is the function that provided the left/right sweeping movement of the servo when you ran this code:

```
def sweep(count=4):                                # (10)
    for i in range(count):
        right()
        sleep(MOVEMENT_DELAY_SECS)
        left()
        sleep(MOVEMENT_DELAY_SECS)
```

In this function, we see the use of `sleep(MOVEMENT_DELAY_SECS)`, which is necessary to give the servo time to complete each rotation request due to the asynchronous nature of servos. If you were to comment out the two `sleep()` calls, you will find that the servo rotates to the left and stops. This happens because as the `for` loop iterates (without `sleep()`), each `left()` call overrides the previous `right()` call, and so on, and it's `left()` that is called last before the loop completes.

We've just seen how to control a servo using PiGPIO and its servo-orientated PWM function, `set_servo_pulsewidth()`. If you are interested in how a servo implementation looks with the `set_PWM_frequency()` and `set_PWM_dutycycle()` functions, you'll find a file in the `chapter10` folder named `servo_alt.py`. It's functionally equivalent to the `servo.py` code we have just covered.

This now concludes our servo examples. The knowledge you have learned together with the code examples will provide you with everything you need to start using servos in your own projects! Our focus has been on using angular motion servos; however, the core of what you have learned will also be adaptable with some trial and error and experimenting (mostly around identifying the correct pulse widths) for use with a *continuous rotation servo*, which I'll briefly mention in the next section.

Let's conclude our discussion of servos with a brief consideration of the different types of servos.

Different types of servos

Our example used a common 3-wire, 180-degree angular servo. While this is a very common type of servo, there are other variations as well, including continuous rotation servos, servos with more than three wires, and special purpose servos:

- **Continuous rotation servos**: Have 3 wires and work on the same PWM principles as a 3-wire angular servo, except the PWM pulse width determines the rotational *direction* (clockwise/counter-clockwise) and *speed* of the servo.

Due to their internal control circuitry and gearing, continuous rotation servos are a convenient low-speed/high-torque alternative to a DC motor and H-Bridge controller (which we will be covering in the next section).

- **4-wire servos**: These come with one set of three wires and a fourth loose wire. This fourth wire is an analog output of the servo that can be used to detect the angle. It's useful if you need to know your servo's resting angle when you start your program.

> Servos track their position using an embedded potentiometer. This fourth wire is attached to such a potentiometer.

- **Special purpose or heavy-duty industrial use servos**: Have different wiring configurations and usage requirements – for example, they may not have the internal circuitry to decode PWM signals and require the user to supply and create the circuit to perform this function.

We have now learned how common hobby-style servos work, and also discovered how to set their angle of rotation in Python using PWM. In the next section, we will learn more about DC motors and how to control them using an IC known as an H-Bridge.

Using an H-Bridge IC to control a motor

In `Chapter 7`, *Turning Things On and Off*, we learned how to use a transistor to turn a DC motor on and off, and we also saw how to control the motor's speed using PWM. One limitation of our single transistor circuit was that the motor only rotated in one direction. In this section, we will explore a way to let us spin our motor in both the forward and backward directions – using what is known as an *H-Bridge* circuit.

> The H in H-Bridge comes from the perception that a basic H-Bridge circuit schematic (created from four individual transistors) make a letter H.

If you search around sites such as eBay for an H-Bridge module, you will identify many ready-made modules for the same purpose that we will cover in this section. What we will do is build a replica module on our breadboard. Once you have your breadboard replica working and understand how it works, you will be in a position to understand the construction of these ready-made modules.

We can create an H-Bridge to drive our motor in a few ways:

- Just use a pre-built module (modules and ICs may also be called or labeled motor drivers, or motor controllers). This is the easiest way.

- Create an H-Bridge circuit using discrete components – for example, four transistors, many diodes, a handful of resistors, and a lot of wire to connect them all. This is the hardest way.

- Use an IC (that internally combines all the necessary discrete parts).

 A servo, just like we used in the previous section, is made up of a DC motor connected to an H-Bridge-style circuit that allows the motor to move forward and backward to create the servo's left and right rotation.

We will opt for the last option and use an L293D, which is a common and low-cost H-Bridge IC that we can use to build a motor controller circuit.

Here are the basic specifications for the L293D extracted from its datasheet:

- Continuous current of 600 mA, 1.2 A peak/pulsed. As a reminder, we explored motors and current use in Chapter 7, *Turning Things On and Off*.
- It can control a motor with a voltage between 4.5 volts and 36 volts.
- It includes internal fly-back diodes, so we do not need to add our own. This is what the D means in L293**D**. If you need a refresher on fly-back diodes, please also see Chapter 7, *Turning Things On and Off*.
- It comprises two channels, so it is capable of driving two DC motors simultaneously.

 If you are looking to purchase a different motor driver IC for a project (for example, if you need one with more current), remember to check the datasheet to see whether it has fly-back diodes embedded, or else you will need to provide your own.

Let's build our circuit to control our motors.

Building the motor driver circuit

In this section, we will build our H-Bridge circuit that we will use to control two DC motors. The following schematic describes the circuit we will create. While this circuit looks busy, most of our work will be simply connecting the legs of the L293D IC to our Raspberry Pi, power source, and motors:

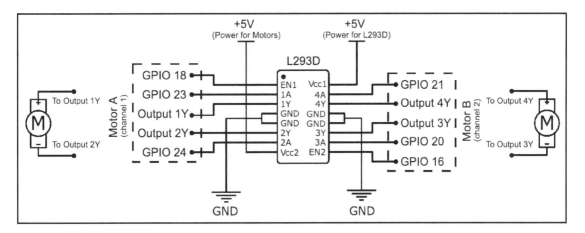

Figure 10.5 – L293D and motor schematic diagram

As there are a lot of wire connections to get through, we will build this circuit on our breadboard in four parts.

We will be using an IC in our circuit build. Many ICs (including the L293D) are sensitive to static **electricity discharge** (**ESD**), and if exposed to static discharge, they can be damaged. As a general rule, you should avoid touching the pins/legs of an IC with your fingers so that any static charge you have in your body does not get discharged to the IC.

Let's get started with the first part, as illustrated in the following diagram:

Figure 10.6 – L293D breadboard layout (Part 1 of 3)

Here are the steps to follow to start our breadboard build. The step numbers match the numbers in black circles in *Figure 10.6*:

1. Start by placing the L293D IC in your breadboard, making sure that that IC is orientated correctly with pin/leg 1 facing toward the top of your breadboard. Pin 1 of an IC is commonly indicated by a small circular indentation or dot beside the pin. In our illustration, this dot is white for visibility; however, it'll most likely be the same color as the casing on your IC. In the absence of a dot, there is also commonly a cutout section on one end of an IC. Pin 1 is the top-left pin when you hold the IC with the cutout facing *away* from you.

2. Connect a 5-volt pin on your Raspberry Pi to the positive rail of the left-hand side power rail.

3. Connect a GND pin on your Raspberry Pi to the negative rail of the left-hand side power rail.

4. Connect GPIO 18 to pin 1 of the L293D.

5. Connect GPIO 23 to pin 2 of the L293D.

6. Connect GPIO 24 to pin 7 of the L293D.

7. Connect a jumper lead to pin 3 of the L293D. The other end of this lead (labeled **Output 1Y**) is not connected to anything for the moment.

8. Connect a jumper lead to pin 6 of the L293D. The other end of this lead (labeled **Output 2Y**) is not connected to anything for the moment.

9. Using a jumper wire, connect pin 4 and pin 5 on the L293D together.

10. Finally, connect pin 4 and pin 5 of the L293D to the negative rail of the left-hand side power rail.

The bulk of the work we just performed involved the wiring of *channel 1* of the L293D. As a reminder, the L293D has two output channels, which, for the content in this section, means we can control two DC motors.

If you refer back to *Figure 10.6*, you will notice the wires (placed at *steps 7* and *8*) comprise the output for channel 1. Later in this section, we will attach a motor to these wires. Furthermore, in the diagram, you will notice that GPIOs 18, 23, and 24 are labeled as Channel 1 Control GPIOs. We will learn how these GPIOs are used to control the larger channel 1 motor when we discuss the code that accompanies this circuit.

Moving on, the next part of our build largely involves wiring up channel 2 of the L293D. This is more or less a mirror of the wiring we just performed:

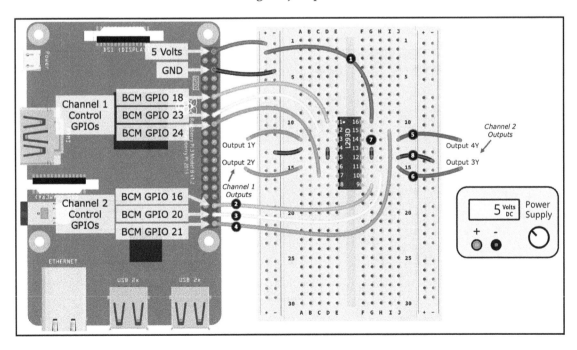

Figure 10.7 – L293D breadboard layout (Part 2 of 3)

Here are the steps to follow to complete the second part of our breadboard build. The step numbers match the numbers in black circles in *Figure 10.7*:

1. Connect pin 16 of the L293D to the positive rail of the left-hand side power rail. This 5-volt connection to pin 16 provides the power for the *IC's internal circuitry* – it is not the power source for the channel outputs (that is our motors). We will connect the external power source to the IC in part 3 of the build for powering the channels' motors.
2. Connect GPIO 16 to pin 9 of the L293D.
3. Connect GPIO 20 to pin 10 of the L293D.
4. Connect GPIO 21 to pin 15 of the L293D.
5. Connect a jumper lead to pin 14 of the L293D. The other end of this lead (labeled **Output 4Y**) is not connected to anything for the moment.
6. Connect a jumper lead to pin 11 of the L293D. The other end of this lead (labeled **Output 3Y**) is not connected to anything for the moment.
7. Using a jumper wire, connect pin 12 and pin 13 on the L293D together.
8. Finally, connect pin 12 and pin 13 of the L293D to the negative rail of the right-hand side power rail.

Now that we have wired the channel 2 output, our third task is to connect the external power supply:

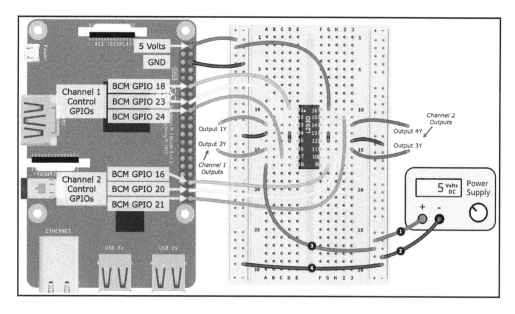

Figure 10.8 – L293D breadboard layout (Part 3 of 3)

Here are the steps to follow to complete the third part of our breadboard build. The step numbers match the numbers in black circles in *Figure 10.8*:

1. Connect the positive output terminal of your power supply to the positive rail of the right-hand side power rail.
2. Connect the negative output terminal of your power supply to the negative rail of the right-hand side power rail.
3. Connect pin 8 of the L293D to the positive rail of the right-hand side power rail. Pin 8 of the L293D provides the input power used to drive the output channels.
4. Finally, using a jumper wire, connect the negative rails of the left-hand side and right-hand side power rails.

This is our breadboard layout complete. However, there is one final task where we connect our motors. Following the example in the following diagram, you can connect a motor to each output channel:

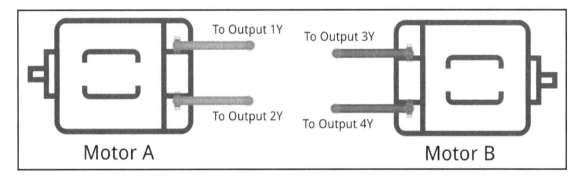

Figure 10.9 – L293D motor connections

Well done! That was a lot of wiring. I imagine that the tangle of wires you now have on your breadboard does not look nearly as graceful as the illustrations! Please do take the time to double-check your wirings for this circuit, as an incorrectly placed wire will prevent the circuit from working as intended.

During our circuit build, in part 3, *step 3*, we connected an external 5-volt power source to pin 8 of the L293D. This is the power used to drive each output channel, and hence our motors. If you ever wish to use motors that require a voltage different to 5 volts, you can alter this supply voltage to suit your needs, subject to the condition that the source voltage for the L293D must be within the range of 4.5 volts to 36 volts. Also remember (as mentioned at the start of this section) that your motors should not draw more than a 600 mA continuous current (fully on) or 1.2 A peak current (for instance, when using PWM, which we will cover when we get to the code).

If you read a datasheet for the L293D, it may be entitled *Quadruple Half-H Drivers*. Datasheets for driver type ICs can have all sorts of different titles and wordings. The important point here is that to drive our motor forward and backward, we require a full H-Bridge circuit, hence, for the L293D: Quad=4 and half=0.5, so *4 x 0.5 = 2* – that is, 2 full H-Bridges – therefore, we can control 2 motors.

Once you have created your breadboard circuit and connected your motors, we will run the example code and discuss how it works.

Running the example H-Bridge code to control a motor

Now that you have created your H-Bridge driver circuit and connected your motors, let's run the code that will make the motors spin.

There are two files for this section, and they can be found in `chapter10/motor_class.py` and `chapter10/motor.py`. Run the code found in `chapter10/motor.py` and your motors will turn on, change speeds, and change direction.

Place a piece of tape on the shaft of your motors to make it easier to see when they rotate and in what direction.

When you have confirmed that your circuit works with the example code, we will next proceed and discuss the code. Since the L293D can drive two motors, the common code has been abstracted out into `motor_class.py`, which is imported and used by `motor.py` to drive our two individual motors.

We'll start by looking at `motor.py`.

motor.py

Starting at line 1, we import PiGPIO and the `Motor` class defined in the `motor_class.py` file, before defining several variables describing how we are connecting the L293D to our Raspberry Pi's GPIO pins:

```
import pigpio                    # (1)
from time import sleep
from motor_class import Motor
```

```
# Motor A
CHANNEL_1_ENABLE_GPIO = 18          # (2)
INPUT_1Y_GPIO = 23
INPUT_2Y_GPIO = 24

# Motor B
CHANNEL_2_ENABLE_GPIO = 16          # (3)
INPUT_3Y_GPIO = 20
INPUT_4Y_GPIO = 21
```

Referring back to *Figure 10.3* and *Figure 10.4*, if we consider the **Motor A** (channel 1) side of the circuits, we see that the logic pins are connected to GPIOs 23 and 24 at line 2 – INPUT_1Y_GPIO = 23 and INPUT_2Y_GPIO = 24. These logic pins (together with the enable pin that we will cover shortly) are used to set the state and rotational direction of the motor. The truth table for these states is shown as follows.

This table was sourced from the L293D datasheet and reformatted and supplemented to match our code and circuit:

Row #	Enable GPIO	Logic 1 GPIO	Logic 2 GPIO	Motor Function
1	HIGH or > 0% duty cycle	Low	High	Turns right
2	HIGH or > 0% duty cycle	High	Low	Turns left
3	HIGH or > 0% duty cycle	Low	Low	Break
4	HIGH or > 0% duty cycle	High	High	Break
5	LOW or 0% duty cycle	N/A	N/A	Motor off

The L293D has two enable pins – one for each channel (that is, one for each motor) – for instance, CHANNEL_1_ENABLE_GPIO = 18 at line 3 in the preceding code. The enable pins are like a master switch for each channel. When the enable pin is set high, it turns the associated channel on, thus applying power to the motor. Alternatively, we can control the speed of a motor if we instead pulse the enable pin using PWM. We'll see the code that works with the logic and enables pins shortly when we explore the motor_class.py file.

Next, we will create a single instance of `pigpio.pi()`, as shown in line 4, and then we will create two instances of `Motor` to represent our two physical motors:

```
pi = pigpio.pi()                          # (4)
motor_A = Motor(pi, CHANNEL_1_ENABLE_GPIO, INPUT_1Y_GPIO, INPUT_2Y_GPIO)
motor_B = Motor(pi, CHANNEL_2_ENABLE_GPIO, INPUT_3Y_GPIO, INPUT_4Y_GPIO)
```

After we have created the `motor_A` and `motor_B` classes, we perform a few actions with these class to control the motors, as shown in the following code, starting at line 5 – this is what you witnessed in the previous section when you ran the code:

```
print("Motor A and B Speed 50, Right")
motor_A.set_speed(50)                                # (5)
motor_A.right()
motor_B.set_speed(50)
motor_B.right()
sleep(2)

#... truncated ...

print("Motor A Classic Brake, Motor B PWM Brake")
motor_A.brake()                                      # (6)
motor_B.brake_pwm(brake_speed=100, delay_millisecs=50)
sleep(2)
```

Take note of the braking at line 6 and observe the motors. Did one motor brake better than the other? We will discuss this further when we cover the two brake functions toward the end of the next section.

Let's move on and look at `motor_class.py`. This is where the code that integrates our Raspberry Pi with the L293D is found.

motor_class.py

First, we see the `Motor` class definition and its constructor:

```
class Motor:

  def __init__(self, pi, enable_gpio, logic_1_gpio, logic_2_gpio):

    self.pi = pi
    self.enable_gpio = enable_gpio
    self.logic_1_gpio = logic_1_gpio
    self.logic_2_gpio = logic_2_gpio

    pi.set_PWM_range(self.enable_gpio, 100) # speed is 0..100        # (1)
```

```
# Set default state - motor not spinning and
# set for right direction.
self.set_speed(0) # Motor off                               # (2)
self.right()
```

At line 1, we are defining the PiGPIO PWM duty cycle range for the enable pin to be in the range `0..100`. This defines the maximum range value (that is, `100`) that we can use with the `set_speed()` function that we'll come to shortly.

The range `0..100` means we have 101 discrete integer PWM steps, which maps conveniently to a 0% to 100% duty cycle. If you specify a higher number, this does not mean more duty cycles (or more motor speed); it just changes the granularity of the steps – for example, the default PWM range of `0..255` gives us 256 discrete steps, where 255 = 100% duty cycle.

 Remember what we're about to discuss covers one channel (one motor) of the L293D IC circuit. Everything we cover applies to the other channel too – it's just the GPIO pins and IC pins that change.

Our constructor finishes by initializing the motor to be off (zero speed) and defaults the motor to the right rotational direction, as shown in the preceding code at line 2.

Next, we encounter several functions that we use to make our motor(s) spin. We see at line 3 and line 4 the `right()` and `left()` methods, which alter the high/low states of the logic pins of the L293D, according to rows 1 and 2 in the preceding table:

```
def right(self, speed=None):              # (3)
    if speed is not None:
        self.set_speed(speed)

    self.pi.write(self.logic_1_gpio, pigpio.LOW)
    self.pi.write(self.logic_2_gpio, pigpio.HIGH)


def left(self, speed=None):               # (4)
    if speed is not None:
        self.set_speed(speed)

    self.pi.write(self.logic_1_gpio, pigpio.HIGH)
    self.pi.write(self.logic_2_gpio, pigpio.LOW)
```

We can check whether our motor is set to rotate left or right by querying the current states of the logic pins, as shown in `is_right()` at line 5. Notice that the queried GPIO states in `is_right()` match the states set in `right()`:

```
def is_right(self):                                     # (5)
    return not self.pi.read(self.logic_1_gpio)    # LOW
            and self.pi.read(self.logic_2_gpio)    # HIGH
```

We see the use of `set_PWM_dutycycle()` in the `set_speed()` method in the following code at line 6, where we set the speed of our motor by pulsing the enable pin of the L293D. Pulsing the enable pin is done using the same basic principles we used back in Chapter 7, *Turning Things On and Off*, when we pulsed a transistor to set our motor's speed:

```
def set_speed(self, speed):                             # (6)
    assert 0<=speed<=100
    self.pi.set_PWM_dutycycle(self.enable_gpio, speed)
```

You can stop the motor by setting the speed to 0, which effectively is cutting off the motor's power (0% duty cycle = pin low).

Moving forward, we find two methods named `brake()` and `brake_pwm()` at lines 7 and 8, which can be used to stop the motor *quickly*. The difference between braking and stopping a motor by cutting its power (that is, `set_speed(0)`) is that `set_speed(0)` allows the motor to slow down gradually over time – which is the state at row 5 in the preceding table:

```
def brake(self):                    # (7)
    was_right = self.is_right() # To restore direction after braking
    self.set_speed(100)
    self.pi.write(self.logic_1_gpio, pigpio.LOW)
    self.pi.write(self.logic_2_gpio, pigpio.LOW)
    self.set_speed(0)

    if was_right:
        self.right()
    else:
        self.left()
```

When you ran this code in the previous section, and if you experiment with the two brake functions on your own, my guess is that you will find `brake()` does not work well (if at all), while the `brake_pwm()` function does:

```
def brake_pwm(self, brake_speed=100, delay_millisecs=50):    # (8)
    was_right = None # To restore direction after braking
    if self.is_right():
        self.left(brake_speed)
        was_right = True
```

```
else:
    self.right(brake_speed)
    was_right = False
sleep(delay_millisecs / 1000)
self.set_speed(0)
if was_right:
    self.right()
else:
    self.left()
```

Let's discuss why we have defined two different braking methods and why one works better than the other.

The implementation of `brake()` is the classic way a motor brake is implemented, where both logic GPIOs are set high or low together, as in rows 3 or 4 in the preceding table. The catch, however, is that the performance of this logic can vary depending on the IC you are using (how it's constructed internally), your motor, and the voltage and current use are using. For our example, we are using a small motor (with no load on its shaft), small voltage and currents, and an L293D IC. The net of all this is that classic braking does not work well, if at all.

We're using the L293D IC because of its popularity, availability, and low cost. It's been in production for many years, and you will have no problem finding example circuits and code based around this IC for all sorts of applications. It's not the most efficient IC, however. This is a contributing factor in classic braking not working in some scenarios.

The `break_pwm(reverse_speed, delay_secs)` implementation takes a different and more reliable approach to braking by applying a small and opposite voltage to the motor. You can use the `brake_speed` and `delay_millisecs` parameters to tune the braking if required – too little speed and delay and the brake will not work, too much and the motor will reverse direction.

Have you noticed that at full speed (that is, `set_speed(100)`), your motor spins slower than if it were connected directly to 5 volts? There is a ~2 voltage drop inherent in the L293D. Even though V_{cc1} (motor power source) is connected to 5 volts, the motor is not getting this full 5 volts (it's more like ~3 volts). If you are using a variable power supply (that is, not a 3.3 V/5 V breadboard power supply), you can increase the input voltage to V_{cc1} to around 7 volts. This will then see the motor getting around 5 volts (you can use your multimeter to verify this).

Congratulations! You have just learned how to operate a servo and master the control of a DC motor in terms of speed and the direction of braking. The circuits, code, and skills you have just acquired can be adapted to many applications where you need to create motion and angular movement – for example, a robotic car or arm. You could even use these skills to retrofit motorized toys and other motorized gadgets and make them controllable by your Raspberry Pi.

If you would like to extend your knowledge further, you might like to explore how to create an H-Bridge circuit from individual components – such as transistors, resistors, and diodes. While there are various ways to accomplish this circuit, we covered the core basics in terms of concepts and components between this chapter and our use of transistors back in `Chapter 7`, *Turning Things On and Off*.

Well done! We covered a lot in this section as we learned how to use an L293D H-Bridge to make a DC motor spin, reverse direction, and brake. In the next section, we will look at an alternative use of the L293D and see how to use it to control a stepper motor.

Introduction to stepper motor control

Stepper motors are a unique type of motor in terms of their precision and torque. Similar to a DC motor, a stepper motor can rotate in both directions continuously, while they can be precisely controlled similar to a servo.

In the following diagram is a 28BYJ-48 stepper motor, together with headpins that can be used to connect the motor to a breadboard:

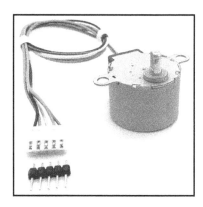

Figure 10.10 – 28BYJ-48 stepper motor

Stepper motor theory and practice can get complex quickly! There are different forms and types of stepper motors and many variables, such as stride angles and gearing, that all need to be accounted for, plus various ways to wire and control them. We can't possibly cover all these parameters here, nor can we go into the low-level details of how stepper motors work.

Instead, we will cover the practical operation of a common and readily available stepper motor, a 28BYJ-48. Once you understand the basic principles as they apply to a 28BYJ-48, you will be well-positioned to broaden your knowledge of stepper motors.

Controlling stepper motors can be confusing and fiddly when you first start using them. Unlike DC motors and servos, you need to appreciate how stepper motors work at both a mechanical and code level to control them.

The basic specifications for our reference 28BYJ-48 are as follows:

- 5 volts (make sure your stepper is 5 volts because the 28BYJ-48 also comes in 12 volts).
- A stride angle of 64, a 1:64 gearing ratio, giving *64 x 64 = 4,096* steps per 360 degree revolution.

Using the stride angle, gearing ratio, and sequence, we can calculate the number of logical steps needed to rotate our stepper motor 360 degrees: *64 x 64 / 8 = 512 steps*.

Next, we will connect our stepper motor to our Raspberry Pi.

Connecting the stepper motor to the L293D circuit

To connect our stepper motor to our Raspberry Pi, we are going to reuse our L293D circuit, as shown in *Figure 10.8* in the previous section. Here is what we need to do:

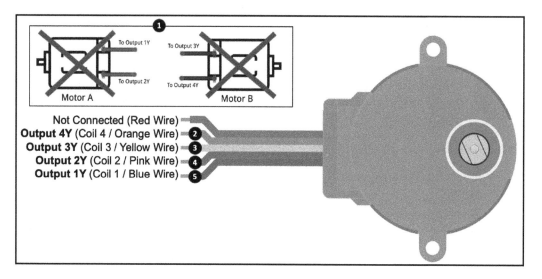

Figure 10.11 – 28BYJ-48 stepper motor wiring connection

The following steps match the numbering shown in *Figure 10.11*. Remember that we are starting with the circuit you completed previously in the section entitled *Building the motor driver circuit* and shown in *Figure 10.8*:

In *steps 2* through *5*, we will connect the stepper motor in our breadboard circuit. A suggestion is to use header pins (as pictured in *Figure 10.10*) to connect your motor to a run of vacant rows on your breadboard, and then connect the output wires from the L293D to the appropriate row matching the wire colors mentioned in the steps.

1. If you have not done so already, disconnect the two DC motors from the existing circuit.
2. Connect the orange wire of your stepper motor to the wire labeled **Output 4Y** in *Figure 10.8*.
3. Connect the yellow wire of your stepper motor to the wire labeled **Output 3Y** in *Figure 10.8*.

4. Connect the pink wire of your stepper motor to the wire labeled **Output 2Y** in *Figure 10.8*.

5. Connect the blue wire of your stepper motor to the wire labeled **Output 1Y** in *Figure 10.8*.

In our example scenario, we are using our L293D H-Bridge to drive our stepper motor as a *bipolar* stepper motor. You will come across the terms *bipolar* and *unipolar* in relation to stepper motors. These terms relate to how the motor is wired, and this influences how you will control them. A discussion of the differences between bipolar and unipolar stepper motors can quickly get complex; however, a simplified distinction at this stage of learning is as follows:

- A *bipolar* stepper motor requires a driving circuit that is capable of reversing the current flow.

- A *unipolar* stepper motor *does not* require a circuit that is capable of reversing the current flow.

In our example with bipolar wiring, we use an H-Bridge circuit because it is capable of reversing current flow to a coil (for example, this is how we made our DC motor reverse direction in the previous section).

The ULN2003 IC is a popular, low-cost Darlington transistor array (with built-in fly-back diodes); you could also use it to drive your stepper motor as a *unipolar* stepper motor. In this setup, you would use the red wire connected to +5 volts because the ULN2003 is unable to reverse current.

With our stepper motor connected, we can continue on to control it with code.

Running and exploring the stepper motor code

The code we are about to run can be found in the `chapter10/stepper.py` file. I recommend reviewing the source code before proceeding so that you have an overall idea of what the file contains.

When you run the code found in the `chapter10/stepper.py` file, your stepper motor should rotate a complete 360 degrees in one direction, and then back again.

Place a piece of tape on the shaft of your stepper motor to make it easier to see when it rotates and in what direction.

Starting at the top of the source file, we define all our GPIO variables, including our enable pins at line 1, plus variables starting at line 2 relating to our stepper motor coil wires. These wires must be **identified and ordered correctly, as coil wire order matters!**

```
CHANNEL_1_ENABLE_GPIO = 18                                    # (1)
CHANNEL_2_ENABLE_GPIO = 16

INPUT_1A_GPIO = 23 # Blue Coil 1 Connected to 1Y              # (2)
INPUT_2A_GPIO = 24 # Pink Coil 2 Connected to 2Y
INPUT_3A_GPIO = 20 # Yellow Coil 3 Connected to 3Y
INPUT_4A_GPIO = 21 # Orange Coil 4 Connected to 4Y

STEP_DELAY_SECS = 0.002                                       # (3)
```

We will see later in code the use of STEP_DELAY_SECS at line 3 to add a slight delay in between coil steps. A higher delay will result in a slower rotation of the stepper motor's shaft; however, too small a number and the shaft may not rotate at all or the rotation may be erratic and stutter. Feel free to experiment with different delay values to suit your needs.

Next, starting at line 4, we group our coil GPIOs into a Python list (array) and initialize these GPIOs as outputs at line 5. We're storing the GPIOs in a list because we will be iterating over these GPIOs later when we use the rotate() function. We also have the off() function at line 6 that we use to turn off all the coils:

```
coil_gpios = [                              # (4)
    INPUT_1A_GPIO,
    INPUT_2A_GPIO,
    INPUT_3A_GPIO,
    INPUT_4A_GPIO
]

# Initialise each coil GPIO as OUTPUT.
for gpio in coil_gpios:                     # (5)
    pi.set_mode(gpio, pigpio.OUTPUT)

def off():
    for gpio in coil_gpios:                 # (6)
        pi.write(gpio, pigpio.LOW) # Coil off

off() # Start with stepper motor off.
```

At line 7, we're setting the two enable GPIO pins `HIGH` in code because we are reusing the circuit from our previous DC motor control example. The alternative non-code approach would be to connect the L293D EN1 and EN2 pins directly to +5 volts (that is, pull them `HIGH` manually):

```
# Enable Channels (always high)
pi.set_mode(CHANNEL_1_ENABLE_GPIO, pigpio.OUTPUT)      # (7)
pi.write(CHANNEL_1_ENABLE_GPIO, pigpio.HIGH)
pi.set_mode(CHANNEL_2_ENABLE_GPIO, pigpio.OUTPUT)
pi.write(CHANNEL_2_ENABLE_GPIO, pigpio.HIGH)
```

Starting at line 8, we define two stepping sequences in a multi-dimension (2 x 2) array named `COIL_HALF_SEQUENCE` and `COIL_FULL_SEQUENCE`, and we thus encounter the parts of the code where it starts to become obvious that stepper motor control is more complex than DC motor or servo control!

A stepping sequence defines how we must turn on (energize) and off (not energized) each coil in the stepper motor to make it step. Each row in the sequence has four elements, each relating to a coil:

```
COIL_HALF_SEQUENCE = [               # (8)
    [0, 1, 1, 1],
    [0, 0, 1, 1],    # (a)
    [1, 0, 1, 1],
    [1, 0, 0, 1],    # (b)
    [1, 1, 0, 1],
    [1, 1, 0, 0],    # (c)
    [1, 1, 1, 0],
    [0, 1, 1, 0] ]   # (d)

COIL_FULL_SEQUENCE = [
    [0, 0, 1, 1],    # (a)
    [1, 0, 0, 1],    # (b)
    [1, 1, 0, 0],    # (c)
    [0, 1, 1, 0] ]   # (d)
```

A sequence with eight steps is known as a *half-step* sequence, while a *full-step* sequence has four rows and is a subset of the half-sequence (match up the *(a)*, *(b)*, *(c)*, and *(d)* rows in the preceding code).

A half-sequence will give you more resolution (for example, 4,096 steps for a 360-degree revolution), while a full-step sequence will give you half the resolution (2,048 steps) but twice the stepping speed.

A stepping sequence for a stepper can usually be found in its datasheet – but not always, as our reference 28BYJ-48 datasheet mentioned in the *Technical requirements* section proves, so sometimes some research may be necessary.

 If a stepper motor is not rotating, but it is making a sound and vibrating, it's a sign that the stepping sequence and coil order is incorrectly matched. This is a common frustration with stepper motors when you try to just connect them blindly and hope they work. To avoid this trial-and-error approach, take the time to identify your stepper motor type and how it is being wired (for example, bipolar or unipolar), and work out the coil numbering and what a suitable coil stepping sequence looks like. Consulting your stepper motor's datasheet is the best place to start.

Next, at line 9, we defined the global variable, `sequence = COIL_HALF_SEQUENCE`, to use a half-step sequence when stepping our motor. You can change this to `sequence = COIL_FULL_SEQUENCE` to use a full-step sequence – all other code remains the same:

```
sequence = COIL_HALF_SEQUENCE          # (9)
#sequence = COIL_FULL_SEQUENCE
```

At line 10, we have the `rotate(steps)` method, which is where all the magic happens, so to speak. Examining and understanding what this method does is the key to understanding how to control our stepper motor. The `steps` parameter can be a positive or a negative number to rotate the stepper motor in the reverse direction:

```
# For rotate() to keep track of the sequence row it is on.
sequence_row = 0

def rotate(steps):                                      # (10)
    global sequence_row
    direction = +1
    if steps < 0:
        direction = -1
```

The core of the `rotate()` function is within the two `for` loops, starting at line 11:

```
# rotate(steps) continued...

    for step in range(abs(steps)):                      # (11)
        coil_states = sequence[sequence_row]            # (12)
        for i in range(len(sequence[sequence_row])):
            gpio = coil_gpios[i]                         # (13)
            state = sequence[sequence_row][i]           # (14)
            pi.write(gpio, state)                       # (15)
            sleep(STEP_DELAY_SECS)
```

As the code loops for `step` iterations, we get the next coil state's form, `sequence[sequence_row]`, at line 12 (for example, `[0, 1, 1, 1]`), before looping through and getting the corresponding coil GPIO at line 13, and its `HIGH`/`LOW` state at line 14. At line 15, we set the `HIGH`/`LOW` state of the coil with `pi.write()`, which makes our motor move (that is, step), before sleeping for a short delay.

Next, starting at line 16, the `sequence_row` index is updated based on the direction of rotation (that is, whether the `steps` parameter was positive or negative):

```
# rotate(steps) continued...

        sequence_row += direction          # (16)
        if sequence_row < 0:
            sequence_row = len(sequence) - 1
        elif sequence_row >= len(sequence):
            sequence_row = 0
```

At the end of this block of code, if there are more steps to complete, the code then goes back to line 11 for the next `for steps in ...` iteration.

Finally, at line 17, we come to the part of the code that made our stepper motor rotate when we ran the example. Remember, if you switch line 9 to be `sequence = COIL_FULL_SEQUENCE`, then the number of steps will be `2048`:

```
if __name__ == '__main__':
    try:                                                    # (17)
        steps = 4096 # Steps for HALF stepping sequence.
        print("{} steps for full 360 degree rotation.".format(steps))
        rotate(steps) # Rotate one direction
        rotate(-steps) # Rotate reverse direction

    finally:
        off() # Turn stepper coils off
        pi.stop() # PiGPIO Cleanup
```

Congratulations! You have just completed a crash course on stepper motor control.

I understand that if you are new to steppers, there is some multi-dimensional thinking required and that you have been introduced to many concepts and terms that we have not been able to cover in detail. Stepper motors will take time to understand; however, once you grasp the basic process of controlling one stepper motor, then you are well on your way to understanding the broader concepts in more detail.

There are many stepper motor tutorials and examples scattered across the internet. The goal of many examples is to just make the stepper motor work, and it's not always clearly explained how this is being achieved due to the underlying complexity. As you read up on stepper motors and explore code examples, remember that the definition of a step can vary greatly and depends on the context in which it is being used. This is a reason why two examples may cite significantly different step numbers for the same stepper motor.

Summary

In this chapter, you learned how to use three common types of motors to create complex movement with your Raspberry Pi – a servo motor for creating an angular moment, a DC motor with an H-Bridge driver to create direction movement and speed control, and a stepper motor for precision movement. If you have grasped the general concepts of each of these types of motors, then you deserve a pat on the back! This is an achievement. While motors are simple in principle and their movement is something we take for granted daily in everyday appliances and toys, as you have discovered, there is a lot going on behind the scenes to make that movement occur.

What you have learned in this chapter, together with the example circuits and code, provides you with a foundation that you can use to start building your own applications where movement and motion are required. A simple and fun project could be to create a program to control a robotic car or robotic arm – you'll find DIY kits and robotic parts for cars and arms on sites such as eBay.

In the next chapter, we will explore ways we can measure distance and detect movement with our Raspberry Pi, Python, and various electronic components.

Questions

As we conclude, here is a list of questions for you to test your knowledge of this chapter's material. You will find the answers in the *Assessments* section of the book:

1. Your servo does not rotate fully to the left or right. Why is this and how can you fix this?
2. Your servo is groaning at one or both of its extreme left/right positions. Why?
3. What advantage does an H-Bridge provide over a single transistor when controlling DC motors?

4. You are using an L293D H-Bridge IC. You follow the instructions as per the datasheet but cannot get your motor to brake. Why?

5. Why do your 5-volt motors spin slower when connected to an H-Bridge using an L293D compared to connecting the motor directly to a 5-volt source?

6. You have a stepper motor that will not work – it vibrates, but will not turn. What could be the problem?

7. Can you drive a stepper motor directly from four Raspberry Pis' GPIO pins?

11
Measuring Distance and Detecting Movement

Welcome to our final core electronics-based chapter. In the previous chapter, we learned how to control three different forms of motors in complex ways. In this chapter, we will direct our attention to detecting movement and measuring the distance with our Raspberry Pi and electronics.

Detecting movement is very useful for automation projects such as turning on lights when you walk into a room or building, an alarm system, building counters, or detecting revolutions of a shaft. We will be looking at two techniques for movement detection, including a **Passive Infrared** (**PIR**) sensor that uses heat detection to detect the presence of a person (or animal), and a digital Hall-effect sensor that detects the presence of a magnetic field (or, more liberally, we can say that the Hall-effect sensor can detect when a magnet moves past it).

Distance measurement is also useful for many projects, from collision detection circuits to measuring water tank levels. We will be looking at two forms of distance measurement, including the use of an ultrasonic sound sensor that can measure distances of around 2 centimeters to 4 meters, and also an analog Hall-effect sensor that can measure the proximity of a magnetic field down to millimeters.

Here is what we will cover in this chapter:

- Detecting movement with a PIR sensor
- Measuring distance with an ultrasonic sensor
- Detecting movement and distance with Hall-effect sensors

Technical requirements

To perform the exercises in this chapter, you will need the following:

- Raspberry Pi 4 Model B
- Raspbian OS Buster (with desktop and recommended software)
- Minimum Python version 3.5

These requirements are what the code examples in this book are based on. It's reasonable to expect that the code examples should work without modification on Raspberry Pi 3 Model B or a different version of Raspbian OS as long as your Python version is 3.5 or higher.

You will find this chapter's source code in the `chapter11` folder in the GitHub repository available at `https://github.com/PacktPublishing/Practical-Python-Programming-for-IoT`.

You will need to execute the following commands in a terminal to set up a virtual environment and install the Python libraries required for the code in this chapter:

```
$ cd chapter11            # Change into this chapter's folder
$ python3 -m venv venv    # Create Python Virtual Environment
$ source venv/bin/activate  # Activate Python Virtual Environment
(venv) $ pip install pip --upgrade       # Upgrade pip
(venv) $ pip install -r requirements.txt # Install dependent packages
```

The following dependencies are installed from `requirements.txt`:

- **PiGPIO**: The PiGPIO GPIO library (`https://pypi.org/project/pigpio`)
- **ADS1X15**: The ADS11x5 ADC library (`https://pypi.org/project/adafruit-circuitpython-ads1x15`)

The electronic components we will need for this chapter's exercises are as follows:

- 1 x 1kΩ resistor
- 1 x 2kΩ resistor
- 1 x HC-SR501 PIR sensor (datasheet: `https://www.alldatasheet.com/datasheet-pdf/pdf/1131987/ETC2/HC-SR501.html`)
- 1 x A3144 Hall-effect sensor (non-latching) (datasheet: `https://www.alldatasheet.com/datasheet-pdf/pdf/55092/ALLEGRO/A3144.html`)
- 1 x AH3503 Hall-effect sensor (ratiometric) (datasheet: `https://www.alldatasheet.com/datasheet-pdf/pdf/1132644/AHNJ/AH3503.html`)

- 1 x HC-SR04 or HC-SR04P ultrasonic distance sensor (datasheet: `https://tinyurl.com/HCSR04DS`)
- A small magnet for use with the Hall-effect sensors

 There are two variations of the HC-SR04 available. The more common HC-SR04, which outputs 5-volt logic and the HC-SR04**P**, which can operate at between 3 volts and 5.5 volts. Either module will be suitable for the exercise in this chapter.

Detecting movement with a PIR sensor

A PIR sensor is a device that can detect infrared light (heat) emitted by an object (for example, a person). We see these types of sensors all around us in applications such as security systems and automatic doors and lights that react to our presence. The *passive* in PIR means the sensor just detects movement. To detect *what* moved and *how*, you would need an active infrared device, such as a thermal camera.

PIR sensors come in a few different forms and varieties; however, their basic usage is the same – they act as a simple digital switch. When they do not detect movement, they output a digital `LOW`, and when movement is detected, they output a digital `HIGH`.

Shown in the following figure is the HC-SR501 PIR sensor module that we will be using for our example. Pictured are the top of the module, the underside, and a common schematic symbol for a PIR sensor:

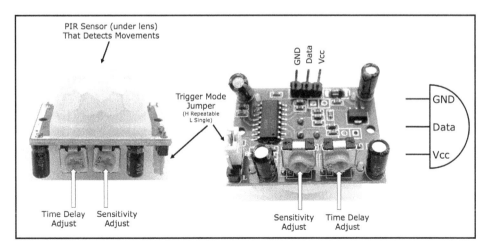

Figure 11.1 – HC-SR501 PIR sensor module

Some PIR sensors, including our HC-SR501, have an onboard setting and calibration adjustments on them. These adjustments are used to change the sensitivity range and triggering mode of the sensor. To use a PIR device without on-board calibration means we would need to handle sensitivity adjustments ourselves in code.

In regard to the HC-SR501, its terminals are as follows:

- **GND**: Connection to ground.
- **Vcc**: Connection to a power source between 5 volts and 20 volts.
- **Data**: Digital output that we connect to a GPIO pin. When the PIR detects movement, this pin goes HIGH; otherwise, it remains LOW in the absence of movement. The HC-SR501 outputs a 3.3-volt signal, even though it requires a 5- to 20-volt power source. As we will see next, the onboard *sensitivity adjust*, *timing adjust* trims, and *trigger mode* jumper influence how, when, and for how long this data pin remains HIGH when movement is detected.

The HC-SR501 onboard settings are as follows:

- **Sensitivity Adjust**: Changes the effective movement sensing range between about 3 meters to about 7 meters. Use a small screwdriver to rotate this setting's dial.
- **Time Delay Adjust**: How long the data terminal remains HIGH after movement is detected. The adjustment range is approximately 5 seconds to 300 seconds. Use a small screwdriver to rotate this setting's dial.
- **Trigger Mode Jumper**: In the presence of continued movement detection, this jumper setting means that after the time delay expires (as set by **Time Delay Adjust**), the data terminal will do the following:
  - Remain HIGH. This is the *repeatable* trigger setting, set by placing the jumper into the **H** position.
  - Revert to LOW. This is the *single-shot* setting, set by placing the jumper into the **L** position.

The best settings for your PIR will depend on how you intend to use it and the environment in which you deploy your sensor. My suggestion is to play around with the setting adjustments after you complete the circuit build and run the example code in the subsequent sections to get a feel for how changing the settings affects the operation of the sensor. Remember to consult the HC-SR501 datasheet for more information on the sensor and its onboard settings.

Let's wire up our PIR sensor and connect it to our Raspberry Pi.

Creating the PIR sensor circuit

In this section, we will connect our PIR sensor to our Raspberry Pi. The following is the schematic diagram of the circuit we are about to build. As you can see, it has relatively straightforward wiring from the perspective of the PIR sensor:

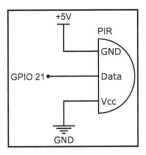

Figure 11.2 – PIR sensor module circuit

Let's connect it to our Raspberry Pi as illustrated in the following figure:

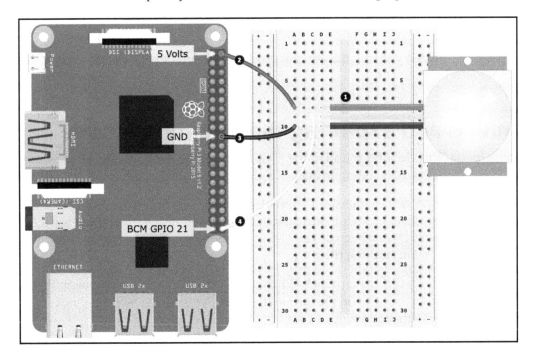

Figure 11.3 – PIR sensor circuit breadboard layout

Here are the steps to follow to create your breadboard build. The step numbers match the numbers in black circles in *Figure 11.3*:

1. Connect each terminal of your PIR sensor to your breadboard. You will need three male-to-male jumper cables.
2. Connect a 5-volt pin on your Raspberry Pi to the same breadboard row used by the PIR's Vcc terminal. PIR sensors only use a little current, so it will be okay to connect the 5-volt Vcc pin directly to your Raspberry Pi.
3. Connect a GND pin on your Raspberry Pi to the same breadboard row used by the PIR's GND terminal.
4. Connect GPIO 21 on your Raspberry Pi to the same breadboard row used by the PIR's data terminal.

 IMPORTANT: Our reference HC-SR501 PIR sensor requires >4.5 volts for its power (Vcc), and outputs 3.3 volts on its **Sig** output pin. If you are using a different PIR sensor, then consult its datasheet and check the output pin voltage. If it is >3.3 volts, you will need to use a voltage divider or logic level shifter. We will cover this exact scenario in the next section when we couple a voltage divider with an HC-SR04 sensor to convert its 5-volt output into a Raspberry Pi-friendly 3.3 volts.

Once you have created your circuit, we will proceed and run our PIR example code, which will let us detect movement.

Running and exploring the PIR sensor code

The code for out PIR circuit is found in the `chapter11/hc-sr501.py` file. Please review the source code before proceeding to get a broad understanding of what this file contains.

 The HC-SR501 datasheet stipulates that the sensor needs around 1 minute after power-on to initialize and stabilize itself. If you try and use the sensor before it becomes stable, you may receive a few erroneous triggers when you start the program.

Run the `hc-sr501.py` file in a terminal. When the HC-SR501 detects movement, the program will print `Triggered` on the terminal, or `Not Triggered` when no movement is detected, as shown in the following output:

```
(venv) $ python hc-sr501.py

PLEASE NOTE - The HC-SR501 Needs 1 minute after power on to initialize
itself.
```

```
Monitoring environment...
Press Control + C to Exit
Triggered.
Not Triggered.
... truncated ...
```

If your program is not responding as expected, try adjusting one or more of the **Sensitivity Adjustment**, **Time Delay Adjustment**, or **Trigger Mode Jumper** settings that we discussed earlier in the section titled *Detecting movement with a PIR sensor*.

You can consider the HC-SR501 as a basic switch. It's either on (HIGH) or off (LOW), just like a common push-button switch. In fact, our code is similar to the PiGPIO button example presented in the *Responding to a button press with PiGPIO* section back in Chapter 2, *Getting Started with Python and IoT*. We'll just brush over the core code parts here; however, if you need a deeper explanation or a refresher, please revisit the PiGPIO sections in Chapter 2, *Getting Started with Python and IoT*.

Let's discuss the example code. Firstly, we start on line 1 by setting up our GPIO pin as an input pin with pull-down enabled, while on line 2, we have debouncing enabled. Our HC-SR501 module won't actually require the pull-down to be activated in code, nor will it require the debouncing; however, I've added it in for completeness:

```
# ... truncated ...
GPIO = 21

# Initialize GPIO
pi.set_mode(GPIO, pigpio.INPUT)                              # (1)
pi.set_pull_up_down(GPIO, pigpio.PUD_DOWN)
pi.set_glitch_filter(GPIO, 10000) # microseconds debounce    # (2)
```

Next, on line 3, we define the callback_handler() function, which will get called whenever the GPIO pin changes its HIGH/LOW state:

```
def callback_handler(gpio, level, tick):                     # (3)
    """ Called whenever a level change occurs on GPIO Pin.
      Parameters defined by PiGPIO pi.callback() """
    global triggered

    if level == pigpio.HIGH:
        triggered = True
        print("Triggered")
    elif level == pigpio.LOW:
        triggered = False
        print("Not Triggered")
```

Finally, on line 4, we register our callback function. It's the second parameter, `pigpio.EITHER_EDGE`, that causes `callback_handler()` to be called whenever GPIO changes to `HIGH` or `LOW`:

```
# Register Callback
callback = pi.callback(GPIO, pigpio.EITHER_EDGE, callback_handler) # (4)
```

For comparison, in `Chapter 2`, *Getting Started with Python and IoT*, for our push-button example, this parameter was `pigpio.FALLING_EDGE`, meaning the callback only got called when the button was pressed, and not when it was released.

As we have seen, a PIR sensor can only detect the proximity of an object – for example, is someone near our sensor? – but it cannot give us an indication of how far or near that object is.

We've now learned how to create and connect a simple PIR sensor circuit to our Raspberry Pi, and how to use it to detect movement in Python. Armed with this knowledge, you can now start building your own motion detection projects, such as turning things on and off when someone or some animal is detected, by combining the examples from `Chapter 7`, *Turning Things On and Off*, or as an important part of your own alarm and monitoring system.

Next, we will look at a sensor that is capable of estimating distance.

Measuring distance with an ultrasonic sensor

In the previous section, we learned how to detect movement with a PIR sensor. As we discovered, our PIR sensor was a digital device that signaled movement detection by making its output a digital `HIGH`.

It's time to learn how to measure distance with our Raspberry Pi. There are a variety of sensors that are capable of performing this task, and they commonly either work with sound or light. Our example will be based around the popular HC-SR04 ultrasonic distance sensor (it works on sound), as pictured in the following figure:

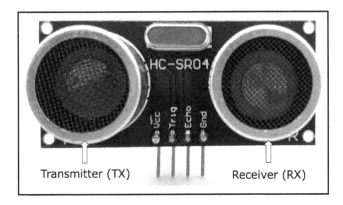

Figure 11.4 – HC-SR04 ultrasonic distance sensor module

A place where you commonly find ultrasonic distance sensors is modern car bumper bars (they're often little round circles, which is a different form factor than the HC-SR04 pictured in the preceding figure). These sensors calculate the distance between your car and a nearby object and, for example, make a beeper inside your car beep faster and faster as you get closer and closer to the object

Another common application is for measuring liquid levels, such as in a water tank. In this scenario, a (waterproof) ultrasonic sensor measures the distance from, for example, the top of the tank to the water level (the sound pulse bounces off the water). The measured distance can then be translated into an estimate of how full the tank is.

Let's take a closer look at our HC-SR04 sensor. The core specifications from the reference HC-SR04 datasheet are as follows:

- Power voltage 5 volts (HC-SR04) or 3 volts to 5.5 volts (HC-SR04P)
- Logic voltage 5 volts (HC-SR04) or 3 volts to 5.5 volts (HC-SR04P)
- Working current 15 mA, resting current 2 mA
- Effective measurement range 2 cm–4 m, with an accuracy of +/- 0.3 cm
- A trigger pulse width of 10 μs (10 microseconds). We'll revisit this pulse width and discuss it more in the section titled *HC-SR04 distance measurement process*.

The SC-SR04 has two round cylinders. They are as follows:

- **T** or **TX**: A transmitter that produces ultrasonic sound pulses
- **R** or **RX**: A receiver that detects ultrasonic sound pulses

We will discuss how the transmitter and receiver pair work to measure distance in the next section.

The HC-SR04 has four terminals, which are as follows:

- **Vcc**: The power source (a Raspberry Pi 5-volt pin will be okay given the max current of 15 mA).
- **GND**: Connection to ground.
- **TRIG**: Trigger *input* terminal – when HIGH, the sensor sends out ultrasonic pulses.
- **ECHO**: Echo *output* terminal – this pin goes HIGH when TRIG is made HIGH, then transitions to LOW when it detects an ultrasonic pulse.

We will discuss the use of the TRIG and ECHO terminals in the section titled *HC-SR04 distance measurement process*.

Now that we understand the basic use of an ultrasonic distance sensor and the basic properties and layout of the HC-SR04, let's discuss how it works.

How an ultrasonic distance sensor works

Let's see how the transmitter (**TX**) and receiver (**RX**) work together to measure distance. The basic operating principle of an ultrasonic sensor is illustrated in the following figure:

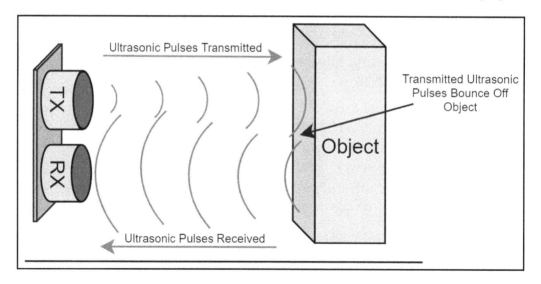

Figure 11.5 – Ultrasonic distance sensor operation

Here is what happens:

1. First, the sensor sends out an ultrasonic pulse from the transmitter (**TX**).
2. If there is an object in front of the sensor, this pulse is bounced off the object and returns to the sensor, and is detected by the receiver (**RX**).
3. By measuring the time between transmitting a pulse and receiving it back, we can calculate the distance between the sensor and the object.

With this high-level understanding of how the sensor works, next, we will go deeper and discuss how to use the TRIG and ECHO terminals on the HC-SR04 together in a process to estimate distance.

HC-SR04 distance measurement process

In this section, we will cover the process used to measure distance with the HC-SR04. Don't get concerned if this does not make immediately sense. I've provided the details here as background material, as this is the logical process that is implemented by our example program to make the sensor work. You will also find the process documented in the sensor's datasheet.

We measure distance with the HC-SR04 through the correct use and monitoring of the TRIG and ECHO pins. The process looks like this:

1. Pull the TRIG pin `HIGH` for 10 microseconds. Pulling TRIG `HIGH` also makes the ECHO pin `HIGH`.
2. Start a timer.
3. Wait for either of the following to happen:
    - ECHO to go `LOW`
    - 38 milliseconds to elapse (from the datasheet, this is the time for >4 meters)
4. Stop the timer.

If 38 milliseconds have passed, we conclude that there is no object in front of the sensor (at least within the effective range of 2 centimeters to 4 meters). Otherwise, we take the elapsed time divided by 2 (because we want the time interval between the sensor and the object, not the sensor to the object and back to the sensor), and then using basic physics, calculate the distance between the sensor and the object using the following formula:

$$d = v \times t$$

Here, we have the following:

- *d* is the distance in meters.
- *v* is the velocity in meters per second, for which we use the speed of sound, which is approximately 343 meters per second at 20°C (68°F).
- *t* is the time in seconds.

 The HC-SR04 will only estimate distance. There are several parameters that influence its accuracy. Firstly, as hinted previously, the speed of sound varies in accordance with temperature. Secondly, the sensor has a resolution of ± 0.3 cm. Furthermore, the size of the object being measured, the angle of the object relative to the sensor, and even the material it is made of can all impact the ECHO timing result and thus the calculated distance.

With this basic understanding of how to use the HC-SR04 to estimate distance, let's build our circuit to connect an HC-SR04 to our Raspberry Pi.

Building the HC-SR04 circuit

It's time to build our HC-SR04 circuit. A schematic of our circuit is shown in the following figure. This wiring will be suitable for both an HC-SR04 or HC-SR04P module:

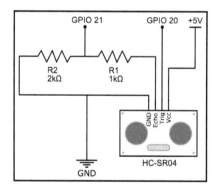

Figure 11.6 – HC-SR04 (5-volt logic ECHO pin) circuit

As a reminder, the HC-SR04 module (or an HC-SR04P wired like this to a 5-volt source) is a 5-volt logic module, and hence you will notice the voltage divider in the circuit created by the two resistors to convert 5 volts into 3.3 volts. If you need a refresher on voltage dividers, we covered them in detail in Chapter 6, *Electronics 101 for the Software Engineer*.

Let's build this circuit on our breadboard:

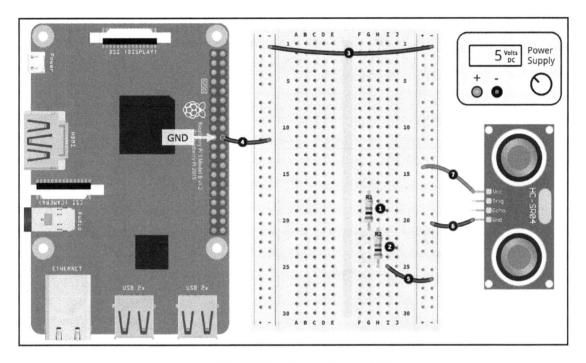

Figure 11.7 – HC-SR04 circuit breadboard layout (part 1 of 2)

Here are the steps to follow to create the first part of your breadboard build. The step numbers match the numbers in black circles in *Figure 11.7*:

1. Place a 1kΩ resistor (R1) into your breadboard.
2. Place a 2kΩ resistor (R2) into your breadboard. A leg of this second resistor shares the same row as a leg of the first resistor. In the illustration, this can be seen in row 21 on the right-hand side bank.
3. Connect the left-hand side and right-hand side negative power rails together.
4. Connect a GND pin on your Raspberry Pi to the negative rail of the left-hand side power rail.
5. Connect the second leg 2kΩ resistor (R2) to the negative rail of the right-hand side power rail.
6. Connect the GND terminal on your HC-SR04 sensor to the negative rail of the right-hand side power rail.
7. Connect the Vcc terminal on your HC-SR04 sensor to the positive rail of the right-hand side power rail.

Make sure the R1 and R2 resistors are connected as shown in the preceding figure – that is, R1 (1kΩ) is connected to the ECHO pin on the HC-SR04. The voltage divider created by R1 and R2 shifts an ECHO pin `HIGH` of 5 volts into ~3.3 volts. If you installed the resistors back to front, the 5 volts get shifted to ~1.67 volts, which is not enough to register a logic `HIGH` on your Raspberry Pi.

Now that we have laid out our basic components and performed a few preliminary wiring connections, let's complete our build:

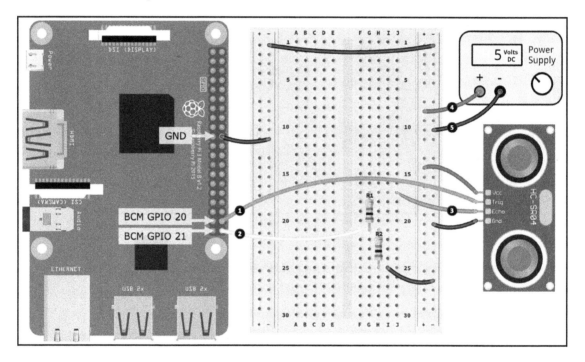

Figure 11.8 – HC-SR04 circuit breadboard layout (part 2 of 2)

Here are the steps to follow. The step numbers match the numbers in black circles in *Figure 11.8*:

1. Connect GPIO 20 on your Raspberry Pi to the Trig terminal on your HC-SR04 sensor.
2. Connect GPIO 21 on your Raspberry Pi to the junction of the 1kΩ (R1) and 2kΩ (R2) resistors. This connection is shown in the illustration at hole **F21**.
3. Connect the Echo terminal of your HC-SR04 sensor to the 1kΩ resistor (R1). This connection is shown at hole **J17**.

4. Connect the positive terminal of a 5-volt power source to the positive rail of the right-hand side power rail.

5. Connect the negative terminal of a 5-volt power source to the negative rail of the right-hand side power rail.

As mentioned, our circuit build will work with both the HC-SR04 and HC-SR04P modules. If you do have the HC-SR04P module, there is a simpler wiring option available to you that you may like to try on your own. Since the HC-SR04P will work at 3.3 volts, here is what you can do:

- Connect Vcc to a 3.3-volt power source or a 3.3-volt pin on your Raspberry Pi.
- Connect the ECHO terminal directly to GPIO 21.
- GND still connects to GND, and TRIG still connects directly to GPIO 20.

Since this configuration is powered at 3.3 volts, the logic output on the ECHO terminal is also 3.3 volts and is therefore safe to connect directly to a Raspberry Pi GPIO pin.

Great! Now that our circuit is complete, next we will run our example program and use the HC-SR04 to measure distance and learn about the code that makes this happen.

Running and exploring the HC-SR04 example code

The example code for the HC-SR04 can be found in the `chapter11/hc-sr04.py` file. Please review the source code before proceeding to get a broad understanding of what this file contains.

Place a solid object in front of the HC-SR04 (about 10 cm) and run the code in a terminal. As you move the object nearer or further from the sensor, the distance printed in the terminal will change, as indicated here:

```
(venv) python hc-sr04.py
Press Control + C to Exit
9.6898cm, 3.8149"
9.7755cm, 3.8486"
10.3342cm, 4.0686"
11.5532cm, 4.5485"
12.3422cm, 4.8591"
...
```

Let's review the code.

Firstly, we define the TRIG_GPIO and ECHO_GPIO pins on line 1, and the VELOCITY constant for the speed of sound at line 2. We're using 343 meters per second.

 Our code is using 343 m/s for the speed of sound, while the datasheet suggests the value 340 m/s. You will also find other HC-SR04 examples and libraries that use slightly different values. These differences are one reason why different code samples and libraries may produce slightly different readings for the same sensor-to-object distance.

On line 3, we define TIMEOUT_SECS = 0.1. The value of 0.1 is a number greater than 38 milliseconds (from the datasheet). Any time greater than this and we conclude that there is no object in front of our HC-SR04 sensor and return the SENSOR_TIMEOUT value, rather than a distance in the get_distance_cms() function, which we will come to shortly:

```
TRIG_GPIO = 20                                              # (1)
ECHO_GPIO = 21

# Speed of Sound in meters per second
# at 20 degrees C (68 degrees F)
VELOCITY = 343                                              # (2)

# Sensor timeout and return value
TIMEOUT_SECS = 0.1 # based on max distance of 4m      # (3)
SENSOR_TIMEOUT  = -1
```

Next, starting on line 4, we find several variables used to help measure the timing of the sensor's ultrasonic pulse and if we have a successful reading:

```
# For timing our ultrasonic pulse
echo_callback = None                                    # (4)
tick_start = -1
tick_end = -1
reading_success = False
```

echo_callback will contain a GPIO callback reference for later clean-up purposes, while tick_start and tick_end hold the start and end timings used to calculate the elapsed time for an ultrasonic pulse-echo. The term tick is used to be consistent with PiGPIO timing functions, which we will come to shortly. reading_success is True only when we have a distance reading before TIMEOUT_SECS elapses.

We use the `trigger()` function shown on line 5 to start our distance measurement. We simply apply the process set out in the datasheet on line 6 – that is, we make the TRIG pin HIGH for 10 µs:

```
def trigger():                                      # (5)
    global reading_success
    reading_success = False

    # Start ultrasonic pulses
    pi.write(TRIG_GPIO, pigpio.HIGH)                # (6)
    sleep(1 / 1000000) # Pause 10 microseconds
    pi.write(TRIG_GPIO, pigpio.LOW)
```

The `get_distance_cms()` function shown at line 7 is our primary function that kicks off the distance measurement process by making a call to `trigger()`, before waiting from line 8 until we have either a successful reading (that is, `reading_success = True`) or `TIMEOUT_SECS` elapses, in which case, we return `SENSOR_TIMEOUT`. While we are waiting, a callback handler named `echo_handler()` is monitoring the `ECHO_GPIO` pin in the background for a successful read. We will discuss `echo_handler()` later in this section:

```
def get_distance_cms()                              # (7)
    trigger()

    timeout = time() + TIMEOUT_SECS                 # (8)
    while not reading_success:
      if time() > timeout:
          return SENSOR_TIMEOUT
      sleep(0.01)
```

When we have a successful reading, our function continues. On line 9, we take the `tick_start` and `tick_end` variables (which will now have values set by the echo callback handler) and calculate the elapsed time. Remember, we're dividing the elapsed time at line 9 by 2 because we want the timing from the sensor to the object, *not* the complete ultrasonic pulse round trip from the sensor to the object, back to the sensor:

```
# ... get_distance_cms() continued

    # Elapsed time in microseconds.
    #Divide by 2 to get time from sensor to object.
    elapsed_microseconds =
            pigpio.tickDiff(tick_start, tick_end) / 2   # (9)

    # Convert to seconds
    elapsed_seconds = elapsed_microseconds / 1000000

    # Calculate distance in meters (d = v * t)
```

```
        distance_in_meters = elapsed_seconds * VELOCITY          # (10)

        distance_in_centimeters = distance_in_meters * 100
        return distance_in_centimeters
```

It is on line 10 where we apply the formula, $d = v \times t$, which we discussed previously, to work out the distance between the sensor and an object.

Next, we encounter the echo_handler() function on line 11, which monitors the ECHO_GPIO pin for changes in state:

```
    def echo_handler(gpio, level, tick):            # (11)
        global tick_start, tick_end, reading_success

        if level == pigpio.HIGH:
            tick_start = tick                       # (12)
        elif level == pigpio.LOW:
            tick_end = tick                         # (13)
            reading_success = True
```

Applying the process set out in the datasheet, we are capturing the time between sending a pulse at line 12 when ECHO_GPIO goes HIGH and receiving it back on line 13 when ECHO_GPIO goes LOW. If we have detected ECHO_GPIO as LOW before the timeout (back on line 8), we set reading_success = True so that get_distance_cms() knows we have a valid reading.

Finally, we register the echo_handler() callback with PiGPIO on line 14. The pigpio.EITHER_EDGE parameter means we want this callback to be called whenever ECHO_GPIO transitions to either a HIGH or LOW state:

```
    echo_callback =
        pi.callback(ECHO_GPIO, pigpio.EITHER_EDGE, echo_handler) # (14)
```

Well done! You've just wired up, tested, and learned how to use the HC-SR04 sensor together with PiGPIO to estimate distances. The circuit and code examples you have just learned could be adapted and used to measure water tank levels, or even as collision detection for a robot (a very common application of an HC-SR04 in amateur robotics), or in any other project you dream up where distance plays a part.

Next, we will briefly explore Hall-effect sensors and learn how they can be used to detect movement and relative distances.

Detecting movement and distance with Hall-effect sensors

Our final practical example in this chapter will illustrate the use of a Hall-effect sensor. Hall-effect sensors are simple components that detect the presence (or absence) of a magnetic field. In contrast to a PIR or distance sensor, you can use a Hall-effect sensor together with a magnet to monitor small-range – and even very rapid – movements. For example, you could attach a small magnet to the shaft of a DC motor and use a Hall-effect sensor to determine the motor's revolutions per minute.

Another common application of a Hall-effect sensor is in mobile phones and tablets. Some phone and tables covers and cases have a small magnet in them. As you open or close the case, your device detects the presence or absence of this magnet with a Hall-effect sensor and automatically turns on or off the display for you.

Hall-effect sensors come in three types, described as follows:

- **Non-latching switch types (digital)**: They output a digital state (that is, HIGH or LOW) in the presence of magnetism and the opposite digital state in its absence. Whether the signal is HIGH or LOW in the presence of magnetism all depends on the sensor and whether it's active LOW or active HIGH (please refer to Chapter 6, *Electronics 101 for the Software Engineer*, if you need a refresher on the concepts of active LOW and active HIGH).
- **Latching switch types (digital)**: They output (and latch to) LOW (or HIGH) when one pole (for example, south) of a magnet is detected, and return to HIGH (or LOW) (unlatch) when the alternative pole (for example, north) is detected.
- **Ratiometric types (analog)**: They output a varying voltage depending on how close they are to a magnetic field.

Some readers may be familiar with a component called a *reed switch*, which is a magnetically controlled switch. At a glance, they seem similar in basic principle and operation to a non-latching Hall-effect sensor. Here are the important differences – unlike a classic reed switch, Hall-effect sensors are a solid-state device (no moving parts), they can be switched/triggered very, very rapidly (thousands of times a second), and they require an appropriate circuit to make them work.

Our examples will use the A3144 (non-latching digital switch) and AH3503 (analog ratiometric) Hall-effect sensors. These specific parts have been chosen due to their availability and low cost; however, the general principles we will discuss will also be applicable to other Hall-effect sensors.

A picture of an A3144 Hall-effect sensor and common schematic symbols are shown in the following figure:

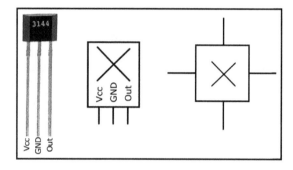

Figure 11.9 – Hall-effect sensor and symbols

You will notice that the far-right symbol has four protruding outputs because some Hall-effect sensors do have four legs. You can expect the outputs of this symbol to be annotated in a schematic diagram appropriate for the sensor it refers to. We will be sticking to the three-legged type sensor and the corresponding three outputs symbol.

The legs of our components are as follows:

- **Vcc**: 5-volt source power.
- **GND**: Ground connection.
- **Out**: 5-volt signal output. Note that the A3144 is active LOW, meaning that in the presence of a magnetic field, the **Out** leg becomes LOW.

The **Out** leg will behave differently depending on the type of Hall-effect sensor:

- **Latching and non-latching switching types**: The **Out** leg will output either digital LOW or a digital HIGH.
- **Ratiometric type**: The output will be a varying voltage (that is, an analog output). Note that the range of varying voltage will not be the full range between 0 to 5 volts, but more likely a range of only a few hundredths of a volt.

Now that we understand the leg configurations of a Hall-effect sensor, let's build our circuit.

Creating a Hall-effect sensor circuit

We will be building the following circuit on our breadboards. Similar to our HC-SR04 example and circuit in *Figure 11.5*, we need to use a voltage divider since our Hall-effect sensor outputs 5-volt logic, which we need to shift down to 3.3 volts:

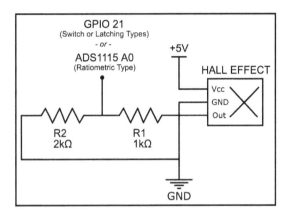

Figure 11.10 – Hall-effect sensor circuit

You will notice that the output of this circuit is dualistic and will depend on which sensor you are using:

- For a *non-latching switch* or *latching switch* type Hall-effect sensor, you will connect the circuit directly to GPIO 21 since the sensor will output a digital HIGH/LOW signal.
- For a *ratiometric* type Hall-effect sensor, you will need to connect the sensor to your Raspberry Pi via your ADS1115 analog-to-digital converter since the sensor outputs a varying analog voltage.

I have not included the ADS1115 wiring in *Figure 11.9* or in the following stepped breadboard layouts. We have already seen how to connect an analog output to our Raspberry Pi using the ADS1115 in previous chapters – refer to Chapter 5, *Connecting Your Raspberry Pi to the Physical World*, and/or Chapter 9, *Measuring Temperature, Humidity, and Light Levels*, for example circuits and code using the ADS1115.

Let's construct this circuit on our breadboard. This layout is for a *switching-type* Hall-effect sensor:

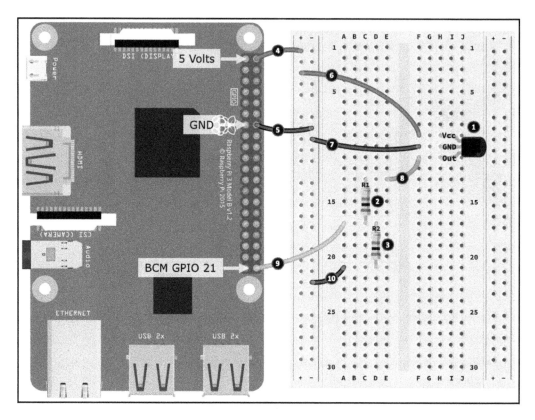

Figure 11.11 – Hall-effect sensor circuit breadboard layout

Here are the steps to follow to complete your breadboard build. The step numbers match the numbers in black circles in *Figure 11.10*:

1. Place your A3144 Hall-effect sensor into your breadboard, paying careful attention to its orientation regarding its legs. Please refer to *Figure 11.8* if you need help identifying the component's legs.
2. Place a 1kΩ resistor (R1) into your breadboard.
3. Place a 2kΩ resistor (R2) into your breadboard. A leg of this second resistor shares the same row as a leg of the first resistor. In the illustration, this can be seen in row 17 on the left-hand side bank.
4. Connect a 5-volt pin from your Raspberry Pi to the positive rail of the left-hand side power rail.

5. Connect a GND pin from your Raspberry Pi to the negative rail of the left-hand side power rail.

6. Connect the Hall-effect sensor's Vcc leg to the positive power rail.

7. Connect the Hall-effect sensor's GND leg to the negative power rail.

8. Connect the Hall-effect sensor's Out leg to the 1kΩ resistor (R1). In the illustration, this is shown at hole **E13**.

9. Connect the junction of the 1kΩ (R1) and 2kΩ (R2) resistors to GPIO 21 on your Raspberry Pi.

10. Connect the left of the 2kΩ resistor (R2) to the negative power rail.

> To use the AH3503 ratiometric type Hall-effect sensor at *step 1* in this circuit, the wire at *step 9* will instead need to be connected to an input port (for example, **A0**) of an ADS1115 module.

Now that we have built our Hall-effect sensor circuit, get a magnet ready, as we're ready to run our example code and see how a magnet triggers the sensor.

Running and exploring the Hall-effect sensor code

You will find the code for Hall-effect sensors in the `chapter11/hall_effect_digital.py` file for switch and latching switch type Hall-effect sensors and the `chapter11/hall_effect_analog.py` file for ratiometric type Hall-effect sensors.

What you will find when you review these two files is the following:

- `chapter11/hall_effect_digital.py` is functionally identical to the PIR code example we covered previously in this chapter in the section titled *Running and exploring the PIR sensor code*. Both the PIR and non-latching/latching Hall-effect sensors are digital switches. The only difference is that our reference Hall-effect sensor is *active* `LOW`.

- `chapter11/hall_effect_analog.py` is similar to other analog-to-digital examples we have seen using the ADS1115 ACD, including the circuit wiring and code from `Chapter 5`, *Connecting Your Raspberry Pi to the Physical World*.

The varying voltage range outputted by the AH3503 ratiometic Hall-effect sensor and measured by your ADC via the voltage divider is likely to be in the range of a few hundred millivolts.

As you run the example code, move a magnet past your Hall-effect sensor. The magnet will need to be close to the casing of the sensor; however, it will not need to physically touch the sensor. How *close* will all depend on the strength of your magnet.

If you cannot get your circuit and code to work, try rotating your magnet to reverse the north/south pole that passes past the sensor. Also note that for a *latching* type Hall-effect sensor, it is common for one pole of the magnet to *latch* (trigger) the sensor, while the opposite pole will *unlatch* (un-trigger) the sensor.

Due to the code similarities, we won't cover the code again here. However, I would like to say that at this point in the book, you now have both the digital and analog base circuits and code available for you to connect up and use any simple analog or digital component. As noted already in this chapter, just be wary of the voltages and currents needed to power the component, and especially what the output voltage is, because if it is more than 3.3 volts, you will need to use a voltage divider or level-shifter.

Summary

In this chapter, we looked at ways to detect movement and estimate distance with our Raspberry Pi. We learned how to use a PIR sensor to detect broad movements, and how a switch-type Hall-effect sensor can be used to detect the movement of a magnetic field. We also discovered how to use an ultrasonic range sensor to estimate absolute distance on a larger scale, and how to use a ratiometric-type Hall-effect sensor to measure relative distances on a small scale.

All our circuits and examples in this chapter have been *input* focused – telling our Raspberry Pi that some event has occurred, such as the detection of a person moving or that a distance is being measured.

You are in a great position now to combine input circuits such as those covered in this chapter (and also in Chapter 9, *Measuring Temperature, Humidity, and Light Levels*), with output-based circuits and examples from Chapter 7, *Turning Things On and Off*, Chapter 8, *Lights, Indicators, and Displaying Information*, and Chapter 10, *Movement with Servos, Motors, and Steppers*, to create end-to-end projects that can both control and measure the environment!

Don't forget about what we learned in `Chapter 2`, *Getting Started with Python and IoT,* `Chapter 3`, *Networking with RESTful APIs and Web Sockets Using Flask,* and `Chapter 4`, *Networking with MQTT, Python, and the Mosquitto MQTT Broker.* These three chapters provide you with the foundations for creating web interfaces and integration to external systems that can control and monitor the environment.

Many of the electronic and code examples presented so far in this book have evolved around a single sensor or actuator. In the next chapter, we will explore several Python-based design patterns that are useful when building more complex automation and IoT projects that involve multiple sensors and/or actuators that need to communicate with one another.

Questions

As we conclude, here is a list of questions for you to test your knowledge of this chapter's material. You will find the answers in the *Assessments* section of the book:

1. Can a PIR sensor detect the direction that an object is moving?
2. What are some factors that can affect the measurement accuracy of an ultrasonic distance sensor?
3. How does the output of a latching or non-latching Hall-effect sensor differ from the output of a ratiometric Hall-effect sensor?
4. In relation to this PiGPIO function call, `callback = pi.callback(GPIO, pigpio.EITHER_EDGE, callback_handler)`, what does the `pigpio.EITHER_EDGE` parameter mean?
5. In a 5-volt to 3.3-volt resistor-based voltage divider consisting of a 1k Ω and 2k Ω resistor, why is important to connect the two resistor values the correct way around in a circuit?
6. Both the HC-SR04 ultrasonic distance sensor and the HC-SR501 PIR sensor were powered using 5 volts connected to their respective Vcc pins. Why did we use a voltage divider with the HC-SR04 to drop the output from 5 volts to 3.3 volts, but not with the HC-SR501?

12
Advanced IoT Programming Concepts - Threads, AsyncIO, and Event Loops

In the previous chapter, we learned how to detect movement with a PIR sensor, as well as measure distances and detect movement with ultrasonic sensors and Hall-effect sensors.

In this chapter, we will discuss alternative ways of *structuring* our Python programs when we are working with electronic sensors (input devices) and actuators (output devices). We will cover the classic event-loop approach to programming, before moving on to more advanced approaches, including the use of threads in Python, the publisher/subscriber model, and finally, asynchronous I/O programming with Python.

I guarantee you that there are many, many blog posts and tutorials across the internet covering these topics; however, what we will cover in this chapter will be uniquely focused on practical electronic interfacing. Our approach in this chapter will involve creating a simple circuit with a push-button, a potentiometer, and two LEDs that we will make flash at different rates, and presenting four different coding approaches to make the circuit work.

Here is what we will cover in this chapter:

- Building and testing our circuit
- Exploring an event-loop approach
- Exploring a threaded approach
- Exploring a publisher-subscriber alternative
- Exploring an AsyncIO approach

Technical requirements

To perform the exercises in this chapter, you will need the following:

- Raspberry Pi 4 Model B
- Raspbian OS Buster (with desktop and recommended software)
- Minimum Python version 3.5

These requirements are what the code examples in this book are based on. It's reasonable to expect that the code examples should work without modification on Raspberry Pi 3 Model B or a different version of Raspbian OS as long as your Python version is 3.5 or higher.

You will find this chapter's source code in the `chapter12` folder in the GitHub repository available at `https://github.com/PacktPublishing/Practical-Python-Programming-for-IoT`.

You will need to execute the following commands in a terminal to set up a virtual environment and install the Python libraries required for the code in this chapter:

```
$ cd chapter12              # Change into this chapter's folder
$ python3 -m venv venv      # Create Python Virtual Environment
$ source venv/bin/activate  # Activate Python Virtual Environment
(venv) $ pip install pip --upgrade      # Upgrade pip
(venv) $ pip install -r requirements.txt  # Install dependent packages
```

The following dependencies are installed from `requirements.txt`:

- **PiGPIO**: The PiGPIO GPIO library (`https://pypi.org/project/pigpio`)
- **ADS1X15**: The ADS1x15 ADC library (`https://pypi.org/project/adafruit-circuitpython-ads1x15`)
- **PyPubSub**: In-process messaging and events (`https://pypi.org/project/PyPubSub`)

The electronic components we will need for this chapter's exercises are as follows:

- 2 x red LEDs
- 2 x 200 Ω resistors
- 1 x push-button switch
- 1 x ADS1115 module
- 1 x 10k Ω potentiometer

To maximize your learning in this chapter, there are some assumptions made regarding pre-existing knowledge and experience:

- From an electronic interfacing perspective, I will assume that you have read the preceding 11 chapters of this book and are comfortable working with the PiGPIO and ADS1115 Python libraries featured throughout this book.
- From a programming perspective, I am assuming existing knowledge of **Object-Oriented Programming (OOP)** techniques and how they are implemented in Python.
- Familiarity with the concepts *event-loop, threads, publisher-subscriber,* and *synchronous versus asynchronous* paradigms will also be advantageous.

If any of the preceding topics are unfamiliar, you will find many online tutorials available covering these topics in great detail. Please see the *Further reading* section at the end of the chapter for suggestions.

Building and testing our circuit

I'm going to present the circuit and programs for this chapter in the form of a practical exercise. Let's pretend for a moment that we have been asked to design and build a *gizmo* that has the following requirements:

- It has two LEDs that blink.
- A potentiometer is used to adjust the rate that the LED(s) blink.
- When the program starts, both LEDs will blink at the same rate determined by the position of the potentiometer.
- A blinking rate of 0 seconds means an LED is off, while the maximum blinking rate of 5 seconds means an LED is on for 5 seconds, then off for 5 seconds, before repeating the cycle.
- A push-button is used to select which LED changes its blinking rate when the potentiometer is adjusted.
- When the push-button is pressed and held for 0.5 seconds, all LEDs synchronize to the same rate, determined by the potentiometer's position.
- Ideally, the program code should easily scale to support more LEDs with minimal coding effort.

Here is a scenario illustrating the gizmo's use:

1. After applying power (and the program starts), all LEDs start to blink at a rate of 2.5 seconds because the potentiometer's dial is at the midpoint (50%) of its rotation.
2. The user adjusts the potentiometer to make the *first* LED blink at a rate of 4 seconds.
3. Next, the user briefly presses and releases the push-button so that the potentiometer will change the *second* LED's blinking rate.
4. Now, the user adjusts the potentiometer so that the *second* LED blinks at a rate of 0.5 seconds.
5. Finally, the user presses and holds the button down for 0.5 seconds to make both the *first* and *second* LED blink in unison at a rate of 0.5 seconds (the rate set by the potentiometer at *step 4*).

Now for the challenge I mentioned – before we get into this chapter's circuit and code, I challenge you to stop reading now and try to create a circuit and write a program that implements the preceding requirements.

You will find a short video demonstrating these requirements at `https://youtu.be/seKkF61OE8U`.

I anticipate that you will encounter challenges and have questions about the best approach to take. There is no one best approach; however, by having your own implementation – whether it works or not – you will have something to compare and contrast with the four solutions that I will present during this chapter. I'm confident that if you have a go yourself first, then you will gain a deeper understanding and more insight. Hey, perhaps you'll create an even better solution!

If you need suggestions to help get you started, here they are:

- We first covered LEDs and push-buttons in `Chapter 2`, *Getting Started with Python and IoT*.
- We first covered potentiometers and analog input using an ADS1115 module in `Chapter 5`, *Connecting Your Raspberry Pi to the Physical World*.

When you are ready, we will look at a circuit that fulfills the aforementioned requirements.

Building the reference circuit

In *Figure 12.1* is a circuit that meets the requirements we just listed. It has a push-button, a potentiometer in the form of a voltage divider connected to an ADS1115 analog-to-digital converter, and two LEDs connected by current limiting resistors. Adding additional LEDs will be as simple as wiring more LED and resistors pairs between GND and a free GPIO pin:

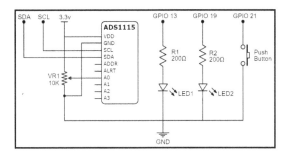

Figure 12.1 – Reference circuit schematic

If you have not already created a similar circuit on your own, we will create this circuit now on your breadboard. We will build this circuit in three parts. Let's get started:

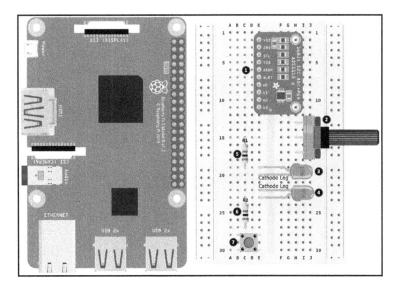

Figure 12.2 – Reference circuit (part 1 of 3)

Here are the steps to follow to create the first part of our breadboard build where we place the components. The step numbers match the numbers in black circles in *Figure 12.2*:

1. Place the ADS1115 module into your breadboard.
2. Place the potentiometer into your breadboard.
3. Place an LED into your breadboard, taking care to orientate the LED's legs as illustrated.
4. Place a second LED into your breadboard, taking care to orientate the LED's legs as illustrated.
5. Place a 200Ω resistor (R1) into your breadboard. One end of this resistor shares the same row as the anode leg of the LED placed in *step 3*.
6. Place another 200Ω resistor (R2) into your breadboard. One end of this resistor shares the same row as the anode leg of the second LED you placed in *step 5*.
7. Place the push-button into your breadboard.

Now that we have placed the components into the breadboard, let's start wiring them:

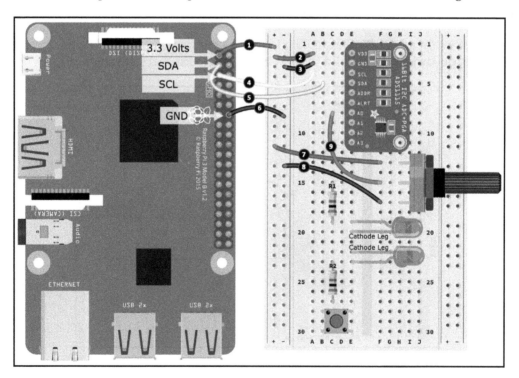

Figure 12.3 – Reference circuit (part 2 of 3)

Here are the steps to follow to continue with the second part of our breadboard build. The step numbers match the numbers in black circles in *Figure 12.3*:

1. Connect a 3.3-volt pin from your Raspberry Pi to the positive rail of the left-hand side power rail.
2. Connect the Vdd terminal of the ADS1115 to the positive rail of the left-hand side power rail.
3. Connect the GND terminal of the ADS1115 to the negative rail of the left-hand side power rail.
4. Connect the SCL terminal of the ADS1115 to the SCL pin on your Raspberry Pi.
5. Connect the SDA terminal of the ADS1115 to the SDA pin on your Raspberry Pi.
6. Connect a GND pin on your Raspberry Pi to the negative rail of the left-hand side power rail.
7. Connect an outer terminal of the potentiometer to the positive rail of the left-hand side power rail.
8. Connect another outer terminal of the potentiometer to the negative rail of the left-hand side power rail.
9. Connect the center terminal of the potentiometer to port **A0** of the ADS1115.

Can you recall that the potentiometer in this configuration is creating a variable voltage divider? If not, you may want to revisit `Chapter 6`, *Electronics 101 for the Software Engineer*. Furthermore, if you would like a detailed refresher on the ADS1115 module, please refer to `Chapter 5`, *Connecting your Raspberry Pi to the Physical World*.

Let's continue with our build:

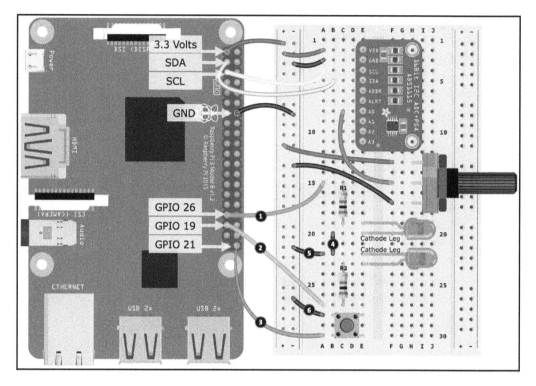

Figure 12.4 – Reference circuit (part 3 of 3)

Here are the steps to follow to continue with the final part of our breadboard build. The step numbers match the numbers in black circles in *Figure 12.4*:

1. Connect GPIO 26 from your Raspberry Pi to the 200 Ω resistor (R1).
2. Connect GPIO 19 from your Raspberry Pi to the second 200 Ω resistor (R2).
3. Connect GPIO 21 from your Raspberry Pi to one leg of the push-button.
4. Connect the two cathode legs of the LEDs together.
5. Connect the cathode legs of the LEDs to the negative rail of the left-hand side power rail.
6. Connect the second leg of the push-button to the negative rail of the left-hand side power rail.

Now that we have finished our circuit build, we are ready to run the sample code to make the circuit work.

Running the examples

This chapter comes with four different versions of code that can work with the circuit shown previously in *Figure 12.1.* You will find the code in the `chapter12` folder organized by version:

- `chapter12/version1_eventloop` is an *event-loop*-based example.
- `chapter12/version2_thread` is a *thread and callback*-based example.
- `chapter12/version3_pubsub` is a *publisher-subscriber*-based example.
- `chapter12/version4_asyncio` is an **Asynchronous IO** *(AsyncIO)*-based example.

All versions are functionally equivalent; however, they differ in their code structure and design. We will discuss each version in greater detail after we test our circuit.

Here are the steps to follow to run each version (starting with version 1) and test the circuit:

1. Change to the `version1_eventloop` folder.
2. Briefly look over the `main.py` source file, and any additional Python files in the folder, to get a feel for what they contain and how the program is structured.
3. Run `main.py` in a terminal (remember to switch into the chapter's virtual environment first).

 At this point, if you receive errors regarding I2C or ADS11x5, remember that there is the **i2cdetect** tool, which can be used to confirm that an I2C device such as the ADS1115 is correctly connected and visible to your Raspberry Pi. Refer to `Chapter 5`, *Connecting Your Raspberry Pi to the Physical World*, for more information.

4. Turn the potentiometer dial and observe the *first* LED's blinking rate changes.
5. Press the button briefly.
6. Turn the potentiometer dial and observe the *second* LED's blinking rate changes.
7. Press and hold the button for 0.5 seconds, and observe that both LEDs now blink in unison at the same rate.

The following is an example of the terminal output you will receive:

```
(venv) $ cd version1_eventloop
(venv) $ python main.py
INFO:Main:Version 1 - Event Loop Example. Press Control + C To Exit.
INFO:Main:Setting rate for all LEDs to 2.5
INFO:Main:Turning the Potentiometer dial will change the rate for LED #0
```

```
INFO:Main:Changing LED #0 rate to 2.6
INFO:Main:Changing LED #0 rate to 2.7
INFO:Main:Turning the Potentiometer dial will change the rate for LED #1
INFO:Main:Changing LED #1 rate to 2.6
INFO:Main:Changing LED #1 rate to 2.5
# Truncated
INFO:Main:Changing LED #1 rate to 0.5
INFO:Main:Changing rate for all LEDs to 0.5
```

8. Press *Ctrl* + *C* in your terminal to exit the program.
9. Repeat *steps 1* through *8* for `version2_threads`, `version3_pubsub`, and `version4_asyncio`.

You have just tested and glanced at the source code of four different programs (perhaps five, if you challenged yourself to create your own) that all achieve exactly the same end result but in different ways.

Now it's time to understand how these programs are built. Let's begin with the *event-loop* version of the program.

Exploring the event-loop approach

We will start our code exploration by discussing an event-loop-based approach to building the sample gizmo that we just tested in the previous section.

The code for the event-loop-based approach can be found in the `chapter12/version1_eventloop` folder. You will find one file named `main.py`. Please take the time now to stop and read through the code contained in `main.py` to get a basic understanding of how the program is structured and how it works. Alternatively, you could add breakpoints or insert `print()` statements into the code and run it again to understand how it works.

How did it go, and what did you notice? If you thought *yuck* or got lost in the web of loops, `if` statements, and state variables, then well done! This means you have invested the time to consider this approach and how the code is constructed.

What I mean by an event-loop approach is demonstrated in the code by the `while True:` loop abbreviated on line 1:

```
# chapter12/version1_eventloop
#
# Setup and initialization code goes before while loop.
#
```

```
if __name__ == "__main__":
    # Start of "Event Loop"
    while True:                                    # (1)
        #
        # ... Main body of logic and code is within the while loop...
        #
        sleep(SLEEP_DELAY)
```

Granted, I could have used functions and even external classes to reduce the quantity (and possibly enhance the readability) of the code within the `while` loop, however, the overall design paradigm remains the same – the body of the program control is sitting in a perpetual loop.

 If you are familiar with Arduino programming, you will be intimately familiar with this approach to programming. That's why I titled this section *event-loop* due to the similarity of approach and the popularity of the term. Notwithstanding, note that the term *event-loop* has a wider context within Python, as we will see when we look at the AsyncIO (version 4) of our program.

You may have realized that this event-loop approach to programming has been used by many of the examples throughout this book. Three examples are as follows:

- When we wanted a timed event such as blinking an LED (`Chapter 2`, *Getting Started with Python and IoT*)
- Polling the DHT 11 or DHT 22 temperature/humidity sensor (`Chapter 9`, *Measuring Temperature, Humidity, and Light Levels*)
- Polling the ADS1115 analog-to-digital converter connected to a **Light-Dependent-Resistor** (**LDR**) (also `Chapter 9`, *Measuring Temperature, Humidity, and Light Levels*)

In this context, for a single focused example, event-loops make sense. They even make sense purely for convenience when you're hacking about and trying out new ideas and learning about a new actuator or sensor. However, as demonstrated by our `version1_eventloop/main.py` program, as soon as you add in multiple components (such as a potentiometer, two LEDs, and a push-button) and want to make them work together for a definite purpose, the code gets complex fast.

For instance, consider the following code on line 3, which is responsible for blinking all the LEDs, and remember that this block of code is evaluated once per loop iteration and is responsible for blinking every LED:

```
#
# Blink the LEDs.
```

```
#
now = time()                                              # (3)
for i in range(len(LED_GPIOS)):
    if led_rates[i] <= 0:
        pi.write(LED_GPIOS[i], pigpio.LOW) # LED Off.
    elif now >= led_toggle_at_time[i]:
        pi.write(LED_GPIOS[i], not pi.read(LED_GPIOS[i])) # Toggle LED
        led_toggle_at_time[i] = now + led_rates[i]
```

Compare this to a vanilla alternative (similar to what we will see in other approaches), which at a moment's glance is significantly easier to understand:

```
while True:
    pi.write(led_gpio, not pi.read(led_gpio)) # Toggle LED GPIO High/Low
    sleep(delay)
```

If you also consider the following block of code, starting on line 2, which is responsible for detecting button presses, then you find nearly 40 lines of code (in the actual main.py file) just to detect what the button is doing:

```
while True:
    button_pressed = pi.read(BUTTON_GPIO) == pigpio.LOW        # (2)

    if button_pressed and not button_held:
        # Button has been pressed.
        # ... Truncated ...
    elif not button_pressed:
        if was_pressed and not button_held:
            # Button has been released
            # ... Truncated ...
    if button_hold_timer >= BUTTON_HOLD_SECS and not button_held:
        # Button has been held down
        # ... Truncated ...

    # ... Truncated ...
```

You will count multiple variables at play – button_pressed, button_held, was_pressed, and button_hold_timer – that are all evaluated at every while loop iteration and are there primarily to detect a *button-hold* event. I'm sure you can appreciate that writing and debugging this code like this can be tedious and error-prone.

We could have used a `PiGPIO` *callback* to handle button presses outside of the `while` loop, or even a GPIO Zero `Button` class. Both approaches would help reduce the complexity of the button-handling logic. Likewise, maybe we could have mixed in a GPIO Zero `LED` class to handle the LED blinking. However, if we did, our example would not be a purely event-loop-based example.

Now, I'm not saying that event-loops are a bad or wrong approach. They have their uses, they are needed, and, in essence, we create one every time we use a `while` loop or another looping construct – so the base ideal is everywhere, but it's just not an ideal approach to building complex programs, because this approach makes them harder to understand, maintain, and debug.

Whenever you find that your program is heading down this event-loop path, stop and reflect, because it might be time to consider refactoring your code to employ a different – and more maintainable – approach, such as a threaded/callback approach, which we will look at next.

Exploring a threaded approach

Now that we have explored an event-loop-based approach to creating our program, let's consider an alternative approach built using threads, callbacks, and OOP and see how this approach improves code readability and maintainability and promotes code reuse.

The code for the *threaded*-based approach can be found in the `chapter12/version2_threads` folder. You will find four files – the main program, `main.py`, and three class definitions: `LED.py`, `BUTTON.py`, and `POT.py`.

Please take the time now to stop and read through the code contained in `main.py` to get a basic understanding of how the program is structured and how it works. Then, proceed to review `LED.py`, `BUTTON.py`, and `POT.py`.

How did it go, and what did you notice? I'd guess that you found this version of the program (while reading through `main.py`) much quicker and easier to understand and noticed that there is no cumbersome and complex `while` loop, but instead a `pause()` call, which is necessary to stop our program from exiting, as summarized on line 3:

```
# chapter12/version2_threads/main.py
if __name__ == "__main__":                                    # (3)
        # Initialize all LEDs
        # ... Truncated ...
```

```
                # No While loop!
                # It's our BUTTON, LED and POT classes and the
                # registered callbacks doing all the work.
                pause()
```

In this program example, we have employed object-oriented techniques and componentized our program using three classes:

- A button class (BUTTON.py), which takes care of all the button logic
- A potentiometer class (POT.py), which takes care of all the potentiometer and analog-to-digital conversion logic
- A LED class (LED.py), which is responsible for making a *single* LED flash

By using an OOP approach, our main.py code is greatly simplified. Its role is now to create and initialize class instances and house the callback handlers and logic that make our program work.

Consider the following OOP approach for our push-button:

```
    # chapter12/version2_threads/main.py
    # Callback Handler when button is pressed, released or held down.
    def button_handler(the_button, state):
        global led_index
        if state == BUTTON.PRESSED:                                  # (1)
            #... Truncated ...
        elif state == BUTTON.HOLD:                                   # (2)
            #... Truncated

    # Creating button Instance
    button = BUTTON(gpio=BUTTON_GPIO,
                    pi=pi,
                    callback=button_handler)
```

Compared to the button-handing code from the event-loop example, this is greatly simplified and much more readable – it's pretty explicit where and how this code is responding to the button pressed at line 1 and button holds on line 2.

Let's consider the BUTTON class, which is defined in the BUTTON.py file. This class is an enhancing wrapper around a PiGPIO callback function that turns the HIGH/LOW states of the button's GPIO pin into PRESSED, RELEASED, and HOLD events, as summarized in the following code at line 1 in BUTTON.py:

```
    # chapter12/version2_threads/BUTTON.py
    def _callback_handler(self, gpio, level, tick): # PiGPIO Callback  # (1)

        if level == pigpio.LOW: # level is LOW -> Button is pressed
```

```
    if self.callback: self.callback(self, BUTTON.PRESSED)

    # While button is pressed start a timer to detect
    # if it remains pressed for self.hold_secs
    timer = 0                                              # (2)
    while (timer < self.hold_secs) and not self.pi.read(self.gpio):
        sleep(0.01)
        timer += 0.01

    # Button is still pressed after self.hold_secs
    if not self.pi.read(self.gpio):
        if self.callback: self.callback(self, BUTTON.HOLD)

else: # level is HIGH -> Button released
    if self.callback: self.callback(self, BUTTON.RELEASED)
```

Compared to the button-handling code of the event-loop example, we did not introduce
and interrogate multiple state variables to detect the button-hold event, but instead, this
logic is reduced to a simple and linear approach at line 2.

Next, as we consider the POT class (defined in POT.py) and LED class (defined in
LED.py), we will see threads come into our program.

 Did you know that even in a multi-threaded Python program, only one
thread is active at a time? While it seems counter-intuitive, it was a design
decision known as the **Global Interpreter Lock** (**GIL**) made back when
the Python language was first created. If you want to learn more about the
GIL and the many other forms of achieving concurrency with Python, you
will find resources in the *Further reading* section of this chapter.

The following is the thread run method for the POT class, which can be found in
the POT.py source file, and illustrates, starting on line 1, the approach of intermediately
polling the ADS1115 ADC to determine the potentiometer's position. We've seen this
polling example several times already throughout this book, starting back in Chapter 5,
Connecting Your Raspberry Pi to the Physical World, where we first discussed analog-to-digital
conversion, the ADS1115 module, and potentiometers:

```
# chapter12/version2_threads/POT.py
def run(self):
    while self.is_polling:                             # (1)
        current_value = self.get_value()
        if self.last_value != current_value:           # (2)
            if self.callback:
                self.callback(self, current_value)     # (3)
            self.last_value = current_value
```

```
                    timer = 0
                    while timer < self.poll_secs:  # Sleep for a while
                        sleep(0.01)
                        timer += 0.01
                # self.is_polling has become False and the Thread ends.
                self.__thread = None
```

The difference with our code here is that we are monitoring the ADC for voltage changes on line 2 (for example, when a user turns the potentiometer), and turning them into a callback on line 3, which you will have seen handled in `main.py` when you reviewed the source code in that file.

Let's now discuss how we are implementing the `version2` LED-related code. As you are aware, the basic code pattern for blinking an LED on and off at a defined rate involves a `while` loop and a `sleep` statement. This is the approach taken in the LED class, as seen in the `run()` method on line 3 in `LED.py`:

```
# chapter12/version2_threads/LED.py
def run(self):                                              # (3)
    """ Do the blinking (this is the run() method for our Thread) """
    while self.is_blinking:
        # Toggle LED On/Off
        self.pi.write(self.gpio, not self.pi.read(self.gpio))

        # Works, but LED responsiveness to rate chances can be sluggish.
        # sleep(self.blink_rate_secs)

        # Better approach - LED responds to changes in near real-time.
        timer = 0
        while timer < self.blink_rate_secs:
            sleep(0.01)
            timer += 0.01

    # self.is_blinking has become False and the Thread ends.
    self._thread = None
```

I am sure you will agree that this is easier to understand than the approach taken by the event-loop approach we discussed in the previous section. It is important to remember, however, that the event-loop approach was working with and altering the blinking rate of *all* LEDs together in a *single* block of code, and within a *single* thread – the program's main thread.

Notice the two sleep approaches shown in the preceding code. While the first approach using `sleep(self.blink_rate_secs)` is common and tempting, the caveat is that it blocks the thread for the full duration of the sleep. As a result, the LED will not respond to rate changes immediately and will feel sluggish to a user when they turn the potentiometer. The second approach, commended `#Better approach`, alleviates this issue and allows the LED to respond to rate changes in (near) real time.

Our `version2` program example using the LED class with its own internal thread now means that we have multiple threads – one per LED – all making the LEDs blink independently to one another.

Can you think of any potential problems this may introduce? Okay, it might be obvious if you have read through the `version2` source files – it's the synchronization of all LEDs to blink at the same rate in unison when the button is held for 0.5 seconds!

By introducing multiple threads, we have introduced multiple timers (that is, the `sleep()` statement), so each thread is blinking on its own independent schedule, and not from a common reference point in terms of a starting timebase.

This means that if we simply called `led.set_rate(n)` on multiple LEDs, while they would all blink on and off at the rate *n*, they would not necessarily blink in unison.

A simple solution to this issue is to synchronize the turning off of all LEDs before we start them blinking at the same rate. That is, we start them blinking from a common state (that is, off), and start them blinking together.

This approach is shown in the following code snippet starting at line 1 in `LED.py`. The core of the synchronization is achieved by the `led._thread.join()` statements on line 2:

```
# chapter12/version2_threads/LED.py
@classmethod                                              # (1)
def set_rate_all(cls, rate):
    for led in cls.instances: # Turn off all LEDs.
        led.set_rate(0)

    for led in cls.instances:
        if led._thread:
            led._thread.join()                            # (2)

    # We do not get to this point in code until all
    # LED Threads are complete (and LEDS are all off)
    for led in cls.instances:  # Start LED's blinking
        led.set_rate(rate)
```

This is a good first pass at synchronization, and for practical purposes, it works well for our situation. As mentioned, all we are doing is ensuring our LEDs start blinking together from an off state at the same time (well, very, very, very close to the same time, subject to the time taken for Python to iterate through the `for` loops).

Try commenting out `led._thread.join()` and the embodying `for` loop on line 2 in the preceding code and run the program. Make the LEDs blink at different rates, then try to synchronize them by holding down the button. Does it always work?

However, it must be noted that we are still dealing with multiple threads and independent timers to make our LEDs blink, so the potential for a time drift to occur is present. If this ever presented a practical issue, we would then need to explore alternative techniques to synchronize the time in each thread, or we could create and use a single class to manage multiple LEDs together (basically using the approach from the event-loop example, only refactoring it into a class and a thread).

The takeaway here regarding threads is that when you introduce threads to your applications, you can introduce timing issues that *may* be designed around or synchronized.

If your first pass at a prototype or new program involves an event-loop-based approach (as I often do), then as you refactor that code out into classes and threads, always think about any timing and synchronizing issues that may arise. Discovering synchronization-related bugs by accident during testing (or worse, when in production) is frustrating as they can be hard to reliably replicate, and could result in the need for extensive rework.

We've just seen how to create our sample gizmo program using OOP techniques, threads, and callbacks. We've seen how this approach results in easier to read and maintain code, and we also discovered the additional requirement and effort needed to synchronize threaded code. Next, we will look at the third variation of our program, which is based around a publisher-subscriber model.

Exploring the publisher-subscriber alternative

Now that we have seen an approach to creating our program using threads, callbacks, and OOP techniques, let's consider a third approach using a *publisher-subscriber* model.

The code for the publisher-subscriber approach can be found in the `chapter12/version3_pubsub` folder. You will find four files – the main program, `main.py`, and three class definitions: `LED.py`, `BUTTON.py`, and `POT.py`.

Please take the time now to stop and read through the code contained in `main.py` to get a basic understanding of how the program is structured and how it works. Then, proceed to review `LED.py`, `BUTTON.py`, and `POT.py`.

What you will have noticed is that the overall program structure (especially the class files) is very similar to the `version2` thread/callback example that we covered in the previous heading.

You may also have realized that this approach is very similar in concept to the publisher/subscribing method employed by MQTT, which we discussed in detail in `Chapter 4`, *Networking with MQTT, Python, and the Mosquitto MQTT Broker*. The main difference is that in our current `version3` example, our publisher-subscribing context is confined just to our program run-time environment, not a network-distributed set of programs, which was the scenario for our MQTT examples.

I have implemented the publishing-subscribing layer in `version3` using the `PyPubSub` Python library, which is available from `pypi.org` and is installed using `pip`. We will not discuss this library in any detail, as the overall concepts and use of this type of library should already be familiar to you, and if not, I have no doubt that you will immediately understand what's going on once you review the `version3` source code files (if you have not already done so).

There are alternative PubSub libraries available for Python through PyPi.org. The choice to use `PyPubSub` for this example was due to the quality of its documentation and the examples provided there. You will find a link to this library in the *Technical requirements* section at the start of this chapter.

Due to the similarity of the `version2` (threaded approach) and `version3` (publisher-subscriber approach) examples, we will not discuss each code file in detail, other than to point out that the core differences:

- In `version2` (threaded), this is how our `led`, `button`, and `pot` class instances communicate with one another:
    - We registered callback handlers in `main.py` on the `button` and `pot` class instances.
    - `button` and `pot` send events (for example, a button press or potentiometer adjustment) via this callback mechanism.
    - We interacted with the LED class instances directly using the `set_rate()` instance method and the `set_rate_all()` class method.
- In `version3` (publisher-subscriber), here is the intra-class communication structure and design:
    - Every class instance is very loosely coupled.
    - There are no callbacks.
    - We do not interact with any class instances directly after they are created and registered with `PyPubSub`.
    - All communication between classes and threads occurs using the messaging layer provided by `PyPubSub`.

Now, to be honest, our gizmo program does not benefit from a publisher-subscriber approach. My personal preference is to adopt the callback version for a small program like this one. However, I have provided the publisher-subscriber alternative implementation as a point of reference so that you have this alternative to consider for your own needs.

Where a publisher-subscriber approach shines is in more complex programs where you have many components (and here I mean software components, not necessarily electronics components) that need to share data and can do so in an asynchronous PubSub-style nature.

 We're presenting the coding and design approaches in this chapter in four very discrete and focused examples. In practice, however, it's common to combine these approaches (and other design patterns) in a hybrid and mixed fashion when creating your programs. Remember, the approach or combination of approaches to use is whatever makes the most sense for what you are trying to achieve.

As we have just discussed, and you will have seen as you reviewed the `version3` code, a publisher-subscriber approach to our gizmo program is a simple variation of the thread and callback approach, where instead of using callbacks and interacting with class instances directly, we standardize all code communication to a messaging layer. Next, we will look at our final approach to coding our gizmo program, this time taking the AsyncIO approach.

Exploring an AsyncIO approach

So far in this chapter, we have seen three different programming approaches to achieving the same end goal. Our fourth and final approach will be built using the AsyncIO libraries offered by Python 3. As we will see, this approach shares similarities and differences with our previous approaches, and also adds an extra dimension to our code and how it operates.

Speaking from my own experience, this approach can feel complex, cumbersome, and confusing the first time you experience asynchronous programming in Python. Yes, there is a steep learning curve to asynchronous programming (and we can only barely scratch the surface in this section). However, as you learn to master the concepts and gain practical experience, you may start to discover that it is an elegant and graceful way to create programs!

 If you are new to asynchronous programming in Python, you will find curated tutorial links in the *Further reading* section to deepen your learning. It is my intention in this section to give you a simple working AsyncIO program that focuses on electronic interfacing, which you can use as a reference as you learn more about this style of programming.

The code for the asynchronous-based approach can be found in the `chapter12/version4_asyncio` folder. You will find four files – the main program, `main.py`, and three class definitions: `LED.py`, `BUTTON.py`, and `POT.py`.

Please take the time now to stop and read through the code contained in `main.py` to get a basic understanding of how the program is structured and how it works. Then proceed to review `LED.py`, `BUTTON.py`, and `POT.py`.

If you are also a JavaScript developer – particularly Node.js – you will already know that JavaScript is an asynchronous programming language; however, it looks and feels very different from what you are seeing in Python! I can assure you that the principles are the same. Here is a key reason why they feel very different – JavaScript is *asynchronous by default*. As any experienced Node.js developer knows, we often have to go to (often extreme) lengths in code to make parts of our code behave synchronously. The opposite is true for Python – it's *synchronous by default*, and we need to extend extra programming effort to make parts of our code behave asynchronously.

As you read through the source code files, I want you to think about our `version4` AsyncIO program as having elements of both the `version1` event-loop-based program and the `version2` threaded/callback program. Here is a summary of the key differences and similarities:

- The overall program structure is very similar to the `version2` thread/callback example.
- At the end of `main.py`, we have a few new lines of code that we have not seen in this book before – for example, `loop = asyncio.get_event_loop()`.
- Like the `version2` program, we have used OOP techniques to factor our components into classes, which also have a `run()` method – but notice how there is no thread instance in these classes and no code related to starting a thread.
- In the class definition files, `LED.py`, `BUTTON.py`, and `POT.py`, we have the `async` and `await` keywords sprinkled around and in the `run()` function, and a delay of 0 seconds in the `while` loop – that is, `asyncio.sleep(0)` – so we're not really sleeping at all!
- In `BUTTON.py`, we are no longer using the PiGPIO callback to monitor a button being pressed, but instead polling the button GPIO in a `while` loop.

The Python 3 AsyncIO library has evolved significantly over time (and still is evolving), with new API conventions, the addition of higher-level functionality. and deprecated functions. Due to this evolution, code can get out of date with the latest API conventions quickly, and two code examples illustrating the same underlying concepts can be using seemingly different APIs. I highly recommend you glance through the latest Python AsyncIO library API documentation as it will give you hints and examples of newer versus older API practices, which may help you better interpret code examples.

I will explain how this program works by walking you through the high-level program flow in a simplified way. When you can grasp the general idea of what is happening, you are well on your way to understanding asynchronous programming in Python.

 You will also find a file named `chapter12/version4_asyncio/main_py37.py`. This is a Python 3.7+ version of our program. It uses an API available since Python 3.7. If you look through this file, the differences are clearly commented.

At the end of the `main.py` file, we see the following code:

```
if __name__ == "__main__":
        # .... truncated ....

        # Get (create) an event loop.
        loop = asyncio.get_event_loop()          # (1)

        # Register the LEDs.
        for led in LEDS:
            loop.create_task(led.run())          # (2)

        # Register Button and Pot
        loop.create_task(pot.run())              # (3)
        loop.create_task(button.run())           # (4)

        # Start the event loop.
        loop.run_forever()                       # (5)
```

An asynchronous program in Python evolves around the event-loop. We see this created at line 1 and started at line 5. We'll come back to the registrations occurring in between at lines 2, 3, and 4 momentarily.

The overall principle of this asynchronous event-loop is similar to our version1 event-loop example; however, the semantics are different. Both versions are single-threaded, and both sets of code do *go around in a loop*. In version1, this was very explicit because our main body of code was contained in an outer `while` loop. In our asynchronous version4, it's more implicit, and has a core difference – it's non-blocking *if programmed correctly*, and as we will see soon, this is the purpose of the `await asyncio.sleep()` calls in the class `run()` methods.

As mentioned, we have registered our class `run()` methods with the loop on lines 2, 3, and 4. After we start the event-loop on line 5, here is what happens in simplified terms:

1. The *first* LED's `run()` function (shown in the following code) is called:

```
# version4_asyncio/LED.py
async def run(self):
    """ Do the blinking """
    while True:                                              # (1)
        if self.toggle_at > 0 and
            (time() >= self.toggle_at):                      # (2)
            self.pi.write(self.gpio, not self.pi.read(self.gpio))
            self.toggle_at += self.blink_rate_secs

        await asyncio.sleep(0)                               # (3)
```

2. It enters the `while` loop on line 1 and toggles the LED on or off from line 2, depending on the blinking rate.

3. Next, it gets to line 3, `await asyncio.sleep(0)`, and *yields* control. At this point, the `run()` method is effectively paused, and another `while` loop iteration does not start.

4. Control is passed over the *second* LED's `run()` function, and it runs through it's `while` loop once until it reaches `await asyncio.sleep(0)`. It then yields control.

5. Now, the pot instance's `run()` method (shown in the following code) gets a turn to run:

```
async def run(self):
    """ Poll ADC for Voltage Changes """
    while True:
        # Check if the Potentiometer has been adjusted.
        current_value = self.get_value()
        if self.last_value != current_value:

            if self.callback:
                self.callback(self, current_value)

            self.last_value = current_value

        await asyncio.sleep(0)
```

6. The `run()` method performs one iteration of the `while` loop until it reaches `await asyncio.sleep(0)`. It then yields control.

7. Control is passed to the `button` instance's `run()` method (partly shown in the following code), which has multiple `await asyncio.sleep(0)` statements:

```
async def run(self):
    while True:
        level = self.pi.read(self.gpio) # LOW(0) or HIGH(1)

        # Waiting for a GPIO level change.
        while level == self.__last_level:
            await asyncio.sleep(0)

            # ... truncated ...

            while (time() < hold_timeout_at) and \
                    not self.pi.read(self.gpio):
                await asyncio.sleep(0)

        # ... truncated ...
        await asyncio.sleep(0)
```

8. As soon as the button's `run()` method reaches any instance of `await asyncio.sleep(0)`, it yields control.

9. Now, all our registered `run()` methods have had a chance to run, so the *first* LED's `run()` method will take control again and perform one `while` loop iteration until it reaches `await asyncio.sleep(0)`. Again, at this point it *yields* control and the *second* LED's `run()` method gets another turn to run...and the process continues over and over, with each `run()` method getting a turn to run in a round-robin fashion.

Let's tie up a few loose ends where you will likely have questions:

- What about the button's `run()` function with its many `await asyncio.sleep(0)` statements?

  When control is yielded at any `await asyncio.sleep(0)` statement, the function yields at this point. The next time the `run()` button gets control, the code will continue from the next statement beneath the `await asyncio.sleep(0)` statement that yielded.

- Why is the sleep delay 0 seconds?

  Awaiting a zero-delay sleep is the simplest way to yield control (and please note that it is the `sleep()` function from the `asyncio` library, not the `sleep()` function from the `time` library). However, you can `await` any asynchronous method, but this is beyond the scope for our simple example.

  I have used zero-second delays for this example for simplicity in explaining how the program works, but you can use non-zero delays. All this means is that the yielding `run()` function would sleep for this period – the event-loop will not give it a turn to run until this period expires.

- What about the `async` and `await` keywords – how do I know where to use them?

  This certainly comes with practice; however, here are the basic design rules:

    - If you are registering a function (for example, `run()`) with the event-loop, the function must start with the `async` keyword.
    - Any `async` function must contain at least one `await` statement.

Writing and learning asynchronous programs takes practice and experimentation. One of the initial design challenges you will face is knowing where to put `await` statements (and how many), and how long you should yield control for. I encourage you to play with the `version4` code base, add in your own debugging `print()` or logging statements, and just experiment and tinker until you get a feel for how it all fits together. At some point, you'll have that *aha* moment, and at that point, you have just opened the door to further explore the many advanced features offered by the Python AsyncIO libraries.

Now that we have seen how an asynchronous program is structured and behaves at runtime, I want to give you something to experiment with and ponder.

An asynchronous experiment

Let's try an experiment. Maybe you've wondered how `version4` (AsyncIO) is a bit like our `version1` (event-loop) code, only it's been refactored into classes just like the `version2` (threaded) code. So, couldn't we just refactor the code in the `version1` `while` loop into classes, create and call a function them (for example, `run()`) in the `while` loop, and not bother with all the asynchronous stuff and its extra library and syntax?

Let's try. You will find a version just like this in the `chapter12/version5_eventloop2` folder. Try running this version, and see what happens. You'll find that the first LED blinks, the second one is always on, and that the button and potentiometer do not work.

Can you work out why?

Here's the simple answer: in `main.py`, once the first LED's `run()` function is called, we're stuck in its `while` loop forever!

The call to `sleep()` (from the `time` library) does not yield control; it just halts the LED's `run()` method for the duration before the next `while` loop iteration occurs.

Hence, this is an example of why we say synchronous programs are blocking (no yielding of control), and why asynchronous programs are non-blocking (they yield control and give other code a chance to run).

I hope you have enjoyed our exploration of four alternative ways of structuring electronic-interfacing programs – and one way we shouldn't. Let's conclude by recapping what we have learned in this chapter.

Summary

In this chapter, we looked at four different way of structuring a Python program that interface with electronics. We learned about an event-loop approach to programming, two variations on a thread-based approach – callbacks and a publisher-subscriber model – and finished by looking at how an AsyncIO approach to programming works.

Each of the four examples we covered was very discrete and specific in its approach. While we briefly discussed the relative benefits and pitfalls of each approach along the way, it's worth remembering that in practice, your projects will likely use a mixture of these (and potentially other) approaches, depending on the programming and interfacing goals you are trying to achieve.

In the next chapter, we will turn our attention toward IoT platforms and present a discussion of the various options and alternatives that are available for building IoT programs.

Questions

As we conclude, here is a list of questions for you to test your knowledge of this chapter's material. You will find the answers in the *Assessments* section of the book:

1. When is a publisher-subscriber model a good design approach?
2. What is the Python GIL, and what implication does it present for classic threading?
3. Why is a pure event-loop usually a poor choice for complex applications?
4. Is an event-loop approach a bad idea? Why or why not?
5. What is the purpose of the `thread.join()` function call?
6. You have used a thread to poll your new analog component via an analog-to-digital converter. However, you find that your code behaves sluggishly to changes in the component. What could be the problem?
7. Which is the superior approach to designing an IoT or electronic interfacing application in Python – using an event-loop, a thread/callback, the publisher-subscriber model, or an AsyncIO-based approach?

Further reading

The `realpython.com` website has a range of excellent tutorials covering all things concurrency in Python, including the following:

- What is the Python GIL? `https://realpython.com/python-gil`
- Speed Up Your Python Program with Concurrency: `https://realpython.com/python-concurrency`
- An Intro to Threading in Python: `https://realpython.com/intro-to-python-threading`
- Async IO in Python: A Complete Walkthrough: `https://realpython.com/async-io-python`

The following are relevant links from the official Python (3.7) API documentation:

- Threading: `https://docs.python.org/3.7/library/threading.html`
- The AsyncIO library: `https://docs.python.org/3.7/library/asyncio.htm`
- Developing with AsyncIO: `https://docs.python.org/3.7/library/asyncio-dev.html`
- Concurrency in Python: `https://docs.python.org/3.7/library/concurrency.html`

13
IoT Visualization and Automation Platforms

In the previous chapter, we looked at alternative approaches to structuring a Python program that interfaces with electronics. This included an event loop approach, two thread-based approaches showing the use of callbacks and a publisher-subscriber model, and an asynchronous I/O approach.

In this chapter, we will be discussing IoT and automation platforms that you can use with your Raspberry Pi. The terms *IoT platform* and *automation platform* are very broad concepts, so for the purpose of this chapter, what I mean by these terms is any software service – cloud-based or locally installable – that provides you with a ready-made ecosystem to create powerful, flexible, and fun IoT-based projects.

Our primary focus will be on the **If-This-Then-That** (**IFTTT**) automation platform, which I suspect many of you will have some familiarity with, and the ThingSpeak platform for data visualization. I have chosen these two services because they both offer a free pricing tier and allow us to create and explore simple demonstrations and examples that you can build upon. However, besides these, I'll also discuss a few other IoT and automation platforms that I have experience with that will allow you to build even more powerful IoT solutions.

The following topics will be covered in this chapter:

- Triggering an IFTTT Applet from your Raspberry Pi
- Actioning your Raspberry Pi from an IFTTT Applet
- Visualizing data with the ThingSpeak platform
- Other IoT and automation platforms for further exploration

Let's get started!

Technical requirements

To perform the exercises in this chapter, you will need the following:

- Raspberry Pi 4 Model B
- Raspbian OS Buster (with a desktop and recommended software)
- Python version 3.5 at a minimum

These requirements are what the code examples in this book are based on. It's reasonable to expect that the code examples should work without modification on a Raspberry Pi 3 Model B or a different version of Raspbian OS, as long as your Python version is 3.5 or higher.

You will find this chapter's source code in the chapter13 folder in this book's GitHub repository, which is available here: https://github.com/PacktPublishing/Practical-Python-Programming-for-IoT.

You will need to execute the following commands in a Terminal to set up a virtual environment and install the Python libraries required for the code in this chapter:

```
$ cd chapter13              # Change into this chapter's folder
$ python3 -m venv venv      # Create Python Virtual Environment
$ source venv/bin/activate  # Activate Python Virtual Environment
(venv) $ pip install pip --upgrade         # Upgrade pip
(venv) $ pip install -r requirements.txt   # Install dependent packages
```

The following dependencies will be installed from requirements.txt:

- **PiGPIO**: The PiGPIO GPIO library (https://pypi.org/project/pigpio)
- **The Paho MQTT library**: https://pypi.org/project/paho-mqtt
- **The Requests HTTP library**: https://pypi.org/project/requests
- **The PiGPIO-based DHT library**: https://pypi.org/project/pigpio-dht

The electronic components we will need for this chapter's exercises are as follows:

- 1 x DHT11 (lower accuracy) or a DHT22 (higher accuracy) temperature and humidity sensor
- 1 x red LED
- Resistors:
  - 1 x 200Ω resistor
  - 1 x 10kΩ resistor (optional)

Triggering an IFTTT Applet from your Raspberry Pi

Many of you may already be familiar with the **If-This-Than-That** (**IFTTT**) web service (ifttt.com), where you can create simple workflow automation chains called *Applets*. An Applet responds to changes in one web service (the *This*), which then triggers an action on another web service (the *That*).

Here are some common examples of Applet configurations (called *Recipes):*

- Send yourself an email whenever a particular Twitter hashtag is published.
- Turn a smart light bulb on or off at a certain time of the day.
- Open your internet-connected garage door using your phone's GPS when you are approaching your house.
- Log how long you spend in the office in a spreadsheet.
- ...and thousands upon thousands of other examples!

As we will learn in this section and the next, our Raspberry Pi can assume the role of both the *This* or the *That,* to either trigger an Applet or perform an action in response to a triggered Applet.

The following is a visual representation of what we will cover in this section; that is, making our Raspberry Pi assume the *This* role in an IFTTT workflow:

Figure 13.1 – Raspberry Pi assuming the *This* role in an IFTTT Applet workflow

Our forthcoming Python example will monitor the current temperature (the *This),* and at a specific temperature will request a special IFTTT Webhook URL. This URL request triggers our Applet, which then sends out an email (the *That).* We will discuss Webhooks in greater detail shortly when we build our first IFTTT Applet.

First, we need to create and test our example circuit, which we will do next.

Creating the temperature monitoring circuit

For this example, we will be reusing the DHT11/DHT22 temperature circuit we created in `Chapter 9`, *Measuring Temperature, Humidity, and Light Levels*.

Here is what we need to do:

1. Build the circuit illustrated in *Figure 9.2*.
2. Connect the data pin to GPIO 24 (in `Chapter 9`, *Measuring Temperature, Humidity, and Light Levels*, we used GPIO 21, but we will use GPIO 21 for a LED later in this chapter).

Once you have built your circuit, we can continue and build our first IFTTT Applet.

Creating and configuring an IFTTT Applet

To create our IFTTT Applet, there are many steps that we need to follow. Many of these steps are simple and generic, irrespective of the type of Applet you are creating. While we will step through these generic steps, we won't go into them in great detail, as I am sure you will be more than capable of understanding what is going on during the process. Instead, what we will focus on is the unique steps and sections of IFTTT that relate to integrating our Raspberry Pi.

Please note that the `https://ifttt.com/` free pricing tier limits the number of Applet that you can have active at once. At the time of writing, the maximum was three active Applets. We will be creating four Applets in this and the next chapter combined, so you will need to archive at least one Applet on IFTTT as you work through the next chapter in order to stay on the IFTTT free pricing tier.

Here are the steps we need to follow:

1. Log into or create your IFTTT account. If you do not already have an IFTTT account, please visit `ifttt.com/join` and follow the on-screen instructions.

We are performing these steps on the IFTTT website, `ifttt.com`. The process to follow for the IFTTT phone and tablet apps will be different.

2. Once logged into IFTTT, click on your profile avatar icon (shown highlighted with a square in the following screenshot) to reveal a menu:

Figure 13.2 – Profile avatar icon

3. Next, click the **Create** option in the profile menu, as shown here:

Figure 13.3 – Profile menu

4. The next page you will be presented with will be the **Create your own** page. Here, click the + icon between the words **If** and **This**:

Figure 13.4 – The Create your own page – part 1

5. Now, you will be asked to **Choose a service**. The service we need to choose to integrate with our Raspberry Pi is called the **WebHook** service, as shown here:

Figure 13.5 – The Choose a service page

6. Once you have found and identified the Webhook service, click on the **Webhooks** icon to continue.

7. The next page you will be presented with will be the **Choose a trigger** page, as shown in the following screenshot. Here, click on the **Receive a web request** option:

Figure 13.6 – The Choose trigger page

8. Next, you will be presented with the **Complete trigger fields** page, as shown here:

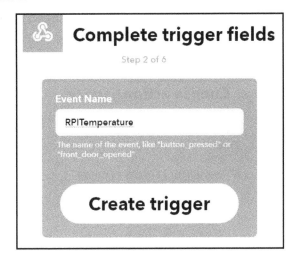

Figure 13.7 – The Complete trigger fields page

The **Event Name** field is of importance for our Raspberry Pi integration. In the Python code that we will cover shortly, we must ensure that the event name that's used by the code matches what we type into this page. For our example, we are naming our event **RPITemperature**.

9. After entering **RPITemperature** into the **Event Name** box, click the **Create trigger** button to continue.

A Webhooks's **Event Name** is its unique identifier (for your IFTTT account). If you are creating many Webhooks, then you will need to use a different **Event Name** to distinguish between them.

10. Next, you will be presented with the **Create Your Own** page once more. This time, you'll see that the *This* is now the Webhook icon:

Figure 13.8 – The Create your own page – part 2

We are now halfway through configuring our IFTTT Applet. Now that we have configured our Webhook trigger, we need to configure our action, which will be to send an email. After creating the emailing action, we will revisit the Webhook trigger and discover the URL and parameters that are used to trigger this Webhook event.

11. Next, click on the + icon between the words **Then** and **That**. You will see the **Choose action service** page. On this page, search for **Email** and click on the **Email** icon:

Figure 13.9 – The Choose action service page

12. When you see the **Choose action** page shown in the following screenshot, select the **Send me an email** option:

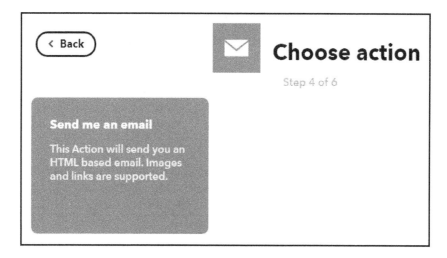

Figure 13.10 – The Choose action page

13. Next, you will be presented with the **Complete action fields** page. Please fill in the **Subject** and **Body** text fields, as shown in the following screenshot. You will find an example email that was produced by this action later in this chapter:

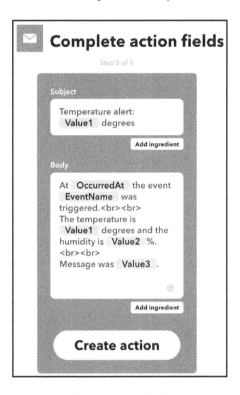

Figure 13.11 – The Complete action fields page

In the preceding screenshot, you will notice that some of the text is surrounded by gray boxes; for example, **Value1** and **OccuredAt**. These are known as *ingredients* and are replaced dynamically when the Applet is triggered. As we will see shortly in code, we will be replacing the **Value1**, **Value2**, and **Value3** ingredients with the current temperature, humidity, and a message, respectively.

14. When you have filled in the **Subject** and **Body** text fields, click the **Create action** button.

15. Finally, click on the **Finish** button on the **Review and finish** page, as shown here:

Figure 13.12 – The Review and finish page

Congratulations! You've just created an IFTTT Applet that sends an email when we trigger it using our Raspberry Pi. But how do we do that? That's what we will learn about in the next section.

Triggering an IFTTT Webhook

Now that we have created our IFTTT Applet, we need to take a few more steps to learn how to trigger our Webhook. These steps boil down to knowing where to navigate to within IFTTT to discover your unique Webhook URL.

Here are the steps we need to follow:

1. First, we need to navigate to the **Webhooks** page. There are a couple of ways we can do this, and I'll leave it up to you which route you take:

    - Navigate your web browser to the Webhook services URL; that is, `ifttt.com/maker_webhook`.

- Alternatively, the navigation steps to take to get to this web page are as follows:

    1. Click on the profile avatar icon (as shown previously in *Figure 13.2*).

    2. In the menu that appears, choose the **My Services** item (refer to *Figure 13.3*).

    3. On the page that appears, find and click on the **Webhooks** item.

Irrespective of the path you take, you will see the page shown in the following screenshot:

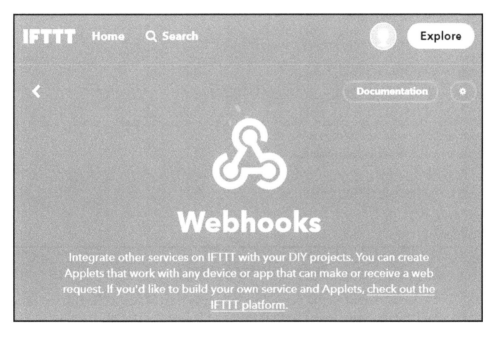

Figure 13.13 – The Webhooks page

2. Click on the **Documentation** button located in the top-right corner of the page. You will be presented with the Webhook documentation page shown here:

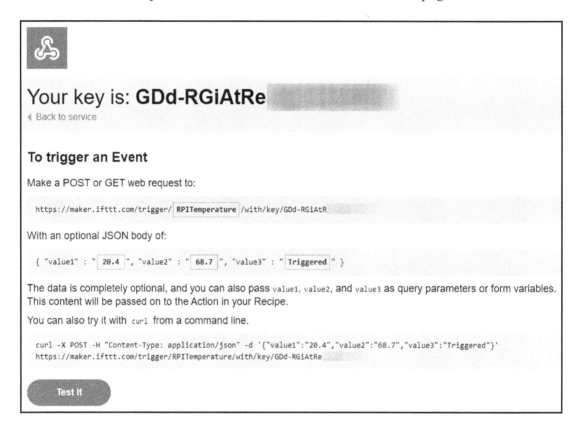

Figure 13.14 – The Webhook documentation page

 Please note that in the preceding example page, I have filled in the **{Event}** and **JSON Body** fields so that they can be referenced during our discussion. Your fields will be initially empty.

This page holds the key pieces of information that we need in order to integrate this Webhook trigger with our Raspberry Pi. Here are the key parts of this page:

- **Your key**: This is your account's Webhook API key and forms part of your unique Webhook URL.

- **GET or POST request URL**: Your unique Webhook URL. The unique combination of your API key and **Event Name** is what associates the URL with a triggerable IFTTT event. To integrate with our Raspberry Pi, this is the URL we need to construct and request. We'll cover this shortly in code.
- **Event name**: The name of the event you want to trigger.
- **JSON body**: Each triggerable Webhook can contain a maximum of three data parameters presented in JSON format, and they must be named **value1**, **value2**, and **value3**.
- **cURL command-line example**: Run this example in a Terminal to trigger the **RPITemperature** event (and you will receive an email).
- **The Test It button**: Clicking this button will trigger the **RPITemperature** event (and you will receive an email).

Now that we have created our IFTTT Applet and discovered where to find the Webhook URL and how it is constructed, we can now delve into the Python code that will trigger our IFTTT Applet.

Triggering an IFTTT Applet in Python

We're about to explore a simple application based around the DHT 11/DHT 22 circuits and code we first saw in Chapter 9, *Measuring Temperature, Humidity, and Light Levels*. You can find this code in the chapter13/ifttt_dht_trigger_email.py file.

This code will monitor the temperature using a DHT 11 or DHT 22 sensor, and if a pre-configured high or low threshold is breached, the code will invoke your IFTTT Webhook URL, which will then send you an email, similar to the one shown in the following screenshot. This corresponds to the email subject and body text you configured in the previous section, in *step 13*:

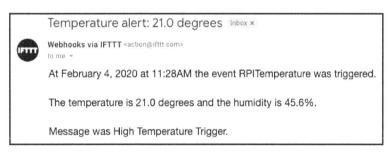

Figure 13.15 – Example IFTTT email

Before we can run our sample application code, there are a few configuration steps we need to perform. Let's take a look:

1. Open the `chapter13/ifttt_dht_trigger_email.py` file for editing.
2. Locate the following segment of code indicated by lines (1) and (2). Confirm that your DHT sensor is connected to the appropriate GPIO pin and that the correct DHT11 or DHT22 instance is being used based on the sensor that you have:

```
# DHT Temperature/Humidity Sensor GPIO.
GPIO = 24                                                   # (1)


# Configure DHT sensor - Uncomment appropriate line
# based on the sensor you have.
dht = DHT11(GPIO, use_internal_pullup=True, timeout_secs=0.5) # (2)
#dht = DHT22(GPIO, use_internal_pullup=True, timeout_secs=0.5)
```

3. Now, locate the following segments of code, indicated by lines (3), (4), and (5), and update the `USE_DEGREES_CELSIUS`, `HIGH_TEMP_TRIGGER`, and `LOW_TEMP_TRIGGER` variables to values that make sense in your location:

```
USE_DEGREES_CELSIUS = True # False to use Fahrenheit   # (3)
HIGH_TEMP_TRIGGER   = 20 # Degrees                     # (4)
LOW_TEMP_TRIGGER    = 19 # Degrees                     # (5)
```

Your IFTTT Applet will be triggered and send an email when the temperature reaches `HIGH_TEMP_TRIGGER` degrees or drops to `LOW_TEMP_TRIGGER` degrees. The reason for high and low temperature triggers is to create a small temperature buffer to prevent the code triggering multiple emails if the temperature were to oscillate above and below a single value.

4. Next, locate the following section of code starting at line (6) and update the details shown – specifically your IFTTT API key, which we identified in the previous section in *step 2*:

```
EVENT = "RPITemperature"                       # (6)
API_KEY = "<ADD YOUR IFTTT API KEY HERE>"
```

That's all our configuration done. You'll notice line (7), which is where we construct the IFTTT Webhook URL using our API key and event name:

```
URL = "https://maker.ifttt.com/trigger/{}/with/key/{}".format(EVENT,
API_KEY) # (7)
```

The remaining code in the file polls the DHT11 or DHT22 sensor, compares the reading to the `HIGH_TEMP_TRIGGER` and `HIGH_TEMP_TRIGGER` values, and if the temperature has been breached, constructs a `requests` object and calls the IFTTT Webhook URL to trigger your Applet. We will not cover that code here since it should be self-explanatory based on your previous experience with the DHT11/DHT22 sensors and the Python `requests` library.

With our code configured, it's time to run the program in a Terminal. You will receive an output similar to the following:

```
(venv) $ python ifttt_dht_trigger_email.py
INFO:root:Press Control + C To Exit.
INFO:root:Sensor result {'temp_c': 19.6, 'temp_f': 67.3, 'humidity': 43.7,
'valid': True}
INFO:root:Sensor result {'temp_c': 20.7, 'temp_f': 69.3, 'humidity': 42.9,
'valid': True}
INFO:root:Temperature 20.7 is >= 20, triggering event RPITemperature
INFO:root:Response Congratulations! You've fired the RPITemperature event
INFO:root:Successful Request.
```

Our example here also shows the IFTTT Applet being triggered when the temperature goes above 20 degrees.

This now completes our IFTTT example using our Raspberry Pi in the *This* role to trigger an IFTTT Applet. The basic process we covered illustrates how easy this is to achieve! We sent an email, but you can follow the same overall process to create other IFTTT recipes that trigger other actions, such as turning on smart lights and appliances, adding rows to Google spreadsheets, and creating a Facebook post. You might like to check out `https://ifttt.com/discover` for a host of ideas and possibilities. Remember that from our perspective and our learning, it's a *Webhook* trigger we can use from our Raspberry Pi to action ideas like these. Have fun!

Next, we will look at the opposite scenario to see how we can action our Raspberry Pi.

Actioning your Raspberry Pi from an IFTTT Applet

The previous section taught us how to trigger an IFTTT Applet from our Raspberry Pi. In this section, we will learn how to action our Raspberry Pi from an IFTTT Applet.

For our example, we will create an IFTTT Applet that will trigger when an email is received. We'll use the subject of this email to control an LED that is connected to a GPIO pin.

We will be using an IFTTT Webhook service, as we did previously, only this time the Webhook service will be installed on the *That* side of our Applet and will request a URL that we specify. This basic idea is illustrated in the following diagram:

Figure 13.16 – Raspberry Pi assuming the *That* role in an IFTTT Applet

Let's look at two possible methods we can use with the IFTTT Webhook service to request a URL that can then be seen by our Raspberry Pi's Python code.

Method 1 – using the dweet.io service as an intermediary

One method to integrate the IFTTT with our Raspberry Pi is to use the dweet.io service. We covered dweet.io, along with Python examples, in `Chapter 2`, *Getting Started with Python and IoT*.

In brief, here is how we will use dweet.io alongside IFTTT and our Python code:

1. In our IFTTT Webhook, we'll use a dweet.io URL to publish a dweet (containing an instruction to turn the LED on, off, or make it blink).
2. Our Raspberry Pi will run Python code to retrieve the dweet published by the IFTTT Webhook.
3. Our code will then control the LED based on the command specified in the dweet.

This is the method we will use for our example. The advantage of this method is that we do not need to worry about configuring firewalls and port forwarding rules on your router. Plus, it means we can run the example in environments – for example, at work – where router configurations may not be practical or even possible.

The code that we will be using for this dweet.io-based integration can be found in the `chapter13/dweet_led.py` file, which is an exact copy of the `chapter02/dweet_led.py` file from `Chapter 2`, *Getting Started with Python and IoT*.

Method 2 – creating a Flask-RESTful service

To use this method, we would need to create a RESTful service, similar to what we did in `Chapter 3`, *Networking with RESTful APIs and Web Socket Services Using Flask* (the code that can be found in `chapter02/flask_api_server.py`, which changes the brightness of a LED (rather than setting it to on/off/blinking), would be a great starting point).

We would also need to expose our Raspberry Pi to the public internet, which would require us to open a port and create a port forwarding rule in our local firewall or router. Then, together with our public IP (or domain name), we could construct a URL and use this directly with the IFTTT Webhook service.

> For prototyping ideas and creating demos, a simple alternative to opening up firewalls and creating port forwarding rules could be to use a service such as Local Tunnels (`localtunnel.github.io/www`) or ngrok (`ngrok.com`), which can help you expose a device to the internet.

Since this method requires configuration and setup on your end that is beyond what we can practically do as part of this chapter, we will stick with the dweet.io approach shown in the previous section.

Next, we will create a circuit that we can use with our second IFTTT Applet, which we will build shortly.

Creating the LED circuit

Our forthcoming example will require an LED, as well as a series resistor connected to a GPIO pin (GPIO 21, for our example). I'm confident that, given the number of times we've built LED circuits already in this book, you could wire this up on your own with no problems! (And in case you do need a reminder, see *Figure 2.7* in `Chapter 2`, *Getting Started with Python and IoT.*)

> Keep the DHT 11/DHT 22 circuit you created for our first IFTTT Applet example because we will reuse this circuit again later in this chapter.

When you have your circuit ready, we will continue and run our sample program.

Running the IFTTT and LED Python program

In this section, we will run our program and obtain a unique thing name and URL for use with the dweet.io service.

Here are the steps to follow:

1. Run the code that can be found in the chapter13/dweet_led.py file in a Terminal. You will receive an output similar to the following (your *thing name* and therefore your URLs will be different):

```
(venv) $ python dweet_led.py
INFO:main:Created new thing name 749b5e60
LED Control URLs - Try them in your web browser:
  On : https://dweet.io/dweet/for/749b5e60?state=on
  Off : https://dweet.io/dweet/for/749b5e60?state=off
  Blink : https://dweet.io/dweet/for/749b5e60?state=blink
```

As we mentioned previously, chapter13/dweet_led.py is an exact copy of the same program we discussed in Chapter 2, *Getting Started with Python and IoT*. If you need more context around how this program works, please revisit that chapter and the code discussion contained therein.

2. Keep your Terminal open with the program running as we will need to copy one of the URLs in the next section. We'll also need the program running to test our upcoming integration.

Next, we will create another IFTTT Applet to integrate with this program via dweet.io.

Creating the IFTTT Applet

We are about to create another IFTTT Applet. The overall process is very similar to the one we followed for the Applet we created previously, except our Raspberry Pi (via Webhook integration) will be at the *That* end of the Applet, as shown in *Figure 13.16*.

Here are the steps we need to follow to create our next Applet. I've left out many of the common screenshots this time around due to their similarity with our previous IFTTT Applet creation process:

1. Once logged into IFTTT, click on your profile avatar icon and select **Create** from the drop-down menu.
2. On the **If + This Then Than** page, press the + icon.
3. In the **Choose a service** page, search for and select the **Email** service.
4. On the **Choose trigger** page, select **Send IFTTT an email tagged** (make sure it's the option with the word in it *tagged*).
5. On the next page, enter **LED** as the **Tag** input and click the **Create trigger** button:

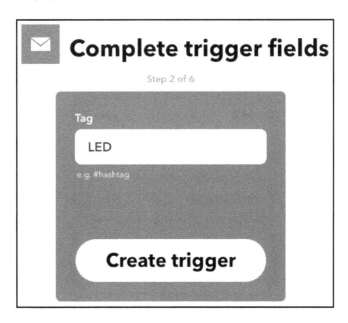

Figure 13.17 – The Complete trigger fields page

6. On the **If <email icon> This Then + Than** page, press the + icon.
7. On the **Choose action service** page, search for and select the **Webhooks** service.
8. Next, on the **Choose action** page, select **Make a web request**.

9. The next page you'll come across is called **Complete action fields**. This is where we'll use the dweet URL that our program printed to the Terminal in the previous section:

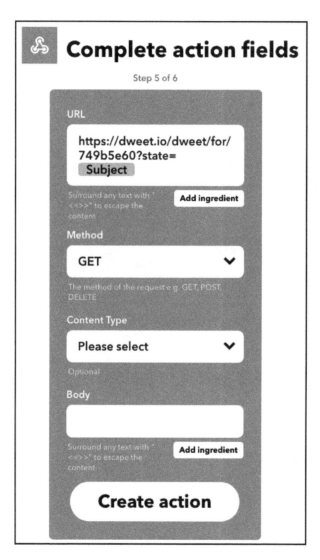

Figure 13.18 – The Complete action fields page

Here are the sub-steps you need to follow to complete the fields on this page:

1. Copy the **On** URL from your Terminal (for example, `https://dweet.io/dweet/for/749b5e60?state=on` – noting that your *thing name* will be different).
2. Paste this URL into the IFTTT **URL** field.
3. In the **URL** field, delete the word **on** (so the URL is now **https://dweet.io/dweet/for/749b5e60?state=**).
4. Click the **Add ingredient** button (under the **URL** field) and choose **Subject** (so that the URL is now **https://dweet.io/dweet/for/749b5e60?state={{Subject}}**).
5. The other fields can be left as their default values.
6. Click the **Create action** button:

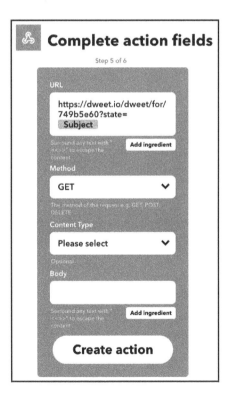

Figure 13.19 – The Complete action fields page

7. Finally, on the **Review and finish** page, click the **Finish** button.

Well done! We've now created our second Applet. Next, we will use this Applet to control our LED by sending an email instructing the LED to turn on, off, or blink.

Controlling the LED from an email

Now that we have created our Applet to control our LED using an email, it's time to test out the integration.

Here are the steps to create the email:

1. Make sure the program in the `chapter13/dweet_led.py` file is still running in your Terminal.
2. Open your favorite email program and create a new email.
3. Use `trigger@applet.ifttt.com` as the email's **To** address.

 When sending a trigger email to IFTTT, it must come from the same email address that you use with IFTTT (you can visit `https://ifttt.com/settings` to check your email address).

4. As the subject, use one of the following to control the LED:

- `#LED On`
- `#LED Off`
- `#LED Blink`

 IFTTT strips off the **#LED** tag, so our `dweet_led.py` program only receives the text **On**, **Off**, or **Blink**. The leading space is stripped off in our Python code.

The following screenshot shows an example email that will make the LED blink:

13.20 – Trigger email example

5. Send the email.
6. Wait a moment and the LED will change state.

Now that we've learned how to control our LED via email using IFTTT, let's quickly cover a few troubleshooting tips.

IFTTT troubleshooting

If your IFTTT Applets do not appear to be triggering and actioning, here are a few troubleshooting avenues for you to explore and try:

- In `dweet_led.py`, try the following:
    - Turn on debug logging; for example, `logger.setLevel(logging.DEBUG)`.
    - Change the dweet retrieval method located near the end of the source file. If you are using `stream_dweets_forever()`, try `poll_dweets_forever()` instead, since it is more resilient to transient connectivity issues.
- On the IFTTT website, you can inspect the activity log for any Applet by doing the following:
    1. Navigating to the **My Services** option under the profile menu
    2. Selecting a service (for example, **Webhooks**)
    3. Selecting the Applet you want to inspect
    4. Clicking the **Settings** button
    5. Clicking the **View activity** button and/or trying the **Check now** button
- You can also check the following IFTTT resources:
    - *Common errors and troubleshooting tips*, available at `https://help.ifttt.com/hc/en-us/articles/115010194547-Common-errors-and-troubleshooting-tips`
    - *Troubleshooting Applets & Services*, available at `https://help.ifttt.com/hc/en-us/categories/115001569887-Troubleshooting-Applets-Services`.

 IFTTT also has a *Best Practices* page available at `https://help.ifttt.com/hc/en-us/categories/115001569787-Best-Practices` where you can learn more about the platform.

As we discussed in the *Triggering an IFTTT Applet from your Raspberry Pi* section, for IFTTT *triggers,* you can adopt the same overall process we just covered for actioning your Raspberry Pi from any IFTTT recipe. Again, check out `https://ifttt.com/discover` for some ideas, and this time, remember that from our perspective, we use a *Webhook* action in our IFTTT recipes to control our Raspberry Pi. Here's an example – use Google Assistant to voice control your Raspberry Pi! Oh, wait a moment – we'll be doing this in the next chapter, `Chapter 14`, *Tying It All Together – An IoT Christmas Tree*!

We've now explored how to integrate our Raspberry Pi with IFTTT in two ways – as the *This* role to trigger an Applet and in the *That* role, whereby we can action our Raspberry Pi from a triggered Applet. Next, we will look at a way to create an IoT dashboard that we can use to visualize data.

Visualizing data with the ThingSpeak platform

We have just learned how to create simple automation using the IFTTT platform. In this section, we will integrate with the ThingSpeak platform to visually display temperature and humidity data that we'll collect using our DHT 11 or DHT 22 sensors. We will be using the DHT 11/DHT 22 circuit we created earlier in this chapter.

ThingSpeak (`thingspeak.com`) is a data visualization, aggregation, and analysis platform. We will be focusing on the data visualization aspect, and specifically on how to integrate our Raspberry Pi into this platform.

I've chosen ThingSpeak for our example in this section for a couple of reasons – it's simple and easy to set up and integrate with, and for simple data visualizations like the ones we will be doing, it's free. There are many other visualization platforms available, and they all have their own unique features, pricing structures, and complexities. I've included a few suggestions in the *Other IoT and automation platforms for further exploration* section for you to explore.

 If you wish to explore the aggregation and analysis features in more depth, you can find many quality examples, tutorials, and documentation by just searching for ThingSpeak. As a suggestion, start your investigation at `https://au.mathworks.com/help/thingspeak`.

An example of the dashboard we will be creating can be seen in the following screenshot. Notice the **Channel Settings** and **API Keys** items shown in the **Tab** bar – we will be referring to these tabs shortly:

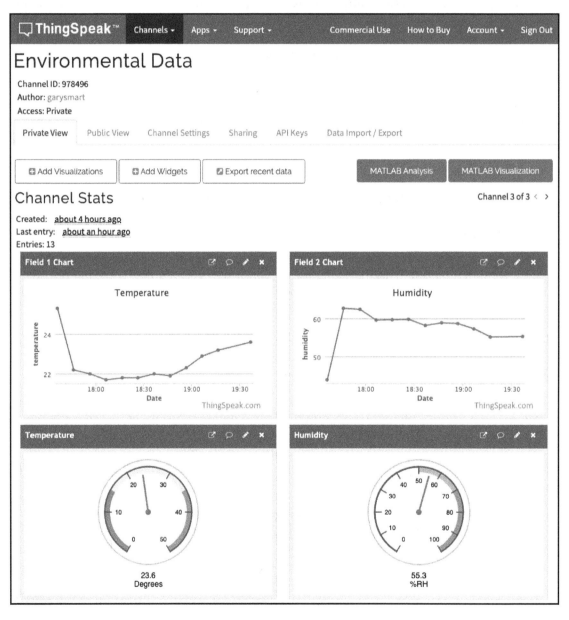

Figure 13.21 – The ThingSpeak channel dashboard

Our first stop before we can integrate our Raspberry Pi and send data to ThingSpeak is to configure the platform for our integration.

Configuring the ThinkSpeak platform

Configuring ThinkSpeak is relatively simple – in fact, it's one of the most straightforward platforms in its class I have come across. Here are the steps that we need to follow:

1. First, you will need to create a ThingSpeak account for yourself. Visit their website, `thingspeak.com`, and click on the **Sign Up** button.
2. Once you have created your ThinkSpeak account and logged into the platform, you should land on the **My Channels** page; that is, `https://thingspeak.com/channels`.

> In the ThingSpeak ecosystem, a *channel* is a virtual place where we store our data, dashboards, and visualizations. It's analogous to a workspace.

3. Next, we need to create a new channel by clicking on the **New Channel** button:

Figure 13.22 – ThingSpeak channel configuration

On the **New Channel** page, enter the following details:

- **Name**: `Environmental Data` (or any name of your choice)
- **Field1**: `temperature`
- **Field2**: `humidity`

You can leave all the other fields as their default values.

> If you need to review or change your channel settings later, they can be found on the **Channel Settings** tab, as shown previously in *Figure 13.19*.

4. Once you have filled in the fields, scroll to the bottom of the page and click the **Save Channel** button. You will be presented with a page similar to the one pictured in *Figure 13.19*, except it will be blank with no data.

To add the two gauges seen in *Figure 13.19*, to this page, do the following:

1. Press the **Add Widgets** button.
2. Select the **Gauge** icon and press **Next.**
3. In the **Configure widget parameters** dialog, type in a name for the gauge (for example, `temperature`) and select the appropriate field number (**Field1** for temperature, **Field2** for humidity, respectively).
4. You can adjust and experiment with the other parameters as you desire to set max/min ranges, coloring, and other display properties for your gauge.
5. Repeat the process for the second gauge.

> Don't worry if the gauges (or charts) display **Field value unavailable**. This is correct since we have not sent any temperature or humidity data to ThingSpeak yet.

5. Now, it's time to obtain an API key and channel ID, which we will need in order to configure our forthcoming Python code. Click on to the **API Keys** tab:

Figure 13.21 – The API Keys tab

Here is the information we need to collect for our Python program:

- **Write API Key** (because we will be *writing* data to the platform)
- Channel ID (this is listed on all ThinkSpeak pages, near the top)

Now that we have created and configured a simple ThinkSpeak channel and collected our API key and Channel ID, we can move onto our Python code.

Configuring and running the ThinkSpeak Python program

We have provided two sample programs that integrate with ThinkSpeak. They are as follows:

- `chapter13/thingspeak_dht_mqtt.py`: An example that uses MQTT to send data into a ThinkSpeak channel.

- `chapter13/thingspeak_dht_http.py`: An example that uses the Python **requests** library to make RESTful API calls that send data to a ThinkSpeak channel.

The core concepts of these two programs were discussed in earlier chapters. For your reference, they are as follows:

- **MQTT**: We discussed the Paho-MQTT library in Chapter 4, *Networking with MQTT, Python, and the Mosquitto MQTT Broker*. A key difference for this chapter is that we are using the Paho-MQTT *simplifying client wrapper* to publish MQTT messages instead of a full life cycle example.
- We covered RESTful APIs and the **requests** library in Chapter 2, *Getting Started with Python and IoT*.
- The code related to the DHT 11/DHT 22 temperature and humidity sensor was covered in Chapter 9, *Measuring Temperature, Humidity, and Light Levels*.

Let's configure these programs, run them, and see the data appear in ThingSpeak. We'll walk through the example code provided in chapter13/thingspeak_dht_mqtt.py; however, the overall process will be the same for chapter13/thingspeak_dht_http.py:

1. Open the chapter13/thingspeak_dht_mqtt.py file for editing.
2. Near the top of the file, identify the following code starting at line (1) and confirm your DHT sensor is connected to the correct GPIO pin and that the correct sensor instance is enabled in code:

```
# DHT Temperature/Humidity Sensor
GPIO = 24                                                    # (1)
#dht = DHT11(GPIO, use_internal_pullup=True, timeout_secs=0.5)
dht = DHT22(GPIO, use_internal_pullup=True, timeout_secs=0.5)
```

3. Next, identify the following code segment starting at line (2) and update it with your ThingSpeak write API key, Channel ID, and time zone. Note that CHANNEL_ID is only used in the MQTT integration (so it does not appear in the thingspeak_dht_http.py file):

```
# ThingSpeak Configuration
WRITE_API_KEY = "" # <<<< ADD YOUR WRITE API KEY HERE    # (2)
CHANNEL_ID = ""    # <<<< ADD YOUR CHANNEL ID HERE

# See for values
https://au.mathworks.com/help/thingspeak/time-zones-reference.html
TIME_ZONE = "Australia/Melbourne"
```

4. Save your file and run the program. You should receive an output similar to the following:

```
(venv) $ python thing_speak_dht_mqtt.py
INFO:root:Collecting Data and Sending to ThingSpeak every 600
```

```
seconds. Press Control + C to Exit
INFO:root:Sensor result {'temp_c': 25.3, 'temp_f': 77.5,
'humidity': 43.9, 'valid': True}
INFO:root:Published to mqtt.thingspeak.com
```

5. Within seconds, you should see your data appear on your ThingSpeak dashboard!

Congratulations! With that, you have created a ThingSpeak dashboard to visualize data that's been collected by your Raspberry Pi. Visualizing data is a frequent requirement for many monitoring IoT projects, whether it be simple indicator displays such as gauges or producing historic graphs to visualize trends. How you approach visualization for your data all depends on your requirements; however, the one thing that's common to all these requirements is that there are many ready-to-go services such as ThingSpeak to help you achieve this as an alternative to custom coding dashboard and visualization applications yourself.

Now, I will conclude this chapter with a brief discussion of other popular IoT platforms that you may like to explore and use in your future projects.

Other IoT and automation platforms for further exploration

So far in this chapter, we have seen IFTTT and ThingSpeak in action, as well as how to integrate them with our Raspberry Pi. We saw how to use IFTTT to create simple workflows and how we can visualize data with ThingSpeak – two very different ideas, but nonetheless, they are both IoT platforms.

Both these platforms are immensely powerful and offer a wide range of features and possibilities beyond what we can cover in a single chapter, so I do encourage you to seek out their documentation and examples to advance your learning.

There are many other IoT platforms, applications, and frameworks that are available. This section will provide a short, curated list based on my experience. They all fit in nicely with this book's Python- and Raspberry Pi-based themes.

Zapier

We've already seen IFFF in action. IFTTT is more consumer-focused in terms of the services that it supports, plus as we have seen, we are limited to a single *This* trigger and a single *That* action.

Zappier is very similar in principle to IFTTT, but with a more business-orientated focus, including a range of services and integrations not available with IFTTT (there will be services and integrations that are unique to IFTTT also). Furthermore, Zapier is also capable of much more complex workflows for triggering events and actions.

You will find it relatively simple to reimplement our two IFTTT examples from this chapter in Zappier.

Website: `https://zapier.com`.

IFTTT platform

In this chapter, we used IFTTT as an end user and performed our integrations using Webhooks. If you are a business wishing to create gadgets you want to expose as first-class IFTTT services, then you should check out the IFTTT platform.

Website: `https://platform.ifttt.com`.

ThingsBoard IoT platform

ThingsBoard is an open source IoT platform that you can download and host on your Raspberry Pi. On the surface, it will allow you to build dashboards and data visualizations, just as we did in ThingSpeak. Compared to ThingSpeak, you will find that ThingsBoard has a steeper learning curve when it comes to creating your first dashboard; however, you will also find that it offers a more extensive set of widgets and customization options. Plus, unlike ThingSpeak, which can only consume data, ThingsBoard allows you to embed controls into a dashboard that lets you interact with your Raspberry Pi using MQTT.

From experience, working your way through the ThingsBoard documentation and tutorials (many are available as videos) is a must if you want to learn how to use this platform since on your first visit to its UI, it's not immediately obvious what you need to do.

Here are a few specific resources from their website:

- Raspberry Pi installation instructions: `https://thingsboard.io/docs/user-guide/install/rpi` (don't worry if it says Raspberry Pi 3; it will still work on a 4)
- Getting started guide: `https://thingsboard.io/docs/getting-started-guides/helloworld`

While there are no Python-specific examples in the getting started guide, there are Mosquito MQTT examples and cURL examples that demonstrate the RESTful API. A suggestion would be to use the two ThingSpeak code examples presented in this chapter as a starting point and adopt them to use the ThingBoard-specific MQTT and/or RESTful APIs.

Website: `https://thingsboard.io`.

Home Assistant

Home Assistant is a pure Python home automation suite. Out of the box, Home Assistant can connect with a wide range of internet-enabled devices such as lights, doors, fridges, and coffee machines – to mention only a few.

Home Assistant gets a mention here, not only because it is built with Python, but because it allows us to integrate directly with the host Raspberry Pi's GPIO pins, as well as with a remote Raspberry Pi's GPIO pins using PiGPIO's remote GPIO feature. Plus, there are MQTT and RESTful API integration options available.

While simple in concept and end user operation, there is a highish learning curve (and a fair amount of experimentation needed) when it comes to configuring Home Assistant since most of the integrations are performed by manually editing **YAML Ain't Markup Language** (**YAML**) files directly.

In relation to GPIO integrations, I have selected some resources from their website to get you started. I recommend reading the glossary first as it will help you better understand the Home Assistant terminology and therefore help you better understand other parts of the documentation:

- Installation: There are a variety of ways that Home Assistant can be installed. For testing the platform and building a GPIO integration, I suggest the "Virtual Environment" option, documented at `https://www.home-assistant.io/docs/installation/virtualenv`.

- **Glossary:** https://www.home-assistant.io/docs/glossary.
- **Available Raspberry Pi integrations:** https://www.home-assistant.io/integrations/#search/Raspberry%20Pi.

Website: https://www.home-assistant.io.

Amazon Web Services (AWS)

Another suggestion is Amazon Web Services, specifically two services – IoT Core and Elastic Beanstalk. These options will provide you with immense flexibility and a near-endless number of options when it comes to creating IoT applications. IoT Core is Amazon's IoT platform where you can create dashboards, workflows, and integrations, while Elastic Beanstalk is their cloud platform where you can host your own programs – including Python – in the cloud.

Amazon Web Services is an advanced development platform, so you will need to invest weeks into learning how it works and how to build and deploy applications using it, but I can promise you that you will learn a lot during the process! Plus, their documentation and tutorials are very high quality.

Amazon IoT Core: https://aws.amazon.com/iot-core.

Amazon Elastic Beanstalk: https://aws.amazon.com/elasticbeanstalk.

Microsoft Azure, IBM Watson, and Google Cloud

Finally, I do want to mention these other IT giants, who all offer their own cloud and IoT platforms. My suggestion regarding AWS is purely due to my more in-depth experience with this platform. The comparative platforms offered by Microsoft, IBM, and Google are also high quality and backed with excellent documentation and tutorials, so if your personal preference is with one of these providers, you are still in good hands.

Summary

In this chapter, we explored and learned how to use our Raspberry Pi with both the IFTTT and ThinkSpeak IoT platforms. We created two IFTTT examples where our Raspberry Pi performed the *This* role in an IFTTT Applet to start an IFTTT workflow. We also saw how to use our Raspberry Pi in the *That* role so that it can be actioned by an IFTTT Applet. Next, we covered an example of how to integrate with the ThinkSpeak IoT platform to visualize temperature and humidity data collected by our Raspberry Pi. Finally, we discussed other IoT platform options that you may like to investigate and experiment with.

We certainly only covered the basics of what is possible with visualization and automation platforms in this chapter. I encourage you to seek our further IFTTT examples and ideas you can experiment with, and also explore the other platforms that we mentioned. And remember, while every platform will be different and have its own integration considerations, the commonly accepted standards to achieve integration boil down to RESTful APIs and MQTT, both of which you now have experience with!

In the next chapter, we will cover a comprehensive end-to-end example to pull together many of the concepts and examples that we have covered throughout this book.

Questions

As we conclude this chapter, here is a list of questions for you to test your knowledge regarding this chapter's material. You will find the answers in the *Assessments* section of the *Appendix*:

1. With our first IFTTT Applet, where we monitored the temperature, why did we use a different high and low temperature value to trigger our Applet and send an email?
2. What was the advantage of using an intermediary service such as dweet.io with our IFTTT Webhook service?
3. What are some of the core differences between IFTTT and Zapier?
4. Can you control your Raspberry Pi from a ThingSpeak dashboard?
5. In relation to data, what is the limitation of the IFTTT Webhook service when used as an action (that is, on the *That* side of an applet)?
6. You want to prototype the switching on and off of an over-the-counter smart light bulb based on a Raspberry Pi's GPIO pin state. What platforms could you use?

Tying It All Together - An IoT Christmas Tree

14

Welcome to our final chapter! We will round out this book by pulling together various topics and ideas from earlier chapters to build a multifaceted IoT program. Specifically, we will be building an internet-controllable Christmas tree, an *IoTree,* if you don't mind the pun!

Our approach in this chapter will be to reuse two circuits from previous chapters to create Christmas tree lighting (using an APA102 LED strip) and a rocking mechanism to make the tree shake (we will use a servo) and jingle (well, it'll jingle as it shakes if you decorate the tree with bells!). We will then revisit and adapt our learning about RESTful APIs and MQTT to create two ways in which we can control the lighting and servo over a network or the internet. We will then revisit dweet.io and **If-This-Then-That** (**IFTTT**) and build IFTTT Applets to control the tree via email and your voice using Google Assistant!

Here is what we will cover in this chapter:

- Overview of the IoT Christmas tree
- Building the IoTree circuit
- Configuring, running, and using the Tree API service
- Configuring, running, and using the Tree MQTT service
- Integrating the IoTree with dweet.io
- Integrating with email and Google Assistant via IFTTT
- Ideas and suggestions to extend your IoTree

Technical requirements

To perform the exercises in this chapter, you will need the following:

- Raspberry Pi 4 Model B
- Raspbian OS Buster (with desktop and recommended software)
- Minimum Python version 3.5

These requirements are what the code examples in this book are based on. It's reasonable to expect that the code examples should work without modification on a Raspberry Pi 3 Model B or a different version of Raspbian OS as long as your Python version is 3.5 or higher.

To complete the section titled *Integration with Google Assistant,* at a minimum, you will need the following prerequisites:

- A Google account (if you have a Gmail email account, that's all you need)
- An Android phone or the *Google Assistant* app for iOS

You will find this chapter's source code in the `chapter14` folder in the GitHub repository available here: `https://github.com/PacktPublishing/Practical-Python-Programming-for-IoT`.

You will need to execute the following commands in a terminal to set up a virtual environment and install the Python libraries required for the code in this chapter:

```
$ cd chapter14            # Change into this chapter's folder
$ python3 -m venv venv    # Create Python Virtual Environment
$ source venv/bin/activate  # Activate Python Virtual Environment
(venv) $ pip install pip --upgrade      # Upgrade pip
(venv) $ pip install -r requirements.txt  # Install dependent packages
```

The following dependencies are installed from `requirements.txt`:

- **PiGPIO**: The PiGPIO GPIO library (`https://pypi.org/project/pigpio`)
- **Flask-RESTful**: A Flask extension for creating RESTful API services (`https://pypi.org/project/Flask-RESTful`)
- **The Paho MQTT client**: `https://pypi.org/project/paho-mqtt`
- **Pillow**: **Python Imaging Library** (**PIL**) (`https://pypi.org/project/Pillow`)
- **The Luma LED Matrix library**: `https://pypi.org/project/luma.led_matrix`

- **Requests**: A high-level Python library for making HTTP requests (`https://pypi.org/project/requests`)
- **PyPubSub**: In-process messaging and events (`https://pypi.org/project/PyPubSub`)

The electronic components we will need for this chapter's exercises are as follows:

- 1 x MG90S hobby servo (or equivalent 3-wire, 5-volt hobby servo)
- 1 x APA102 RGB LED strip
- 1 x logic level shifter module
- External power supply (at a minimum a 3.3 V/5 V breadboard-mountable power supply)

 A video showing this tree in action is available at `https://youtu.be/15Xfuf_99Io`. Please note that this tree uses RGB LEDs and an alternating blinking animation for the lights. We'll be using an APA102 LED strip in this chapter that is capable of creating more animation effects. The demo tree can also play a tune, which we will not cover in this chapter (although you'll easily be able to add that feature if you wish by adopting the RTTTL example from `Chapter 8`, *Lights, Indicators, and Displaying Information*).

Overview of the IoT Christmas tree

Before we commence our chapter by building circuits and looking at code, let's take a moment to understand what our IoTree will do and how we will be building it. The tree pictured in *Figure 14.1* is representative of what you could create after completing this chapter:

Figure 14.1 – IoTree example

Now, I'll need to let you know up front that we're only covering the electronics and programming of the IoTree. You'll need to apply your initiative and bring your maker skills to the table to build the tree and bring it to life. I suggest using a small table-top Christmas tree since part of our build involves a servo to *shake* the tree. Our hobby-grade servo is powerful enough to shake a small tree; however, it's unlikely that it could shake a full-size Christmas tree (you'll need to research and get a more powerful servo if you aspire to upgrade our build to a larger tree – and please send me a picture if you do!).

Our base-level tree will comprise the following electronic components:

- An APA102 LED light strip for the tree lights (we covered the APA102 LED strip in Chapter 8, *Lights, Indicators, and Displaying Information*).
- A servo to make the tree *shake* and *jingle* – for this, you will need some bell ornaments on the tree that will *jingle* when the tree shakes (we covered servos in Chapter 10, *Movement with Servos, Motors, and Steppers*).

Programmatically and structurally, our tree program will be drawing on the following concepts we've learned about:

- **The dweet.io service**: First covered in `Chapter 2`, *Getting Started with Python and IoT*, and revisited in `Chapter 13`, *IoT Visualization and Automation Platforms*
- **RESTful API with Flask-RESTful**: From `Chapter 3`, *Networking with RESTful APIs and Web Sockets Using Flask*
- **Message Queue Telemetry Transport (MQTT)**: Covered in `Chapter 4`, *Networking with MQTT, Python, and the Mosquitto MQTT Broker*.
- **A thread and Publisher-Subscriber (PubSub) approach to IoT programs**: Covered in `Chapter 12`, *Advanced IoT Programming Concepts – Threads, AsyncIO, and Event Loops*
- **The IFTTT IoT platform**: Covered in `Chapter 13`, *IoT Visualization and Automation Platforms*

As we proceed through this chapter, we are going to assume you have an understanding of the concepts from each of the aforementioned chapters, and that you have performed the exercises presented in each chapter, including building the circuits and understanding the circuit and code-level concepts that make the circuits work.

Our first task will be to build the circuit needed for our IoTree, which we will do next.

Building the IoTree circuit

It's time to get building! Please construct the circuit illustrated in *Figure 14.2*:

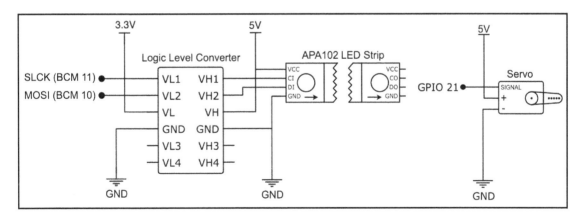

Figure 14.2 – IoTree circuit schematic diagram

This circuit hopefully looks familiar. It's a combination of two circuits that we have seen before:

- The APA102 (with a logic level shifter) circuit from *Figure 8.4*, in `Chapter 8`, *Lights, Indicators, and Displaying Information*
- The servo circuit from *Figure 10.2*, in `Chapter 10`, *Movement with Servos, Motors, and Steppers*

Please consult these respective chapters if you need step-by-step instructions on building this circuit on your breadboard.

> Please remember that you will need to use an external power supply to power your APA102 and servo, as they will draw too much current to use the 5-volt pin on your Raspberry Pi.

When you have completed your circuit build, next let's briefly discuss three programs that can be used to control this circuit.

Three IoTree service programs

There are three separate programs to accompany our IoTree, each taking a slightly different approach to work with our lights and servo. The programs are as follows:

- **The Tree API service** (found in the `chapter14/tree_api_service` folder): This program provides a RESTful API created with Flask-RESTful to control the lights and servo. It also includes a basic HTML and JavaScript web app that uses the API. We will discuss the Tree API service further in the section titled *Configuring, running, and using the Tree API service*.
- **The Tree MQTT service** (found in the `chapter14/tree_mqtt_service` folder): This program will allow us to control the lights and servo by publishing MQTT messages. We will discuss the Tree MQTT service further in the section titled *Configuring, running, and using the Tree MQTT service*.
- **The dweet integration service** (found in the `chapter14/dweet_integration_service` folder): This program receives dweets and republishes them as MQTT messages. We can use this program together with the *Tree MQTT service* program to control our lights and servo using dweet.io, which thus provides us with an easy way to integrate our IoTree with a service such as IFTTT. We will discuss the dweet integration service more in the section titled *Integrating the IoTree with dweet.io*.

Now that we have briefly discussed the programs that make up this chapter's examples, let's configure and run our Tree API service and use it to make the lights and servo work.

Configuring, running, and using the Tree API service

The Tree API service program provides a RESTful API service for controlling our IoTree's APA102 LED strip and servo. You can find the Tree API service program in the chapter14/tree_api_service folder. It contains the following files:

- README.md: The full API documentation with examples for the Tree API service program.
- main.py: This is the program's main entry point.
- config.py: Program configuration.
- apa102.py: A Python class that integrates with the APA102 LED strip. The core of this code is very similar to the APA102 Python code we explored back in Chapter 8, *Lights, Indicators, and Displaying Information*, only now it is structured as a Python class, uses a thread to run light animations, plus has a few other small additions, such as code to make the LEDs blink.
- apa102_api.py: Flask-RESTful resource classes that provide the APA102 API. It draws upon the Flask-RESTful code and examples from Chapter 3, *Networking with RESTful APIs and Web Sockets Using Flask*.
- servo.py: A Python class for controlling the servo. It draws upon the servo code we covered back in Chapter 10, *Movement with Servos, Motors, and Steppers*.
- servo_api.py: Flask-RESTful resource classes that provide the servo API.
- templates: This folder contains the example web app's index.html file.
- static: This folder contains the static JavaScript libraries and an image used by the web app.

A diagram depicting the Tree API service program architecture is shown in *Figure 14.3*:

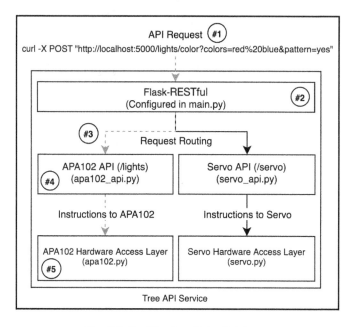

Figure 14.3 – Tree API service architecture block diagram

Here is the high-level operation of the Tree API service for the API request shown by the dotted line in the preceding diagram:

1. An external client makes a POST request to the `/lights/colors` endpoint at **#1**.
2. The request is handled by the Flask framework/server at **#2**. (The Flask and Flask-RESTful setup can be found in `main.py`.)
3. The `/lights/*` endpoint is routed to the appropriate Flask-RESTful resource at **#3** (APA102 – that is, the *light* – resources are defined in `apa102_api.py`). The endpoint setup and resource registration with Flask-RESTful are found in `main.py`.
4. At **#4**, the appropriate resource is invoked (in this example, it will be `ColorControl.post()`), which then parses and validates the query string parameters (that is, `colors=red%20blue&pattern=yes`).
5. Finally, at **#5**, `ColorControl.post()` then calls the appropriate methods in an instance of APA102 (defined in `apa102.py`, and set up in `main.py`) that directly interfaces with and updates the physical APA102 LED strip with the repeating pattern of red and blue.

Now that we have an understanding of how our Tree API service works, before we can run our Tree API service, first we need to check its configuration. We'll do that next.

Configuring the Tree API service

The Tree API service configuration is found in the `chapter14/tree_api_service/config.py` file. There are many configuration options in this file, and they mostly relate to the configuration of the APA102 (discussed in `Chapter 8`, *Lights, Indicators, and Displaying Information*) and the servo (discussed in `Chapter 10`, *Movement with Servos, Motors, and Steppers*). You will find this file and the configuration options well commented.

The default configuration will be adequate for running an example locally on your Raspberry Pi; however, the one configuration parameter you should check is `APA102_NUM_LEDS = 60`. If your APA102 LED strip contains a different number of LEDs, please update this configuration appropriately.

Let's run the Tree API service program and create some light (and movement)!

Running the Tree API service

It's now time to run the Tree API service program and send it RESTful API requests to make it work. Here are the steps to run and test our Tree API service:

1. Change into the `chapter14/tree_api_service` folder and start the `main.py` script, as shown:

```
# Terminal 1
(venv) $ cd tree_api_service
(venv) $ python main.py
* Serving Flask app "main" (lazy loading)
... truncated ...
INFO:werkzeug: * Running on http://0.0.0.0:5000/ (Press CTRL+C to
quit)
```

2. Next, open a second terminal and run the following `curl` command to set the repeating light pattern sequence to `red, blue, black`:

```
# Terminal 2
$ curl -X POST
"http://localhost:5000/lights/color?colors=red,blue,black&pattern=y
es"
```

3. Also in *Terminal 2*, run this next command to start making the lights animate:

```
# Terminal 2
$ curl -X POST
"http://localhost:5000/lights/animation?mode=left&speed=5"
```

Other animation modes you can use for the `mode` parameter, in addition to `left`, include `right`, `blink`, `rainbow`, and `stop`. The `speed` parameter takes a value between 1 and 10.

4. To clear or reset the LED strip, run the following command, again in *Terminal 2*:

```
# Terminal 2
$ curl -X POST "http://localhost:5000/lights/clear"
```

5. To make the servo sweep (that is, to make the tree *shake)*, run the following command in *Terminal 2*:

```
# Terminal 2
$ curl -X POST "http://localhost:5000/servo/sweep"
```

The servo should sweep back and forth a number of times. If you want to make the servo sweep more times or need to increase its range of movement, then you can adjust the `SERVO_SWEEP_COUNT` and `SERVO_SWEEP_DEGREES` configuration parameters in the `chapter14/tree_api_service/config.py` file.

If you find your LEDs dimming, flickering, or otherwise behaving erratically when you make the servo move, or your servo twitches as you change the APA102 LEDs, chances are that your external power supply cannot deliver enough current to run both the LEDs and servo simultaneously. As in interim measure, if you don't have another power supply, try reducing the number of LEDs (`APA102_NUM_LEDS` in `config.py`) and/or reducing the LED contrast (`APA102_DEFAULT_CONTRAST`, also in `config.py`). This will lower the current requirements of the LED strip.

6. Finally, let's run the web app and control our IoTree from a web browser by opening a web browser on your Raspberry Pi desktop and navigating to the URL `http://localhost:5000`. You should see a web page similar to the one pictured here:

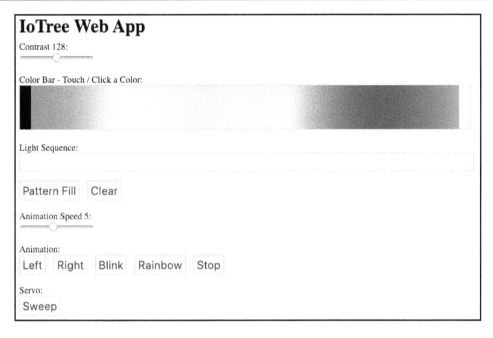

Figure 14.4 – Example IoTree web app

Try the following actions:

- Click on colors in the **color bar** and watch that color get pushed to the APA102 LED strip.
- Click the **Pattern Fill** button to fill the APA102 LED strip with the selected colors.
- Click **Left** to start an animation.

The JavaScript behind this web app (found in `chapter14/tree_api_service/templates/index.html`) is simply calling our IoTree API similar to what we have already done using `curl`, only it's doing it using jQuery. jQuery and JavaScript are beyond the scope of this book; however, they are briefly touched on in `Chapter 3`, *Networking with RESTful APIs and Web Sockets Using Flask.*

 You will find the full set of API documentation for the IoTree with `curl` examples in the `chapter14/tree_api_service/README.md` file.

Our RESTful API implementation provides the basic API endpoints that we need for this chapter; however, I am more than confident that you will be able to expand and adapt this example for your own projects or add new functionality to your IoTree. I'll provide suggestions on how you can expand your IoTree based on what you have learned in this book toward the end of the chapter in the section titled *Ideas and suggestions to extend your IoTree*.

Now that we have run and seen how to control our IoTree's lights and servo with a RESTful API, next we will look at an alternative service implementation that will allow us to control our IoTree using MQTT.

Configuring, running, and using the Tree MQTT service

The Tree MQTT service program provides an MQTT interface for controlling our tree's APA102 LED strip and servo by publishing MQTT messages to MQTT topics. You can find the Tree MQTT service program in the `chapter14/tree_mqtt_service` folder, and it contains the following files:

- `README.md`: A full list of MQTT topics and message formats for controlling your IoTree.
- `main.py`: This is the program's main entry point.
- `config.py`: Program configuration.
- `apa102.py`: This is an exact copy of the `chapter14/tree_api_service/apa102.py`. file
- `servo.py`: This is an exact copy of the `chapter14/tree_api_service/servo.py` file.
- `mqtt_listener_client.py`: This is a class that connects to an MQTT broker and subscribes to a topic that will receive messages to control the APA102 and servo. When MQTT messages are received, they are turned into a PubSub message and published using the `PyPubSub` library, which we discussed in `Chapter 12`, *Advanced IoT Programming Concepts - Threads, AsyncIO, and Event Loops*.
- `apa102_controller.py`: This code receives PubSub messages sent by `mqtt_listener_client.py` and updates the APA102 LED strip as appropriate.
- `servo_controller.py`: This code receives PubSub messages sent by `mqtt_listener_client.py` and controls the servo.

A diagram depicting the Tree MQTT service program architecture is shown in *Figure 14.5*:

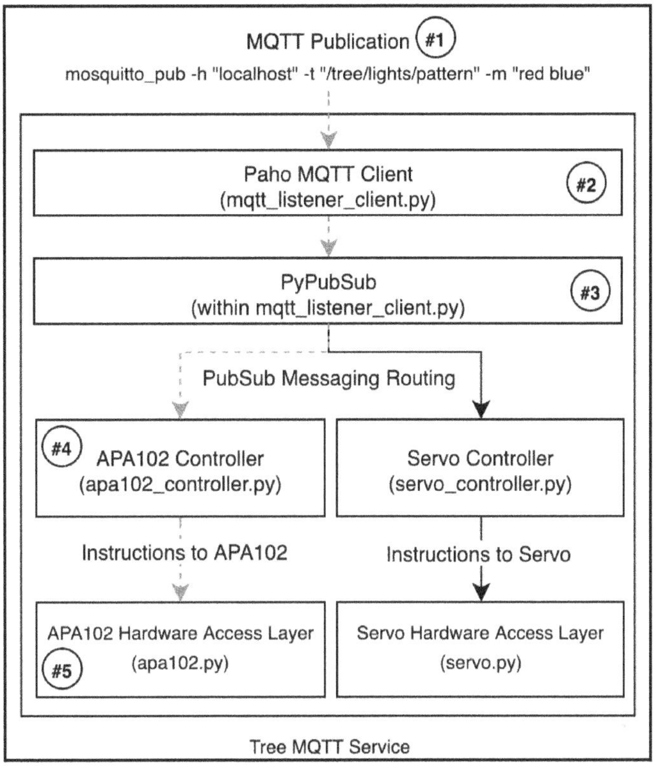

Figure 14.5 – Tree MQTT service architecture block diagram

Here is the high-level operation of the Tree MQTT service for the MQTT publication depicted by the dotted line in the preceding diagram:

1. A `red blue` message is published on to the `tree/lights/pattern` topic at **#1**.
2. The message is received by the Paho-MQTT client at **#2**. The topic and message is parsed in the `on_message()` method in `mqtt_listener_client.py` and mapped into a local PubSub topic *pattern* using the `MQTT_TO_PUBSUB_TOPIC_MAPPINGS` mapping dictionary found in `config.py`.
3. The mapped message and parsed data are dispatched using the `PyPubSub` library at **#3**.

4. The `PyPubSub` subscription in `apa102_controller.py` receives the *pattern* topic and its payload data at **#4**

5. `apa102_controller.py` handles the message and data at **#5** and calls the appropriate methods on an APA102 instance (defined in `apa102.py`) that directly interfaces and updates the physical APA102 LED strip with the repeating pattern of red and blue.

In case you are wondering, the decision to use `PyPubSub` and re-dispatch MQTT messages in `mqtt_listener_client.py` was a design decision based on my personal preferences to decouple MQTT-related code and hardware control-related code, with the goal of making the application easier to read and maintain. An alternative – and equally valid – approach could have been to use `apa102.py` and `servo.py` within `mqtt_listener_client.py` in direct response to the MQTT messages received.

Now that we have an understanding of how our Tree MQTT service works, before we can run our Tree MQTT service, first we need to check its configuration. We'll do that next.

Configuring the Tree MQTT service

The Tree MQTT service configuration is found in the `chapter14/tree_mqtt_service/config.py` file. Similar to the Tree API service, they mostly relate to the configuration of the APA102 and the servo. You will also find this file and its configuration options well commented.

The default configuration will be adequate for running an example locally on your Raspberry Pi; however, just as we did for the Tree API service configuration, please check and update the `APA102_NUM_LEDS = 60` parameter as appropriate.

If you also needed to change any of the `APA102_DEFAULT_CONTRAST`, `SERVO_SWEEP_COUNT`, or `SERVO_SWEEP_DEGREES` parameters while running the Tree API example, please also update these values now for the MQTT example.

Once you have made any necessary changes to the configuration, we will proceed and run our Tree MQTT service program and publish MQTT messages to make our IoTree work.

Running the Tree MQTT service program

It's now time to run the Tree MQTT service program and publish MQTT messages that will control our IoTree. Here are the steps to run and test our Tree MQTT service:

1. We must have the Mosquitto MQTT broker service installed and running on our Raspberry Pi, plus the Mosquitto MQTT clients tools. Please refer to `Chapter 4`, *Networking with MQTT, Python, and the Mosquitto MQTT Broker*, if you need to check your installation.

2. Change into the `chapter14/tree_mqtt_service` folder and start the `main.py` script, as shown:

```
# Terminal 1
(venv) $ cd tree_mqtt_service
(venv) $ python main.py
INFO:root:Connecting to MQTT Broker localhost:1883
INFO:MQTTListener:Connected to MQTT Broker
```

3. Next, open a second terminal and send an MQTT message using the following command:

```
# Terminal 2
$ mosquitto_pub -h "localhost" -t "tree/lights/pattern" -m "red
blue black"
```

The LED strip will light up with the repeating color pattern – red, blue, black (black means that the LED is off).

Try experimenting with the `--retain` or `-r` retained message option to `mosquirro_pub`. If you publish a retained message, it gets re-delivered to your Tree MQTT services when it connects to the MQTT broker and subscribes to the `tree/#` topic. This provides a way for your IoTree to restore its last state in between restarts.

4. Now, run the following command in *Terminal 2* to make the LED strip animate:

```
# Terminal 2
$ mosquitto_pub -h "localhost" -t "tree/lights/animation" -m "left"
```

5. To clear or reset the LED strip, run the following command, again in *Terminal 2*:

```
# Terminal 2
$ mosquitto_pub -h "localhost" -t "tree/lights/clear" -m ""
```

In this example (and also the next one in *step 6*), we don't have any message content; however, we still need to pass an empty message with the −m " " option (or, alternatively, −n); otherwise, `mosquitto_pub` will abort.

6. Finally, try the following to sweep the servo:

```
# Terminal 2
$ mosquitto_pub -h "localhost" -t "tree/servo/sweep" -m ""
```

The servo will sweep back and forth according to the values set for `SERVO_SWEEP_COUNT` or `SERVO_SWEEP_DEGREES` in `chapter14/tree_mqtt_service/config.py`.

You will find the full set of MQTT topics and message formats that are recognized by the Tree MQTT service, complete with `mosquitto_pub` examples, in the `chapter14/tree_mqtt_service/README.md` file.

Similar to our RESTful API example, our MQTT example provides the minimum functionality that we need for this chapter but does provide a basic framework that you can expand on for your own future projects, or if you extend your IoTree's features.

Now that we have run and seen how to control our IoTree's lights and servo with MQTT, let's look at an integration service that we can use to couple our Tree MQTT service with dweet.io.

Integrating the IoTree with dweet.io

The *dweet integration service*, found in the `chatper14/dweet_integration_service` folder, is a Python-based integration service that receives dweets and re-publishes them as messages to MQTT topics. This service provides us with a simple approach to integrate a service such as IFTTT with our Tree MQTT service program.

The dweet integration service is made up of the following files:

- `main.py`: The main program entry point.
- `config.py`: The configuration parameters.
- `thing_name.txt`: Where your thing name is saved. This file will be created when you first start the program.
- `dweet_listener.py`: The core program code.

The core of our dweet service is found in the `dweet_listener.py` file. If you inspect this file, you will notice that it is almost identical to the `dweet_led.py` file covered in both `Chapter 2`, *Getting Started with Python and IoT*, and `Chapter 13`, *IoT Visualization and Automation Platforms* (except it's now wrapped as a Python class).

The core difference is found in the `process_dweet()` method, shown at line (1) in the following code, where instead of directly controlling a LED, we instead intercept the dweet and then re-publish it to MQTT topics:

```
def process_dweet(self, dweet):          # (1)

    # ...Truncated...
    # command is "<action> <data1> <data2> ... <dataN>"
    command = dweet['command'].strip()
    # ...Truncated...

    # elements (List) <action>,<data1>,<data2>,...,<dataN>
    elements = command.split(" ")
    action = elements[0].lower()
    data = " ".join(elements[1:])

    self.publish_mqtt(action, data)       # (2)
```

The `publish_mqtt()` method, shown at line (2) in the preceding code and at line (3) in the following code, then turns our parsed command string into an MQTT topic based on the `ACTION_TOPIC_MAPPINGS` setting found in `chapter14/dweet_mqtt_service/config.py` and publishes the message:

```
def publish_mqtt(self, action, data):                      # (3)
    if action in self.action_topic_mappings:
        # Map Action into MQTT Topic
        # (Eg mode --> tree/lights/mode).
        # See config.py for mappings.

        topic = self.action_topic_mappings[action]
        retain = topic in self.mqtt_topic_retain_message   # (4)
        # ... truncated ...
        publish.single(topic, data, qos=0,                 # (5)
                    client_id=self.mqtt_client_id,
                    retain=retain, hostname=self.mqtt_host,
                    port=self.mqtt_port)
    # ... truncated ...
```

Notice, at line (5), that we are using a Paho-MQTT `publish.single()` convenience method, rather that than the fully fledged MQTT client approach we used in `Chapter 4`, *Networking with MQTT, Python, and the Mosquitto MQTT Broker* (and that was also used in the Tree MQTT service program).

At the moment, I just want to point out line (4), where we set the `retain` variable (also notice its use in `publish.single()`). We will discuss this message retention more in the following section when we discuss the service configuration file.

A diagram depicting the Tree service program architecture is shown in *Figure 14.6*:

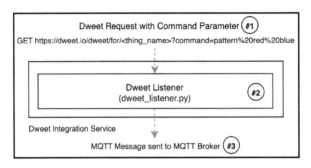

Figure 14.6 – dweet integration service architecture block diagram

Here is the high-level operation of the dweet integration service for the request shown by the blue dotted line in the preceding diagram:

1. A dweet is created at **#1**.
2. `dweet_listener.py` receives the dweet at **#2** and parses the data contained in the `command` parameter. The action contained within the commend is mapped into an MQTT topic using the `ACTION_TOPIC_MAPPINGS` mapping dictionary found in `config.py`.
3. A message is published to the MQTT broker to the mapped MQTT topic at **#3**. The message's *retained* flag is set according to the `TOPIC_RETAIN_MESSAGE` mapping dictionary found in `config.py`.

After the publication of the MQTT message, if your Tree MQTT service is running and connected to the same MQTT broker, it will receive the MQTT message and update your IoTree accordingly.

Now that we have an understanding of how our dweet integration service works, before we can run our dweet integration service, first we need to check its configuration. We'll do that next.

Configuring the Tree MQTT service

The dweet integration service configuration is found in
the `chapter14/dweet_integration_service/config.py` file. There are a number of
configuration options relating to how the service works, and the defaults will be adequate
for running this service locally on your Raspberry Pi where you also have your Mosquitto
MQTT broker running. The configuration parameters are well commented in this file;
however, I will make mention of the `ACTION_TOPIC_MAPPINGS`
and `TOPIC_RETAIN_MESSAGE` parameters:

```
ACTION_TOPIC_MAPPINGS = {
    "clear": "tree/lights/clear",
    "push": "tree/lights/push",
    ... truncated ...
}
```

The dweet integration service maps *dweeted commands* into *MQTT topics*. It's
the `ACTION_TOPIC_MAPPINGS` configuration parameter that determines how commands
are mapped into MQTT topics. We'll discuss this idea of *commands* in the next section.

> The MQTT topics mapped and used by the dweet integration service must
> match those used by a Tree MQTT service. The default configurations for
> each service use the same topics.

The `TOPIC_RETAIN_MESSAGE` configuration shown in the following code determines which
MQTT topics will have their message's *retained* flag set. It's this configuration (`True` or
`False`) that is used to set the `retained` parameter on `single.publish()`, as we pointed
out in the previous section:

```
TOPIC_RETAIN_MESSAGE = {
    "tree/lights/clear": False,
    "tree/lights/animation": True,
    ... truncated ...
}
```

Now that we have discussed the configuration file, let's start our dweet integration service
and send it dweets that will control our IoTree.

Running the dweet integration service program

Our dweet integration service works by receiving dweets in a predefined format and turns them into MQTT topics and messages as per the configuration parameters we discussed in the previous section. We'll discuss this dweet format shortly as we run and test the dweet integration service. Here are the steps we need to follow:

1. Firstly, make sure you have the *Tree MQTT service* program from the previous section running in a terminal. It is the Tree MQTT service that will receive and process the MQTT messages published by the dweet integration service.

2. Next, navigate to the `chapter14/dweet_integration_service` folder in a new terminal and start the `main.py` program, as shown (remember your thing name will be different):

```
(venv) $ cd dweet_service
(venv) $ python main.py
INFO:DweetListener:Created new thing name ab5f2504
INFO:DweetListener:Dweet Listener initialized. Publish command
dweets to 'https://dweet.io/dweet/for/ab5f2504?command=...'
```

3. Copy and paste the following URLs into a web browser to control your IoTree. Use the thing name shown in your output in place of the `<thing_name>` text:

   - `https://dweet.io/dweet/for/<thing_name>?command=pattern%20red%20blue%20black`
   - `https://dweet.io/dweet/for/<thing_name>?command=animation%20left`
   - `https://dweet.io/dweet/for/<thing_name>?command=speed%2010`
   - `https://dweet.io/dweet/for/<thing_name>?command=clear`
   - `https://dweet.io/dweet/for/<thing_name>?command=sweep`

 It may take a few moments between calling one of these URLs and it being received by your dweet integration service.

As you will see in the `command` parameter in the preceding URLs, the format of our dweets is `<action> <data1> <data2> <dataN>`.

You will find the full set of dweet command strings recognized by the default configuration in `config.py`, complete with example URLs, in the `chapter14/dweet_integration_service/README.md` file.

Well done! We've just created a simple integration service using dweet.io and MQTT and learned a simple and non-invasive approach that allows us to control our tree over the internet that did not require you to make any network or firewall configurations.

When designing an IoT project and considering how data is moved around the internet and networks, it's common to find that you need to design and build some form of integration to bridge systems that are built on different transport mechanisms. Our example in this section illustrates a scenario where we bridge an MQTT service (our IoTree MQTT service) with a polling-based RESTful API service (dweet.io). While every integration has its own requirements, hopefully this example has provided you with a rough roadmap and approach that you can adapt and build upon in the future when you encounter these scenarios.

Now that we have our dweet integration service running and have tested that it's working, let's see how we can use it together with the IFTTT platform.

Integrating with email and Google Assistant via IFTTT

Now comes the really fun part – let's make our tree controllable over the internet. As a spoiler, I'm not going to hold your hand through this integration because the core concepts on using dweet.io and IFTTT together were explained in detail in Chapter 13, *IoT Visualization and Automation Platforms*. In particular, we learned how to integrate our Raspberry Pi with IFTTT and email to control a LED.

What I will do, however, is give you screenshots of my IFTTT configuration so that you can verify what you set up. Plus, as a bonus, I'll also give you a tip and screenshot on how to integrate with Google Assistant so that you can voice-control your IoTree!

At the time of writing, IFTTT has a Google Assistant service that can take arbitrary spoken text (in IFTTT lingo, an *ingredient*). I did check out Alexa integration but unfortunately, the Alexa IFTTT service could not take arbitrary input and so was not compatible with our example.

First, we will look at a few pointers on how to integrate our IoTree with email.

Integration with email

The process for integrating with email or Twitter is the same as what we covered in `Chapter 13`, *IoT Visualization and Automation Platforms*, with the following changes:

1. Rather than using `LED` as the hashtag (the **Complete Trigger Fields Page** step in IFTTT), use `TREE`. This way, your email subject can be something such as `#TREE pattern red blue` or `#TREE animation blink`.

2. When configuring the **That** webhook service, you need to use the dweet URL printed on the terminal previously when you ran the dweet integration service. An example from my configuration is shown in the following figure. Remember the *thing name* in your URL will be different:

Figure 14.7 – Webhook configuration

3. Once you have completed setting up your IFTTT Applet, try emailing `trigger@applet.ifttt.com` with the following subject:

- `#TREE pattern red blue black`
- `#TREE animation left`

A few moments after emailing or tweeting the `#TREE pattern red blue black` command, your tree's lights will change to these colors in a repeating pattern. Similarly, a few moments after emailing or tweeting `#TREE animation left`, your tree lights will start animating.

Remember, you will need to have both the Tree MQTT service and dweet integration service running in terminals for this example to work. It may also take a few moments after sending an email or posting a tweet before your IoTree changes.

Once you have been able to control your IoTree with email, next we'll look at the steps necessary to add voice control using Google Assistant.

Integration with Google Assistant

Let's make our IoTree voice-controllable using Google Assistant.

Google Assistant comes in many other forms, including Google Home, Google Nest, and Google Mini. These products will also work with the IFTTT Google Assistant integration and your IoTree as long as they are signed in to the same Google Account you use with IFTTT.

To create our integration, we need to link your Google account with the IFTTT Google Assistant service and call a dweet.io URL when it receives commands. Here are the high-level steps to follow:

1. Log in to your IFTTT account.
2. Create a new Applet.
3. For the **This** part of the Applet, use **Google Assistant Service**.
4. Next, you will be asked to connect and allow IFTTT to use your Google account. Follow the on-screen instructions to connect IFTTT and your Google account.

5. Now it's time to select the Google Assistant trigger. Choose **Say a phrase with a text ingredient**. A sample trigger configuration is shown in *Figure 14.8*:

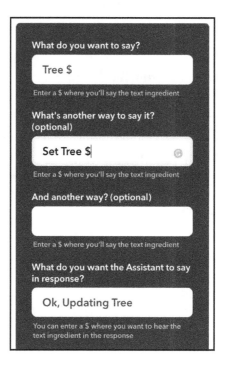

Figure 14.8 – Google Assistant trigger example

It's the **$** sign in **Tree $** shown in the preceding screenshot that gets turned into an IFTTT ingredient that we will use with our webhook service (which we'll see in a later step).

With this trigger configuration, you can say commands such as the following to control your IoTree:

- "Tree pattern red blue black"
- "Set tree animation blink"
- "Tree clear"

6. It's time to configure the **That** part of the IFTTT Applet. Search for and select **WebHook**.

7. Configuration of the webhook service is the same as the process we covered previously under the *Integration with email* heading in *step 2*, and as shown in *Figure 14.7*.

8. Continue and complete the creation of your IFTTT Applet.
9. Ask your Google Assistant the following commands:

- "Tree pattern red blue black"
- "Tree animation blink"
- "Tree clear"
- "Tree sweep" (or "tree jingle")
- Or any other command documented in the `chapter14/dweet_integration_service/README.md` file

 Remember, it may take a moment after Google Assistant acknowledges your request for your IoTree to start changing.

Here is a screenshot of my Google Assistant dialog on my iPhone:

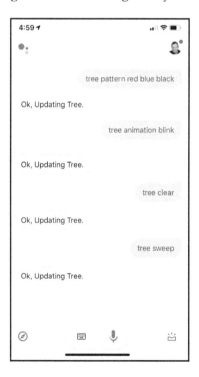

Figure 14.9 – Google Assistant dialog to control the IoTree

If the integration is working, Google Assistant will respond with *"Ok, Updating Tree"*(or whatever text you used at *step 5*), and moments later, your IoTree will respond.

The important thing to remember is that we must speak commands exactly as they are interpreted by the dweet integration service – for example, as they would appear in the command parameter to a dweet URL, such
as `https://dweet.io/dweet/for/<thing_name>?command=pattern red blue black`.

Remember to prefix them with the word "Tree" (or "Set Tree"). This text is what triggers your IFTTT Applet. Just speaking a command alone will not trigger your Applet.

If you use an Android phone or the Google Assistant app for iOS, you will be able to see how your spoken words are turned into textual commands, which can help you troubleshoot commands that are not working or are misunderstood.

You've just learned how to create three IFTTT integrations to control your IoTree using email and your voice, and you can easily adapt the same basic ideas and processes to control and automate other electronic circuits we've seen in this book.

Furthermore, as we discussed in `Chapter 13`, *IoT Visualization and Automation Platforms*, IFTTT provides many *triggers* and *actions* that you can combine to build automation workflow *Applets*. Between this chapter and the previous one, you have now created several Applets, so I have every confidence that you'll be able to explore the IFTTT ecosystem and create all sorts of interesting Applets that work together with your Raspberry Pi.

Before we conclude this chapter (and the book!), I want to leave you with a few ideas and experiments you can conduct to further expand your IoTree's capabilities.

Ideas and suggestions to extend your IoTree

The code and electronics we have used throughout this chapter have given us a foundation that we can build upon. This might be to extend your IoTree, or as the basis for other IoT projects.

Here are a few suggestions you can try:

- Add and integrate a PIR sensor that plays an RTTTL tune whenever anyone walks past your IoTree. After all, what electronic Christmas gadget is complete unless it drives everyone crazy by playing tunes over and over and over and over...

- Add and integrate an RGB LED to the top of the tree (maybe inside a transparent star), or use RGB LEDs in place of – or together with – the APA102 LED strip.

- Build multiple IoTrees. If you use MQTT, they'll synchronize!

- Try to build a WebSocket integration and an accompanying web app.

- The current dweet Google Assistant integration requires you to speak commands exactly. Can you create an upgrade that is a little *fuzzier* – that is, that can parse spoken text and work out what command is spoken?

- We used dweet.io (together with MQTT) in our IFTTT examples, so we did not have to worry about firewall configurations. You might want to investigate opening up a firewall port at your place or investigate services such as LocalTunnels (`https://localtunnel.github.io/www`) or ngrok (`https://ngrok.com`). These approaches will allow you to use IFTTT webhooks to directly communicate with your IoTree's RESTful API. However, do remember that our RESTful API examples are not secured – they are not using HTTPS and there is no authentication mechanism such as a username and password to restrict access to the APIs, so you might want to also research how to secure a Flask-based API and perform these upgrades first.

Obviously, these are just a few of my suggestions. We've covered many circuits during our journey, so use your imagination and see what you come up with – and have fun!

Summary

Congratulations! We have now reached the end of the chapter and the end of the book!

In this chapter, we ran through the electronics and tested programs that control those electronics that create the basis of an IoT Christmas tree. We've seen a RESTful API that can control our IoTree's lights and servo, as well as a comparable MQTT implementation. We also looked at a dweet.io-to-MQTT integration service, which we coupled with IFTTT to provide a mechanism to control out IoTree using email and Google Assistant.

Throughout our journey in this book, we have covered many concepts and technologies, including a variety of networking techniques, electronic and interfacing fundamentals, and a range of practical examples using sensors and actuators with your Raspberry Pi. We have also looked at automation and visualization platforms and finished off, in this chapter, with one example of tying our learnings together.

I had a couple of core intentions in mind when I wrote this book. One of my intentions was to share and explain the reasons behind *how* we connect sensors and actuators to a Raspberry Pi, and *why* we accompany them with additional components such as resistors to create voltage dividers. My second core intention was to provide you with a variety of networking techniques and options that are applicable to IoT projects.

I believe that the software and hardware fundamentals, together with practical examples you have learned throughout our journey, will provide you with many skills and insights to not only help you design and build your own complex IoT projects but to also understand, at a fundamental level, how existing IoT projects work at a software, networking and electronics level.

It is my sincere hope that you have enjoyed this book, learned a lot, and picked up many practical tips along the way! All the best on your IoT journey, and I hope you create some amazing things!

Questions

As we conclude, here is a list of questions for you to test your knowledge of this chapter's material. You will find the answers in the *Assessments* section of the *Appendix*:

1. Why, in our MQTT service example, did we use `PyPubSub` to re-dispatch MQTT messages?

2. Why is using the Google Assistant app on a phone (or tablet) useful during development when integrating with or debugging an IFTTT Google Assistant Applet?

3. You are working on an existing weather monitoring project that uses MQTT as its network transport layer to connect many distributed devices. You have been asked to integrate the application with an IFTTT service. How do you do this?

4. You want to build multiple IoTrees and have them all work together in unison. What are two approaches you can take to achieve this outcome?

5. Why did we use the free `dweet.io` service in this chapter? Would you use this approach in a commercial IoT project?

6. We want to test a RESTful API service from the command line. What command-line tool can we use?

7. What feature of MQTT can you use to have IoTrees initialize automatically when their Raspberry Pis are powered on or rebooted?

8. Further to *Question 7*, what are some of the considerations you will need to make regarding the Mosquitto MQTT broker setup and deployments to achieve this outcome?

Assessments

Chapter 1

1. To keep your project-specific Python packages and dependencies isolated from other projects and the system-level Python packages.
2. No. You can always regenerate a virtual environment and reinstall packages.
3. To keep a list of all the Python packages (and versions) that your Python projects rely on. Having a maintained `requirements.txt` file allows you to reinstall all packages easily with the command `pip install -r requirements.txt`.
4. Make sure you are using the absolute path to the Python interpreter that is in the `bin` folder of your virtual environment.
5. It activates a virtual environment so that all users of Python and pip are sandboxed to the virtual environment.
6. `deactivate`. If you type `exit` (and we all do it sometimes!), it exits the Terminal window or closes your remote SSH session! Grrrrr.
7. Yes, just change into the `projects` folder and activate the virtual environment.
8. Python IDLE, but remember you need to use `python -m idlelib.idle [filename]` & in a virtual environment.
9. Check that the I2C interface has been enabled in Raspbian.

Chapter 2

1. Sort by answer number so that you do not damage other components or the resistor... unless you understand how the different values will affect the electronic circuit and it's safe to do so.
2. False. GPIO Zero is a wrapper on top of other GPIO libraries. It's designed to be easy to use for beginners by hiding away lower-level GPIO interfacing details.
3. False. In many scenarios, you are better off using mature higher-level packages as they will help speed up development. The Python API documentation also recommends this approach.
4. No. An LED has positive (anode) and negative (cathode) terminals (legs) and must be connected the correct way around.

5. There's a chance that there is a mismatch between the devices' time zone handling.
6. `signal.pause()`

Chapter 3

1. We can create and configure an instance of `RequestParser`. We use this instance in our controller's handler methods such as `.get()` or `.post()` to validate the client's request.
2. WebSockets – a client and server built using Web Sockets can initiate a request to one another in either direction. This is in contrast to a RESTful API service where only the client can initiate a request to the server.
3. Flask-SocketIO does not include an in-built validation class like Flask-RESTful. You have to perform input validation manually. Alternatively, you could also find a suitable third-party Python module to use from PyPi.org.
4. The `templates` folder is the default location where the Flask framework looks for template files. It's in this location where we store our HTML pages and templates.
5. We should initialize event listeners and the web page content in the document ready function, which is called once the web page has been completely loaded.
6. The command is `curl`. It is installed by default on most Unix-based operating systems.
7. Changing the value property changes the PWM duty cycle for the LED. We visualize this as changing the brightness of the LED.

Chapter 4

1. **MQTT**, or **Message Queue Telemetry Protocol**, is a lightweight messaging protocol frequently used in distributed IoT networks.
2. Check the QoS levels, making sure they are either level 1 or 2.
3. A `Will` message will be published on behalf of a client if that client abruptly disconnects from the broker without cleanly closing the connection first.
4. Both the published message and subscribing clients must use at least QoS level 1, which ensures messages are delivered one or more times.

5. Ideally, nothing should need to change in your Python code other than perhaps the broker host and port because MQTT is an open standard. The proviso is that the new broker is configured similarly to the broker being replaced – for example, both brokers are configured similarly to provide message retention or durable connection features to clients.

6. You should subscribe to topics in an on successful connection-type handler. This way, if the client loses its broker connection, it can automatically reestablish topic subscriptions when it reconnects.

Chapter 5

1. **SPI** (**Serial Peripheral Interface Circuit**). LED strips and matrices are common examples.

2. You can refer to the device's official datasheet, or use the command-line tool i2cdetect, which lists the addresses of all connected I2C devices.

3. Make sure you are using the correct pin numbering scheme expected by the library, and/or make sure you have configured the library to use the scheme you prefer if the library provides this option.

4. The driver library is not built upon PiGPIO and therefore does not support remote GPIO.

5. False. All GPIO pins are rated for 3.3 volts. Connecting any voltage higher than this can damage your Raspberry Pi.

6. The library you are using to drive the servo is most likely using software PWM to generate the PWM signals for the servo. Software PWM signals can be distorted when the Raspberry Pi's CPU gets busy.

7. If you are powering the servos from the 5-volt pin of your Raspberry Pi, it'll indicate that you are drawing too much power, effectively robbing the power from the Raspberry Pi. Ideally, the servos should be powered from an external power source.

Chapter 6

1. Generally speaking, yes. It's safe to try because a higher resistance results in a lower current in the circuit (Ohm's law) and 330Ω is relatively close to the desired 200Ω resistor.

2. The higher resistance has resulted in less current to the point that there is not enough current for the circuit to operate reliably.

3. The amount of power to be dissipated by the resistor exceeds the resistor's power rating. In addition to using Ohm's law to determine a resistor value, you also need to calculate the expected power dissipation of the resistor and ensure that the resistor's power rating (in watts) exceeds your calculated value.

4. 1 (one). An input GPIO pin connected to +3.3 volts is a logical high.

5. GPIO 21 is floating. It's not pulled up to +3.3 volts by a physical resistor or via code using a function call such as `pi.set_pull_up_down(21, pigpio.PUD_UP)`.

6. You must use a logic level converter. This could be a simple resistor-based voltage divider, a dedicated logic level converter IC or module, or any other form that can appropriately shift down 5 volts to 3.3 volts.

7. False. A resistor voltage divider can only step down a voltage. However, remember that it may be possible to drive a 5-volt logic device using 3.3 volts as long as the 5-volt device registers 3.3 volts as a logical high.

Chapter 7

1. MOSFETs are voltage-controlled components, while BJTs are current-controlled components.

2. You do not have a pull-down resistor on the MOSFET's gate leg, so it's left floating. The MOSFET discharges slowly and this is reflected as the motor is spinning down. Using a pull-down resistor ensures the MOSFET discharges promptly and becomes off.

3. (a) Make sure the G, S, and D legs are connected correctly because different package styles (for example, T092 versus TP220) have their legs ordered differently.
   (b) You also want to make sure that the MOSFET is logic-level compatible so that it can be controlled using a 3.3-volt voltage source.
   (c) Ensure that the voltage divider created between the pull-down resistor and the current limiting resistor allows >~3 volts into the MOSFET's gate leg.

4. Optocouplers and relays electrically isolate the input and output sides of a circuit. Transistors are in-circuit, and while they allow a low-current device to control a larger current device, both devices are still both electrically connected (for example, you will see a common ground connection).

5. Active low is where you make a GPIO low to turn on or activate the connected circuit. Active high is the opposite, in that we make the GPIO pin high to activate the connected circuit.

6. Code activated pull-down only becomes pull-down when the code is run, so the MOSFET gate is basically left floating until the code is run.

7. The stall current is the current used by the motor when its staff has been, well, stalled – for example, forcefully stopped from turning. This is the maximum current that a motor will draw.

8. There is no difference – they are two terms used interchangeably to describe the current a motor uses when it is spinning freely with no load attached to the motor's shaft.

Chapter 8

1. Check that your power supply can deliver enough current (and voltage) to your LED strip. Current requirements increase in proportion with the number of LEDs you want to illuminate, and the color and brightness they are set to. An insufficient current can mean that the internal red/green/blue LEDs are not illuminated correctly and thus the colors are not as you expected.

2. The absence of a Slave Select or Client Enable pin means that the APA102 takes full control of the SPI interface. This means that you cannot connect more than one SPI slave to an SPI pin (unless you employ additional electronics).

3. First, check that your logic level converter is connected correctly. Secondly, it's possible that the logic level converter cannot convert logic levels fast enough to keep up with the SPI interface. Try lowering the SPI bus speed.

4. We use the **PIL** (**Python Imaging Library**) to create an in-memory image representing what we want to display. We then send this image to the OLED display for rendering.

5. **RTTTL** means **Ring Tone Text Transfer Language**, which is a ring-tone music format created by Nokia.

Chapter 9

1. The DHT22 is a more accurate sensor, and it is capable of sensing a greater range of temperatures and humanities.

2. The external pull-up resistor is optional because our Raspberry Pi can use its internal embedded pull-up resistor.

3. An LDR is a light-sensitive resistor. When used as part of a voltage-divider circuit, we turn the varying resistance into a varying voltage. This voltage can then be detected by an analog-to-digital converter such as the ADS1115, which is connected to your Raspberry Pi.

4. Try varying the resistance of the fixed resistor in the voltage-divider circuit. Try higher-value resistances to make the LDR more sensitive in darker conditions. Try lower-resistance values to make the LDR more sensitive to brighter conditions.

5. No two LDRs are identical when it comes to the resistances they measure. If you swap out an LDR in a circuit, re-calibrate the code just to be sure.

6. Water conducts electricity. It acts as a resistor between the two probe wires. This resistance is converted to a voltage by the voltage divider, and this is detectable by the ADS1115 ADC.

Chapter 10

1. We typically find default reference pulse widths of 1 ms for left, and 2 ms for rights used for the servos. In reality, the servos may need slightly adjusted pulse widths to reach their extreme rotation positions.

2. You are applying a pulse width that is trying to rotate your servo beyond its physical limits.

3. An H-bridge allows us to also change the rotation of a motor and apply a brake to quickly stop the motor spinning.

4. Many factors affect the reliability of braking, including the IC and your motor. You can adopt PWM-style braking as an alternative braking technique.

5. Vibrating but not turning is often the symptom of a mismatch between the coil energizing order and the coil stepping sequence. You need to identify and ensure the stepper motor's coils are connected correctly and match the stepping sequence. Consulting your stepper motor's datasheet is the best place to start.

6. The L293D has a voltage drop of around 2 volts, so your motor is only getting around 3 volts. To compensate for this voltage drop, you would need a power source of 7 volts.

7. No. The GPIO pins only supply 3.3 volts. While this might be just enough to rotate a 5-volt stepper motor, the current requirements of a stepper motor will exceed the safe limits of the Raspberry Pi GPIO pins.

Chapter 11

1. No. A **passive infrared** (**PIR**) sensor can only detect abstract movement. You will need an active-type infrared sensor or a device like a thermal camera (and a lot more complex code) to extract richer movement information.

2. An ultrasonic sensor measures the round-trip timing of ultrasonic pulses, which is then used to calculate distance. Factors that affect the ultrasonic pulse timing or the speed-of-sound constant used therefore affect the calculated distance. Some examples include temperature since this affects the speed of sound, the material of the detected object (for example, does it absorb sound?), the size of the object, and its angle relative to the sensor.

3. Both latching and non-latching Hall effect sensors output a digital signal – their output pin is either HIGH or LOW. In contrast, ratiometric Hall effect sensors output an analog signal (varying voltage) relative to how close they are to a magnetic field.

4. The `callback_handler` function will be called whenever GPIO transitions to either a HIGH or LOW state.

5. So that the relative voltage drop across the resistor that sits between the 5-volt source and the voltage-divider output (between the two resistors) is 3.3 volts, that is, 5 volts * 2kΩ/(1kΩ + 2kΩ) = ~3.3 volts. If you reversed the resistor values in the circuit, the voltage-divider output would be ~1.7 volts, that is, 5 volts * 1kΩ/(1kΩ + 2kΩ) = ~1.7 volts.

6. After consulting the datasheet for the HC-SR501 PIR sensor, we learn that its output pin always works at 3.3 volts even though it's powered from 5 volts, thus we did not need a voltage divider. (Note that, in practice, we ideally would also confirm this by our measurement.)

Chapter 12

1. A publish-subscribe approach promotes a highly decoupled approach to programming. This can be beneficial when you have many components (for example, sensors) publishing data that simply needs to be consumed elsewhere in your program.

2. **GIL** stands for **Global Interpreter Lock**. It's a design aspect of the Python programming language that means only one thread ever has access to the Python interpreter at a time.

3. A pure event loop (for example, one long while loop) can get complex as your program grows. The need for many state variables and non-trivial and intervening conditional tests (for example, if statements) can make the program logic hard to follow and debug.

4. No. Every approach has its purpose. Event loops are fine when they are small and focused. It's only when they become large and are performing multiple actions that they become complex.

5. When you are programming with threads, calling `join()` on another thread joins that thread to your current thread. Your current thread then blocks until all joined threads run methods complete. This is a simple way of synchronizing the completion of multiple threads.

6. Perhaps you are using a `sleep` statement (from the time library), such as `sleep(duration)`, which blocks for the full duration. Try using the approach in the following example, which will allow your program to remain responsive to a change in the value of `duration`:

```
duration = 1    # 1 second
timer = 0
while timer < duration:
    timer += 0.01
    sleep(0.01)
```

7. No approach is superior. There is always more than one way to reach your programming goal in Python. The best approach, or combination of approaches, all depends on your project and what you are trying to achieve. The best approach can also be the one that is best for you based on your personal preferences and preferred programming style.

Chapter 13

1. We used different temperatures to create a buffer so that we would not generate multiple triggers (and multiple emails) if the temperature hovered around a single temperature value.

2. Using an intermediary meant we did not need to worry about a firewall, port forwarding, and other configurations necessary to expose your Raspberry Pi to the public internet.

3. IFTTT is more consumer-focused, while Zapper is more business-focused in terms of the integrations it provides. Zapper will also allow you to create a more complex workflow, trigger, and action scenarios.

4. No. ThingSpeak only consumes data to display on a dashboard. Some platforms, such as ThingBoard, will allow you to send data back to a device for the purposes of controlling that device.

5. There is a maximum of three JSON properties available – `Value1`, `Value2`, and `Value3`.

6. From ease and speed of development perspectives, IFTTT or Zapper would be a good choice, but you could certainly use AWS or one of the other major IoT platforms, or even Home Assistant.

Chapter 14

1. The use of PyPubSub was a design decision to decouple MQTT-related code and logic from hardware control code and logic, with the goal of making the code cleaner and easier to maintain.

2. The commands you speak when using the Google Assistant app are shown on your device as text, so it's easy to see how Google Assistant heard your spoken commands, and what was sent as textual commands to your IFTTT Applet.

3. You will need to build an integration service that marshals data between MQTT and the RESTful APIs (or, alternatively, identify a thirty-party service that does this – for example, check out `https://io.adafruit.com` and their IFTTT service). IFTTT offers RESTful webhooks as an option to build custom integrations, however, it does not offer an MQTT option.

4. One option is to use MQTT, just like the example we covered in this chapter. If you connect multiple IoTrees using MQTT to a central MQTT broker, they all receive instructions together. A second option could be to build a WebSockets-based service and application (we covered this approach in *Chapter 3, Networking with RESTful APIs and Web Sockets Using Flask*).

5. We used the free `dweet.io` service for practical convenience so what we did not have to worry about firewalls, port forwarding, and router configurations at your place (just in case this is something you are not experienced with). The free `dweet.io` service offers no security or privacy, so it is undesirable for many projects. If you like the idea of `dweet.io`, there is `dweetpro.io`, a paid alternative that offers security and many other features that are not available in the free version.

6. `CURL` is a popular command-line tool that can be used to test RESTful APIs. Postman (`getpostman.com`) is a popular GUI tool that can also be used for the same purpose.

7. If you use the retained message features of the MQTT broker, each IoTree will receive the last message (for example, what color pattern to show) when it connects and therefore can initialize itself. We covered retained messages in `Chapter 4`, *Networking with MQTT, Python, and the Mosquitto MQTT Broker.*

8. If your MQTT broker is running on the same Raspberry Pi as an IoTree and you restart this Raspberry Pi, all retained messages will be lost unless the Mosquitto MQTT broker has persistence enabled in its configuration. (Our configuration from `Chapter 4`, *Networking with MQTT, Python, and the Mosquitto MQTT Broker,* ensured persistence is enabled).

Other Books You May Enjoy

If you enjoyed this book, you may be interested in these other books by Packt:

Hands-On Internet of Things with MQTT

Tim Pulver

ISBN: 978-1-78934-178-2

- Explore MQTT programming with Arduino
- Discover how to make your prototypes talk to each other
- Send MQTT messages from your smartphone to your prototypes
- Discover how you can make websites interact with your prototypes
- Learn about MQTT servers, libraries, and apps
- Explore tools such as laser cutting and 3D printing in order to build robust prototype cases

Internet of Things Projects with ESP32

Agus Kurniawan

ISBN: 978-1-78995-687-0

- Understand how to build a sensor monitoring logger
- Create a weather station to sense temperature and humidity using ESP32
- Build your own Wi-Fi wardriving with ESP32. Use BLE to make interactions between ESP32 and Android
- Understand how to create connections to interact between ESP32 and mobile applications
- Learn how to interact between ESP32 boards and cloud servers
- Build an IoT Application-based ESP32 board

Leave a review - let other readers know what you think

Please share your thoughts on this book with others by leaving a review on the site that you bought it from. If you purchased the book from Amazon, please leave us an honest review on this book's Amazon page. This is vital so that other potential readers can see and use your unbiased opinion to make purchasing decisions, we can understand what our customers think about our products, and our authors can see your feedback on the title that they have worked with Packt to create. It will only take a few minutes of your time, but is valuable to other potential customers, our authors, and Packt. Thank you!

Index

www.ingramcontent.com/pod-product-compliance
Lightning Source LLC
Chambersburg PA
CBHW081453050326
40690CB00015B/2780